National Security and Counterintelligence in the Era of Cyber Espionage

Eugenie de Silva
University of Leicester, UK & Virginia Research Institute, USA

A volume in the Advances in Digital Crime, Forensics, and Cyber Terrorism (ADCFCT) Book Series

Information Science REFERENCE
An Imprint of IGI Global

Published in the United States of America by
Information Science Reference (an imprint of IGI Global)
701 E. Chocolate Avenue
Hershey PA, USA 17033
Tel: 717-533-8845
Fax: 717-533-8661
E-mail: cust@igi-global.com
Web site: http://www.igi-global.com

Library of Congress Cataloging-in-Publication Data

Names: Silva, Eugenie de, 1998 editor.
Title: National security and counterintelligence in the era of cyber espionage / Eugenie de Silva, editor.
Description: Hershey : Information Science Reference, 2016. | Includes bibliographical references and index.
Identifiers: LCCN 2015037651| ISBN 9781466696617 (hardcover) | ISBN 9781466696624 (ebook)
Subjects: LCSH: Computer crimes. | Intelligence service. | Intelligence service--Computer networks. | National security--Law and legislation.
Classification: LCC HV6773 .N387 2016 | DDC 327.120285/4678--dc23 LC record available at http://lccn.loc.gov/2015037651

This book is published in the IGI Global book series Advances in Digital Crime, Forensics, and Cyber Terrorism (ADCF-CT) (ISSN: 2327-0381; eISSN: 2327-0373)

British Cataloguing in Publication Data
A Cataloguing in Publication record for this book is available from the British Library.

For electronic access to this publication, please contact: eresources@igi-global.com.

Advances in Digital Crime, Forensics, and Cyber Terrorism (ADCFCT) Book Series

Bryan Christiansen
PryMarke, LLC, USA

ISSN: 2327-0381
EISSN: 2327-0373

Mission

The digital revolution has allowed for greater global connectivity and has improved the way we share and present information. With this new ease of communication and access also come many new challenges and threats as cyber crime and digital perpetrators are constantly developing new ways to attack systems and gain access to private information.

The **Advances in Digital Crime, Forensics, and Cyber Terrorism (ADCFCT) Book Series** seeks to publish the latest research in diverse fields pertaining to crime, warfare, terrorism and forensics in the digital sphere. By advancing research available in these fields, the **ADCFCT** aims to present researchers, academicians, and students with the most current available knowledge and assist security and law enforcement professionals with a better understanding of the current tools, applications, and methodologies being implemented and discussed in the field.

Coverage

- Encryption
- Hacking
- Vulnerability
- Watermarking
- Cryptography
- Criminology
- Mobile Device Forensics
- Global Threat Intelligence
- Identity Theft
- Cyber warfare

IGI Global is currently accepting manuscripts for publication within this series. To submit a proposal for a volume in this series, please contact our Acquisition Editors at Acquisitions@igi-global.com or visit: http://www.igi-global.com/publish/.

The Advances in Digital Crime, Forensics, and Cyber Terrorism (ADCFCT) Book Series (ISSN 2327-0381) is published by IGI Global, 701 E. Chocolate Avenue, Hershey, PA 17033-1240, USA, www.igi-global.com. This series is composed of titles available for purchase individually; each title is edited to be contextually exclusive from any other title within the series. For pricing and ordering information please visit http://www.igi-global.com/book-series/advances-digital-crime-forensics-cyber/73676. Postmaster: Send all address changes to above address.

Titles in this Series

For a list of additional titles in this series, please visit: www.igi-global.com

Cybersecurity Policies and Strategies for Cyberwarfare Prevention
Jean-Loup Richet (University of Nantes, France)
Information Science Reference • copyright 2015 • 393pp • H/C (ISBN: 9781466684560) • US $245.00 (our price)

New Threats and Countermeasures in Digital Crime and Cyber Terrorism
Maurice Dawson (University of Missouri–St. Louis, USA) and Marwan Omar (Nawroz University, Iraq)
Information Science Reference • copyright 2015 • 369pp • H/C (ISBN: 9781466683457) • US $200.00 (our price)

Handbook of Research on Digital Crime, Cyberspace Security, and Information Assurance
Maria Manuela Cruz-Cunha (Polytechnic Institute of Cavado and Ave, Portugal) and Irene Maria Portela (Polytechnic Institute of Cávado and Ave, Portugal)
Information Science Reference • copyright 2015 • 602pp • H/C (ISBN: 9781466663244) • US $385.00 (our price)

The Psychology of Cyber Crime Concepts and Principles
Gráinne Kirwan (Dun Laoghaire Institute of Art, Design and Technology, Ireland) and Andrew Power (Dun Laoghaire Institute of Art, Design and Technology, Ireland)
Information Science Reference • copyright 2012 • 372pp • H/C (ISBN: 9781613503508) • US $195.00 (our price)

Cyber Crime and the Victimization of Women Laws, Rights and Regulations
Debarati Halder (Centre for Cyber Victim Counselling (CCVC), India) and K. Jaishankar (Manonmaniam Sundaranar University, India)
Information Science Reference • copyright 2012 • 264pp • H/C (ISBN: 9781609608309) • US $195.00 (our price)

Digital Forensics for the Health Sciences Applications in Practice and Research
Andriani Daskalaki (Max Planck Institute for Molecular Genetics, Germany)
Medical Information Science Reference • copyright 2011 • 418pp • H/C (ISBN: 9781609604837) • US $245.00 (our price)

Cyber Security, Cyber Crime and Cyber Forensics Applications and Perspectives
Raghu Santanam (Arizona State University, USA) M. Sethumadhavan (Amrita University, India) and Mohit Virendra (Brocade Communications Systems, USA)
Information Science Reference • copyright 2011 • 296pp • H/C (ISBN: 9781609601232) • US $180.00 (our price)

Handbook of Research on Computational Forensics, Digital Crime, and Investigation Methods and Solutions
Chang-Tsun Li (University of Warwick, UK)
Information Science Reference • copyright 2010 • 620pp • H/C (ISBN: 9781605668369) • US $295.00 (our price)

IGI GLOBAL
DISSEMINATOR OF KNOWLEDGE
www.igi-global.com

701 E. Chocolate Ave., Hershey, PA 17033
Order online at www.igi-global.com or call 717-533-8845 x100
To place a standing order for titles released in this series, contact: cust@igi-global.com
Mon-Fri 8:00 am - 5:00 pm (est) or fax 24 hours a day 717-533-8661

Editorial Advisory Board

Table of Contents

Detailed Table of Contents

Foreword

I had the privilege of participating in a graduation ceremony during which Miss Eugenie de Silva received a Master's Degree at the age of 15. Later, when she asked if I would do the foreword to this book, I told her it would be an honor for two reasons. First, I was really impressed with how far this young woman had come in her academic career and with what she plans to accomplish. Second, and most importantly, I thought this book, *National Security and Counterintelligence in the Era of Cyber Espionage*, covers one of the most important topics of our time.

We have entered a new era in which rapid advances in information technology are stretching our collective imagination, driving innovation, and stimulating much needed public debate at all levels. Like so many of the great technological advances in history—the printing press, electricity, and manned flight—advances in information technology bring amazing advantage and opportunity, while presenting new complexity and intertwined political, social, and economic challenges.

The development of cyberspace is but the most recent manifestation of the manner in which technology can transform the human experience. Cyberspace offers current and future generations with tremendous opportunities to invent, explore, grow, and learn, in ways that can better the human condition. But with these potential benefits comes risk. We need responsible policymakers, entrepreneurs, scientists, and scholars who will study and work to address the new problems that can accompany progress.

This book is an important contribution toward that end. The purpose of this edited volume is to provide readers, especially those doing serious work on cyber-related issues, a broad overview of some of the most important challenges posed by cyberspace, as well as thoughts as to how we might frame and address them.

To accomplish this, Eugenie assembled an impressive group of people from around the world, with different responsibilities and perspectives, and with tremendous expertise. These eighteen individuals include acknowledged scholars and practitioners from the United Kingdom, Australia, Israel, and the United States.

This book is arranged in three major sections. Each section has five chapters written by thought leaders from academia and related communities of practice.

Section 1 covers current threats. The authors of these chapters highlight several of the main security concerns currently faced by law enforcement and intelligence officials, introducing readers to an array of threats that extends beyond what is widely discussed in the media. Included in this section are discussions of the following: terrorist use of the internet; the differing views of the US and China on cybersecurity; threats to the energy sector and electrical grid; and threats posed by cyber espionage. The authors in this section review past events in the security arena as well as develop novel analyses that relate to current and evolving threats.

Section 2 contains various views on the meaning of security in the digital age and suggestions as to how it may be enhanced. The authors help readers to think about what can be learned from past events such as the theft of national security data by former US security contractor Edward Snowden, present thoughts on how to benefit from recent developments in the field, and indicate future research directions that may be most fruitful in strengthening security. Some of the specific topics discussed in these chapters are: the ethical issues associated with countering uses of the internet for radicalization; insider threats; the types of data targeted in cyber espionage; and recommendations as to how states can address privacy concerns.

Section 3 presents readers with frameworks and ideas relating to the implementation of new security measures. The authors provide recommendations as to how law enforcement and intelligence officials may implement novel techniques and strategies—such as new laws and educational approaches—to enhance security, especially in technologically-dependent societies. Key issues discussed include: national data breach laws; using the internet to combat terrorism; international cooperation in cyber security; the utility of using theory drawn from multiple disciplines to understand intelligence in a big data environment; and detecting deception.

As someone who has seen first-hand the complex policy problems posed by cyberspace—as the Director of the National Security Agency from 2005 to 2014 and the Commander, US Cyber Command from 2010 to 2014—I know the importance of the issues raised in this volume. I have personally seen the national security dangers that cyberspace presents, and I am deeply concerned about the security of the United States and its allies in this area.

These experiences, as well as the three preceding decades I spent in military intelligence, reaffirmed the importance of partnering with talented thought leaders like those who have shared their ideas in this book. While I have an unwavering confidence in the intelligence professionals with whom I served in the US government and respect the critical role of the US Intelligence Community in safeguarding national security, I am convinced that advances in cybersecurity must also draw upon experts from a variety of fields and perspectives.

Technology continues to get faster, more capable, and more accessible. We should all be concerned with and informed about the unintended or deliberate misuse of rapidly advancing capabilities. The development of effective laws, policies, and governance at all levels will continue to struggle to keep up with society's use of cyberspace. Books like this help us stay informed and provide a fuller understanding of the complexity of this domain.

Increased reporting in the media regarding major cyber attacks and data breaches is correctly increasing the attention paid—in corporate boardrooms and within the general population—to cyber security. The ideas explored in this book span economic advantage, ethical principles, political and military affairs, national security, privacy, influence, regulation and reform, espionage, criminal activity, roles and relationships, critical infrastructure protection, conflict resolution strategies, information sharing, advanced data analytics, detection methodologies, trends, and the use of the Internet for extremist recruiting and radicalization. This long list of diverse concerns appropriately reveals the complexity and importance of furthering our ability to use the tremendous potential offered by cyberspace in a safe manner.

I am impressed with the thoughtfulness and diversity of views presented in this book. With continued focus and action in the areas of intelligence, national security, and cyber security there is hope for rapid progress. The thoughts assembled here are a great example of the talent that exists to meet these challenges, refine the global narrative, and present workable answers going forward at multiple levels.

Miss Eugenie de Silva and her colleagues have done a superb job in bringing together some extremely important thoughts, ideas, and opportunities that we can all draw upon as cyberspace continues to evolve.

Keith B. Alexander
IronNet Cybersecurity, USA

Keith B. Alexander. *At IronNet Cybersecurity, as the CEO and President, GEN (Ret) Alexander provides strategic vision to corporate leaders on cybersecurity issues through development of cutting edge technology, consulting and education/training. Mr. Alexander served as the first Commander, U.S. Cyber Command (USCYBERCOM) from 2010 to 2014 and the 16th Director, National Security Agency (NSA) from 2005-2014. As Commander, USCYBERCOM, he was responsible for planning, coordinating and conducting operations and defending Department of Defense (DoD) computer networks as well as the defense of the nation from cyber attacks. As the Director, NSA, he was responsible for a DoD agency with national foreign intelligence requirements, military combat support, and U.S. national security information system protection responsibilities. Mr. Alexander holds a Bachelor of Science degree from the U.S. Military Academy, as well as holding a Master of Science in Business Administration from Boston University; a Master of Science in Systems Technology (Electronic Warfare) and Physics from the Naval Post Graduate School; and National Security Strategy from the National Defense University.*

Preface

In a perfect world, there would be no need for restrictive maintenance of social order as there would be no crime, terrorism, destruction, or mayhem. Au contraire, the development of such an idealistic world will never come to fruition without the devotion and dedication of all humankind. A concerted effort on the part of educators, intelligence officials, security personnel, politicians, economists, scientists, and other professionals, in addition to members of the general public, is paramount to establishing a harmonious, global environment that fosters acceptance and understanding. Of course, it is quite simple to argue that the achievement of perfect law and order within any society is a pipe-dream, yet to lose hope on such a positive goal is to lose hope on the progress of humanity. It is certainly more optimistic and useful to aim for the attainment of a mammoth goal than to limit humanity and never make an effort based on preconceived notions that the goal is out of reach. Whilst the progress will be a cumulative effort, it is important to recognize the contributions of members of the security arena. As long as there is crime and as long as some individuals act outside the bounds of legality, security officials will be tirelessly working, at times without recognition, to maintain order.

For individuals who have made the decision to enter the security field and thus work in an environment wherein their safety is not guaranteed, the technologically reliant twenty-first century has raised a multitude of new issues. For the general public, technology has become the focal point of most activities; it has paved the way to make the world in one's pocket a virtual reality. The speed at which individuals can share information is incomparable to that which was previously available. In fact, individuals can now share information whilst remaining anonymous, which has, unfortunately, opened the door for some to share malicious opinions and threats or even carry out illegal activities without any worries of backlash. The newfound flexibility of the cyber arena has become so embedded in daily life activities that it has become one of the fundamental examples used in arguments pertaining to human rights to privacy. The revolutionary force of technology has not only paved the way for "rights to privacy" discussions, but it also has led to the politicization of such arguments in a manner that has imposed an oppressive spotlight on surveillance, secrecy, and oversight. Nevertheless, one should bear in mind that surveillance, security, and oversight have been prevalent for centuries and have simply adapted to the ever-changing times.

As far back as the 1700s, the First Continental Congress even made clear the importance of maintaining secrecy with regard to their confidential proceedings. Secrecy and the covert nature of government activities are underlying features of the field; whilst this must be accepted and considered, this book serves as a way for individuals, especially members of the public, to gain insight to the current workings and dynamics of the field. Classified information is, plainly, not accessible by the public, which makes this book "National Security and Counterintelligence in the Era of Cyber Espionage," a compelling read; this book provides analytical assessments derived from information that allow readers to touch upon that which may generally be classified or may be considered as classified.

The cyber arena is used by security officials to protect the nation, but is also used by criminals who yearn to achieve their own goals by undermining the law. It is the complex and diverse nature of the cyber arena that makes difficult the task of protecting individuals from evolving threats to humanity. Due to the criminal exploitation of cyberspace, one could logically expect that future criminal activity will cause more destruction and devastation than was previously possible. The new era of cyber espionage has made it imperative that security officials continuously monitor cyber systems, since the cyber world is more complex than the physical reality of daily life. Whereas physical activities are monitored by long-standing security procedures and surveillance, cyber activities enter new virtual ground that has not, in its entirety, been subject to oversight and strategic rules and regulations. Cyberspace is filled with data and millions of individuals who use advanced technology for a multitude of reasons. Businesses, academic institutions, research facilities, etc. use cyberspace to fulfill reasonable objectives, whereas there are others who manipulate the dynamics of cyberspace in an effort to shield their illegal activities and overstep the bounds of legal framework. Not only do individuals utilize the anonymity offered through cyberspace, but they also take advantage of the fact that coordinating legal efforts across cyberspace is a tremendous task encumbered by the complications in ensuring that law enforcement cooperate with one another to effectively prosecute guilty parties at national and international levels.

The use of cyberspace, as aforementioned, has resulted in discussions related to privacy. The issues of conducting surveillance by searching through one's social media or similar online profiles have made many individuals quite uncomfortable and wary of security personnel; however, as is made clear through this book, cyberspace is a mammoth arena that not only welcomes professionals and law-abiding citizens, but also provides a safe-haven for criminals that seek to wreak havoc. It is the fact that cyberspace is essentially the home to such individuals of varying backgrounds that makes detailed surveillance, within legal regulations, imperative.

One way in which to look at cyberspace is to take into consideration a public road, such as an interstate. When one is driving on the public interstate in one's own car, one must obey the driving laws, while understanding that other drivers may decide to break those laws at any given moment. While driving, it is reasonable to assume that one's car is personal property, yet the license plate on the back of that car and the voluntary driving on a public road make it understandable that the license plate has now become public knowledge accessible by law enforcement officers to scan and check; additionally, one has automatically assumed a position wherein they may be stopped by a law enforcement officer who feels that one's driving or behavior is suspicious or not in alignment with the law. In fact, one need not even be driving, one needs to simply park a car on public property, at which point a law enforcement officer may follow the plain view doctrine in the USA, which is an exception to a warrant and allows evidence of a crime to be seized. A car is private property; accordingly, individuals have the rights to privacy, yet over time individuals have become accustomed to the norm that the rights to privacy are limited when in certain situations that require greater surveillance, such as public roads wherein the safety of citizens may be compromised if law enforcement do not actively maintain oversight. Along these lines, cyberspace is the digital public road, as it transfers data. Therefore, while one's own computer or phone may be private property, when one accesses the Internet or uses wireless data, one is automatically entering a public domain; a domain that is larger in comparison to any physical road, which brings about even greater risks. When one uses social media sites or any page on the Internet or through mobile data, one must realize that there are millions of other individuals also using those same avenues to wreak havoc and overthrow legal and social order. Thus, law enforcement officers conduct surveillance and essentially use a digital plain view doctrine wherein information that is plainly evidence of a crime could be collected.

In order to factually contribute to on-going discussions pertaining to the intelligence field, this book draws together experts from around the world. The chapters offer diverse perspectives of the security arena in the twenty-first century. The topic of intelligence in the current age, of course, is vast; thus, this book is broken down into three distinct components; (1) current threats, (2) understanding the field, (3) novel implementations and forward thinking. Each of these three sections expands on topics that I, the editor, deemed to be the most important; the individual chapters not only contribute to the existing body of literature, but also provide readers with an opportunity to understand the unique dynamics of intelligence and security in a simplified manner. The aim of this book is to encourage more members of the public to be actively informed about the continuously evolving intelligence and security fields; it is further hoped that this book will spark more rigorous, academic debates and discussions about security and heightened intelligence systems amongst individuals from varying backgrounds. Currently, it is clear that there are biased discussions about security matters that have flooded social media and the Internet; whilst freedom of speech allows such discussions to continue, they should not be considered as the basis upon which the subject is assessed. Therefore, this book serves as a firm foundation for individuals to understand security matters based on referenced, academic research. This book does not elaborate on personal views, nor does it provide biased assessments based on ideological standpoints. The professionals in this book have recognized the necessity of objectivity and have maintained unbiased perspectives in their presentation of facts and research data.

The first section of this book places a focus on current threats. The authors of these chapters have highlighted several of the main threats currently faced by law enforcement and intelligence personnel. The aim of these chapters was to provide readers with an opportunity to view a wide range of threats that are currently present. The authors have used this opportunity to take into consideration past events in the security arena, and then develop novel analyses that relate to current threats. These chapters highlight the diversification of the field ranging from threats to the electrical grid to terrorist use of the Internet and counterespionage. These chapters contribute to a holistic view of the field that nullifies the perception that cyber security simply means protecting computers and other similar technology from hacking; these chapters allow one to recognize the variety of activities that cyber security entails. This section is a prime example of the ways in which experts choose to focus on various aspects of the field, yet equally recognize that the expansions in technology are the chief reasons why the security domain has been faced with many challenges. These chapters not only prove how the field has evolved, but also highlight how current practices must continue to evolve to ensure the safety of citizens. This section is an excellent reference for those who desire a firm understanding of the field, yet also want to understand the diversity and a range of issues within the field.

In chapter one, the author introduced readers to the impact of the Information Revolution, especially as it pertains to terrorists' use of the Internet. This chapter, appropriately titled, "The Mirror has Two Faces: Terrorist Use of the Internet and the Challenges of Governing Cyberspace," expands on an impressive, professional analysis of an "asymmetric information war" and the ways in which technology has been exploited to further transnational terrorist activities. Unfortunately, technology has been a convenient means of enhancing terrorist operations; in fact, the advances in technology have provided greater opportunities for terrorists to access the Internet. Terrorists recruit and radicalize through the Internet, spread propaganda, and even conduct transnational criminal activity under the guise of anonymity. Thus, this chapter is useful in understanding current issues in protecting Internet users, and how tactical and strategic activities must be focused on evolving threats from terrorists who take advantage of the Internet.

Although it is certainly true that terrorists use the Internet and novel technology to achieve their objectives, it is also equally true that state-actors or state-owned industries can be involved in cyber espionage. The second chapter, "US-China Relations: Cyber Espionage and Cultural Bias," provides outstanding research into a unique perspective of cyber espionage. According to the authors of this chapter, a majority of individuals may believe that China is conducting cyber espionage and essentially initiating a cyber war against the US, yet the authors highlight that the US also conducts cyber espionage on China. The authors have taken the opportunity to focus on the necessity of more improved understandings of national cultures that would ultimately contribute to rational discussions and progress, especially in relation to economics, security, and the evolving new role of cyber espionage. Whilst this chapter focuses on China and the US, it effectively presents an overview of the ways in which state actors also play a role in the use of technology and cyberspace to conduct cyber espionage to achieve goals.

The first two chapters immediately provide an understanding of how state and non-state actors use cyberspace; however, the third chapter then highlights another aspect of the cyber arena by focusing on the electrical grid. When one ponders issues, such as cyber espionage, cyber warfare, or even cyberspace in its entirety, the electrical grid may not be the most obvious issue, since it has not been discussed in the media in detail. The authors of this chapter, which is titled, "The USA Electrical Grid: Public Perception, Cyber Attacks, and Inclement Weather," move away from the trend in chapters one and two, which focused on who or what is using cyberspace or conducting cyber espionage. The authors of chapter three focus on how illegal cyber activity can have wide scale consequences that could include damage to the electrical grid, which would affect all citizens in the US. The chapter highlights ways in that these issues could be prevented, and also notes the recent development of batteries for one's home that would allow individuals to no longer be reliant on the electrical grid. In particular, this chapter also highlights the ways in which public perception has an effect on how intelligence and security issues are viewed and handled.

Of course, the intelligence field was placed under a magnifying glass by the public consequent to the Edward Snowden case. Snowden, a former contractor for the National Security Agency, illegally leaked classified documents to the public. Many members of the public viewed this as an opportunity to understand how intelligence activities are conducted and highlight any possible illegal activities within the intelligence field; however, the Snowden case is, in actuality, an excellent example of how insider-threats are major issues in government and institutions/businesses in the twenty-first century. Along these lines, the fourth chapter provides insight to the intriguing topic of insider-threat detection methods and security precautions in corporate espionage and cyber espionage. The chapter, aptly titled, "Insider-Threat Detection in Corporate Espionage and Cyber-Espionage," explores insider-threats in the form of data scientists, penetration testers, and data analysts who may use their education, experience, and access to gather information.

As one advances through the book, the next chapter effectively highlights the conclusion of section one by focusing on how espionage has evolved over time, yet has at a general level remained the same even in the digital age. This chapter, "Teaching New Dogs Old Tricks: The Basics of Espionage Transcend Time," examines how detection and prevention at early stages are the way forward in mitigating cyber threats and cyber espionage. Through a reliance on continuous risk assessments that identify threats, the authors propose that most threats can be countered. This chapter appropriately ends section one by highlighting the tremendous tasks and activities that are necessary to prevent the disastrous consequences of cyber espionage and cyber attacks.

The second section of this book provides readers with a broader opportunity to understand the field. The authors of these chapters have presented their views of security in the digital age by maintaining a focus on developments in the field and how current cyber security practices could be improved. Although the authors do include future research directions and highlight what they feel may be most appropriate to strengthen the security discipline, these chapters primarily present readers with a way to realize the recent developments in the field, while also showing readers what could be learned from past events in field, such as the Snowden debacle. In comparison to the first section of this book, section two offers more detailed descriptions of the field by also highlighting more aspects of the cyber security field. Section two places a spotlight on the overview of the field in a more descriptive manner that moves away from the current politicization of the field. Although intelligence and politics are inherently intertwined, the authors have done an outstanding job of presenting facts in an objective platform. This section is an outstanding literary compilation for readers, especially for students, in the intelligence field who yearn to gain a basic understanding of the vast discipline of cyber security. Each of the chapters in this section has been written by authors from four different countries, which has resulted in an extremely diverse section that is inundated with varying facts and analytical assessments.

Within this section of the book, chapter six begins with an outstanding review of digital intelligence written from a British perspective from one of the most qualified individuals to discuss such a matter, Sir David Omand, the former head of the GCHQ. Sir David, in his chapter, "Understanding Digital Intelligence: A British View," has eloquently elaborated on digital intelligence in manner that focuses on ethical principles and human rights. Additionally, this chapter also focuses on a three-layer model of security activity on the Internet: securing the use of the Internet for everyday economic and social life and for political and military affairs; the activity of law enforcement attempting to manage criminal threats on the Internet; and the work of secret intelligence and security agencies exploiting the Internet to gain information on their targets, especially in support of law enforcement. Although this chapter essentially highlights a British view, it presents novel interpretations and analyses that could be globally initiated.

To further understand the field in the technology-dependent society, chapter seven provides an overview and discussion of how social media and the Internet have facilitated various movements around the globe. This chapter, "Surveillance and Resistance: Online Radicalization and the Political Response," will be a favorite for any individual who seeks a clear, fact-based analysis of how liberal, political democracies have difficulties in censoring certain groups and the ideas they promote that do not align with or protect national interests. This chapter is not only thought provoking, but it is also a direct example of the wide-ranging nature of the intelligence field. The expert author of this chapter, from Australia, provides a unique view of the field that many researchers fail to take into consideration.

Contributing to the diversity of this section and the book in its entirety is chapter eight, titled "Developing Discourse and Tools for Alternative Content to Prevent Terror," which has been written by two impressive researchers from Israel. This chapter provides a wonderful discussion of propaganda and the ways in which terrorists may manipulate the openness and multiculturalism of Western countries. This chapter is useful in understanding how cyberspace has made radicalization and recruitment an easier task than ever before. Through this chapter, the authors have also proposed the use of inclusive cultural and religious policy that promotes intra-community dialog to prevent radicalization.

Finally from this section, chapter nine, "The Value of Personal Information," which is written by three authors from the USA provides an extensively detailed overview of five types of information that are targeted during cyber-attacks, and why the information is important. This chapter effectively concludes section two, since it provides a final understanding of the field in a manner that is directly related to cyberspace and specific components of cyber espionage and cyber attacks.

The third section of this book focuses on novel implementations and forward thinking. The authors of these chapters have placed a priority on presenting readers with novel framework and ways in which to implement new security measures. The authors have highlighted their professional views of how law enforcement and intelligence officials may implement novel techniques and strategies (e.g. new laws and educational framework) to enhance security, especially in a technologically dependent society. This section is particularly useful for those who seek diverse opinions on how to combat terrorism and maintain security stability. For instance, these chapters include how to use peace education to prevent terrorism through online education, in addition to the necessity of a federal data breach notification law. These chapters further contribute to the notion that whilst all members of the security arena work toward achieving the ultimate goal of protecting citizens, the members each have individual and unique ideas with regard to how the goal may be most appropriately achieved. It is paramount for readers to further realize that the future of the security arena is also partly influenced by the public. Those within the field guide the process, yet the public also has the power to put forth notions that may be used to improve security practices. By initiating public discussions, it becomes possible to ensure appropriate oversight of all the necessary surveillance programs. It also ensure that those within the field realize that they are also subject to rules and regulations; accordingly, it helps to ascertain that those within the field realize that their positions do not entitle them to act above the law. This section is especially useful for researchers in the field who are seeking to investigate novel data pertaining to the security arena.

Section three begins with chapter ten, which is titled, "Application of Mathematical Modeling for the Secure and Intelligent Energy Infrastructure." This chapter adopts a novel perspective that essentially ties into chapter three pertaining to the electrical grid. Whilst the prior chapter provides a qualitative discussion of the electrical grid, this chapter provides a quantitative solution to the issue by providing the preliminary framework of a new mathematical model. This chapter offers an opportunity to learn more about the structure of security, in addition to understanding the unique ways that researchers assess situations. Not all political or security researchers rely on qualitative assessments; rather, many such researchers prefer quantitative methodologies to provide more structured assessments. This is a very useful chapter for researchers who are seeking new topics in which to conduct research and investigate.

Chapter eleven, "The Need for a Federal National Data Breach Notification Law," once again moves back to the qualitative discussions of the field by focusing on extremely important notions in the intelligence and security fields: uniformity and quality assurance. This chapter proposed a federal national data breach notification law, which would ascertain that various issues, such as insider threats, do not result in overwhelming losses of confidential data that could compromise the security and safety of a country. This chapter is useful in the wake of issues, such as those raised by Snowden. Moreover, this chapter also elucidates how cyber attacks and related issues should be reported to the public or those individuals who are the victims of the cyber attacks. This chapter further proves the ways in which many individuals within the security and intelligence fields strive to find ways to make intelligence and security activities acceptable to the public without compromising the security of activities or the lives of those involved. In fact, the next chapter further explicates the ways in which members of the public can be actively involved in the maintenance of security, without having to be directly involved in intelligence agencies or security organizations.

Chapter twelve, "Combating Terrorism Through Peace Education: Online Educational Perspective," is especially useful for students or individuals who are interested in learning about an academic pathway in peace education through online learning that would provide flexibility to balance personal, professional, and academic activities whilst also contributing to the security of a nation. Peace education is a form of education that focuses on peaceful resolutions; hence, the authors of this chapter have focused on the ways in which the integration of peace education into educational curricula or special online peace education degree programs can contribute to the fight against terrorism. The reliance on online learning is especially useful as technology continues to advance, and as individuals maintain their busy lifestyles whilst earning higher education in order to be competitive to earn job positions. This chapter also complements the other chapters by promoting academic pathways that would rationally teach the new generation to rely on non-violent resolutions to issues.

Drawing near to the end of this compilation of experts, chapter thirteen, "The Role of State Actors in Cyberspace: Can State Actors Find Their Role in Cyberspace?" specifically complements chapter two which pertained to state actors in cyberspace. This chapter explicitly provides a detailed assessment of many issues in cyberspace, such as attribution and motivation. Furthermore, this chapter also touches upon the issue of ensuring an effective network amongst law enforcement to protect citizens across all borders. As aforementioned, the effort to ensure that law enforcement effectively work with one another and cooperate can be a difficult task; thus, this chapter is beneficial as a framework to explore continued efforts to implement a multilateral network to enforce the security of citizens across borders in cyberspace.

Chapter fourteen, "Intelligence Studies, Theory, and Intergroup Conflict Resolution: Theory and Beyond," continues with the chapter trend of identifying ways to improve the field and security of nations. The authors of this chapter have specifically focused on shifting the current practices in the intelligence and security fields to rely on primarily multidisciplinary methods, specifically by integrating social psychological approaches. The intelligence field may primarily seem to be directly correlated to military operations or other distinct security activities (e.g. covert action); however, the intelligence arena actually has a direct link to psychology, which must be recognized. Those in the discipline must be able to appropriately work with individuals on a daily basis, which requires at least a basic understanding of psychology. Therefore, this chapter serves as a meaningful resource for those who desire to learn about the diversification of the intelligence field, especially with regard to conflict resolution.

Finally, chapter fifteen, "Detecting Individual-Level Deception in the Digital Age: The DETECT Model ©" is the final chapter in this book. This chapter covers a novel model developed to detect individual-level deception for law enforcement officers who come into contact with members of the public on a daily basis. This chapter proposes the use of new, proven-successful model that allows for the timely detection of individual-level deception even in a technologically advanced world. This chapter also contributes to the field by providing individuals with an opportunity to realize the novel contributions to the field that have been designed in an effort to maintain security and aid in the positive advancement of the intelligence field.

The evolution of this book has resulted in a compilation of expert research that is aimed at an audience willing to read about the current security arena with an open-mind. The research can be used as a reference book for academics or practitioners within the field, but it may also be used for those without a firm background in the topic. The diversity of the chapters and the scholarly writing has left little to ambiguity and ensured a centered piece of literary art. It is especially fascinating to recognize how the authors have overlapping notions of the current issues within field, yet also have varying ideas pertaining to solutions. By perusing each of these chapters, one can recognize the individuality expressed through the work, in addition to how one's own beliefs and opinions align or contrast with the authors' views. As one reads through these chapters, it is important to have an open-mind, but also consider how the chapters directly relate to one's own life. Cyber security is not that which is isolated to those who hold positions within the field; thus, as members of the public, individuals can be largely involved without ever acquiring a position in the field. By reading the presented chapters, it becomes easier to recognize what changes one can make to one's own life in order to contribute to the stability of a country and the security of citizens. Even the smallest of actions can result in the contribution to the bigger goal of securing the globe. Therefore, these chapters provide open-source information that can be used to develop strategies to strengthen cyberspace in a manner that would provide the general public with greater freedom, whilst also ensuring that criminal activity is appropriately handled and prosecuted.

Of course, as the editor of this book, I had the privilege of reading each of the chapters more than once over the course of several months. I am humbled and honored to have worked with each of the authors. I witnessed the hard work and dedication of each of these authors who, at times, had to overcome personal and professional challenges in order to finalize their work in the midst of their busy schedules. Each of these authors represent distinct experts in their relevant fields; thus, their contribution to this book has resulted in a unique, one-of-a-kind academic, reference book. As you read through this book, it will become possible to recognize the individuality and varying styles of the authors, which makes this book much more entertaining and enjoyable.

I am also greatly indebted to General (ret.) Keith Alexander who took the time out of his extremely busy schedule to provide a foreword for this book. I had the honor of meeting General (ret.) Alexander and his beautiful wife at my first Master's degree graduation; when I asked him to provide a foreword, I did not expect a prompt affirmation. Thus, when General (ret.) Alexander agreed to provide a foreword and did so in such a timely manner, I was truly honored that the man whom I had admired for his professionalism as the Director of the National Security Agency (NSA) would provide me with a foreword for my first academic, reference book. Through this preface, I would like to extend my heartfelt gratitude and thanks to General (ret.) Alexander, in addition to each of the authors within this book. Without these individuals, this book would never have come to fruition.

I must also extend my thanks to four individuals who helped me over the course of my own personal, academic, and professional journeys; Dr. Joseph DiRenzo, Dr. Bruce Hay, Dr. Joseph Bond, and Dr. Eugene de Silva (otherwise known as my father). Dr. DiRenzo acted as my research supervisor for my first Master's degree from the American Military University; it was his guidance that prepared me to conduct in-depth research in the intelligence field. His comments never failed to open my eyes to new perspectives. Dr. Bruce Hay, on the other hand, acted as my supervisor for my second Master's degree from Harvard. Hay's comments made it possible for me to develop a thesis that was accepted upon my first submission. The late Dr. Bond was an outstanding professor at Harvard who devoted his time to his students; he was a true professional who exemplified the high standards of academia. Moreover, Dr. Eugene de Silva, my father, is simply an amazing man. Without his support, it would not have been possible for me to achieve my goals. During hard times, my father has always been by my side to guide me on the right path in life. Words cannot express my love for my father; therefore, through my work in the security arena in an effort to help and protect my nation, I hope that I am able to continue to make my father proud. Finally, I must thank IGI Global Publishers for providing me with my first opportunity to be the editor of an academic, reference book in my chosen field. Additionally, thanks to the Virginia Research Institute, E and E Enterprises, LLC, and the National Accrediting Commission for Martial Arts which have provided me with the necessary funding to conduct research and progress, in addition to providing me with the required resources to maintain my research pursuits.

The future of intelligence and security is subject to change at a moments notice, but one can always be certain that experts, such as the authors within this book, will always be working to maintain structure and security. As time progresses, the challenges with which security officials are faced will also evolve. The security arena is not a stable field, but it can become more stable over the years with the help of more individuals engaging in fact-based analyses and discussions. As is the case with any topic, individuals will not always agree on certain perspectives, but security matters will benefit from accepting mindsets that resolve disagreements based on objective, factual assessments. Thus, it is hoped that this book will spark novel discussions, in addition to expanding on current debates. The authors of this book have set a firm foundation for future research, and have presented novel ideas that deserve widespread attention and consideration.

I hope that the readers of this book enjoy the diversity of academic research herein presented.

Eugenie de Silva
University of Leicester, UK & Virginia Research Institute, USA
January 10, 2015

Section 1
Current Threats

Chapter 1
The Mirror Has Two Faces:
Terrorist Use of the Internet and the Challenges of Governing Cyberspace

Shefali Virkar
University of Oxford, UK

ABSTRACT

The Information Revolution has greatly impacted how nation-states and societies relate to one another; particularly wherein new, or hitherto less powerful, actors have emerged to bypass and influence established channels of power, altering the manner in which nation-states define their interests, power bases, security, and increasingly, their innate ability to govern and control flows of information. This book chapter investigates the 'winner-takes-all' hypothesis relative to how the Internet, its associated platforms, and technologies have been harnessed to enhance the activities of both transnational terrorist networks and the organisations, clusters, and individuals dedicated to researching and combating them. The issues covered by this research raise important questions about the nature and the use of technology by state and non-state actors in an asymmetric 'information war'; of how ideas of terrorism, surveillance, and censorship are conceptualised, and manner in which the role of the nation-state in countering and pre-empting threats to national security has been redefined.

DOI: 10.4018/978-1-4666-9661-7.ch001

INTRODUCTION

The Information Revolution and the advent of the new Information and Communication Technologies has significantly impacted how nation-states and societies relate to one another, and has underlined several challenges to international governance and security. These include the creation of global electronic platforms where new, or hitherto less powerful, actors have emerged to influence policy agendas; bypassing established channels of participation, changing the conception of how nation-states define their interests, their power bases, and their security, and increasingly challenging states' ability to govern and control the dissemination of information.

Ten years since its emergence as a mainstream global medium, the Internet plays an active role in both contentious political debates and the dissemination of alternative visions for a new order in world politics. Today, therefore, the issue is no longer *whether* the Internet and the World Wide Web have altered the world we live in, but instead *how* the study of them thereof might enhance our understanding of the political changes they bring. Unlike print or other broadcast media, which have largely remained the clearly designated territory of communications scholars, the study of the Internet and its associated new Information and Communications Technologies has attracted researchers from various scholarly backgrounds and disciplines to explore its implications for political, social, and economic change from the unique perspective of their own particular field of expertise.

With social scientists starting recently to examine the political impact of the new digital technologies on everyday living, concepts such as power and governance and their relationship to networks of communication, conflict, and excellence have become increasingly important and have entered common parlance when examined within the context of digital communications technology. When considered in this regard, the world has also seen the rise of a new type of conflict, *the Information War*, which involves the disruption of information networks through the proliferation of aggressive software and the use the Internet and its associated applications by loosely organised groups of dissidents to communicate and to co-ordinate attacks. Recent investigations spurred on by the global *War on Terror* have further thrown into sharp focus international terrorist networks' usage of the Internet, not only as a communications platform and as a vehicle for the dissemination of propaganda, but also as an active element in their recruitment strategies and as a tool for delivering remote instruction and training.

BACKGROUND

This book chapter investigates the 'winner-takes-all' hypothesis in relation to how the Internet and its associated platforms and technologies have been harnessed to enhance the activities of both transnational terrorist networks and the organisations, clusters, and individuals dedicated to researching and combating them. The attacks of September 11, 2001 on the United States of America, followed closely by numerous instances of terrorist-related activity around the world, demonstrated that modern-day terrorist networks are widely interconnected and connected to each other, and are able to harness effectively the flexibility afforded by the Internet and its associated technologies in order to achieve key aims, goals, and objectives.

Transnational terrorism has always been a security issue of great sovereign concern, and dissident groups have consistently taken advantage of the potentialities of the new digital communications media in direct opposition to the fundamental constitution of the nation-state. With scholars, practitioners, and researchers increasingly using the Web- and Internet-based search engines and databases to locate highly specialised information, knowledge, and sources of expertise, the question also stands of whether digital data collection and the use of online data resources to understand and to combat terrorism enhances the range of available channels of excellence and expertise and improves state-citizen relations, or if their frequent use and overuse results in an eventual oversimplification of terrorist typologies that is bound to become a more pressing concern for the community in the not-so-distant future. In this respect, the issues central to the understanding of terrorism and terrorist-related networks and activities might be best addressed by examining the impact of the Internet and its related digital platforms and applications on society and the body politic through the double lens of power and governance.

Through a discussion of these core concepts, the chapter seeks to enable scholarship to further comprehend the shift in global power relations and the new forms of governance and regulation that appear and then co-exist in a digitised world. The central themes covered by this research raise important questions about the nature of the Internet and its particular use by both state and non-state actors; of how ideas of national and international security, surveillance, and censorship are conceptualised, and the manner in which the role of the nation-state in countering and pre-empting threats to national security and sovereignty has been fulfilled and redefined. In particular, the work examines whether the increases seen in transnational acts of terrorism, and their corresponding scholarly, practitioner, and state-sovereign responses, might be considered as a general trend towards an escalation in the asymmetric 'information war' waged against Western-liberal democracies, the degree to which the *War on Terror* has manifested itself and is being fought online, and the nature and ways in which traditional security tactics and strategies have been altered in direct response.

PLUGGING IN: A BRIEF HISTORY OF THE INTERNET

In 1962, an academic at the Massachusetts Institute of Technology (M.I.T.), J.C.R. Licklider, circulated a series of memos elaborating an idea that he called the "Galactic Network", a concept that envisioned "a globally interconnected set of computers through which everyone could quickly access data and programs from any site." He later became the first person to head the computer research programme at the Advanced Research Project Agency (ARPA), a division of the U.S. Department of Defence, where he quickly convinced his successors about of the importance of his idea. His ideas soon converged with those of Paul Baran, an engineer at the American think-tank RAND Corp., whose work stemmed from the concern that a leader of an unfriendly state would be tempted to take advantage of the ease with which military communications could be disrupted, and launch a pre-emptive nuclear strike on the USA circumventing its current digital arrangement. As an alternative to conventional circuit switching technology, therefore, which focused on a single line of communication, Baran suggested the creation of a nationwide network of computers to head off such a catastrophe (Abbate, 2001).

Licklider and Baran's ideas were soon put to the test with the creation of the ARPANET, which commenced operations in the early 1970s. The aim of ARPANET was to make research on military defence related issues efficient by enabling researchers and their government sponsors to share resources without having to physically deliver them. The informal collegial, non-hierarchical working relationships that evolved were the chief cause of ARPANET's early success, ultimately resulting in that of the Internet and its associated technologies as we know it today (Warkentin, 2001). ARPANET's users were also involved in its development: the most significant addition being the introduction of *electronic mail* or *e-mail*, an application that very soon became the most popular feature of the project. From a means of sharing data, the ARPANET thus became a medium of instantaneous and rapid communication.

The late 1980s saw a boom in the sale of personal computers (PCs) and a gradual opening of the Internet to public access. The creation of the World Wide Web in the mid-1990s, following the almost complete privatisation of the ARPANET a few years earlier, completed the transformation of the Internet from a purely defence-related research tool into a popular communication medium that allowed for "information gathering, social interaction, entertainment, and self-expression" as well as the overall interaction of many with many on a global scale. Today, the Internet is shaping and is constantly being shaped by the activities of its users like never before. It is inexpensive and increasingly popular - current estimates suggest that over 2.5 billion people were online as of September 2012, up from a little over 600 million in September 2002 (Internet World Stats, 2012). From its inception, the people and groups who use the Internet have had their own 'agendas, resources, and visions' for its future, making its history 'a tale of collaboration and conflict amongst a remarkable variety of players' (Abbate, 2001).

The explosion in the number of civil society networks dependent on the Internet and its associated technologies over the last few years has been touted as one of the most dramatic and intriguing changes in current world politics (Warkentin, 2001). These groups and their ideas proliferate across borders, and infiltrate nearly all major political arenas, thereby altering the landscape of international political economy with their promise of forging a global civil society that is altogether more just and equitable. Delivering this promise, however, depends on the ability of these groups and networks to communicate with each other quickly over vast expanses of space and time; and it is in this endeavour that new communication technologies, particularly the Internet, have played and will continue to play, a crucial role (Frangonikolopoulos, 2012). One of the more innovative means used by global civil society for mobilisation and communication has been the Internet, which, since its initial inception and subsequent commercialisation, has provided unprecedented opportunities for the exchange of information outside the control of the dominant mainstream media (Fenton, 2007). The prevalence of such information and resources not other available in the mainstream media, and stemming from alternative sources that may otherwise not be heard or easily accessed, has thus the potential to greatly enhance the quality of action in global civil society and the tools available to actors involved in social and political grassroots struggles.

Political observers and social critics are divided, however, as to the nature and ultimate significance of such citizen networks; with the more optimistic (encompassing a broad spectrum ranging from Gramscians to liberals) seeing these networks as being by-and-large positive expressions of democracy in arenas dominated by nation-states and cross-border companies and as having an ever increasing significance on world affairs (Diebert, 2000). A second line of argument takes a more cautious approach, and vocalises an oft-muted concern that, instead of citizen-focused mass democracy, the global arena will be dotted with millions and millions of niche interests. More particularly, there are those who associate the advent of the Internet with the idea of the information 'haves' and 'have-nots', and are wary of the consequences ensuing from the so-called 'digital divide' (Zinnbauer, 2001). Finally, there those who believe that, far from being constructive, the Internet is harmful to true global civil society, and in that an increasingly digital society results in a gradual decline in an individual's social circle and in the ultimate destruction of social capital which can only be built up and maintained through continuous face-to-face interaction (Huysman & Wulf, 2004).

THE INTERNET AND THE NEW DIGITAL COMMUNICATIONS TECHNOLOGIES: ISSUES OF POWER AND OF GOVERNANCE IN A DIGITISED WORLD

In the study of politics and international affairs, the notion of 'governance' has become an extremely fashionable and adaptable concept. Even when considered on its own, it is important to keep in mind that the term conceptually embodies and is underpinned by certain pivotal, fundamental ideas about control, authority, and the exercise of executive power. Placed within the study of the global political implications of the Internet and digital technologies, with particular attention paid to terrorism and the actor-networks central to the defiance of sovereign state power, much remains about the understanding and the implications of the theoretical conceptualisation of governance that is still in its infancy and that we do not understand. To better explain how the structures of the Internet are conceived and conceptualised within the context and the study of terrorism and terrorist-related behaviour and activities, of how actor and group participation and the actions within them are enabled, facilitated, and enhanced, and of the manner and the ways in which distributional outcomes are achieved and ultimately understood, the importance of citizen participation and sovereign power, and by association, the various forms of governance within the broader framework of democracy and the new digital communications technologies needs to be first addressed.

The idea of governance, and by extension Electronic Governance or e-Governance, may therefore be said to comprise of two distinct but complementary elements: that of e-Government – which encompasses all the formal institutional and legal structures of a country, and e-Democracy – which can be said to refer to the participative and deliberative processes which operate within those structures (Virkar, 2007). Broadly speaking, on the one hand, e-Government itself may be divided into two distinct areas: (1) e-Administration, which refers to the improvement of government processes and to the streamlining of the internal workings of the public sector often using ICT-based information systems, and (2) e-Services, which refers to the improved delivery of public services to citizens through multiple electronic platforms (Virkar, 2011). On the other, the concept of e-Democracy may be further subdivided into two distinct areas: e-Engagement (or e-Participation), which emphasises opportunities for greater consultation and dialogue between government and citizens, and e-Voting, the expression of fundamental democratic rights and duties online (Virkar, 2007).

e-Engagement as a policy, if defined by an express intent to increase the participation of citizens in decision-making through the use of digital media, would consequently involve the institutionalised provision of resources to facilitate the responsible and collaborative decision making involved ultimately in institutional and social change. Whilst the earliest speculations about the Internet and Democracy emphasised the potential for direct, unmediated participation (OECD 2001) and the transformative nature of the process of public engagement, this chapter follows the view of scholars such as Coleman and Gotze (2001) that whilst e-Democracy is incompatible with a political culture of élitism, it is not about replacing what has evolved so far but instead, rather than seeking to radically transform governance along any particular ideological line, it aims to complement the institutions and processes of representative democracy.

For different reasons, however, there has always been considerable disagreement amongst social scientists over understanding power and the exercise of authority in a highly digitised world. Disputes have historically pivoted around the definition, scope, domain, effects and the meaning of both the capacity and the exercise of authority (Dahl, 1989). In this regard, the notion of power has been thought of as inherently contestable, even underestimated as a category of political analysis. Discussed within the context of this chapter, the point is not to search for a single or dominant notion of power that would command either universal acceptance or application, but is instead to open scholars and practitioner communities concerned with the Internet and with terrorism to a more rigorous and sustained examination of this key fundamental concept.

In this view, facilitating the involvement of different sections of society in the process of government is now seen as a democratic prerequisite in many advanced liberal democracies, with some commentators such as Fishkin (1995) highlighting the need for 'mass deliberation', and emphasising the need for people and their representatives to be brought together to collaborate on issues of mutual interest. The recent exponential growth in access to new Information and Communication Technologies (ICTs), and the expansion of a newly-created digital environment wherein people shop, talk, and otherwise spend large parts of their lives in online spaces, has opened up a plethora of new opportunities for interaction between power elites and the various constituent elements of civil society. At the same time, their rapid proliferation has raised important questions and triggered debates as to *who* is able to participate and to *what* extent they may do so, as well as the *types* of participation such technologies make possible at different levels of government and their impact on different government institutions and democratic processes (Virkar, 2011).

Explored within the contextual framework of Government 2.0, governance may be considered as the active participation of citizens in political and civic processes, facilitated and enhanced through the use of *Web 2.0 Technologies*, a term referring to the collection of social media through which individuals and actor groups become active agents in the creation, organization, editing, combining, sharing, commenting, and rating of Web-based content, as well as in the formation of social and other networks of excellence through various in-group interactions and inter-linkages to each other.

Technologies used include blogs, wikis, social networking hubs, (such as Facebook and MySpace), Web- based communication modes like chatting and online chat groups, photo-sharing tools such as Flickr and Picasa, video casting and sharing platforms like YouTube, audio-sharing media such as Podcasts, mashups, widgets, virtual worlds, microblogs like Twitter, and the social annotation and bookmarking of Web sites (Virkar, 2014). The emphasis is, therefore, on both active participation and on an *outside-in wisdom of crowds approach*, wherein data and information are created by a network of users outside of an organizational boundary in a collaborative, interactive manner. This perspective is markedly different from the *inside-out, authoritative, know-all* approach typical to the Web 1.0 era, whereby an organization or apex body becomes the key creator and organizer of content for consumption, and wherein people are considered mere passive consumers of information or part of a larger passive-receptive audience only (Chun et.al, 2010).

Given this, therefore, have transnational civil society networks (including those active in the proselytizing and propagation of terrorism and civil disobedience on- and offline) been able to harness the potential benefits of the Internet and of online networking to mount international campaigns for political, social, and economic change? Or is the power of the Internet and the new digital technologies merely a chimera, unable to deliver on its promises? As the structure and scale of the Internet has evolved since its initial inception, and the spectrum of associated digital platforms, technologies, and applications expanded over time, both researchers and practitioners have speculated over and frequently debated the various levels, modes, mannerisms, and mechanisms appropriate for harnessing and governing the medium. Within this set of given circumstances, it may be argued that the study of both power and of governance have become increasingly 'fitting' as frameworks used to conceptualise and understand terrorism in an increasingly digitised world; capturing as they do base ideas of collective rule-making and authoritative decision-making within multiple hierarchies.

THE MIRROR HAS TWO FACES: TERRORISTS, HACKTIVISTS, CYBER ACTIVISTS, SCHOLARS AND THEIR USE OF THE INTERNET

The Internet may be put to a variety of uses by civil society organisations (Arquilla & Ronfeldt, 2001). The five main modes of Internet usage listed and elucidated upon below. These modes are by no means unrelated, and are frequently used in combination by civil society networks to enhance their efficacy (Harwood & Lay, 2001).

- **Collection:** The Internet is a vast storehouse of information, most of it available for free. Today, fact-sheets, policy statements, legislative documents, academic papers, critiques and analyses, and other items relating to a wide variety issues are available for download online. Activists can get hold of whatever material they need at the click of a button, using one of the many search engines, e-mail lists, or chat services available online. News channels providing almost minute-to-minute updates are also available, and prove especially invaluable to groups wishing to monitor ongoing events. In addition, websites provide activists with information on how to use the Internet, its associated applications and digital technologies more effectively.
- **Publication:** Organisations use the Internet to post and distribute information for public consumption. They can create interactive websites that provide global audiences may include fact-sheets, reports, lectures, and interviews. They may publish online journals, create mailing lists, online discussion groups, and bulletin boards. By using the Internet to publish and disseminate information, civil society groups can take advantage of its relatively low costs whilst at the same time reaching out a global audience. The interwoven nature of the World Wide Web, with its links, attachments, and hypertext, enhances its effectiveness as a medium of effective and far-reaching information dissemination.
- **Dialogue and Debate:** E-mail, newsgroups, web forums, chat rooms, and the like provide to civil society multiple forums for the discussion and debate of various issues. For instance, the use of chat rooms has been a subject of robust debate amongst social scientists; with some scholars touting on the one hand virtual discussions as being as good for the building of social capital amongst network members as face-to-face conversations, and with others believing that the only outcome of such impersonal communications is a gradual decline in the quality of interpersonal relationships.
- **Organising and Mobilising:** Advocacy groups use the Internet to increase awareness and mobilise people to rally around an issue. The Net also enables groups to co-ordinate action among members and with other organisations and individuals, across borders and across time-zones. Plans of action may be circulated via e-mail or posted on websites, which exist solely to facilitate better co-ordination between different members of a network.
- **Lobbying Decision-Makers:** The Internet facilitates the lobbying of those in power, and has contributed to the success of many online campaigns. In particular, the use of e-mail has become

very popular with, for example, e-mails containing sample protest letters being sent to people on electronic mailing lists, or through the setting up of e-mail boxes by activist groups to gather signatures for petitions. These days, almost everyone who's anyone in the echelons of power and civil society has an e-mail address, and some websites meticulously compile a list of such government officials and urge people to write in to them. It is not clear, however, just how successful such lobbying campaigns are. It is possible that, with e-mail software to block certain types of incoming electronic mail, and the use of standard, automatically generated replies used to respond to electronic petitions, campaign success depends on how well augmented the use of the Internet and associated platforms is with more traditional offline methods; backing the argument made by some that the Internet alone is not an adequate tool for public political movement.

There are, however, several disadvantages or potential drawbacks to the use of the Internet that can limit its usefulness to grassroots groups engaged in political action. More specifically, many of these "downsides" depend on what facets of the Internet are used and the context within which they are applied. Much like the advantages of the Internet discussed above, some have to do with the medium's unique characteristics.

- **The Internet is a Single Source of Communication:** Although the Internet was designed for robustness during the time of emergency, disruptions in the global network of networks can and have occurred. In July 1997, for example, Internet traffic "ground to a halt" across much of the United States because of a freak combination of technical and human errors, forewarning what some Internet experts believed could someday be a more catastrophic meltdown (Chandrasekaran & Corcoran, 1997). Similarly, at a micro-level, Internet crashes and outages are a regular feature of everyday life the world over. Other, older, technologies such as the facsimile and the telephone continue to have an advantage over the Internet in particular situations, particularly if a sender needs immediate acknowledgement or if information is required urgently or covertly or both (Larmer, 1995).
- **Communications Over the Internet Can Be Easily Monitored:** Public platforms and Internet websites are easy to monitor and control, particularly by state organisations or individuals with the appropriate technical know-how. Further, private one-to-one electronic messages may be slightly more secure, however, these again can be hacked by anyone with sufficient technical knowledge. Whilst data encryption packages may provide a solution to individuals and organisations exchanging private or classified information, these programmes and their related technologies might for a while remain out of reach of the majority of Internet users (Danitz & Stobel, 2001).
- **Opponents May Try to Use the Internet for Sabotage:** This disadvantage is related to many of the concerns discussed above, but represents a more active use of the Internet by activists, hacktivists and cyber criminals alike to trick, disrupt, or otherwise sow dissension (de Armond, 2001). This is because the Internet allows for anonymity, and makes it possible for provocateurs posing as someone or something else to try to cause dissension or sidetrack the campaign by posting messages for that purpose (Kalathil & Boas, 2010).
- **Information on the Internet is Unmediated:** One of the advantages of the Internet for activists and many other users, of course, is the fact that it allows them to dispense with the traditional filters for news and information (Virkar, 2014). It allows users to self-select information they are interested in and retrieve data in far more detail than available in a newspaper or, certainly, a tele-

vision programme. This same lack of structure, however, can present dangers, allowing for wide and rapid dissemination of information that is of questionable accuracy, being factually incorrect or propagandistic, including material that is racist, sexist, or otherwise hateful and incendiary (Arquilla & Ronfeldt, 2001).

- **Access to the Internet and Technical Know-How is Not Equal:** Not all who wish to play a role in a campaign for change, have access to the most modern tools of communication, including computers, modems, and the necessary telephone lines or other means to connect to the Internet. As already noted, access to encryption methods that allow for more secure communication may be limited, and technical knowledge concentrated in a small pool of hacktivists bent on causing destruction (Norris, 2001).
- **The Internet Cannot Replace Face-to-Face Contact:** Put simply, the Internet and other communications media cannot replace human interaction. Rather, the Internet has its own set of advantages and disadvantages, with Internet campaigns, because of their decentralized electronic nature, being decidedly unstable (Juris, 2005). Whilst the use of the Internet may supplement face-to-face interactions, it cannot wholly substitute for them as personal interactions constitute nearly-all initial campaigning groundwork (Kalathil & Boas, 2010).

TERRORIST NETWORKS AND THE NETWORKING OF SECURITY OPERATIONS & INTELLIGENCE: CONNECTING FOR SUCCESS

The Internet is altering the landscape of political discourse and advocacy in a way no other technology has done before (Virkar, 2014). It has proved of great use to those who wish to influence foreign policy and the international decision-making process, particularly non-state actors - both individuals and organisations. Cyber activism (otherwise known as Internet activism or *hackitivism*) involves *a normal, non-disruptive use of the Internet in support of an agenda or cause*, such as the use of the Web as an information resource, the construction of user-friendly websites and the posting of material for public viewing, the use of e-mail to disseminate information and electronic publications and letters, and the use of the World Wide Web as a place to discuss issues, form alliances, and to plan and co-ordinate activities (Jordan & Taylor, 2004). Coupled with a steadily growing online community, the Internet has become a powerful, inexpensive medium through which ideas and agendas may be communicated. The beauty of the Internet lies in its ability to cross national boundaries, enabling people and organisations from diverse geographical regions to come together to influence foreign policy anywhere in the world (Denning, 2001).

Today, many virtual communities are focused on shared political beliefs, and there are a number of websites encouraging online activism (Wall, 2007). The owners of some websites, such as Netaction.com, have even published online 'how-to' guides and training programmes, which *inter-alia* aim to adapt and popularise the use of e-mail, cyberspace networking, internet relay chats, instant messaging and intranets as a means of expanding and sustaining the cyber activist community. As The Virtual Activist training manual proclaims:

... Although you'll need some special skills to build and maintain a Web site, e-mail is easily mastered even if you have little or no technical expertise. If you can read and write and your computer has a modem, you can be a Virtual Activist! (Krause et. al., 2007)

The successful use of the Internet by civil society organisations lies chiefly in the key organisational process of *networking*. A critical concept, particularly in the context of collective action in the Information Age, the idea of a network is fundamental to an understanding of the dynamics of both online communication and collaboration and to the work that civil society organisations carry on offline (Wall, 2007). In theory, a network consists chiefly of a number of nodes connected to each other in a loose, horizontal, flexible structure that may expand and integrate new nodes and satellites, as long as communication and information flows between the key nodes is maintained (Castells, 1996).

It is easy to infer, therefore, that the emergence of the Internet would greatly benefit the setting up and maintenance of civil society networks in the today's world. Effective use of the Internet and its associated technologies does indeed seem to mitigate traditional difficulties of conventional civil society networks, particularly those issues pertaining to the co-ordination of functions, focusing its resources on specific goals and restraints placed on it due to its size and complexity (Van Laer & Van Aelst, 2010). Scholars of digital society such as Castells often credit the Internet as being the technological basis of form that civil society networks take in the Information Age. Accordingly, the use of technology results in networks having a potent combination of "flexibility and task performance, co-ordinated decision-making and decentralised execution, of individual expression and global horizontal communication which provide a superior form for human action" (Castells, 2001:2).

How Terror Uses the Internet: Issues, Threats, and Options

In direct contrast to what Resnick (1999) describes as the 'Political Uses of the Net', or the employment of the Internet by ordinary citizens, political activists, organised interests, governments and others to achieve political goals, the analysis below concerns itself with the utilisation of the Internet by terrorist groups and networks intent on harnessing the capabilities and capacities of the new digital information and communication technologies to capitalise on scaled-up economies of power and authoritarian control. Five core uses of the Internet and of Web-based technologies and associated applications might be identified and are further elucidated upon in this section: Information Provision, Financing and Fund-Raising, Presence-Building and Enhanced Networking, Recruitment and Training, and Data Mining and Information Sharing.

Information Provision

The advent of the Internet, and in particular the development of the World Wide Web and rich multimedia digital content, has significantly increased the opportunities for terrorists to pursue their activities online and has enhanced their efforts to engage in publicity, propaganda and, ultimately, in psychological warfare (Conway, 2006). This pursuance may manifest itself in the form of paid-for or funded websites that provide historical information, in the proliferation of profiles of leaders over other popular social media networks or platforms, or in the online dissemination of manifestos and other types of ideological propaganda (Theohary & Rollins, 2011). Terrorist organisations may also use the Internet as a tool of psychological warfare, using the medium to spread disinformation, to deliver threats, and to disseminate highly graphic or disturbing visual images (Bosco, 2013).

Prior to the Internet becoming the foremost mainstream medium of international communication, terrorists' hopes of attracting publicity for their causes and activities depended almost-solely on their garnering the attention of other, traditional mass media: television, radio, or the print media (Conway, 2006). Such attention still remains attractive, however, the more conventional media still retain high 'selection thresholds' or multistage processes of editorial selection that terrorists often cannot reach (Weimann, 2004). On the contrary, the same criteria do not apply to terrorists' own websites, and to public access to media time or bandwidth over the Internet in general (Theohary & Rollins, 2011). In this regard, the Internet offers terrorist groups an unprecedented level of direct control in the management of their organisations and over the content of their message(s); extending considerably both their legitimacy and their ability to manipulate and to shape how different target audiences perceive them and their professed opponents.

Financing and Fundraising

Money is the life-blood of terrorist activity. Terrorist networks and organisations require high levels of sustainable financing to fund what is commonly termed 'the engine of the armed struggle' (Napoleoni, 2004). The structure of the Internet, the platform's global reach, and its capacity for instantaneous and interactive communication has already made the medium attractive to a host of non-violent political organisations and civil society actors as channel for increased financial donations and transactions (Biersteker & Eckert, 2008). In much the same way, terrorist organisations and networks seek financing for their operations and activities, both via their individual websites and through harnessing the infrastructure of the Internet to engage with society at large and to effectively and clandestinely mobilise resources illegally.

In this respect, terrorist groups and networks may finance members and their numerous operations through either Direct Solicitation via (Terrorist) Websites, whereby a terrorist group or organisation requests funds from the public directly as Web-surfers who visit their sites in the form of either general statements underlining the organisation's need for money, or more direct solicitations that urge supporters and/or believers to donate immediately by either supplying bank account details or via an Internet payment gateway (Theohary & Rollins, 2011); the Exploitation of e-Commerce Tools and Entities, wherein terrorist-affiliated entities and individuals have establish Internet-related or –based business fronts as a means of raising money to support their activities; or the Creation and Establishment of Charities and Humanitarian Causes, referring to the use of charities as undercover fund raising vehicles, either by infiltrating branches of existing organisations to raise funds clandestinely, or by establishing new charities that allegedly profess humanitarian aims and purposes (Conway, 2006).

Presence-Building and Enhanced Networking

Another objective of terrorist use of the Internet refers to groups' efforts to flatten their organisational structures and to act in a more decentralised manner through taking advantage of that facet of the medium's structure which allows dispersed actors to communicate quickly with each other and coordinate activities and operations effectively at low cost (Conway, 2006). The current architecture of the Internet allows not only for rapid intra-group communication, but also for the creation of lasting inter-group linkages; in which respect the medium enhances terrorists' capacities to transform the internal hierarchies of their organisations and to build global links within the alternative spaces it provides for communication, discussion, and other rich-media based interaction (Bosco, 2013).

The Internet and its associated platforms and technologies are set to transform terrorist organisations and networks in a number of different ways. Firstly, the medium may do so by Transforming Organisational Structures, whereby information-age network designs, wherein there is no single, central leadership, command or headquarters, replace traditional hierarchical structures of terror, and where greater efforts are channelled into building arrays of digitally-connected transnational alliances (Bosco, 2013); secondly through changes to Planning and Coordination, wherein hyper-modern I.T. systems, particularly those involving the new digital communications technologies, become essential in establishing and for sustaining effective and efficient terrorist networks, organisations, and institutions (Conway, 2006); and finally through the Mitigation of Risk, particularly that of detection by law enforcement, with the Internet offering terrorists and terrorist groups a means by which they might interact both freely and anonymously, together with the opportunity to evolve and become more decentralised.

Recruitment and Training

Online recruitment by terrorist organisations is reputed to be widespread and frequent (Theohary & Rollins, 2011). More especially, the Internet offers a number of ways in which terrorist groups and organisations might effectively mobilise sympathisers from within the general public and recruit new members who more actively support the terrorist cause or activity in question. The new digital communications technologies and their associated platforms make information gathering altogether easier for potential recruits to access and understand, whilst the global reach and interactivity of the Web allows groups to publicise events to more people and to be contacted directly and clandestinely (Conway, 2011). Finally, through the use of discussion forums and other interactive platforms, it is also possible for members of the public, whether as supporters or detractors of a group or cause, to engage in active debate with one another (Bosco, 2013).

Data Mining and Information Sharing

A final major use of Internet and its related technologies and applications by terrorists and terrorist organisations is that of and data gathering and information seeking (Conway, 2006). This refers, in particular, to the capacity of Internet users across all demographics to access huge volumes of information, previously extremely difficult to retrieve as a result of its being stored in widely differing formats and locations. Unlike the other uses mentioned and discussed previously, terrorists' information gathering activities rely not only on the operation and development of their own websites as vehicles for the creation and dissemination of propaganda, but also on the collection and evaluation of data contributed by others to 'the vast digital library', that is the World Wide Web (Bosco, 2013). Information gathering by terrorist networks may either take the form of Data Mining, or information-seeking behaviour that involves the in-depth and extensive use of the Internet and Web-based resources by terrorists in order to collect and assemble detailed information about specific topical issues, opportunities for funding, or potential targets; or of a more direct Sharing of Information, which refers to the sum total use of more general online information collection practices by terrorists (Theohary & Rollins, 2011).

LAW ENFORCEMENT, INTELLIGENCE, AND CLANDESTINE INFORMATION-GATHERING ONLINE: FIGHTING BACK

The Internet, and cyberspace more generally speaking, can demonstrably act as a significant source of unrestrained, clandestine power for terrorist groups. When considered within the context of being an essential, if not indispensable, tool to proponents of cyber activism and socio-political revolution, the regular use of and the heavy reliance on the Internet as an all-purpose medium of mass communication is, however, a double-edged sword for terrorists and terrorist networks. These organisations are not the only groups utilising the Internet to forge connections internationally and to forward their goals, indeed the new digital platforms and technologies can act as valuable, instrumental sources of power for anti-terrorist forces also (Theohary & Rollins, 2011).

Since the 9/11 terrorist attacks of 2001, a number of civil society groups and organisations have undertaken initiatives to disrupt terrorist use of the Internet and its associated platforms and applications, building on the small number of similar efforts undertaken by law enforcement prior to the turn of the millennium (Bosco, 2013). In this respect, national Intelligence and Law Enforcement agencies have been the chief instigators of such initiatives, and have been joined in their endeavours by other government agencies as well as concerned individuals, activists, and groups of hacktivists comprising the remainder of global civil society (Conway, 2006).

It stands to reason logically, therefore, that the more frequently terrorist groups use the Internet to move information and money around the globe, and the greater the dependence of these organisations is on the medium to recruit internationally, the more data is readily accessible and the wider the spectrum of tools is made freely available with which to trail them. Whilst advances in digital technologies have improved without a doubt the means by which covertly-obtained information is gathered together with the degree of its quality of content, the Internet also serves as consistent provider of open source knowledge and general intelligence for national intelligence agencies,

UNDERSTANDING TERRORISM 2.0: RECONFIGURING ACCESS TO KNOWLEDGE AND TO NETWORKS OF EXCELLENCE & EXPERTISE ONLINE

It is widely believed that the rapid diffusion of the Internet and the World Wide Web has transformed knowledge and expertise by widening access and making information available globally. Whilst there has been an exponential increase in the production and usage of networked digital resources, little is known about the reach and impact of this form of distributed knowledge. Some have argued that Information Technology could have a 'democratizing' impact on knowledge and information (Dahl, 1989); yet others have countered in the opposite: that in the online world these resources have, in fact, become concentrated in a 'winner-takes-all' effect that has a significant and lasting impact on the study and the understanding of global phenomena (Hindman et. al., 2003). There is thus a need to determine the extent to which the Internet is reshaping access to knowledge and resources world-wide (Dutton et. al., 2003), particularly in the science that is Terrorism scholarship, where the Internet is fast becoming the primary medium for communication and collaboration between scholars and practitioners.

In this chapter, we address the issue of 'winner-takes-all' in relation to the use of online resources within the related research domains of Terrorism, Terrorist-related activities, and actor-group led behaviours, motivations, goals, rules of play, and *modus operandi*. Together, these domains represent a broad interdisciplinary mix of an urgent global issue, addressed by both natural and human sciences. As these topics are also arguably highly current and relevant to an international stage, they provide a good case for examining whether access to scientific expertise is being reconfigured by the new digital information and communication technologies, and whether and how practitioner communities in the domain area are further reorganised towards the better understanding of a complex phenomenon they are constituted to counterpoint and to combat.

A popular approach for studying the dynamics of knowledge domains and the online presence of actors in those domains is webmetric analysis (Park & Thelwall, 2005). Hyperlink studies in social science research, generally referred to as webmetric analysis, draws on techniques and frameworks from the information science field of bibliometrics. To this end, this research synthesised webmetric data (detailed results of the webmetric analysis are reported in Schroeder et al. (2005)) with data gathered from an interview series with UK-based academic researchers. The following section focuses on the analysis of primary interview data, and the extent to which available webmetric or "Google" representations of the current information environment of each domain overlapped with respondents' mental models of the core institutions, people, and resources in their respective sub-domains. The aim of the interviews was to obtain a well-rounded understanding of how researchers use online and paper-based resources; including how they combine online and offline sources of information, the manner in which search engines are chosen, accessed, and used, and the general typography of those resource websites preferred and utilised most frequently.

As the production and use of online resources used to comprehend and to counter the various facets of terrorism continues to grow, it will become increasingly important to understand whether digital search-and-sort can find its way through these different types of hitherto-uncharted landscapes. For topics and sub-disciplines, such as those examined here, which in some way cross the boundaries of established domains, disciplines, fields of expertise and phenomena, there is the additional question of the extent to which online resources coupled with developments in communications technology will transcend or reconfigure established bounds of excellence and expertise. Such a shift will necessitate libraries and publishers, not to speak of the researchers and institutions who produce and use material online, to re-align their strategies for organising services and content accordingly.

TERRORISM, THE INTERNET, AND THE SCHOLARLY WEB: FROM UNCHARTED WILDERNESS TO WELL-DEFINED LANDSCAPE

As a domain of scholarship and practitioner advocacy, the study of terrorism and of terrorist networks is particularly pivotal, being both highly topical and international in scope. This observation, it may be argued, holds true across the world, regardless of the differences, subtleties, and nuances prevalent, particularly in terms of practitioner communities, target audiences, resources, research concerns, institutions, information sources and patterns of dissemination, across each separate sub-domain or sub-discipline (Reid & Chen, 2007). For instance, although some areas within the domain-field have more of a narrower, local or national orientation in terms of resources and audiences as compared to others, the broader information environment is by and large found to be pluridisciplinary in terms of its constituent epistemic structures with each possessing a unique policy-related orientation in terms of their disseparate outcomes.

More specifically, it has been noted that researchers concerned with the study of Terrorism in its various forms come from such diverse disciplines and perspectives as the natural sciences, human clinical disciplines, religious studies, political science and international relations (Fry et. al., 2008). Their research interests range from religious violence to *modus operandi* to weaponry and fire-armaments to international security. In terms of geographic orientation the domain and its sub-disciplines have been described as being *glocal* in its scope and relevance, given that this phenomenon has both a global dimension when the research organization is, for example, taking a world-wide approach to the topic, and local one when the focus is on a particular set of people, incidents, organizations, or similar (Reid & Chen, 2007).

Within the given framework, this book chapter proposes to analyse the dimensions and impact of the 'winner-takes-all' effect manifest in the use of online sources of data and other digital resources necessary to understand, predict, and combat the phenomenon Terrorism and Terrorist-related behaviours and activities across four, clearly-differentiated phenomena within scholarly and practitioner communities, across the scholarly web and other offline networks of scholarship and expertise: the decreasing use of libraries, the changing face of networks of excellence, web-search behaviour and other web-based search strategies, and differing perceptions regarding the nature and role of online gatekeepers.

The Decreasing Use of Libraries

Information and Library eScience scholarship has shown that, overall, both scholars and practitioner communities concerned with the study of terrorism and terrorist-related activities are unanimously in favour of the use of the Internet and World Wide Web for finding key data and information related to their work (Meyer & Schroeder, 2009). Case study responses across the canon confirm that these researchers and communities use the web *"all the time"*, *"all the time, for everything"*, and that they describe the Internet as a *"vital tool"* in relation to their subject mastery (Reid & Chen, 2008). In practice, however, there has nevertheless been great variation demonstrated in how these individuals and groups have used online resources and sources once accessed (Fry et. al. 2008).

A recent study conducted by Fry, Virkar, and Schroeder (2008) indicated that networks of scholarship on terrorism and those of related practitioner excellence used search engines not just to find published material on and around their topic, but also for locating so-called 'grey' data and literature, for exploring and evaluating a new, often current subject-specialist domain, and for finding out more about the research activities of other individuals, groups, communities, and networks (Fry et. al., 2008). Researchers in the field domain also registered a distinct decline in the use of libraries and other offline sources of information. Variants of this observation ranged from those respondents who now almost never use libraries to others who simply noted that more material is available online now than ever before. Within the domain of Terrorism research persist the dual findings that there may not only exist significant differences in the type of online material sought depending on the task at hand, but also the *fait accompli* that researchers also need different materials at different times. In this respect, the frequency and the priority rating attributed to a search might change, and differences in the type of material sought may be determined by whether the topic under examination is either immediately current or more slanted towards the historical.

For example, researchers of terrorism interviewed for the study conducted by Fry et. al. indicated that whilst they sometimes located journal articles and books (and other secondary materials) online, they at other times looked mainly for speeches, rich media formats and content, together with other kinds of primary documentation and resource material (Fry et. al., 2008). Futher, participants noted that legal cases and trial documentation related to acts and incidents of terrorism are usually not made available "until the draft has been approved and becomes law"; therefore pre-empting the pivotal necessity of printed papers and books. This also holds true the case of historians of terrorism, whereas "for those who are studying current trends of movements…current responses and reactions by government…the [Internet] is an absolutely vital source" (Fry et. al., 2008).

Networks of Excellence

In addition to the gaps identified by researchers in response to the direct validation of the webmetric data and the digital mapping of online information environments, there has across the scholarly domain been noted a discrepancy between the organisations, institutions, people involved with these networks and communities, and the resources that they reported using during the course of participant study-based interviews and evaluations of available Google representations (Hillis et. al., 2013). This observation has held particularly true for the web-pages of academics and academic institutions that the respondents frequently use and which constitutes key hubs and nodes in representations of the scholarly web. Fry et. al. (2008) noted particularly that in cases where participants were asked to recognise or identify key resource websites from a given list, or to name organisations and institutions or groups or individual people that stood a chance of appearing in a list of the top thirty search engine hit results, those remembered and ultimately identified were found unlikely to feature in the final list of the top 10 results presented at the interview.

A key example of this finding is the position of the M.I.P.T database, used by a large number of terrorism scholars as a first point of enquiry for the sourcing of primary data (Fry et. al., 2008). Branded by its content producers as the 'Terrorism Knowledge Base', the M.I.P.T database is run by a non-profit organisation of the same name, with a broad remit to both prevent terrorism in the U.S.A., and to provide generalised and universal access to accurate statistics and information about global terrorist activities and incidents (Reid & Chen, 2008). It is an interesting finding to note that, should a Google search be run using the keyword '*Terrorism*', regardless of the inherent popularity of website within the community and its intrinsic centrality to research on the subject, the M.I.P.T. database appears as the 11th search result and not within the top ten hits, being typically the first link on the second page of results (Fry et. al., 2008). Such a result is indicative of the difference between perception and actual web-presence, and could be considered crucial in terms of online visibility and representations of digital information environments (Hillis et. al., 2013).

Web Search Behaviour and Other Web-based Search Strategies

Users of online information sources and resources tend often to hold different perceptions regarding the relevance of digital material and content at different stages of information seeking. Fry and Talja (2007) have linked directed searching to the scatter of relevant material online across domain boundaries, and comparative findings reported across the related disciplines of Internet Studies and Library Science seem to corroborate their central argument (Fry et.al, 2008). During the early stages of search formulation, users tends to be more receptive to the topically relevant items presented to them, whereas in the later stages of information-seeking that follow query formulation, the user tends to be more discriminating whilst identifying items pertinent only to their personal information needs (Kuhltau, 1993).

In this regard, ensuring the validity of primary data, in particular figures and statistics, is a particularly important concern for researchers of Terrorism who feel that, owing to the highly sensitive nature of the issues that they deal with, as well as the difficulties they face in identifying 'legitimate' sources of data, any information collected from a search should be subjected to a stringent quality control process (Fry et. al., 2008). Further, studies conducted within the domain of eResearch and Library Science indicate that persistence with a particular set of results also depends on whether the researchers participant to the study believed that it was worth sifting through a large volume of irrelevant material to unearth 'gems', or not (Hillis et. al., 2013).

In particular, Terrorism researchers have been found more likely to persist with a particular set of search results, 'excavating' links in a similar way to the interdisciplinary humanities scholars observed by Palmer and Neumann (2002), wherein the importance of following a two stage quality control process is emphasised: in the first instance the use of a researcher's own judgement to determine what they felt was valid from within a list of search results, and in the second, a cross-checking the accuracy of the data by corroborating it with other sources of information, particularly with experienced colleagues in the field (Fry et. al., 2008).

For researchers of Terrorism and related sub-disciplines it has been further found that, in terms of web-search strategies, the search engine Google plays a more central role in exploring the object of research and identifying relevant sources of information than for most other subject domains of global import (Meyer & Schroeder, 2009). This may be due to the amorphous, shadowy nature of the subject matter itself – websites of terrorist groups and the message-boards, chatrooms, and blogs associated with them are constantly being shut down by national intelligence agencies, only to resurface with new web-addresses, and the only way to locate these and other sources like them is for researchers to 'excavate' old key words and resources across a range of databases and domain boundaries.

The Nature and Role of Online Gatekeepers

The digital information environment of researchers concerned with the exploration of terrorism has been found was similar to that of several other key global research domains, wherein, whilst non-governmental and not-for-profit organizations play a central role in disseminating primary information resources, publishers still have an enduring role as the pivotal gatekeepers to academic research. It is well documented that, within the research domain, the dissemination of research via books and other printed matter plays a major role within the scholarly communication system, and still remains closely interrelated to the recognition and reward system across practitioner communities and networks of expertise (Reid & Chen, 2008). Research methods used within the field of terrorism are of a sensitive sort, which may account to some extent for the sustained importance of the traditional gatekeepers such as publishers, printers, and book houses.

Interestingly, although publishers play a key dissemination and access role within the research domain, they are noticeably absent from any Google representation of the scholarly web, which may reflect their overall low visibility in the wider domain websphere. This variation in the characteristics and role of gatekeepers in the information environment of the given subject domain, in contrast to other current or cutting-edge domains of global significance, appears to be influenced directly by a number of domain-specific intellectual and social factors (Fry et. al., 2008). This includes the various types of data used by researchers in their respective subject sub-specialisms; where news sources and public speeches constitute key sources of primary information, but a heavy reliance on secondary sources such as academic publications is also found. Academic homepages in the field have a much lower information valency; a variation that may also be explained by the nature of the domain's websphere, and in terms of the extent to which it is academically oriented and oriented towards not-for-profit organizations (Fry, 2006).

THE WINNER TAKES IT ALL: UNDOMESTICATED RESEARCH WILDERNESS OR VERITABLE TERRORIST HAVEN?

The winner-takes-all effect manifest in the use of online sources of data and other resources necessary to propagate, encourage, understand, and combat the phenomenon that is Terrorism has been examined by this research across four broad, clearly differentiated axes: geographic orientation of knowledge domains; strength or weakness of networks of excellence; the scatter of material across disciplinary boundaries; and the role and digital presence of traditional and newly-emergent gatekeepers. The variations posited possible within the prevalent information environment of the domain, wherein resources are scattered across a diverse range of gatekeepers and resources, make it important not just to identify a concentration or democratization effect online, but rather to also refine the parameters that define the circumstances and conditions under which the search for expertise on this domain of global importance, and the quest for national and international cyber security and governance will be dominated by certain results and exhibit particular biases. This environment can be a well-organized landscape or a less-well charted wilderness (Fry et. al., 2008).

Concepts are often contested and fundamentals hard to define, which leads to more open-ended undirected searches and increased uncertainty with regard to, one the one hand an exact determination of the appropriate keywords to search, and on the other, an accurate identification of the individuals, groups, and networks classed as perpetrators of acts and incidents of international terrorism. In these domains access to online resources is more likely to depend on the indexing algorithms of Internet search engines and the online presence of particular institutions, organizations, people and resources. Real terrorists, terrorist organisations, and terrorist networks are automatically overwhelmed, and are often noticeably absent as top level hit results. Rather than searches being directed at a particular specialized definition or concept, efforts to combat terrorism via online networks of expertise are often thus stymied by a concerted lack of availability of genuine or comprehensive information on anything bar that concerning individual researchers, institutions, or, at best, general themes and *liet motifs*.

The type of information environment identified for the domain of terrorism and terrorist-related activities through the research presented in this chapter may, therefore, be seen at once as alternating between an 'undomesticated research wilderness' and a 'veritable terrorist haven', and the manifestation of a lopsided balance of power between terrorist networks and the communities constituted to combat them. As the production, dissemination, and use of online resources continues to grow, and the number and significance of electronic platforms designed to aid and abet governance augments, it will become increasingly important to determine whether information-seeking and research on Terrorism can find its way through the different types of digital landscapes. For the issues and topics looked out for, in both the scholarly domain and across practitioner fields, which in some way cross the boundaries of established disciplines, there is the additional question of the extent to which the availability and the veracity of online resources will transcend or reconfigure established bounds of expertise, power, and authority. Such a shift will necessitate governments, libraries, and publishers – not to speak of the researchers and institutions that produce and use material online - to re-align their strategies accordingly for the better organization, provision, and dissemination of services and content accordingly.

DIRECTIONS FOR FURTHER RESEARCH: TERRORISM AND THE FUTURE OF THE INTERNET

Never before in history has any invention shot from obscurity to global fame in the way the Internet has done. Never before has any new technology given us a peek into the future in quite the same way: a peek into a highly interconnected world where the cost of transmitting and accessing an infinite amount of information is reduced to virtually nothing, where physical boundaries are no longer limits to human action, and constrained physical space is replaced by a virtual 'cyberspace' which is not subject to traditional hierarchies and power relations. And where there is place for all regardless of sex, nationality, ethnicity, or religion. In short, the Internet promises a rapid movement towards a just and prosperous world, and the development of a truly global civil society. The contemporary world is in the midst of a historical change.

At the same time, there are roadblocks to be overcome if the Internet is to deliver on its promises and not cater to the contrarian needs and requirements of the multitude of dissident groups and terrorist networks that populate it. In direct opposition to the claims of *cyber romantics*, equality and empowerment are not inevitable consequences of the use of technology. The present bias of the Internet towards the West, with the predominance of English as the major *lingua franca* online, reinforces the existing digital divide and reflects the lopsided power relationships in contemporary world politics. This imbalance is a formidable barrier to a truly global civil society, and there is no guarantee that it will be rectified in the near future. Furthermore, issues of Internet regulation and security have, particularly after its effective use by terrorist networks such as Al-Qaeda, become hotly debated issues.

In the Information Age, societies are interconnected. The days of closed-door negotiations and secret repression are drawing to an end. As national governments across the world have found out the hard way, the digital technology has empowered those terrorist organisations and advocacy groups that have embraced the Internet and are now electronically networked across borders. Information technology has become, and looks set to remain, a critical ingredient of networking activity in today's world. Civil society networks, buttressed by the power of the Internet and digital platforms, can defy existing boundaries. We can no longer remain isolated from the networks of power and resistance that envelop our interconnected world.

Transnational terrorist movements of the 21st century have recognised this, and are increasingly expanding their presence on the Internet. From the more traditional movements such as the Irish Republican Army (I.R.A.), to more recent ones that involve scattered groups of people operating clandestinely under a banner that has no real name, there is a growing acknowledgement of the Internet's dynamism and versatility, and its advantages as a medium of communication. The ease with which information can be exchanged and fluency of the logistics planned between partners thousands of miles apart, promises new opportunities for vigorous coalition-building and other similar activist activities.

CONCLUSION

The world at large is exactly what is at stake. Geographical borders seem to be of no importance whatsoever to the new media - they simply haven't been invited to the global ICT party. - Sarai Report to The Waag

The Internet, together with its associated platforms and technologies, is often guilty of propagating a strong bias that marginalises the digital spread and reach of local and regional output, issues, and topics, in contrast and direct juxtaposition with content and material related to more globally-oriented, pressing, and significant concerns. Even if this bias does not openly enunciate the imbalances of power that the virtually-total anonymity of the medium affords, is nevertheless closely connected, as both the level of organisation of information online and the extent to which it is genuine are directly related to the degree of 'boundedness' of the information landscape and to the limits that circumscribe accessibility and the availability of ultimate authority.

The Internet is, at the same time, an increasingly important tool for facilitating and cementing the social relations that serve as the future basis for global civil society. The Information Age has given way today to new powers and new responsibilities and to a whole host of local, national, and international actors who, through embracing the Internet and digital technologies, are fast becoming central to the new, electronically networked civil society responsible for stability and governance in the digital age. Whilst Internet access in the developed world far outstrips that of the developing world, predictions for the growth in the number of users remain phenomenal, and the potential of the Internet as a weapon to combat underdevelopment and inequality in the future is immense. The Internet today, therefore, constitutes a significant part of socio-political interactions, and will continue to play an increasingly important role in the shaping of world politics in the years to come.

REFERENCES

Abbate, J. (2001). Government, Business, and the Making of the Internet. *Business History Review* (Special Issue), *75*(1), 147-176.

Arquilla, J., & Ronfeldt, D. (2001). Networks and Netwars: The Future of Terror, Crime, and Militancy. Santa Monica, C.A.: RAND Publications.

Biersteker, T. J., & Eckert, S. E. (2007). *Countering the Financing of Terrorism*. Oxford: Routledge Press.

Bosco, F. (2013). Terrorist Use of the Internet. In U. Gürbuz (Ed.), *Capacity Building in the Fight Against Terrorism* (pp. 39–46). Amsterdam: IOS Press.

Castells, M. (1996). The Information Age: Economy. Society and Culture: Vol. 1. *The Rise of the Network Society*. Oxford: Blackwell Publishing.

Chandrasekaran, R., & Corcoran, E. (1997, July 18). Human Errors Block E-Mail, Web Sites in Internet Failure: Garbled Address Files From Va. Firm Blamed. *The Washington Post,* A1.

Chun, S., Shulman, S., Sandoval, R., & Hovy, E. (2010). Government 2.0: Making Connections between Citizens, Data and Government. *Information Polity Journal, 15*(1–2), 1–9.

Conway, M. (2006). Terrorism and the Internet: New Media - New Threat? *Parliamentary Affairs, 59*(2), 283–298. doi:10.1093/pa/gsl009

Dahl, R. (1989). Democracy and its Critics. New Haven, C.T.: Yale University Press.

Danitz, T., & Stobel, W. P. (2001). Networking Dissent: Cyber Activists Use the Internet to Promote Democracy in Burma. In J. Arquilla & D. Ronfeldt (Eds.), Networks and Netwars: The Future of Terror, Crime, and Militancy (pp. 129-170). Santa Monica, C.A.: RAND Publications.

de Armond, P. (2001). Netwar in the Emerald City: WTO Protest Strategy and Tactics. In J. Arquilla & D. Ronfeldt (Eds.), Networks and Netwars: The Future of Terror, Crime, and Militancy (pp. 201-238). Santa Monica, C.A.: RAND Publications.

Deibert, R. J. (2000). International Plug 'n Play?: Citizen Activism, the Internet and Global Public Policy. *International Studies Perspectives, 1*(3), 255–272. doi:10.1111/1528-3577.00026

Deibert, R. J. (2002). The Politics of Internet Design: Securing the Foundations for Global Civil Society Networks. *Institute of Intergovernmental Relations Conference Paper*. Retrieved from http://www.iigr.ca/conferences/archive/pdfs1/deibert.pdf

Denning, D. E. (2001). Activism, Hactivism and Cyberterrorism: The Internet as a Tool for Influencing Foreign Policy. In J. Arquilla & D. Ronfeldt (Eds.), Networks and Netwars: The Future of Crime, Terrorism and Militancy (pp. 171-199). Santa Monica, C.A.: RAND Publications.

Dutton, W. H., Gillet, S. E., McKnight, L. W., & Peltu, M. (2003, August). Broadband Internet: The Power to Reconfigure Access. *Oxford Internet Institute Forum Discussion Paper No. 1*.

Fenton, N. (2007). Contesting Global Capital, New Media, Solidarity and the Role of a Social Imaginary. In B. Cammaerts & N. Carpentier (Eds.), *Reclaiming the Media: Communication Rights and Democratic Media Roles* (pp. 225–242). Brussels: ECREA Series - Intellect.

Fishkin, J. S. (1995). *The Voice of the People*. New Haven, N.J.: Yale University Press.

Frangonikolopoulos, C. A. (2012). Global Civil Society and Deliberation in the Digital Age. *International Journal Electronic Governance*, *5*(1), 11–23. doi:10.1504/IJEG.2012.047440

Fry, J. (2006). Studying the Scholarly Web: How Disciplinary Culture Shapes Online Representations. *International Journal of Scientometrics, Informetrics and Bibliometrics, 10*(1).

Fry, J., & Talja, S. (2007). The Intellectual and Social Organization of Academic Fields and the Shaping of Digital Resources. *Journal of Information Science*, *33*(2), 115–133. doi:10.1177/0165551506068153

Fry, J., Virkar, S., & Schroeder, R. (2008). Search Engines and Expertise about Global Issues: Well-defined Landscape or Undomesticated Wilderness? In A. Spink & M. Zimmer (Eds.), *Web Search: Multidisciplinary Perspectives* (pp. 255–275). Berlin, Heidelberg: Springer Link-Verlag. doi:10.1007/978-3-540-75829-7_14

Harwood, P. G., & Lay, C. J. (2001, August-September). Surfing Alone: The Internet as a Facilitator of Social and Political Capital? *Paper prepared for the 2001 Annual Meeting of American Political Science Association.*

Hillis, K., Petit, M., & Jarrett, K. (2013). *Google and the Culture of Search*. New York, N.Y.: Routledge Press.

Hindman, M., Tsioutsiouliklis, K., & Johnson, J. (2003). Googlearchy: How a Few Heavily-Linked Sites Dominate Politics on the Web. Proceedings of the *Annual Meeting of the Midwest Political Science Association*, Volume 4.

Huysman, M., & Wulf, V. (2004). *Social Capital and Information Technology. Cambridge M.A*. M.I.T Press.

Jordan, T., & Taylor, P. A. (2004). *Hacktivism and Cyberwars: Rebels with a Cause?* London: Routledge Press.

Juris, J. S. (2005). The New Digital Media and Activist Networking within Anti–Corporate Globalization Movements. *The Annals of the American Academy of Political and Social Science*, *597*(1), 189–208. doi:10.1177/0002716204270338

Kalathil, S., & Boas, T. C. (2010). *Open Networks, Closed Regimes: The Impact of the Internet on Authoritarian Rule*. Washington, D.C.: Carnegie Endowment for International Peace.

Kuhltau, C. C. (1993). *Seeking Meaning: a Process Approach to Library and Information Services*. Norwood, N.J.: Ablex Publishing Inc.

Meyer, E. T., & Schroeder, R. (2009). The World Wide Web of Research and Access to Knowledge. *Knowledge Management Research & Practice*, *7*(3), 218–233. doi:10.1057/kmrp.2009.13

Napoleoni, L. (2004). Money and Terrorism. *Strategic Insights*, *3*(4), 47–50.

Norris, P. (2001). *Digital Divide: Civic Engagement, Information Poverty, and the Internet*. Cambridge: Cambridge University Press. doi:10.1017/CBO9781139164887

Palmer, C. L., & Neumann, L. J. (2002). The Information Work of Interdisciplinary Humanities Scholars: Exploration and Translation. *Library Quarterly: Information, Community. Policy*, *72*(1), 85–117.

Park, H. W., & Thelwall, M. (2005). The Network Approach to Web Hyperlink Research and its Utility for Science Communication. In C. Hine (Ed.), *Virtual methods: Issues in Social Research on the Internet* (pp. 171–181). Oxford: Berg Publishers.

Reid, E., & Chen, H. (2008). Domain Mapping of Contemporary Terrorism Research. In H. Chen, E. Reid, J. Sinai, A. Silke, & B. Ganor (Eds.), *Terrorism Informatics: Knowledge Management and Data Mining for Homeland Security* (pp. 3–26). New York, N.Y.: Springer Link US. doi:10.1007/978-0-387-71613-8_1

Resnick, D. (1999). Politics on the Internet: The Normalization of Cyberspace. In C. Toulouse & T. W. Luke (Eds.), *The Politics of Cyberspace* (pp. 55–56). London: Routledge Press.

Schneider, S. M., & Foot, K. A. (2002). Online Structure for Political Action: Exploring Presidential Web sites from the 2000 American Election. *Javnost - The Public Journal of the European Institute for Communication and Culture*, *9*(2), 43–60.

Schroeder, R., Caldas, A., Mesch, G., & Dutton, W. H. (2005, June 22-24). The World Wide Web of Science: Reconfiguring Access to Information. *Proceedings of the First International Conference on e-Social Science*, Manchester. Retrieved from: http://www.oii.ox.ac.uk/research/project.cfm?id=22

Theohary, C. A., & Rollins, J. (2011, March 8). Terrorist Use of the Internet: Information Operations in Cyberspace. CRS Report for Congress, Congressional Research Service.

Uimonen, P. (2003). Networks of Global Interaction. *Cambridge Review of International Affairs*, *16*(2), 273–286. doi:10.1080/09557570302054

Van Laer, J., & Van Aelst, P. (2010). Internet and Social Movement Action Repertoires. *Information Communication and Society*, *13*(8), 1146–1171. doi:10.1080/13691181003628307

Virkar, S. (2007). (Dis)connected Citizenship: Exploring Barriers to eConsultation in Europe. *Deliverable 2 of the Breaking Barriers to e-Government: Overcoming Obstacles to Improving European Public Services Project*.

Virkar, S. (2011). *The Politics of Implementing e-Government for Development: The Ecology of Games Shaping Property Tax Administration in Bangalore City* [Unpublished Doctoral Thesis]. University of Oxford.

Virkar, S. (2014). Re-engaging the Public in the Digital Age: e-Consultation Initiatives in the Government 2.0 Landscape. In M. Khosrow (Ed.), Encyclopedia of Information Science and Technology (3rd ed., pp.427-435). Hershey, P.A.: IGI Global.

Wall, M. A. (2007). Social Movements and Email: Expressions of Online Identity in the Globalization Protests. *New Media & Society*, *9*(2), 258–277. doi:10.1177/1461444807075007

Wartenkin, C. (2001). *Reshaping World Politics: NGOs, the Internet and Global Civil Society*. Oxford: Rowman and Littlefield.

Weimann, G. (2004, March). [REMOVED HYPERLINK FIELD]Www.terror.net: How Modern Terrorism Uses the Internet, *United States Institute of Peace Special Report 116*.

Weimann, G. (2006). Virtual Disputes: The Use of the Internet for Terrorist Debates. *Studies in Conflict and Terrorism*, *29*(7), 623–639. doi:10.1080/10576100600912258

Zinnbauer, D. (2001). Internet, Civil Society and Global Governance: The Neglected Political Dimension of the Digital Divide. *Information and Security: An International Journal*, *7*(1), 45–64.

ADDITIONAL READING

Blatherwick, D. E. S. (1987). The International Politics of Telecommunications. Institute of International Studies Research Series, 68. Berkley, C.A.: University of California.

Box, L., & Engelhard, R. (2001). International Civilateral Transformations: ICTs in Development Cooperation. *Paper prepared for the HIVOS Symposium 2001*. Retrieved from www.hivos.nl/downloads/boxdoc.pdf

Cairncross, F. (1997). The Death of Distance: How the Communications Revolution is Changing Our Lives. Boston, M.A.: Harvard Business School Press.

Castells, M. (2001). *The Internet Galaxy: Reflections on the Internet, Business and Society*. Oxford: Oxford University Press. doi:10.1007/978-3-322-89613-1

Centre for Science and Environment. (2013). Global Environmental Negotiations Factsheet: Fact 10 - The Multilateral Agreement on Investment. Retrieved from http://www.cseindia.org/html/eyou/geg/factsheet/fact10.pdf

Conway, S., Combe, I., & Crowther, D. (2003). Strategizing Networks of Power and Influence: The Internet and the Struggle over Contested Space. *Managerial Auditing Journal*, *18*(3), 254–262. doi:10.1108/02686900310469916

Harris, E. (1999, August 5). Web Becomes a Cybertool for Political Activists. *Wall Street Journal*, B11.

Internet Society. (2013). All About the Internet: A Brief History of the Internet. Retrieved from http://www.isoc.org/internet/history/brief.shtml#Origins

Koliba, C. (2000). Collaboration, Technical Assistance and Interactive Media: Trends in U.S. Civil Society. *Institute of Development Studies Civil Society and Governance Case Study Papers (USA), #20*. Retrieved from http://www.ids.ac.uk/ids/civsoc/final/usa/Chris%20Koliba2.doc

Krause, A., Stein, M., Clark, J., Chen, T., Li, J., Dimon, J., . . . Herschman, J. (2006). The Virtual Activist 2.0: A Training Guide. *NetAction.Org*. Retrieved from http://www.netaction.org/training/v-training.html

Kraut, R., Patterson, M., Lundmark, V., Kiesler, S., Mukhopadyay, T., & Scherlis, W. (1998). Internet Paradox: A Social Technology That Reduces Social Involvement and Psychological Well-Being? *The American Psychologist*, *53*(9), 1017–1031. doi:10.1037/0003-066X.53.9.1017 PMID:9841579

Kumar, C. (2000). Transnational Networks and Campaigns for Democracy. In A. M. Florini (Ed.), The Third Force: The Rise of Transnational Civil Society (pp. 115-142). Tokyo: Japan Centre for International Exchange/Washington D.C.: Carnegie Endowment for International Peace

Longworth, R. C. (1999, July 5). Activists on Internet Reshaping Rules for Global Economy. *Chicago Tribune*. Retrieved from http://www.economicjustice.org/resources/media/trib070599.html

McChesney, R. W., Wood, E. M., & Foster, J. B. (1998). *Capitalism and the Information Age: The Political Economy of the Global Communications Revolution*. New York, N.Y.: Monthly Review Press.

OECD. (1997). *Towards A Global Information Society – Global Information Infrastructure, Global Information Society: Policy Requirements*. Paris: Organisation for Economic Cooperation and Development.

Protest.Net. (2013). Retrieved from www.protest.net

Reid, E. F., & Chen, H. (2007). Mapping the Contemporary Terrorism Research Domain. *International Journal of Human-Computer Studies*, *65*(1), 42–56. doi:10.1016/j.ijhcs.2006.08.006

Surman, M., & Reilly, K. (2003, November). Appropriating the Internet for Social Change: Towards the Strategic Use of Networked Technologies by Transnational Civil Society Organisations. *Social Science Research Council Report*. Retrieved from http://www.ssrc.org/programs/itic/publications/knowledge_report/final_entire_surman_reilly.pdf

Tehranian, M., & Falk, R. (1999). *Global Communication & World Politics: Domination, Development and Discourse*. London: Lynne Rienner Publications.

The Economist. (1999). *Economics: Making Sense of the Modern Economy*. London: Profile Books.

The Economist. (2001). *Globalisation: Making Sense of an Integrating World*. London: Profile Books Ltd.

University of Toronto. (2013). G8 Information Centre. Retrieved from http://www.g7.utoronto.ca/

KEY TERMS AND DEFINITIONS

Actor(s): The individuals, groups or other entities whose interactions shape the direction and nature of a particular game being considered.

Bibliometrics or Information Science or Library Science: The phenomenon manifest refers particularly to the use of online sources of data and of other digital resources across the *scholarly web* and across other networks of scholarship, on- and offline, and along four, clearly-differentiated axes within both scholarly and practitioner communities; most notably the decreasing use of libraries, the changing face of networks of excellence, web-search behaviour and other web-based search strategies, and the differing perceptions regarding the nature and role of online gatekeepers.

Cyber-Activism: Cyberactivism or Internet activism refers to the normal, non-disruptive use of the Internet and its associated platforms and technologies in support of an agenda or cause; including those concerned with the use of the World Wide Web as a political, social, economic, or informational resource.

e-Democracy: May be defined by the express intent to increase the participation of citizens in decision-making through the use of digital media and the application of Information and Communication Technologies to political processes. e-Democracy may be subdivided into e-Engagement (or e-Participation), e-Voting, e-Consultation.

e-Governance: Refers to the use of ICTs by government, civil society, and political institutions to engage citizens in political processes and to the promote greater participation of citizens in the public sphere.

e-Government: Refers to the use of Information and Communication Technologies by government departments and agencies to improve internal functioning and public service provision. Broadly speaking, e-government may be divided into 2 distinct areas: e-Administration and e-Services.

Hacking: Refers to a taxonomy of behaviour online, originally described as the innovative use of technology to solve a problem, frequently practiced in the defence or the furtherance of a unique set of norms that have developed as part of the Internet's culture. Hacking may be differentiated from hacktivism, in that the act of hacking lacks either a political focus or explicit objectives.

Hacktivism: Refers to the emergence of popular political action or civil disobedience in cyberspace or the nonviolent use, for the attainment of political ends, of either illegal or legally ambiguous digital tools; including website defacements, information theft, website parodies, DoS attacks, DDoS attacks, virtual sit-ins, and virtual sabotage.

Hacktivist: Refers to an online participant or user who engages in hacker activities to protest against political or corporate policy; towards the attainment of either personal or collective goals that range from the accessing and downloading of data from corporate websites to the defacement of public-facing platforms.

Internet Activism: Cyberactivism or Cyber-Activism refers to the normal, non-disruptive use of the Internet and its associated platforms and technologies in support of an agenda or cause; including those concerned with the use of the World Wide Web as a political, social, economic, or informational resource.

Internet Trolling: The practice of deliberately trying to aggress electronically or to distress participants online through frequently inflammatory and abusive behaviour; usually just to disrupt without direction and to often do so anonymously.

Scholarly Web (The): The Scholarly Websphere or The Scholarly Semantic Web refers to the production and/or the dissemination and/or the delineation of disciplinary knowledge, scholarship, and/or scholarly content online over the Internet; often represented in diagrammatic and/or schematic form.

Scientific Community: Scientific Network or Disciplinary Community or Community of Practice refers to that 'invisible college' or cohesive, networked community pertaining to specific intellectual specialism or particular mode of scientific enquiry.

Technological Addiction: Of which *Internet Addiction Disorder* is a subset, is the non-chemical, behavioural addiction that involves human-machine interaction; wherein the behaviours that manifest can be passive or active, and usually contain both inducing and reinforcing features which may contribute to the promotion of addictive tendencies.

Terrorism: Or Terror (*colloq.*) refers to the act, the action, the activity, or the behavioural or cognitive framework that involves the premeditated use, or the threat of use, of extra-normal, extra-legal, and/or excessive violence or brutality to attain and/or obtain political power, influence, and objectives; especially, through the incitement of negative emotional responses ranging from mild intimidation to extreme fear directed at a large, carefully selected, usually innocent, target participant-audience.

Terrorist(s): Refers to the actor-perpetrator(s) of acts of terrorism and/or the actor-participant(s) in terrorism-related activities and behaviours and cognitive frameworks; including individuals, groups, and/or networks of actors.

Troll(s): The person or set of people who attempt to entertain their kind through the sustained provocation of others or via the propagation of misinformation and other forms of propaganda in order to attain a certain measure of dominance and/or satisfaction; the term may be extended to include any individual within a subversive, transgressive, or dissident faction and/or group, particularly online.

Winner-Takes-All (Hypothesis): Or Winner-Takes-All Effect is defined as a game, an interaction, a situation, or an outcome wherein the most dominant actor present is able to capture or captures a very large share or a majority proportion of existing rewards therein.

Chapter 2
US-China Relations:
Cyber Espionage and Cultural Bias

Clay Wilson
American Public University System, USA

Nicole Drumhiller
American Public University System, USA

ABSTRACT

It is assumed by most observers that China is copying or stealing vast amounts of intellectual property from US military and private industry through its cyber espionage activities, and then sharing that information with state-owned industries, giving them unfair economic advantages. The US also conducts cyber espionage against China and other nations, but chooses to not share the vast collections of intellectual property and data with its own domestic industries. By choosing not to do the same thing as China, the US may be placing itself at an economic disadvantage, and may also mistakenly be accusing China of threatening cyber warfare. What is needed is a clearer understanding of differences in national cultures that contribute to intolerance between the US and China when it comes to economics, threats of war, and the evolving new role of cyber espionage.

DOI: 10.4018/978-1-4666-9661-7.ch002

INTRODUCTION

In recent years relations between the United States and China have become strained over alleged instances of cyber related intellectual property theft and espionage. According to officials within the US Government, "The Chinese government has a national policy of economic espionage in cyberspace…", and, "…the Chinese are the world's most active and persistent practitioners of cyber espionage today." (McConnell, Chertoff, & Lynn, 2012). Some government officials believe that China's masses are simply hungry for economic advancement and that by stealing intellectual property (IP), China can quickly create products that are cheaper than similar items produced in the US and elsewhere. These officials warn that, over the next decade, cyber espionage could have a catastrophic impact on the US economy and global competitiveness (McConnell et al., 2012). Other U.S. military and business officials believe that China has a long-term goal of "preemptive reconnaissance" intended to surpass the US economy and also affect US military planning (Thomas, 2010; Dilanian, 2011).

Former Attorney General Eric Holder reportedly stated that China has been actively hacking Westinghouse, US Steel, Alcoa and more than 60 other companies for half a decade (Hu, 2014). The McAfee security company stated in a February 2013 report that China has launched "coordinated covert and targeted cyber-attacks" against global oil, energy, and petrochemical companies since November 2009 (Barron-Lopez, 2014). U.S. officials have commented that Chinese cyber espionage is done to benefit its state owned companies. This characteristic is seen as outside the traditional bounds of espionage done for national security reasons (Michaels, 2014). Targets for cyber espionage also appear to align with China's stated economic and strategic directives. For example, in recent years the National Security Agency (NSA) and international groups watched as a group of privately employed engineers based in Guangzhou in southern China copied technology and blueprints for missile, satellite, space, and nuclear propulsion systems from businesses in the United States, Canada, Europe, Russia and Africa (Sanger & Perlroth, 2014). A clear distinction of Chinese behavior is that it blurs the lines between traditional espionage done for national security purposes, and economic theft of intellectual property directed against government and business entities. Defense consultant and author James Farwell reportedly stated in March 2013 that while espionage is not against international law, the theft and infringement of intellectual property is. Farwell even suggests that the situation is so egregious that the U.S. should initiate a case against China under the Trade Related Aspects of Intellectual Property Rights (TRIPS) agreement, stating that "… legal proceedings that found China guilty of intellectual-property theft or infringement, could render it liable for billions of dollars in compensation, expose it to multinational economic sanctions and cause it to be branded a pirate state" (McGregor, 2013).

Grievances over cyber espionage are also directed by China against the US and other countries. In particular, Beijing has accused the US of hacking its systems, claiming that Washington has long used the Internet to steal secrets. Reportedly, NSA monitored communications of top Huawei business executives looking for evidence of ties to the Chinese government and military. Huawei is based in China and is a global telecom company that ranks third to Apple and Samsung as a producer of mobile phones. The objective of the NSA surveillance program reportedly was to exploit Huawei's technology so that when the company sold equipment to other countries — including both US allies and other potentially hostile nations— the NSA could later choose to roam through their computer and telephone networks to conduct surveillance and, if ordered by the president, conduct offensive cyber operations. Recent news reports also describe cyber surveillance programs such as "PRISM" where the NSA, as part of its Signals

Intelligence (SIGINT) mission, collected metadata for all telecommunications messages that transited the US involving foreign senders or receivers. In addition, the NSA reportedly has an electronic spying organization called the Tailored Access Operations, which has a mission to gather intelligence by specifically penetrating computers and telecommunications systems in China and other countries (Aid, 2013).

The United States response to the accusation from China shows how the US perceives its own behavior when conducting its own cyber espionage activities. White House spokeswoman Caitlin M. Hayden, reportedly said: "We do not give intelligence we collect to US companies to enhance their international competitiveness or increase their bottom line (Wallace, 2014; Sanger & Perlroth, 2014). The U.S. maintains this separation due to law that is in line with a general philosophy where the separation between public and private affairs means less regulation, which is viewed by many as healthy and generally good for business and innovation. Competitive intelligence is an ethical and legal business practice where information-gathering is done using open sources, such as newspaper articles, or corporate reports about competitors. However, computers and the internet have made it relatively easy to just steal sensitive information outright. Under Title 18 USC, the National Infrastructure Protection Act and the Economic Espionage Act of 1996, the theft or transfer of trade secrets, intellectual property, or other proprietary information through industrial espionage (including cyber espionage) is considered illegal. For this reason, a group of five Chinese military hackers were recently indicted by a grand jury in the Western District of Pennsylvania for computer hacking directed at six American victims in the U.S. nuclear power, metals and solar products industries. The hackers were accused of unauthorized access into their victims' computers to steal information that would be economically beneficial to state-owned enterprises in China (U.S. Department of Justice, 2014).

It has become increasingly obvious that China and many other countries do not accept the American perspective of isolating government espionage practices from business espionage practices. Given the way the business is conducted within the United States, U.S. companies are met with challenges when attempting to operate in China due to the differences in how they approach the concept of intellectual property. Carter administration official, Bob Herzstein has reportedly stated that U.S. companies seeking to operate in China's state-dominated economy have been regularly forced to share their intellectual property and manufacturing knowhow with Chinese competitors (Prestowitz, 2013). He reportedly stated that U.S. firms often are forced to share ownership with state owned companies, to make special deals on supply or sales with local companies, and to clear many investment decisions with bureaucratic authorities. He stated that many of China's businesses are state dominated, and its business culture is vastly different from the free market systems of the United States (Prestowitz, 2013b).

China is not the only country that appears to share cyber espionage data for the benefit of their domestic industries. Many other countries, including several members of the World Trade Organization, also assist their state-owned or partially state-owned companies considered vital to their national economies. For example, Renault is partially owned by the government of France, and Singapore Airlines is partially owned by the government of Singapore. Most of the world's largest oil companies are owned by governments. None of the countries mentioned here draws such a strict line between government and private business as does the U.S. (Prestowitz, 2014). Within the United States, Government involvement in private business, usually by regulation, is viewed as an unnecessary drag on innovation due to imposed inefficiencies. However, some observers have stated America should no longer ignore the importance of using cyber intelligence to keep the U.S. economically competitive. If the NSA started providing some of this cyber intelligence to the private sector, it would greatly benefit U.S. companies and perhaps help them maintain an important economic lead in the global marketplace (Prestowitz, 2014).

The different approaches to cyber espionage and the varying protections for intellectual property rights can be best understood by looking at the differences in historical development of China and the West. The people of China give a great deal of attention to the past, in order to promote strong personal and moral growth in the present. The senior members of Chinese society believe in their responsibility to nurture and direct the junior members by following and exploring the common cultural heritage of all Chinese. Reference to the past in many cases, more importantly than religion or law, defined the limits of proper behavior. The cultural reliance on knowledge from the ancestors, and common heritage, pushed away thinking about intellectual endeavors as private property for personal profit (Alford, 2004, p. 20). In this regard we can begin to see some of the societal differences between China and Europe. These experiences ultimately come to impact the way in which China will interpret information in its surrounding environment. We believe that this difference in perception is fueling the conflict between the United States and China when it comes to the boundaries of cyber theft and espionage within the global arena.

This chapter examines whether the cyber espionage activities of China are perceived mistakenly by the US as a threat toward cyber warfare. This chapter also examines whether US cyber espionage against China and other nations, along with its choice to not share its collections of IP and data with its own domestic industries, combine to place the US at an economic disadvantage. A contributing factor may be the need for a clearer understanding of national cultural differences that may lead to intolerance between the US and China. Ultimately the evolving new role of cyber espionage, and the responses to it, needs to be further examined by the United States.

BACKGROUND

The way in which the U.S. and China approach the concepts of intellectual property and cyber espionage is important to understanding why these states are struggling to come to terms within one another over this issue. For this reason, important to the understanding of U.S.-China relations are those psychological components that allow us to postulate how a state may come to perceive or draw inferences about another's behavior within a particular situation. This presents a challenge since a state itself is not a cognitive being and so it cannot actively perceive the behavior of other states (Herrmann, 1985). However state behavior, and even more specifically conflict between states, has been described through the use of psychological concepts like cognition, perception and imagery for a number of years (Holsti, 1967; Jervis, 1976; Cottam, 1977; George, 1979; Kaplowitz, 1984; Herrmann, 1985; Herrmann, Voss, Schooler, & Ciarrochi, 1997; Herrmann & Keller, 2004; Alexander, Levin, & Henry, 2005). In order to do this we must look at those actors within the state which shape foreign policy decisions (Hermann, 2001). When looking at humans as decision-makers it is important to recognize that they are imperfect beings with a limited capacity to process all of the complexities of their surrounding environment. In order to make sense of their world people utilize information processing strategies to help them function and make decisions within and about their environment. Cottam, Dietz-Uhler, Mastors, and Preston (2004) explain that people seek to discover patterns of information in order to assess why others behave a certain way. Since people need to quickly make decisions, they do not employ any scientific rigor to their assessments and rely upon heuristics or mental short-cuts when organizing their world (Cottam et al., 2004). To draw upon information quickly people develop cognitive categories or schemas about situations, people, or objects. These schemas then help inform and organize bits of information about something including its characteristics and patterns that emerge (Cottam et al., 2004). Ultimately the end result of a person's information processing is the development of "knowledge that can be applied to the users' tasks and will affect the processing of future information" (Vertzberger, 1990, p. 9). A potential issue arises when a person has processed information *incorrectly* as a result of bias or some other cognitive error. This can happen within a wide variety of situations that go beyond the scope of this chapter, however within the foreign policy arena, given the high degree of secrecy and deception employed by state actors, the conditions are acutely conducive for information processing errors and misperception to occur. In his work on misperception and international conflict, Jervis (1988) argues that perceptions can "create their own reality" in the sense that the action or situation itself is less important than one's perception of that action (p. 694). In this regard reality is thus reduced to one's interpretation or perception of the events in question. A person's perception of their environment is largely determined by the lens that impacts the way in which information is interpreted (Fiske &Taylor, 2013).

One of the most common biases, called the fundamental attribution error, occurs when one "over-attributes" another's behavior to dispositional causes like that of personality rather than to situational causes like the operational environment (Cottam et al., 2004; Fiske & Taylor, 2013). "Instead of realizing that external forces – such as social norms or social pressure – influence behaviors, social perceivers often assume that another's behavior indicates that person's stable qualities" (Fiske & Taylor, 2013, p. 169). Differences in perception between China and the West have been studied within the social psychology literature and have described China as being more "situation-centered" where they are more focused and "sensitive to their environments" (Norenzayan, Choi & Nisbett, 1999, p. 241). American's on the other hand are "individual-centered" and thus "expect their environments to be sensitive to them" (Norenzayan et al., 1999, p. 241). Cultural differences such as this can impact societal relationships with one another in a number a ways as their understanding of events, both historical and current, will influence how they interact with, and perceive the intentions of one another (Kundra, 1999). This disconnect in perception is something that we can see in the way in which both China and the West approach issues specific to intellectual property and cyber espionage.

While much has been written on the behavior of states within the international arena, Kaplowitz (1984) explains that states will develop strategies for dealing with others based on not only their perception of the adversary, but also based on ones "self-image." Some of the self-images that are thought to influence foreign policy include,

...how a people sees itself, how it views its history, the 'lesson' it has learned, and its concepts of national purpose and national interest. The sources of self-imagery include early and later socialization at home, in schools, via the media, and through the political process; historical experiences, as conveyed by various political socialization agents, including interpretations of history by important leaders and opinion-makers; configurations of domestic political and social unity or fragmentation; and economic successes or failures. (Kaplowitz, 1984, p. 376)

When considering issues between the United States and China over issues stemming from intellectual property violations and concerns regarding cyber espionage or even "cyber warfare" a question arises over whether or not both the United States and China are on the same page when it comes to interpreting these behaviors as true acts of aggression. Within the political arena it is common practice for states to collect "intelligence" or information on other states or non-state actors to protect their national interests. By common practice, the practice of intelligence and intelligence collection has been going on for thousands of years. In China, the practice of intelligence has had a much respected history stemming from master strategist and General during the "Warring States" period, Sun Tzu. Within *The Art of Warfare* Master Sun writes on the importance of intelligence as a way of winning battles before one steps foot out of the temple and onto the battle field. Prior to engaging in war it is important to first know one's opponent. To demonstrate this Sun Tzu explains that:

He who knows the enemy and himself
Will never in a hundred battles be at risk;

He who does not know the enemy but knows himself
Will sometimes win and sometimes lose;

He who knows neither the enemy nor himself
Will be at risk in every battle (Carr, 2000, pp. 80-81).

The teachings of Sun Tzu have wide reaching applications and are widely studied by military personnel and business leaders alike (Golden, 2011).

In a similar vein, businesses and other non-state organizations also seek out information on their rivals through competitive intelligence (CI) collection. The definition of "competitive intelligence" is often debated however it can be thought of as "the process by which organizations actively gather information about competitors and the competitive environment, and, ideally [sic] applying it to their decision-making and planning processes in order to improve their business performance" (Fleisher & Wright 2009, p. 250). Within China, CI is a fairly new practice, however the Chinese are working to increase their CI competency given their need to sustain their growing market economy. Given the digital revolution, now more than ever intelligence collection can be carried out online or within the wide reaching cyber networks of the world. Though technology is quick to develop, the policies governing it are developing at a much slower pace.

Under the Communist government in China information important to businesses such as "industry growth, manufacturing output, and purchasing power were essentially regarded as trade secrets" (Fleisher & Wright 2009, p. 254). However more recently intelligence collection is perceived as a common practice of gathering information (Fleisher & Wright, 2009). The way in which concepts are understood is an important point to consider when dealing with cultural differences, and has relevancy to U.S.-China relations specifically as it impacts the way in which "intellectual property" is perceived. In particular "Asian companies often consider 'scientific knowledge' to be nonproprietary. This means that protecting a specific process in an alliance or partnership, or business planning exercise, between an Eastern and Western company might lead to culturally anchored misunderstandings" (Fleisher & Wright, 2009, p. 252), something that we can see currently occurring when it comes to allegations of "cyber-attacks" or "cyber-warfare" on the part of China against the United States.

In a study on Chinese CI practices Tao and Prescott (2000) surveyed CI practitioners from the Society of Competitive Intelligence of China (SCIC). When looking at "perceived strategic uncertainties" within China, Tao and Prescott (2000) found that CI practitioners in China ranked economic, customer, and international dimensions as those having high levels of uncertainty, yet technological uncertainty was ranked fairly low. Tao and Prescott (2000) note that this finding stems from the respondents background within the sciences however it may also stem from the fact that technological development is something that receives a great deal of monitoring and analysis among CI groups in China (Tao & Prescott, 2000). Furthermore it might also be the case that since scientific knowledge is perceived as shared knowledge it may not be perceived as something that groups are in competition for *per se* as this is something that could be easily accessed through technological means. When assessing Chinese CI programs Tao and Prescott (2000) found that the main purpose of the CI programs existence was to generate knowledge and understanding of the industry and would be competitors. The second and third reasons for the programs existence were to assess competitor weaknesses and to forecast possible decision-making that would negatively impact their position within the market (Tao & Prescott, 2000). With CI being a fairly new practice, and codes of ethics still being developed, the differing perspectives on intellectual property bring about additional challenges when it comes to diplomacy between the United States and China. "The Western conceptualization of property rights is based on the individual, which China's tradition is based on a collective view of property rights. Thus, new intellectual property is viewed as a gain for society in general. Consequently, the interpretation of ethical behavior is institutionally bound" (Tao & Prescott, 2000, p. 70).

This difference in perspective is something to consider when concerns are raised regarding China's "cyber-warfare" against the United States. In an article by David Gewirtz (2011) on cyber warfare and corporate espionage, Gewirtz examines organizations within China that gained access to and extracted information from oil, energy, and petrochemical companies within the United States. In his description of the so-called "Night Dragon attacks" Gewirtz (2011) explains that hackers were able to gain unrestricted access to "internal IT systems, internal corporate financial and energy data, and the desktops of key executives" (p. 8). The hackers were able to connect through the internet to these different industry systems in a manner that allowed them to download information directly onto their own computers.

The attackers essentially had a direct pipeline to massive amounts of sensitive corporate information, including information relating to oil and gas field bids and operations...[they] also gained command and control access to some of the companies' SCADA (supervisory control and data acquisition) systems, the computers that monitor, operate, and control actual physical processes throughout the energy industry. (Gewirtz, 2011, p. 8)

Rather than use the term "competitive intelligence collection" Gewirtz (2011) refers to this as a "cyber-attack." The way that these issues are labeled within the media and the professional literature can have a direct impact on the way we conceptualize these issues. In an effort to provide added clarity to the discussion of cyber operations and cyber information campaigns Josh Cartin (2014) breaks the concept of offensive cyber operations down into two forms, instrumental and strategic. Cartin (2012) explains that an "instrumental" operation is one that "serves an enabling action in the pursuit of battlefield objectives that may transcend the cyberspace domain...Instrumental cyber operations use information to attack information, but to achieve an effect not necessarily limited to information" (p. 15). A "strategic" operation is not necessarily something that plays a direct role in a military campaign, rather the goal is to influence the perception on one's security (Cartin, 2012). Breaking this down further, Cartin (2012) identifies three different categories of offensive cyber operations including cyber exploitation, cyber disruption, and deception. When considering the case of China, the types of "cyber-attacks" occurring appear to be of the cyber exploitation type, whereby it sets out to break into an opponent's "information system to access, exfiltrate, or monitor privileged information" similar to what an organization might do for competitive intelligence (Cartin, 2012, p. 16).

U.S - CHINA CYBER RELATIONS

Historical Development of Intellectual Property

Business practices, much like that of political practices are influenced by a wide variety of factors including both historical experiences and culture (Fleisher & Wright, 2009; Cottam et al, 2004). For this reason it is important to examine the historical development of intellectual property to better gauge how different interpretations of this concept developed over time. Historically, as printing technology advanced during the Song Dynasty (AD 960-1279), Chinese government officials observed a relative rise in literacy, and sought to restrict the proliferation of printed materials that were deemed offensive to the imperial family. For example, writings using the names of ancestors to the imperial family were considered inappropriate, and were not deemed beneficial to scholars. Reproduction of astronomical charts, viewed as a state concern, was also considered an offense. By 1009, private printers were ordered to submit works for prepublication review to block the private reproduction of some materials where concerns were subject to exclusive state control. The penalties varied for not following the rules for prepublication review. For example, persons failing to obtain the required official state approval were given 100 blows with a heavy bamboo cane. The printing blocks were destroyed. Sometimes the printer was exiled beyond a 500-mile radius of their home. Printers who obtained the prepublication permission often displayed somewhere in their works an announcement or notice of state approval to prevent other unauthorized reproductions – "This book is published by the --**-- family. No one is permitted to reprint [this book]".

Similarly, subsequent dynasties moved to protect trademark by restricting the use of special symbols associated with the imperial family or other officials (the white rabbit, or the 5-toed dragon), especially when these marks were used to denote items made for the exclusive use of the imperial family.

Thus, official efforts to provide protection to intellectual property in China were directed toward sustaining imperial power, and were not concerned with the creation of property rights for individuals.

The Chinese linked the protection of intellectual property with state interests. The objective of protections was to maintain the unequal relationships that go along with privilege and status for different levels or classes of society. There was no objective to maintain a system for profits to the individual through intellectual property rights. Unauthorized reproduction of printed materials previously registered with prepublication approval was considered a disruption of the local peace, and a violation of the officially-granted monopolies (Alford, 2004, p. 14-29).

The development and protection of intellectual property that appeared in the West had no counterpart in imperial Chinese history. There was no consideration that the authors or inventors had a property interest in their creations. In China, the state was focused more on maintaining political power, order and stability, and less on questions of private ownership. Historically, the state may have granted monopoly rights to certain families or guilds, but no laws existed that gave these guilds or families the necessary support to prosecute claims against others to protect their "rights" in the intellectual property. Claims made to the state sometimes resulted in state responses that were intended to maintain fairness, peace and harmony, and not necessarily to find a way to award damages to the offended party.

Chinese philosophy teaches that the essence of human understanding for correct ideas and intellectual endeavors were transmitted as gifts from the ancients, rather than emerging as creations from individuals. Ideas are not created by human beings, but actually come from nature and are then imitated by humans. Imitations therefore are not just copies of things made by individuals, but are imitations of natural law.

Therefore, through the Confucian understanding for guidance toward correct action, it is necessary for all persons to allow themselves to interact with the shared past and heritage from the ancestors. This belief actually curtailed how strongly state authority could act to restrict access to, or copying of expressions that were strongly seen as tied to the common ancestors of China (Alford, 2004, p. 25).

There has been an unavoidable collision between Chinese beliefs and the traditional European ideas of justice and individual control profits from intellectual property (Pang, 2012). Writing and other intellectual endeavors often involve an endless chain of creativity. That endless chain of ideas can be viewed by a culture as gifts flowing from the ancestors, but that flow can be unnaturally restricted or limited by the Western copyright regime. The creative process can also be viewed by another culture as very expensive and time-consuming. For example, if the digital blueprints for new military weapons are easily copied through cyber espionage, the resulting strategic advantages can be lost quickly, and the global balance of power can be easily upset, without having to make the same investments in time and money.

Persistence of Confucian Philosophy

Confucius, the sixth-century B.C. Chinese philosopher and teacher, developed a school of thought that stressed obedience to authority. Confucianism still affects business practices in China. For example, business practice includes harmony, maintenance of proper demeanor, and the preservation of 'face'. In China today there is a strong allegiance to family, ancestor worship, and education that reflects Confucianism's continuing influence, including as a way for criticizing Western democracy (Roberts, 2012).

Chinese researcher, Yan Xuetong, today advocates a state based on the Confucian concept of "humane authority", stating, "The goal of our strategy must be not only to reduce the power gap with the United States but also to provide a better model for society than that given by the United States." Other researchers describe many problems related to Western-style capitalism, including massive budget deficits and an inability to slow global warming. These are viewed as examples of community problems that Western societies, which promote gathering wealth for the individual, are not well equipped to tackle (Roberts, 2012). Other Chinese observers perceive Western attitudes of independence as a sign of "showing off". Within the Confucian philosophy, an individual standing out from the crowd causes disharmony, and showing off is considered poor behavior (Wang & Chee, 2012).

Economic Relations and the Division of the Public and Private Sector in China

During what are called the "Dark Ages" of Europe, China maintained a highly developed culture along with a vast administrative bureaucracy. Gunpowder was invented by China during the eighth century, and the compass in the tenth century. So, for several centuries, it was China who was the world's technology leader with the world's highest per capita income (Brenner, 2011, pp. 67-71). The following table from Golden (2011) helps to demonstrate China's historic economic position relative to that of Japan, India, Western Europe and the United States (see Table 1).

During the early 1800's, Britain became trading partners with China, which was their principal supplier of tea. But, at that time, China was not interested so much in acquiring European goods. China also required payment for tea and other products in sterling, causing money to flow mainly from Europe to China. The British reversed this through choosing to sell opium to China, a product of opium poppies that were grown in colonial India. In 1830s, China closed its ports in an attempt to stop the import of drugs, but the British saw this as a violation of the principles generally associated with free trade. The Royal

Table 1. China, Japan, India, Western Europe, and the US, 1820-2030(Percentage of World GDP)

Year	China	Japan	India	Western Europe	US
1820	33.0	3.0	16.0	17.0	2.0
1913	9.0	3.0	7.0	33.0	19.0
1950	5.0	3.0	4.0	26.0	27.0
1978	4.9	7.6	3.3	21.5	21.7
2001	12.0	7.0	5.0	20.0	21.0
2030	18..4	4.0	10.0	13.0	17.7

Source: Golden, 2011, p. 83

Navy and Marines were dispatched to re-open trade, and this resulted in the Opium Wars of 1839-42 and 1856-60. China was defeated, and its ports were surrendered and reorganized into European concessions under European law (Brenner, 2011).

The Chinese people and leaders have not forgotten the national humiliation due to drug addiction and the military defeats at the hands of Western power, and how that sad history contributed to the upset and reversal of their historic economic progress and prosperity. Prior to the Opium War, China was initially seated in a position of great prosperity by comparison to that of Western Europe and the United States. Since this point in time Cheng (2012) explains that the Chinese "suffered severely under Western imperialism with more than a century of shame and humiliation" (p. 168). This "shame and humiliation" is seemingly the shadow that China is hoping to shake with its economic development. Because of its long and rich history, prior to Western domination, it is easy to understand that the national priorities for China are topped by efforts to raise its population out of poverty. With economic development playing such a strong role in its national interests "any problem that interferes with the sustained development of China's economy is a threat" to its stability (Golden, 2011, p. 92). As a result, China will do whatever it can in order to ensure that sustained development is not disrupted.

Historically, a state-controlled economy has been the norm in China. Imperial Chinese monopolies, which existed into the 20th century, could be viewed as models for today's state owned businesses. Many observers have predicted that China would gradually evolve towards Western-style capitalism, including a stronger separation between the private and public sectors. However, while China's economy continues to grow, there are no signs emerging that the private sector will be separated from government influence (Mandiant, 2013).The move by China toward state owned enterprises was reinforced during the global financial crisis in 2008. During that time, international confidence in the free-market model was placed in doubt. Many countries gave serious consideration to the China model for state owned enterprises as a viable option for greater economic stability. Since the time of that crisis, the Chinese government has reaffirmed its belief in a state owned enterprise system (Chen, 2013).

Technology research firm, Mandiant, recently reported:

In terms of historical impact, it is also important to recognize that espionage has a long and glorious history in China, largely free from the negative connotations and "fairness" baggage that often saddles contemporary Western perceptions of spying. China's political history and popular culture is littered with examples of changing allegiances, profiteering, lies, spying, etc. in the name of victory, which, more often than not, ultimately equals moral legitimacy. This was as true in ancient times during the Warring

States period as it was during the Chinese Revolutionary Civil War in the 20th century; the patterns remain remarkably consistent over the millennia. Such a perspective can also be seen more recently in works like Chaoxian Zhan or Unrestricted Warfare, an influential book authored by members of the PLA, which criticizes as self-serving the restrictions and boundaries Western tradition places on conflict. The authors instead propose an expansion of the definition of warfare to include other avenues like computer network operations or economic warfare in peacetime to benefit a developing country like the PRC.... In light of this perspective, Chinese officials may find it difficult to treat the public and private sectors separately, and to conduct espionage against one but not the other. This traditional lack of separation is an important consideration when trying to predict or discern Chinese political behavior as it relates to espionage....It would be easy for an outsider to judge as irrational the fear PRC officials have of repeating the mistakes that led to multiple disasters over the last century, and/or again being victim to foreign depredations. For this reason, foreign perceptions of Chinese chauvinism or ignorance are often misconstrued. Many times such incidents reflect China's self-realization that its rise has been relatively short and how close the country has been, and perhaps still is, to the precipice. For this reason, the idea of not playing by foreigner's rules, grasping opportunity whenever and wherever available, and building national strength at an almost desperate pace are "rational" responses in the Chinese perspective. (Mandiant, 2013)

China has historically relied on an approach to commerce that never emphasized a distinct divide between public and private business. And, there was no stigma attached to espionage for economic purposes. China has deliberately chosen a path to strengthen its technological and industrial base to avoid past humiliations, and there are plans to resume in the future its past role as a great power (Mandiant, 2013).

Conflicting East-West Perceptions

Given the history of China, there is a disconnect between East and West about whether a boundary actually exists between cyber espionage for national security objectives and cyber espionage for economic gain. Does the U.S. instinctively observe this strict boundary, while China does not? Does one country see a separation between national security and economic gain, while the other views them as one in the same?

Computer access through the Internet eliminates the need for physical presence for technology transfer. Some U.S. officials consider copying of sensitive intellectual property (meaning IP and designs created by Department of Defense contractors) to be the same as theft of state secrets. Cyber espionage which enables technology transfer is considered by U.S. observers as a new method used to prepare the battlefield before warfare. Thus the theft of IP from contractors that support military systems may be considered by U.S. officials an approach to warfare. However, China may view warfare as business, and business as warfare. China may also view cyber espionage and the gathering of IP as following natural laws based on the philosophy of Confucius.

The U.S. perceives that China is seeking an aggressive cyber capability as it 1) sees it as a way to remove political and military pressure coming out of the West and the US, 2) is seeking to enhance its military capacity, and 3) seeks to enhance its lagging technological level in order to move forward economically (Hjortdal, 2011). Cyber as an information warfare tool can be considered an important asymmetric tool for China so that it can have a viable deterrent against U.S. influence (Kanwal, 2009). In particular it is recognized that China is wary over its position with Taiwan, and that a cyber-option could also have serious implications for India as it becomes increasingly dependent on technology (Kanwal, 2009). Kanwal (2009) further describes China's cyber capabilities in general as a way to carry out "acupuncture warfare" of "paralyzing the enemy by attacking the weak link of his command, control, communications and information as if hitting his acupuncture point in kung fu combat" (p. 18).

Within China, there is a deep concern over U.S. "intervention" and interference in the sovereignty of others, and sees this occurring more frequently through the guise of the United Nations, and when the West is unable to accomplish their goals through the UN, they are thought to rally under the NATO flag (Cheng, 2012). "Western powers are perceived as trying to maintain their global domination by relying on their superiority in economics as well as science and technology, and they appear reluctant to embrace cultural diversity and the balanced development of human society" (Cheng, 2012, p. 168). Given its historical experience with Western imperialism it comes as no surprise that China has concerns about Western intervention occurring over Tibet or Taiwan. When considering its national interest China is heavily occupied in ensuring that the economic, scientific, and technological gap between it and the West closes.

Rather than compete for the US position as a main pole in the international system, China appears to be motivated towards seeing a multipolar world built around peaceful co-existence (Cheng, 2012; Golden, 2011). To overcome the stigma of being perceived as a rising threat, China is working to reimage itself under the guise of peaceful development. Similar to its 1950s promotion of the five principals in order to achieve "peaceful co-existence," including respect for territorial boundaries and national sovereignty, non-interference in the affairs of others "equality and mutual benefit, non-aggression and peaceful co-existence" China is attempting to rebrand itself as a leader and advocate for developing nations (Cheng, 2012, p. 174). Rather than exerting imperialistic tendencies China is looking to demonstrate that it is carrying out its modernization in a peaceful manner and that anything other than this would be counterproductive (Cheng, 2012). Furthermore, "to reduce the 'China threat' perception and to emphasize the idea of a 'harmonious world', Chinese leadership tries to re-assure developing countries, especially those who are China's neighbors, that China's economic development would benefit them" (Cheng, 2012, p. 178).

As China continues to develop economically it will do so under the guise of its concept of "comprehensive national power" (CNP) which seeks to blend all aspects of the state in order for it to achieve its goals (Golden, 2011). Under this concept one can see the lack of distinction that China has when it comes to using military or nonmilitary means. Golden (2011) explains that the concept of CNP can be attributed to "ancient Chinese military strategists" when he references Michael Pillsbury's comments that "China's wise ancient strategists never advocated relying only on military power to conquer the enemy, but emphasized combining military power with nonmilitary power related to war in order to get the upper hand (Pillsbury 1991: 10-108)" (Golden, 2011, p. 97). This can help provide an understanding to the Chinese approach to conflict and the tasking of its resources to gain an edge within that conflict. Rather than having a clear distinction between purely military resources and nonmilitary resources, China blurs the lines in an effort to gain a competitive advantage over its adversary.Some have observed that in China, business is war. In China, business is often a matter of national strategy and sometimes also a matter of nationalist sentiment (Prestowitz, 2013). China has now become a major trading partner with the rest of the world. However, the business relationships involved with that partnership can be mutually beneficial, adversarial, and competitive -- all at the same time. Those who make huge economic profits doing business in China are also having their cyber information extracted quietly. It is not uncommon for the business person who travels to China to have their computers bugged, or to have their hotel rooms searched. For China, cyber is just another medium for information warfare (IW). Given China's fears of Western intervention a great deal of China's cyber activities appear to be aimed at monitoring its own people (Cartin, 2012). Perhaps as a way to mitigate an uprising or protest against its authoritarian government, China is using its cyber prowess to demonstrate to its own people the need for such a system of government in order to receive trustworthy information. Such an intent would place some of China's cyber behavior into the realm of deception whereby the goal of an offensive demonstration of cyber power would be to cause "a system to deliver incorrect information, to deliver information incorrectly, or to obscure correct information, would deceive its operators into making misdirected decisions" (Cartin, 2012, p. 16).

Americans, who generally are more direct in their business dealings, may not understand the ambiguity they are faced with when doing business in China. Americans are accustomed to viewing the world as a place where others think as they do, and want to act as they do. In the West, our laws, religion and policy are based on a belief that "Peace" and "War" are mutually exclusive opposites that cannot occur at the same time. We like to think of these conditions as factually based. China challenges this mindset, where their belief is that conflict exists fully even in the midst of a mutually advantageous mindset (Brenner, 2011).

A mutually supportive relationship with China will always involve a constant struggle for unilateral advantage. This relationship will also involve radically different visions of individual liberty and social order. Cyber espionage is therefore to be expected on the part of China, even as the West may have a desire to maintain a global order that protects individual rights in intellectual property. To the nations of the West, upholding this right may be more important than the advantage that could be gained from U.S. violations of our own legal belief system to maintain the separation of public and private business. This viewpoint from a developed country is easy to see, while the viewpoint from a developing country, such as China, may be quite different. While, for the time being, China may not have a much to steal as do the Western countries that are more developed, the leaders in China are determined to close the technological and economic gap between East and West (Brenner, 2011).

SOLUTIONS AND RECOMMENDATIONS

Both the United States and China have a mutual interest in building a strong relationship with one another. Carnegie Endowment (2013) found that a large majority of U.S. elites, "81 percent of government officials to 94 percent of media elites," cited that building a strong relationship with China was important to the future of U.S. foreign policy (p. 35). Within China, the study also found that a majority of elites placed building a strong relationship with the United States as a top priority. "This ranked higher than any other policy priority among all elite categories except government elites, who most frequently cited the need to strongly opposed U.S. arms sales to Taiwan" (Carnegie Endowment, 2013, p. 36).

As a reemerging power China has the potential to be a key leader within the region and the world. As a result of China's increased global involvement and their aggressive economic development policies, China needs to be part of any international decision making body looking to shape cyber policies. The research demonstrates that both the United States and China view cyber espionage in a different light. On the one hand the United States sees a clear separation between commercial enterprise and the military. For this reason the United States alleges that it does not take its cyber espionage practices into the business realm. On the other hand, China views that business and the military both seek to support the success of the state as demonstrated in their concept of "comprehensive national power." Given these differing perspectives, decision makers from both states need to come together to establish tangible policies regarding the use of cyber espionage in order to enhance commercial enterprises.

Negative sentiment that the US feels regarding Chinese competitive intelligence practices can be likened to the negative sentiment that China feels over US arms sales to Taiwan (Carnegie Endowment, 2013). The commercial espionage practices of China have caused the United States to face a problem that it considers a serious threat. While U.S. arms sales to Taiwan are considered by China to be an infringement on their sovereignty. In spite of serious concerns by both parties, the U.S. and China both view a positive relationship with one another as something that is highly desirable. During diplomatic negotiations between these states both issues should be discussed to find mutually beneficial policies.

FUTURE RESEARCH DIRECTIONS

When it comes to technological advancements and cyber technologies, it can be stated that the genie has been officially released from its bottle. States are now able to integrate cyber into their business practices, offensive and defensive military capabilities, etc. The landscape appears to be changing in that business innovations are increasingly relied upon to support military and government capabilities. Further research should investigate the long term implications of these linkages, especially as they relate to our understanding of noncombatants and perhaps even Western philosophies on war and the placement of business within the military industrial complex. Is the U.S. separation of business and military outdated?

As governments increase their cyber capabilities we also have the opportunity to further consider what cyber regulations or "cyber control" might look like. During the Cold War the United States and the former Soviet Union experienced security dilemmas whereby arms development for alleged defensive purposes were viewed by the other as offensive posturing. In order to establish some trust between the two superpowers they developed arms control agreements and confidence building measures to reassure one another that they are following through with their agreements. Can confidence building measures help states with developing cyber capabilities? How can reassurance be created when we move from something concrete and visible like multiple independently targeted reentry vehicles on a missile to something largely invisible to the naked eye like cyber technology? Can the arms control policies between the United States and Russia serve as an example for how cyber capabilities should be managed between the United States and China?

CONCLUSION

It is assumed by most observers that China is copying vast amounts of intellectual property from US military and private industry and also from other nations through its cyber espionage activities. US officials say these activities go beyond traditionally accepted ideas for cyber espionage, where the intent is to protect against military surprises and guard national defense. China is accused of sharing with their industries the vast quantities of IP they collect, and those industries are also largely controlled by the central government. This action amounts to the PRC directing much of its vast national cyber resources and talent into stealing IP and ideas that give its industries unfair economic advantages over other nations. However, the fact is that many other nations also have their own nationally controlled industries and, in ways similar to China, some may also share IP collected through their nationally directed cyber espionage. By choosing to not do the same thing, and by not sharing with its domestic industries the vast collection of IP and data obtained through its own considerable cyber espionage activities conducted against other countries, including China, the U.S. may be placing itself at an economic disadvantage.

China's history shows that traditionally IP has been centrally controlled by the government for the purpose of maintaining social order along with state authority. The development of protections for IP has been a Western value that has no counterpart in China's history. Ideas and creations came to society as gifts from the ancestors. Confucian philosophy for guidance toward correct action showed that it was necessary to interact with a past heritage shared by all. This belief actually curtailed how strongly state authority could restrict access to, or copying of expressions that were strongly seen as tied to the common ancestors of China.

Add to this the cultural beliefs for China, where business and war are seen as the same thing, and where partnerships can coexist along with competition that is adversarial. For Americans, however, laws, religion and policies are based on a belief that "Peace" and "War" are mutually exclusive opposites that cannot occur at the same time. They are also accustomed to viewing the world as a place where others think like they do, and want to act as they do. China and the U.S. do not share similar views about what should be the correct boundaries for cyber espionage. Therefore, actions seen by one side as justified for business may be viewed as steps toward war by the other, and accusations that are regularly traded between these two countries continue to be affected poorly by this cultural disconnect that aggravates misunderstanding.

What is needed is a clearer understanding of differences in national cultures that contribute to intolerance between countries, such as China and the U.S. when it comes to business, threats of war, and the evolving new role of cyber espionage. The U.S. may need to reconsider its current views of cyber espionage, and allow some of the vast amounts of IP and data collected through regular cyber espionage activities to also be shared with industry. We are moving into a new world where the "Internet of Everything" will result in unimaginable conveniences, and also an overwhelming deluge of meta-data concerning every human movement and action, as personal devices record our biological status and household appliances can order our groceries without need for our intervention. It may be time to recognize that cyber espionage has evolved into something new, useful and perhaps essential for modern commerce. We may not like it entirely, but the reality is changing around us.

REFERENCES

Aid, M. (2013, June). Inside the NSA's ultra-secret China hacking group. *Foreign Policy*. Retrieved from http://foreignpolicy.com/2013/06/10/inside-the-nsas-ultra-secret-china-hacking-group/

Alexander, M. G., Levin, S., & Henry, P. J. (2005). Image theory, social identity, and social dominance: Structural characteristics and individual motives underlying international images. *Political Psychology*, *26*(1), 27–45. doi:10.1111/j.1467-9221.2005.00408.x

Alford, W. P. (2004). *To steal a book is an elegant offense*. Stanford, CA: Stanford University Press.

Barron-Lopez, L. (2014, June). Cyber threats put energy sector on red alert. *The Hill*. Retrieved from http://thehill.com/policy/technology/209116-cyber-threats-put-energy-sector-on-red-alert

Brenner, J. (2011). *America the vulnerable: Inside the new threat matrix of digital espionage, crime, and warfare*. New York: Penguin Press.

Carnegie Endowment for International Peace. (2013). *U.S.-China security perceptions survey: findings and implications*. Washington, D.C. Retrieved from http://cusef.org.hk/wp-content/uploads/2014/05/02_eng.pdf

Carr, C. (Ed.). (2000). *The book of war: Sun-Tzu the art of warfare & Karl Von Clausewitz on war*. New York: The Modern Library.

Cartin, J. M. (2014). Don't forget the humans: Toward a 21st century offensive cyber strategy. *Global Security Studies*, *5*(2), 1–26.

Chen, D. (2013). China's state-owned enterprises: How much do we know? From CNOOC to its siblings. *The School of Public Policy*, 6(19), 1-27. Retrieved from http://www.policyschool.ucalgary.ca/sites/default/files/research/china-soes-final.pdf

Cheng, J. Y. S. (2012). Convincing the world of China's tradition to pursue universal harmony. *Journal of Chinese Political Science*, *17*(2), 165–185. doi:10.1007/s11366-012-9191-5

Cottam, M. (1994). *Images &intervention: U.S. policies in Latin America*. Pittsburgh, PA: University of Pittsburgh Press.

Cottam, M., Dietz-Uhler, B., Mastors, E. M., & Preston, T. (2004). *Introduction to political psychology*. Mahwah, New Jersey: Lawrence Erlbaum Associates.

Cottam, R. (1977). *Foreign policy motivation: A general theory and a case study*. Pittsburgh, PA: University of Pittsburgh Press.

Dilanian, K. (2011, October 4). China cyber attacks threaten U.S. security, official says. *Los Angeles Times*. Retrieved from http://articles.latimes.com/2011/oct/04/news/la-pn-china-cyberattacks-20111004

Fleisher, C. S., & Wright, S. (2009). Examining differences in competitive intelligence practice: China, Japan, and the West. *Thunderbird International Business Review*, *51*(3), 249–261. doi:10.1002/tie.20263

George, A. (1979). The causal nexus between cognitive beliefs and decision-making behavior: The 'operational code. In L. S. Falkowski (Ed.), *Psychological Models in International Politics* (pp. 95–124). Boulder, CO: Westview Press.

Gewirtz, D. (2011). Night dragon: Cyberwar meets corporate espionage. *Journal of Counterterrorism & Homeland Security International*, *17*(2), 6–8.

Glaser, B.S. (2014). US-China relations: Managing differences remains and urgent challenge. *Southeast Asian Affairs*, 76-82.

Golden, S. (2011). China's perception of risk and the concept of comprehensive national power. *The Copenhagen Journal of Asian Studies*, *29*(2), 79–109.

He, K. (2012). Undermining adversaries: Unipolarity, threat perception, and negative balancing strategies after the Cold War. *Security Studies*, *21*(2), 154–191. doi:10.1080/09636412.2012.679201

Hermann, M. G. (2001). How decision units shape foreign policy: A theoretical framework. International Studies Association, 47-81.

Herrmann, R. K. (1985). *Perception and behavior in Soviet foreign policy*. Pittsburgh, PA: University of Pittsburgh Press.

Herrmann, R. K., & Keller, J. W. (2004). Beliefs, values, and strategic choice: U.S. leaders' decision to engage, contain, and use force in an era of globalization. *The Journal of Politics*, *66*(2), 557–580. doi:10.1111/j.1468-2508.2004.00164.x

Herrmann, R. K., Voss, J. F., Schooler, T., & Ciarrochi, J. (1997). Images in international relations: An experimental test of cognitive schemata. *International Studies Quarterly*, *41*(3), 403–433. doi:10.1111/0020-8833.00050

Hjortdal, M. (2011). China's use of cyber warfare: Espionage meets strategic deterrence. *Journal of Strategic Security*, *4*(2), 1–24. doi:10.5038/1944-0472.4.2.1

Holsti, O. (1967). Cognitive dynamics and images of the enemy. In D. Finley, O. Holsti, & R. Fagen (Eds.), *Enemy in Politics* (pp. 25–96). Chicago: Rand McNally.

Hu, E. (2014, June 6). The 'cool war' with China is unseen, but comes with consequences. *National Public Radio*. Retrieved from http://www.npr.org/blogs/parallels/2014/06/06/318788569/the-cool-war-with-china-is-unseen-but-comes-with-consequences

Jervis, R. (1976). *Perception and misperception in international politics*. Princeton, NJ: Princeton University Press.

Kanwal, G. (2009). China's emerging cyber war doctrine. *Journal of Defense Studies*, *3*(3), 14–22.

Kaplowitz, N. (1984). Psychopolitical dimensions of international relations: The reciprocal effect of conflict strategies. *International Studies Quarterly*, *28*(4), 373–406. doi:10.2307/2600562

Mandiant. (2013, May 29). *Chinese motivations for corporate espionage: A historical perspective*. Retrieved from https://dl.mandiant.com/EE/library/Whitepaper_China_Motivations_for_Corporate_Espionage.pdf

McConnell, M., Chertoff, M., & Lynn, W. (2012, January 27). China's cyber thievery is national policy - and must be challenged. *The Wall Street Journal*. Retrieved from http://online.wsj.com/news/articles/SB10001424052970203718504577178832338032176

McGregor, J. (2013, April 27). Is the specter of a 'cyber Cold War' real? *The Atlantic*. Retrieved from http://m.theatlantic.com/china/archive/2013/04/is-the-specter-of-a-cyber-cold-war-real/275352/href=

Michaels, J. (2014, May 19). China's theft of business secrets is beyond espionage. *USA Today*. Retrieved from http://www.usatoday.com/story/news/nation/2014/05/19/china-indictment-cyber-espionage/9289829/

Norenzayan, A., Choi, I., & Nisbett, R. E. (1999). Eastern and western perceptions of causality for social behavior: Lay theories about personalities and situations. In D. D. Prentice & D. T. Miller (Eds.), *Cultural Divides: Understanding and Overcoming Group Conflict* (pp. 239–272). New York: Russell Sage Foundation.

Pang, L. (2012). *Creativity and its discontents*. London: Duke University. doi:10.1215/9780822394587

Prestowitz, C. (2010). *The betrayal of American prosperity: Free market delusions, America's decline, and how we must compete in the post-dollar era*. Simon and Schuster Digital Sales Inc.

Prestowitz, C. (2013b, June). The China conundrum. *Foreign Policy*. Retrieved from http://prestowitz.foreignpolicy.com/posts/2013/06/03/the_china_conundrum

Prestowitz, C. (2014, May 25). Got intel, Uncle Sam? Share it with U.S. companies. *Los Angeles Times*. Retrieved from http://www.latimes.com/opinion/op-ed/la-oe-prestowitz-china-hacking-20140526-story.html

Roberts, D. (2012, November 1). Confucius makes a comeback in China. *Bloomberg Business Week*. Retrieved from http://www.businessweek.com/articles/2012-11-01/confucius-makes-a-comeback-in-china

Ronald Deibert. (2011). Ronald Deibert: Tracking the emerging arms race in cyberspace. *The Bulletin of the Atomic Scientists*, *67*(1), 1–8. doi:10.1177/0096340210393703

Sanger, D. E., & Perlroth, N. (2014, March 22). N.S.A. breached Chinese servers seen as security threat. *The New York Times*. Retrieved from http://www.nytimes.com/2014/03/23/world/asia/nsa-breached-chinese-servers-seen-as-spy-peril.html?_r=0

Tao, Q., & Prescott, J. E. (2000). China: Competitive intelligence practices in an emerging market environment. *Competitive Intelligence Review*, *11*(4), 65–78. doi:10.1002/1520-6386(200034)11:4<65::AID-CIR10>3.0.CO;2-N

Thomas, T. L. (2010). *Google confronts China's "three warfares."* Carlisle, PA: US Army War College.

U.S. Department of Justice, Office of Public Affairs. (2014, May 19). U.S. charges five Chinese military hackers for cyber espionage against U.S. corporations and a labor organization for commercial advantage. Retrieved from http://www.justice.gov/opa/pr/us-charges-five-chinese-military-hackers-cyber-espionage-against-us-corporations-and-labor

Vertzberger, Y. Y. I. (1990). *The world in their minds: Information processing, cognition, and perception in foreign policy decision-making*. Stanford, CA: Stanford University Press.

Wallace, G. (2014, March 24). Report: Leaked Snowden documents show NSA hacked Chinese telecom company. *CNN*. Retrieved from http://money.cnn.com/2014/03/23/technology/security/nsa-china-huawei/?iid=EL

Wang, B., & Chee, H. (2012, January 12). China's public sector: a different way of working. *The Guardian*. Retrieved from http://www.theguardian.com/public-leaders-network/blog/2012/jan/03/china-public-sector-leadership

KEY TERMS AND DEFINITIONS

Competitive Intelligence: The legal and active collection of information specific to ones competitors and the competitive environment, traditionally done through open sources.

Cyber Attack: Networked computers with exposed vulnerabilities may be disrupted or taken over by an unauthorized user. Vulnerabilities resulting from poor security practices, inadequate training, or unexpected faults in computer software provide the entry points for an attack. As technology becomes more complex and sophisticated, the surface area for vulnerabilities also expands.

Cyber Espionage: Cyber espionage is enabled due to vulnerabilities that allow unauthorized intrusions into other networked systems. Information can be copied and secretly transferred through the network and onto other computer systems where it can be viewed and exploited by unauthorized users. Cyber espionage is traditionally done by nation states to protect national security by secretly observing and monitoring the computer systems of other nation states to protect against unexpected threats or surprises. However, it can also be done to secretly and actively gain economic, strategic, or military advantage.

Cyber Warfare and Information Warfare: Warfare can occur if a nation state takes control of the computer systems that are critical to another nation state and deliberately causes disruption. Disruption may be incremental, and may affect physical property, financial markets, or psychological stability. However, attribution is usually difficult to determine, and the appropriate level and direction for retaliation may be problematic. Organizations other than a traditional nation state may also have the capability to produce the effects of cyber warfare and information warfare.

Fundamental Attribution Error: The tendency to overly credit the behavior of another to dispositional causes like one's personality rather than to situation causes like one's environment.

Industrial Espionage: Industrial espionage is theft of information for commercial gain. Industrial cyber espionage is enabled through vulnerabilities that allow cyber espionage for this purpose.

Intellectual Property: Concepts may be rendered either as models, documents, plans, images or designs in 2-D and 3-D. When these concepts, especially in digital form, are protected by patent or copyright, they are assigned rights of ownership and become intellectual property. Protected concepts cannot be used or copied without permission of the property owner.

Chapter 3
The USA Electrical Grid:
Public Perception, Cyber Attacks, and Inclement Weather

Eugene de Silva
Virginia Research Institute, USA

Eugenie de Silva
University of Leicester, UK

ABSTRACT

This chapter provides a discussion of the United States (U.S.) electrical grid. In particular, the chapter explicates the vulnerabilities of the electrical grid by placing a focus on public perception, cyber-attacks, and the inclement weather. The authors elaborate on the necessity of contingency plans, heightened security through the utilization of smart grids and microgrids, and improved cooperation between the Intelligence Community (IC) and the public. This chapter further expands on the importance of government agencies establishing community outreach programs to raise public awareness and build a strong relationship between U.S. security agencies and the public. Overall, this chapter highlights the key issues pertaining to the electrical grid, and provides solutions and strategies to resolve them.

DOI: 10.4018/978-1-4666-9661-7.ch003

INTRODUCTION

It has become increasingly apparent that the technologically dependent culture of the United States (U.S.) has heightened risks to national security and intelligence practices. Although the mass majority may not be aware, the threat to critical infrastructure in the U.S. has persisted for years. This chapter explores the vulnerability of the current U.S. electrical grid system, and possible threats that could cripple the entire nation with greater consequences than that have been caused by any of the recent attacks on the U.S. by terrorist/radical groups. The long-term implications and the possible catenation of disasters are discussed whilst also explaining what immediate measures can be taken in this regard.

Due to the overwhelming difficulty in prediction and prevention, cyber-attacks are a particularly effective and dangerous method to gain the upper hand. As technology has advanced, individuals within the security fields have continuously reevaluated their procedures and have sought appropriate mechanisms to protect vital systems from the extreme threats that are cyber-attacks. With a view to enhancing security systems, cyber security officials have honed their skills in order to identify novel measures to detect and deter cyber-attacks; however, protecting U.S. cyber systems is a difficult task, especially due to the sheer size of network systems and the uproar that may result due to public angst toward evolving times that necessitate greater security. However, issues in protecting cyber systems also stem from a lack of trust from the public toward intelligence personnel and agencies that have resulted in poor public relations and have further promulgated a weak intelligence system.

The twenty-first century has witnessed heinous crimes and acts of terror, yet the consequences of these acts will seemingly be lesser in comparison to the effects of possible future cybercrime. An unsecure electrical grid system and a society unwilling to change for their benefit will certainly be the downfall of U.S. society in the near future as U.S. adversaries slowly, but steadily gain the necessary power and knowledge to undermine the integrity of major cyber systems. To turn on any major news outlet on the television in the U.S. is to firstly expose one's self to the partisanship nature of politics and secondly to open one's self to repetitive discussions of the threats posed by state and non-state actors as a result of cyber-attacks. Most recently, the hacking of Sony and the release of allegedly "embarrassing" financial records and incriminating emails highlighted the effects of a cyber-attack even at a considerably low level. It is quite simple to convey the message of the harsh nature of possible cyber-attacks; yet, it is much more difficult to provide a resolution. There are many within the field who seek to improve the stability and security of U.S. cyber systems; however, it certainly seems that the public is wary of the extent to which improvements in the field actually benefit the nation. With this taken into consideration, this chapter also provides a brief reasoning to explain why continuous discussions of the stability of the cyber field to raise awareness will result in heightened cyber standards in the U.S.

The threats of cyber-attacks are undoubtedly present, yet the electrical grid also faces other issues, such as the inclement weather. The effects of climate change, as explained within this chapter, pose major threats to the stability of the electrical grid. The unpredictability of the weather, and the lack of protection from any inclement weather could result in a major breakdown of the grid. The weather, in actuality, may present greater issues than a cyber-attack, due to the inability to avoid weather unlike the ability to deter cyber-attacks that are detected. For example, even if an extreme storm is detected, there is no way to eradicate the storm without allowing nature to run its full course.

Of course, if the weather was simply the issue, then researchers, academics, and practitioners could aim to make this the focus of their investigations to secure the grid. However, this also leads to the issue of political beliefs and ideologies that cause individuals who could play vital roles in the improvement of the system to shy away from the topic. Accordingly, a majority of the U.S. public has apparently dismissed the topic, due to a lack of initiative taken to discuss issues related to the electrical grid. Without much public opinion on the topic, there has been little impetus for politicians to also be involved in the discussion of the issue. The lack of priority placed on this issue by U.S. politicians has also seemingly resulted in limited progress.

BACKGROUND

It was President Barack Obama who stated that "it is now clear this cyber threat is one [of] the most serious economic and national security challenges we face as a nation" ("Cyber War: Sabotaging the System"). Due to the fact that cyber-attacks pose such significant threats, it would seem only logical that the U.S. should prepare and safeguard its systems to a great extent. Nonetheless, this is far from the actual case; for instance, retired Admiral Mike McConnell even denoted that the U.S. is not even prepared for a major cyber-attack, such as one even directed at "bringing down a power grid" ("Cyber War: Sabotaging the System"). Accordingly, it has been reported that there is not even one "overarching" definition of cybercrime, and there has not been one lead agency designated with the responsibilities of combating cybercrimes (Finklea & Theohary, 2013, 1). The fact that there is not one universal definition of cybercrime is analogous to the fact that there is not one universal definition of terrorism. A lack of a definition may result in wavering boundaries with regard to what activities can or cannot be considered as cybercrime or terrorism. In addition, the threats to cyber security are exacerbated by a lack of "universally accepted and enforceable norms of behavior in cyberspace" (Stewart, 2015). These issues have been recognized and, as a result, the Defense Intelligence Agency (DIA) in February of 2015 released a worldwide threat assessment wherein it was noted that "states worldwide are forming 'cyber command' organizations and developing national capabilities" (Stewart, 2015). From a professional perspective, it would seem that these actions are taking place much later than was necessary; however, a concerted effort to reconcile the overarching issues with cyber security will immensely aid in the current security situations.

It has been reported that the number of network posts is "expected to exceed the human population" by the year 2015 ("U.S. Cybersecurity Policy," 2010). As the use of cyber systems progresses to an essentially unthinkable level, greater support will be warranted. As such, the military also plays a role in protecting cyber efforts through commands, such as the USCYBERCOM; as per the directions of the Secretary of Defense, the Commander of U.S. Strategic Commander established this command ("U.S. Cyber Command," 2013). The aims of this command were to coordinate and synchronize activities to "direct the operations and defense of specified Department of Defense information networks" and also conduct full spectrum military operations when necessary ("U.S. Cyber Command," 2013). Accordingly, the military offers opportunities to collect information and conduct activities that would not otherwise be possible. However, threats to U.S. cyber systems persist, and as technology improves, more individuals have gained access to resources that can be used to attack critical infrastructure. Social media has become a major tool for criminals to recruit members, share their ideologies and beliefs, boast about their victories against the law, and also taunt protectors of the law. For example, Mara Salva Trucha 13 (MS13), a transnational criminal organization known for its use of a machete to behead its victims, uses social media to "to attract new members, and also to manage some of their operations trafficking people and goods" (Collins, 2014). Additionally, many cartel members have staunch followers on social media who praise them for their "selfies" that are taken with their guns at their sides (Collins, 2014). This almost twisted support seemingly stems from the cartel's flaunting of wealth, sexual relations, and power; however, the cartels actually are known to upload photographs of the members helping others (e.g. handing out food and tents consequent to a major hurricane) (Collins, 2014). The ability of criminals to mold public view through social media would not have been possible several years ago when technology was less advanced. Yet, the use of technology is not a new strategy for criminals to achieve success. Technology has been so useful that Hezbollah even developed their own video games as propaganda to subtly influence the younger generation to follow Hezbollah's beliefs. Most recently, the Islamic State of Iraq and Syria (ISIS) began to take advantage of the ease of social media to connect with those who can be easily swayed by others to aid in the attainment of ISIS' goals.

Accordingly, technology has given rise to novel opportunities, and thus requires the public to understand the dangers associated with unsecure cyber systems. In an online environment, criminals are offered freedoms to act under false personas and carry out what would otherwise be quite difficult, illegal tasks. Through cyber systems, criminals can act anonymously online, while even conducting transactions that would regularly require crossing borders and facing related challenges. Of course, this also poses the challenge of trying to ensure that law enforcement work with one another, since "the cooperation between law enforcement, revenue services and judiciary is one of the most difficult tasks as far as the transnational criminality is concerned" (Filipkowski, 2008, 17). Moreover, it has been reported that, at times, the victim of a cyber-attack may remain unaware of the attack occurring until many years later (Gelinas, 2010, 1). Hence, technological advances pose hurdles to law enforcement when seeking to adequately identify responsible parties in order to take necessary actions.

As aforementioned, the U.S. military is also involved in cyber activities. However, it seems that there are two major challenges that are posed as a result of the military's role in these cyber activities. The first problem seems to pertain to the speed at which the military can act. For instance, General Martin E. Dempsey stated that the military must improve so that it can "operate at network speed, rather than what I [Gen. Dempsey] call swivel-chair speed" (Shanker, 2013) The second problem that could possibly be identified is the legal restrictions which are enacted to place regulations on the intelligence that can be gathered and the actions that can be taken (Williams, Dunlevy, & Shimeall, 2013). However, these problems can be overcome by including various government agencies in the plan to protect computer networks. This leads to the clear recognition of the necessity of integration and cooperation. Information sharing is a key asset that not only promotes a flourishing environment, but also establishes a sense of respect amongst intelligence and law enforcement officers.

When discussing this topic, it may be useful to take into consideration the old, yet well-known quote that denotes that more is not always better. In the field of intelligence, it may seem better to expand the community and hire more personnel to address intelligence issues; however, there can be negative consequences in expanding the Intelligence Community (IC) too much, such as failures which could include but are not limited to a lack of information sharing, disorganized activities, and higher costs in maintaining the standards of the field. Therefore, it would not be reasonable to try and include many different departments in the effort against cybercrime; however, it is necessary that there is a carefully selected group of departments which focus on defending computer networks and executive offensive attacks. There must be a well-balanced blend of departments which are selected to defend computer networks, since having too little or too many agencies involved would result in a failure to safeguard the systems. For instance, it was General Keith Alexander who stated, "cyber security is a team sport" ("U.S. Cybersecurity Policy," 2010). Accordingly, the utilization of the military alone would not be a well-planned strategy, but it certainly has proved to be useful in collaboration with other intelligence agencies.

It is quite simple to recognize the extent to which state and non-state actors, especially in recent years until 2015, have placed a higher priority on the use of cyber operations. Additionally, the international media frequently repeat the possible consequences of major cyber-attacks aimed at the U.S. Even in academic and professional documents, the extents to which cyber operations are likely have been continuously reported to the public. However, the published reports and media focus on cyber security issues are seemingly repetitive warnings to the masses that have yet to result in major changes or improvements to cyber security. As is argued in this chapter, the media and even academic reports are simply wetting the tongues of the public by failing to devote detailed, analytical discussions to the extent to which the U.S. electrical grid is vulnerable to major cyber-attacks. Although reports, such as the DNI and DIA worldwide threat assessments refer to the ways in which state and non-state actors may execute cyber operations, it seems that the IC has failed to raise sufficient awareness about the U.S. electrical grid. This was hence the reason why this chapter has explicitly focused on the electrical grid and the ways in which the public, media, and IC can effectively raise awareness and further protect current systems.

Definitions

Although this work may not consistently refer to attribution with regard to cyber operation and cyber security, it is imperative that onlookers of the field are aware of at least the basic understanding of the definition of attribution, especially as it is used in this work. Accordingly, for the purpose of this analysis, the definition of attribution as offered by David D. Clark and Susan Landau is used; therefore, "Although attribution generally means assigning a cause to an action, as used here *attribution* refers to identifying the agent responsible for the action (specifically, 'determining the identity or location of an attacker or an attacker's intermediary)'" (2011, 2). The concept of attribution as it relates to cyber cases requires that one fully identify the responsible parties in a manner that would be conducive to establishing a foundation that would cause attackers to refrain from future attacks on the grounds of fear of retaliation (Clark & Landau, 2011, 2). However, as a result of technological advances, it can be quite difficult to identify the responsible party through online systems. This has come to be known as the attribution problem (Clark & Landau, 2011, 2). Although attribution is not heavily discussed within the body of this chapter, it provides contextual knowledge to this topic.

For the purposes of this chapter, the following is a list of compiled definitions of terms either frequently used within this work or explicitly related to the discussed topic.

- **Access:** The ability and opportunity to obtain knowledge of classified sensitive information or to be in a place where one could expect to gain such knowledge ("Terms," 2011, 2).
- **Advanced Persistent Threat:** An extremely proficient, patient, determined, and capable adversary, including two or more of such adversaries working together ("Terms," 2011, 3).
- **Bot Net:** A collection of zombie PCs [personal computers]. Botnet is short for robot network. A botnet can consist of tens or even hundreds of thousands of zombie computers. A single PC in a botnet can automatically send thousands of spam messages per day. The most common spam messages come from zombie computers. ("Terms," 2011, 13).

- **Classified Information:** Any information/data that has been purposefully recognized and designated as to be protected against unauthorized disclosures ("Terms," 2011, 18).
- **Computer Security (COMUSEC):** The protection resulting from all measures to deny unauthorized access and exploitation of friendly computer systems ("Terms," 2011, 26).
- **Critical Asset:** A specific entity that is of such extraordinary importance that its incapacitation or destruction would have a very serious, debilitating effect on the ability of a nation to continue to function effectively ("Terms," 2011, 47).
- **Defector:** A person who has consciously abandoned loyalty to his country and who possess intelligence information of value to another country or countries ("Terms," 2011, 56).

MAIN FOCUS OF THE CHAPTER

In 2013, the U.S. public was made aware of classified intelligence processes as a result of Edward Snowden, a former National Security Agency (NSA) contractor, who stole and leaked confidential reports. The leaks fueled intensive debates with regard to the ethicality and legality of U.S. government monitoring. Whilst Snowden fled to Russia to evade legal charges, the public uproar continued in the U.S., even extending into 2015. Consequently, many researchers, lawyers, and even former intelligence practitioners seemingly took advantage of the extent to which the public was inherently interested in their privacy rights, especially when using social media or technology in general. Although the interest in technology and the legal boundaries of cyber systems could have been used to raise awareness of the reasons why monitoring is necessary and the consequences of failing to monitor cyber activities, those interested in furthering their political, economic, and/or social agenda ruined the opportunity. Therefore, this is another reason why this chapter focuses on the electrical grid in a hope to focus some attention on the possible disastrous consequences of failing to emphasize the necessity of further securing U.S. cyber systems, more specifically securing the electrical grid.

It was in 1882 that Thomas Edison established the first "commercial" electrical power grid (Pierce, 2014). Edison's power grid was known as the "Pearl Street Station," and essentially set the foundation for society to progress in this manner (Pierce, 2014). As far back as 1882 the electrical power grid has been a vital component of life in the U.S.; however, since its inception it has evolved into "three large interconnected systems that move electricity around the country" ("Energy in Brief," 2014). It has been reported that in the beginning of the twentieth century there were "over 4,000 individual electric utilities, each operating in isolation" ("Energy in Brief," 2014). As time progressed, those who worked in the industry made the decision to rely on alternating current (ac), which made it possible to transmit electricity over longer distances in comparison with the previously popular direct current ("Energy in Brief," 2014). As the industry further evolved after World War II, those in the field further determined that it was more appropriate and effective to interconnect transmission systems ("Energy in Brief," 2014). As a result of the evolution of the power industry, three "large interconnected systems evolved in the United States" ("Energy in Brief," 2014). The continuous progress and improvement of the industry allowed those in the U.S. to establish strong electrical systems across the nation.

Although the distinct processes of the electrical grid require technical knowledge, any individual can easily understand the basic outline of the processes. The electricity is first generated in a power plant, and then a transformer raises the voltage of the electricity so that the transmission is effective ("Energy in Brief," 2014). The raising of the voltage ensures that the "carrying capacity" is higher, which further ascertains that there is a lower loss of electricity during the transmission process ("Energy in Brief," 2014). However, prior to being distributed, substation transformers are used to lower the voltage, which ensures that the electricity is safely distributed to businesses and even homes ("Energy in Brief," 2014). The structure of the electrical grid has clearly been appropriately planned and developed. However, it is poorly safeguarded from possible adversarial attacks, which essentially has left the U.S. in an unstable and vulnerable position.

Solely by observing and assessing the steady and substantial growth of the power industry and the electrical grid in the U.S., one could easily recognize that there have been noticeable improvements that have been set in place to adapt with the times. Accordingly, this growth has continued, especially after the passing of the American Recovery and Reinvestment Act of 2009. This Act provided the U.S. Department of Energy (DOE) with several billion dollars to "modernize the electric power grid" ("Energy in Brief," 2014). In addition to providing 4.5 billion dollars for the modernization of the electrical grid, 100 million dollars was provided through the Recovery Act for workforce training ("Energy in Brief," 2014). The finances allocated through the Act aided in the deployment of "existing smart grid technologies, tools, and techniques" ("Energy in Brief," 2014).

Clearly, those in the DOE have taken the initiative to assess all possibilities and determine the most appropriate resources to strengthen the electrical grid. For instance, in order to modernize the electrical grid, smart grids have been implemented. These smart grids "are made possible by two-way communication technology and computer processing that has been used for decades in other industries" ("Smart Grid," n.d.). The smart grids allow individuals to control the devices around the country from one single location; furthermore, due to the computerization of these smart grids, there is enhanced cyber security and improved "handling sources of electricity like wind and solar power and even integrating electric vehicles onto the grid" ("Smart Grid," n.d.). The smart grids provide more power to professionals in the field to manage against cyber-attacks.

On the other hand, it is also important to take into consideration microgrids that, much like smart grids, improve the protection of the electrical grid. Microgrids "are localized grids that can disconnect from the traditional grid to operate autonomously and help mitigate grid disturbances to strengthen grid resilience" ("The Role," n.d.). Furthermore, microgrids also allow for the integration of "renewable sources of energy such as solar and wind and distributed energy resources such as combined heat and power, energy storage, and demand response" ("The Role," n.d.). Accordingly, the microgrids provide support against the inclement weather that can entirely disrupt the electrical grid. And so, in combination, the smart grids and microgrids are certainly the way forward to enhance the electrical grid and protect against possible disasters.

Issues, Controversies, Problems

There are wide array of issues pertaining to the U.S. electrical grid, a majority of which were covered in the previous component of this chapter. These issues, if not resolved, will almost certainly have disastrous effects that could affect the lives of all living in the U.S. Even the simple allocation of billions of dollars to enhance the grid, as aforementioned, highlights the importance of maintaining and consistently improving it to adapt to the current times. Albeit, there are many individuals who have not entirely grasped the concept that the electrical grid is a staple of daily life in the U.S. and is not secure from many threats. Therefore, it is imperative that experts and researchers continue to share this information.

The first issue with which one would be faced in order to improve the electrical grid is the American perception of the electrical grid. Public opinion is vital in the initiation of widespread discussion of issues in the nation. The use of public opinion polls and the sharing of the results in the national media provide politicians, legislators, researchers, and even academics with greater impetus to focus on the issue at-hand. Accordingly, it is quite surprising that a simple search renders no results of public opinion polls on the topic of the electrical grid, especially in 2014 or 2015. Unlike topics of climate change, waging war in Middle Eastern countries, widespread medical concerns, each of which have been discussed in a staggering number of research articles and polls, the topic of the electrical grid has fallen short. In 2012, Robert Strickling from the Macalester University conducted research and presented a report with regard to the electrical grid in Argentina, Brazil, and the U.S. in order to shed light on public opinion, funding, and coordination in the efforts to modernize the electrical grids in these countries. The research was able to highlight that it is correct to assume that public opinion can provide the necessary political momentum to move forward, yet while the U.S. public is generally aware of the electrical grid necessity of modernization, the political "support is giving way to other interests" (Strickling, 2012, p.22). The U.S. is not naïve to the harsh consequences of allowing political, biased opinion to guide actions; however, it seems that the lessons of the past have yet to be entirely realized.

How could the majority in a country that could be plagued by the consequences of the failure of the electrical grid simply dismiss the topic? It is most likely that the failure to have open discussions about the electrical grid is due to a lack of education or knowledge of the subject. According to a study conducted by the National Energy Technology Lab in 2007, "the American public does not fully understand the benefits that the modernization of the electrical grid can bring and so are not willing to make the short-term investment" (Strickling, 2012, p.24). While the public does have a responsibility to learn about the topic and make the necessary changes to aid in the improvement of the system, the public cannot be entirely blamed. If an individual is unaware of the importance of the electrical grid, the extent to which it is vulnerable to attacks, and the devastating consequences of a possible attack, then it is only logical that he/she would not be willing to make any form of investment since they would simply feel that the issue would not pertain to him/her. Therefore, the issue of public opinion and public perception of the electrical grid must be resolved in order to create widespread discussions of the topic and provide politicians and government leaders with greater impetus to appropriately improve the electrical grid.

Moving forward, the second issue that should be at the forefront of all discussions pertaining to the electrical grid is the possibility of cyber-attacks. As discussed in the previous component of this chapter, there are many non-state actors who, albeit most probably do not have the necessary capabilities, have threatened the U.S. of cyber-attacks. The possibility of a cyber-attacks is heightened when the public and the intelligence organizations do not have a strong relationship. However, since the realization of major government surveillance, the U.S. IC may have difficulties in gaining the trust of the public without initiating a reform of current intelligence practices. If the public placed greater trust in their IC, there would be a social movement to contribute to the protection of vital infrastructure, and there may be greater possibilities of more citizens willingly agreeing to allow security agencies to monitor communications and conduct in-depth surveillance. However, considering the extent to which the IC has failed to promote an open-relationship with the public, it is, from a professional perspective, irrational and illogical to expect the public to alter their views at this time. Furthermore, the failure to initiate a more welcoming and open relationship could also result in a higher number of individuals defaulting to extremism or aligning their views with radical ideologies as a result of their frustration with the way in which the nation is handling affairs. In fact, homegrown violent extremism or lone-wolf terrorism could steadily become a major issue that could also result in greater cyber-attacks aimed at the electrical grid, since it would be a simple way to disrupt the U.S. from within.

The third issue that should be taken into consideration is the inclement weather. The weather issues directly correlate with climate change. The unstable nature of the weather will pose immense issues to the electrical grid in comparison to cyber-attacks, since cyber-attacks can be detected and deterred before they disrupt the system, whereas the weather can be unpredictable and cannot be stopped. In fact, the DOE had reported that "[t]he number of outages caused by severe weather is expected to rise as climate change increases the frequency and intensity of hurricanes, blizzards, floods and other extreme weather events" ("Economic Benefits," 2013, p.4). Therefore, to improve the grid, efforts must span beyond the protection against cyber-attacks and must be linked to informing the nation of the effects of climate change. However, to resolve the issues with the grid, one must also take into consideration that "for-profit utility companies" privately own a majority of the grid ("Economic Benefits," 2013, p.6). Since the investor-owned utilities serve a majority of citizens, issues arise about the extent to which these utility owners will take the necessary steps to protect the grid if it is in conflict with their political or economic pursuits. Additionally, in the U.S., there are religious biases that influence the way in which climate change is viewed. There are staunch religious supporters who contradict the notion of climate change and dismiss the scientific evidence gathered to substantiate claims of climate change. This is another way that the overall nature of the nation plays a role in the improvement of the electrical grid. The U.S. is known for religious freedom as a constitutionally granted right to its citizens; however, academic analyses must be placed at the forefront of discussions of security. The right to religion should not equal the right to leave unprotected a majority of the nation solely due to a religious belief that contradicts scientific discoveries.

Although each of the issues pertain to various components of the electrical grid, it is possible to recognize the pattern that the failure to improve the grid is largely the result of the failure of the government to take all the necessary actions and appropriately inform the public. The public does have a responsibility to learn about these issues; however, without any impetus or direct support, it is unlikely that a majority of the public will take an interest in the topic in a timely manner.

SOLUTIONS AND RECOMMENDATIONS

The first issue that was highlighted with the electrical grid was the lack of appropriate public perception and failure to take into consideration public opinion of the topic. A lack of education and knowledge of the subject is mainly the reason why the U.S. majority does not realize the dynamics of the electrical grid. It may be difficult to entirely change public perception in a timely manner to improve the electrical grid simply by campaigning to improve education on the topic. Education is key to improving any society, yet it takes many years to witness substantial improvement by which time the electrical grid will still be vulnerable to attacks. Therefore, in a situation that requires swift and timely changes, it is important to utilize the benefits of a technologically dependent society. Social media campaigns and the use of the media to share stories and analyses of the electrical grid will almost certainly result in more of the population taking an interest and investigating the electrical grid. Facebook, Twitter, Instagram, and Tumblr are quite popular with the younger generation who, if better informed of the electrical grid, would have the necessary voice to effect change across the nation. Many media stations are also known to champion quite specific political views; thus, persuading news stations to discuss the topic may be difficult. However, if social media campaigns are successful, news stations will most probably be forced to discuss the topic and possibly even adopt their own views of the issue, which could result in even greater discussions. It would seem necessary to also question politicians about the electrical grid, yet the bottom-up approach of allowing the public to first discuss the topic, and then the politicians and elected government officials to voice their opinion will allow the public to first make an informed decision without being influenced by the opinions of their politically-motivated leaders.

The second issue, as previously mentioned, was the issue of cyber-attacks, which also relates to a lack of trust between the IC and the public, and homegrown violent extremism and lone-wolf terrorism. This issue, unlike the first issue that required initiation by the public, necessitates the U.S. IC to take the necessary steps to promote information sharing with the public without compromising the covert nature of the intelligence activities. The current IC websites do not provide the public with enough information to captivate their attention or allow the public to feel as though they play a role in the protection of the nation. The way in which the IC handles issues and speaks to the public could seemingly cause the public to feel as though they are subservient and have no say in what actually happens in their government and intelligence sectors. The US IC needs to devote a portion of the budget to public outreach and education; if the youth learned more about the field in high school, then the IC could establish a better prepared nation. Furthermore, the public outreach could also allow the public to feel as though they genuinely matter in relation to security matters. In addition, the IC could also actively engage in publishing to contribute to the existing body of literature in the public domain. Although the IC does share research with the public, it would be much more useful if the IC members continuously shared research in widely viewed public domains, without limiting their research to their own private intelligence websites. Furthermore, as previously mentioned, the continued use of smart grids across the nation will provide greater power to professionals to enhance cyber security.

Moving forward, the third issue that was raised pertained to inclement weather, especially due to climate change. It is unfortunate that in order to counter the harsh consequences of climate change a majority of individuals must agree and work with one another, especially since bipartisanship has proven to be quite difficult in the U.S. in recent years. Thus, in order to resolve the issue, it is important to place a focus on the safeguarding of the electrical grid from any weather, regardless of the cause of the inclement weather. Since it will be difficult to have a discussion about weather and the reason why it is now an important issue on which to focus, it may be possible to establish professional and academic discussions by agreeing on the common ground that the weather (regardless of whether the result of climate change or religious beliefs) can negatively impact the electrical grid. As far back as June of 2011 there have been government reports devoted to the protection of the electrical grid that focused on the weather. Accordingly, the President's "Policy Framework for the 21st Century Grid," (2011) clearly outlined that there should be advanced cooperation amongst local, state, and federal government and law enforcement, in addition to increased consumer awareness. These are necessary steps in the correct direction that need to be further taken seriously in the public domain.

It is possible to argue that it would be useful for politicians, legislators, and other government personnel to take a stance on the issue to initiate public discussions; however, this approach may be harmful to the academic assessment of the subject. By allowing the public to first assess the issue based on their own interpretations and discoveries, there can first be a neutral assessment that is not biased in favor of the views of politicians or officials who are aligned with specific political parties or religious ideologies. This is simply another reason why the media should not initially champion the discussions, since these platforms, although useful to share information with large cohorts of individuals, have tendencies to be subjective.

Another way to handle the issue of the electrical grid is through the continuous assessment of current standards and the continuous improvement of a contingency plan. In order to protect the grid, a team should be allocated the responsibilities of constantly conducting risk assessments to provide up-to-date contingency plans. The contingency planning phase should take into account as many variables as possible to ensure that there is a firm basis to protect the electrical grid. The planning of the contingency plan will require consideration of physical and cyber security of the grid. Currently, it is clear that trained professionals continuously monitor power grids. For instance, it has been reported that, "Modern power grids are continuously monitored by trained system operators equipped with sophisticated monitoring and control systems. Despite such precautionary measures, large blackouts, that affect more than a million consumers, occur quite frequently. To prevent such blackouts, it is important to perform high-order contingency analysis in real time" (Mittal, Hazra, Jain, Goyal, Seetharam, & Sabharwal, 2011, p.1). However, real-time analyses are not only time consuming, but quite expensive. From a professional perspective, it would seem that the benefit gained from continuous contingency analyses would outweigh the finances required to conduct such analyses. This issue would first have to be resolved prior to its initiation; however, in order to provide an alternative to the constant assessment of the electrical grid through contingency analyses, a specific group of experts in the field could collaborate with one another to develop general contingency plans for the most probable incidents. For example, inclement weather is certainly an issue that could shut down the electrical grid; therefore, a group of experts could provide a general plan to resolve the issue in the least amount of time. Although it will not be possible for the experts to manually develop a plan for each and every possible scenario, having general plans for the most probable scenarios can further provide support that may be used as a last resort in extreme cases.

To further strengthen the electrical grid and promote active discussions of the topic, youth in elementary, middle, and high schools could be provided with the opportunities to enter contests to describe contingency plans that could be used in the case of an electrical grid emergency. Although the students will most probably not have the technical knowledge to provide detailed plans, it will engage the younger generation and possibly inspire them to continue to conduct research on the issue. By making the discussion of the topic exciting for all involved, there will be higher possibilities of more improvements. Furthermore, it is even possible that a student's perspective of the issue will touch upon a notion not yet assessed by those in the field. The active engagement of the public will almost certainly establish a trend to learn more and contribute to the nation in this manner.

FUTURE RESEARCH DIRECTIONS

Researchers, students, and practitioners of intelligence, security, law enforcement, and even the environment should take the initiative to conduct research about the electrical grid, especially by directly investigating public perception of the issue. It would be interesting to identify the extent to which the U.S. public entirely understands the subject. Furthermore, future research pursuits could include the determination of what the public believes would be the most appropriate steps forward in relation to the steps that have already been taken thus far to modernize the electrical grid. This could also be a useful opportunity to explore the way in which the public is willing to make changes to their lifestyles that are conducive to the successful improvement of the electrical grid. Along these lines, public opinion polls should be continuously conducted to determine whether public view evolves over time.

Although officials within the nation will better handle the U.S. electrical grid, it is imperative that officials seek advice from international consultants. Furthermore, experts should also determine how the U.S. infrastructure could be more appropriately safeguarded specifically by recognizing how other countries have adopted new technology to improve their security. The geopolitical variations must be accounted for, yet the U.S. could certainly improves its own systems by heeding the advice and directions of fellow members of the international community. Accordingly, researchers could lead this effort by assessing how countries have protected their electrical grids in comparison to the U.S.

Although the improvement of the electrical grid is certainly necessary, other researchers have taken the initiative to create a platform that would allow individuals to power their homes through the use of at-home electrical systems. For instance, Tesla Motors is reportedly creating a battery that could power a house (Risen, 2015). The company noted that that design phase had been completed, and now the battery was in production (Risen, 2015). Therefore, these creations will almost certainly provide citizens with new ways in which to have sustainable power; thus, lessening the reliance on the electrical grid. Additionally, Karl Brauer who is a senior analyst at the Kelley Blue Book automation valuation company even stated, "It's foreseeable in the future that people are going to utilize solar power for their grids during the day and store that energy in a battery in the house for use at night" (Risen, 2015). These immense steps into the future will provide citizens with novel ways to access energy. If researchers will not place a focus on the electrical grid, then placing a priority on similar initiatives will contribute to the resolving of issues related to the electrical grid. If more individuals are provided with the opportunity to have self-powered homes that do not rely on the power of the electrical grid, then it will seemingly be inevitable that a majority of the nation will opt to have their own power sources. Eventually, if these new batteries are successful, then the issues with the electrical grid will become miniscule, since an attack on such a power source would not result in major catastrophes or issues to the public. However, this could also cause issues to power companies, since there would no longer be a need for such organizations. This could lead to job loss that could negatively impact the economy; however, the long-term benefits of batteries for home and business would outweigh these short-term issues.

CONCLUSION

Overall, through this chapter, it is hoped that the readers gained a further understanding of the necessity of placing a priority on the protection of the electrical grid. The electrical grid forms the basis of everyday life in the U.S., which is one of the main reasons why the protection of the system should be at the forefront of political and economic goals. There are many issues with which the electrical grid is faced; many of these issues have resulted from a lack of initiative taken to tactically and strategically improve the grid to minimize vulnerabilities. The electrical grid is not appropriately safeguarded from cyber-attacks or inclement weather.

This chapter has placed a priority on resolving three major issues that directly pertain to the U.S. electrical grid: cyber-attacks, inclement weather, and lack of appropriate public perception. These three issues, if resolved, could lead to the substantial reform and improvement of the electrical grid. The use of smart grids and microgrids would certainly become commonplace if these issues were handled in an appropriate manner. Albeit the actual safeguarding of the electrical grid relies on technical knowledge, the public, media, and political atmosphere of the nation will play a primary role in the time it takes to protect the electrical grid. Moving forward, if researchers do not place a focus on the electrical grid, then support should at least be placed on the development of batteries, such as the one being produced by Tesla Motors, to promote the possibility of self-powered homes and businesses. By moving away from reliance on the electrical grid, then the risks associated with an attack on the grid or inclement weather will be lessened. Nonetheless, until the battery is successfully released and implemented into homes and businesses in the nation, a priority must be placed on raising awareness about the electrical grid and the consequences of neglecting to improve this important resource.

REFERENCES

CBS News. (2010). *Cyber War: Sabotaging the System.* Retrieved from http://www.cbsnews.com/news/cyber-war-sabotaging-the-system-10-06-2010/5/

Center for Strategic and International Studies. (2010). *U.S. Cybersecurity Policy and the Role of U.S. Cybercom: Cyber Security Policy Debate Series.* Retrieved from https://www.nsa.gov/public_info/_files/speeches_testimonies/100603_alexander_transcript.pdf

Clark, D.D. & Landau, S. (2011). Untangling Attribution. *Harvard National Security Journal*, *2*(1), 30.

Collins, K. (2014). *Guns, Gore and Girls: The Rise of Cyber Cartels.* Retrieved from http://www.wired.co.uk/news/archive/2014-11/05/cyber-cartels

Executive Office of the President. (2011). *A Policy Framework for the 21st Century Grid: Enabling Our Secure Energy Future.* Retrieved from http://www.whitehouse.gov/sites/default/files/microsites/ostp/nstc-smart-grid-june2011.pdf

Executive Office of the President. (2013). *Economic Benefits of Increasing Electric Grid Resilience to Weather Outages.* Retrieved from http://energy.gov/sites/prod/files/2013/08/f2/Grid%20Resiliency%20Report_FINAL.pdf

Federation of American Scientists. (2011). *Terms and Definitions of Interest for DoD Counterintelligence Professionals.* Retrieved from http://fas.org/irp/eprint/ci-glossary.pdf

Filipkowski, W. (2008). Cyber Laundering: An Analysis of Typology and Techniques. *International Journal of Criminal Justice Sciences*, 15-27.

Finklea, K., & Theohary, C. A. (2013). *Cybercrime: Conceptual Issues for Congress and U.S. Law Enforcement.* Retrieved from http://fas.org/sgp/crs/misc/R42547.pdf

Gelinas, R. R. (2010). Cyberdeterrence and the Problem of Attribution. Georgetown University, 1-26.

Mittal, A., Hazra, J., Jain, N., Goyal, V., Seetharam, D. P., & Sabharwal, Y. (September, 2011). *Real Time Contingency Analysis for Power Grids.* Paper presented at the 7th International Conference, Euro-Par 2011. Bordeaux, France. doi:10.1007/978-3-642-23397-5_31

Office of Electricity Delivery & Energy Reliability. (n. d.). *Smart Grid.* Retrieved from http://energy.gov/oe/services/technology-development/smart-grid

Office of Electricity Delivery & Energy Reliability. (n. d.). *The Role of Microgrids in Helping to Advance the Nation's Energy System.* Retrieved from http://energy.gov/oe/services/technology-development/smart-grid/role-microgrids-helping-advance-nation-s-energy-system

Pierce, E. R. (2014). *Top 9 Things You Didn't Know About America's Electrical Grid.* Retrieved from http://www.energy.gov/articles/top-9-things-you-didnt-know-about-americas-power-grid

Risen, T. (2015). *Could Apple Compete with Tesla?* Retrieved from http://www.usnews.com/news/articles/2015/02/18/could-apple-compete-with-tesla

Shanker, T. (2013). *Pentagon Is Updating Conflict Rules in Cyberspace.* Retrieved from http://www.nytimes.com/2013/06/28/us/pentagon-is-updating-conflict-rules-in-cyberspace.html?_r=1&

Stewart, V. R. (2015). *Statement for the Record: Worldwide Threat Assessment.* Retrieved from http://www.dia.mil/News/SpeechesandTestimonies/ArticleView/tabid/11449/Article/570863/statement-for-the-record-worldwide-threat-assessment.aspx

Strickling, R. (2012). *Funding, Coordination, and Public Opinion: Political Obstacles to Electrical Grid Modernization in the Americas.* Retrieved from http://regulation.upf.edu/exeter-12-papers/Paper%20156%20-%20Strickling%202012%20-%20Funding,%20Coordination%20and%20Public%20Opinion.pdf

U.S. Energy Information Administration. (2014). *Energy in Brief.* Retrieved from http://www.eia.gov/energy_in_brief/article/power_grid.cfm

U.S. Strategic Command. (2013). *U.S. Cyber Command.* Retrieved from http://www.stratcom.mil/factsheets/Cyber_Command/

Williams, P., Dunlevy, C., & Shimeall, T. (2013). *Intelligence Analysis for Internet Security.* Retrieved from http://www.cert.org/archive/html/Analysis10a.html

KEY TERMS AND DEFINITIONS

Access: The ability and opportunity to obtain knowledge of classified sensitive information or to be in a place where one could expect to gain such knowledge ("Terms," 2011, 2).

Advanced Persistent Threat: An extremely proficient, patient, determined, and capable adversary, including two or more of such adversaries working together ("Terms," 2011, 3).

Bot Net: A collection of zombie PCs [personal computers]. Botnet is short for robot network. A botnet can consist of tens or even hundreds of thousands of zombie computers. A single PC in a botnet can automatically send thousands of spam messages per day. The most common spam messages come from zombie computers. ("Terms," 2011, 13).

Classified Information: Any information/data that has been purposefully recognized and designated as to be protected against unauthorized disclosures ("Terms," 2011, 18).

Computer Security (COMUSEC): The protection resulting from all measures to deny unauthorized access and exploitation of friendly computer systems ("Terms," 2011, 26).

Critical Asset: A specific entity that is of such extraordinary importance that its incapacitation or destruction would have a very serious, debilitating effect on the ability of a nation to continue to function effectively ("Terms," 2011, 47).

Defector: A person who has consciously abandoned loyalty to his country and who possess intelligence information of value to another country or countries ("Terms," 2011, 56).

Chapter 4
Insider-Threat Detection in Corporate Espionage and Cyber-Espionage

Kirk Y Williams
Walden University, USA

ABSTRACT

National Security will always be threatened by individuals internal to the organization in the form of an insider-threat and external to the organization in the form of corporate espionage or cyber-espionage. Therefore, insider-threat detection methods, security precautions, authentication processes, and standard operating procedures for employees should be in place to try to reduce the instances of an insider-threat and/or an external threat breaching the security of an organization, institution, company, or governmental agency. Espionage and cyber-espionage can and does occur; however, it is not usually made public knowledge and when it does, it can have grave effects on the organization, institution, company, or governmental agency in which it occurred. Within this chapter the author explores how an insider-threat in the form of a Data Scientist, Penetration Tester, or Data Analyst can use their education, access, and background to gain access to systems and information that can be of value to external organizations, institutions, companies, and/or governmental agencies.

DOI: 10.4018/978-1-4666-9661-7.ch004

INTRODUCTION

National Security can be affected by many factors and issues that are unseen, foreseeable, seen, and predictable. These factors can come in the form of threats that are external and/or internal to the agency and are increased by the skill set and access granted to the individual(s) or group(s) that can be a threat. Individuals who are internal to an organization are considered an insider-threat if they plan to do harm to the employees, company, or infrastructure of the organization, and their access to systems and information only makes the impact to their actions more harmful to the organization. Insider-threats are problematic and their diverse skill set makes it easier for them to go undetected for longer periods of time. It goes without saying that the person with the background who would be able to harm the organization the most would be the one with the knowledge, experience, skill set, and access to the information that is of value. When insider-threats use their access to information to gain knowledge or information and then gives it to others this is considered espionage. When that information is gained internally or externally via the use of a computer or other form of wireless technology then it is considered cyber-espionage.

Cyber-espionage is a form of espionage that can occur locally, from a distance, or even from the cubicle right next to the person/target of interest. It only requires the use of a system that is connected to an Internet source – cell phone or computer. When compared to corporate espionage, cyber-espionage can have many external and internal agents who can, would, and should be viewed as an insider-threat to an agency, company, organization, or facility. These insiders are considered a threat to the company, agency, and work force that they work in, and their actions can be harmful and financially detrimental to the company and employees that they work with on a daily basis. When trying to determine how the insider-threat would have an effect on the company, it would be better to have an idea about the insider-threat's background and their access to various projects and information to determine what effect they will have on the organization. A look at a few particular positions that companies and agencies are hiring towards –Data Scientist, Penetration Tester, and Data Analyst – can show how such skill sets can be a problem. These positions make an insider-threat more plausible because of their access and their position on projects that can affect national security and the involvement of the company in assuring the continued stability of national security.

With the intent of suggesting ways to look into insider-threat detect, the objective of this chapter is to explore the idea of cyber-espionage and corporate espionage from the viewpoint of the data scientist, penetration tester, and data analyst. Within this chapter the skill sets of three positions are explored, the level and areas of training are explored based on education and research backgrounds, and suggestions are made in regards to encrypting systems, and reducing access to systems based on project involvement, and determining the information that is of value to others outside of the organization, institution, company, or governmental agency.

EDUCATION, EXPERIENCE, AND INTERESTS

A number of threats to national security exist in the form of insider-threats who conduct espionage for companies or for other countries. Factors that affect national security can range from and include incidents that are unintentional to incidents that are intentional. Open conversations outside of the workplace in public settings such as local coffee houses, at lunch counters, in restaurant settings, or the neighborhood bar or grocery stores frequented by anyone other than oneself can result in others overhearing information that should not be exposed to the general public or spoken to anyone outside of the work place. Simply mentioning the information can be seen as spillage or data leaks that can range from minor to severe/grave depending on what was said, who overheard the information, and what information was transmitted. Deliberate, intentional, open conversations with individuals outside of the workplace on issues that can directly affect security measures and the infrastructure of a facility can be seen as a deliberate attempt to harm or affect national security. These incidents can be considered espionage and the use of computers to disclose any information that is secured can be considered cyber-espionage.

The intentional disclosure of information can have a devastating effect depending on the level of information, the type of information, and the amount of information. Usually, regardless of how much information is disclosed or whether the information is used, or what the information pertains too, this information can have a grave effect on national security. Therefore, it is generally good practice to not have open conversations about information that can affect national security outside of designated places within the workplace, outside of designated secure environments, or with others that are not part of the agency or part of the approved secured protocols that govern the communication of secured information. Although unintentional incidents that result in the disclosure of secured information such as the ones described do occur, the unintentional incidents that result in the disclosure of secured information can do more harm and affect national security just as much as the intentional disclosure of secured information.

These threats can be compounded by their access and the information that they gain access to based on their position within their organization, institution, company, or government agency. When these individuals infiltrate their organization, it may not always be with the intention of physically and directly harming the organization, but their actions will undoubtedly harm the organization and potentially the infrastructure of the organization via any type of intrusion; furthermore, any intrusion is an unwanted intrusion. Any and all types of intrusions usually result in a feeling of continued mistrust and a sense of personal loss/violation that leaves one to wonder. *What did they take? How much do they know about me personally and financially? Will they return? Will (or when) will it happen again?* When these types of questions are posed to the people who are in the business of protecting, safeguarding, and securing our information, data, memories, finances, and personal health information this type of intrusion leaves one to wonder, *Is there any place that is safe, and is that place safe from intrusions?*

Analysis of data of someone that engages in corporate espionage or cyber-espionage shows that in order for the targeted attack to be successful it requires individuals who are familiar with the organization, institution, company, or government agency's research, practices, and projects that are of interest. The individuals or groups that are involved would have capabilities that would allow for corporate espionage or cyber-espionage to go unnoticed and especially undocumented. Methods to hide their activities and to remain undetected can be very simple in nature for the insider-threat, and are used on a daily basis for the insider-threat to go undetected. These activities can make it more difficult for the threat to be detected because of the normal nature of individuals to "blend in" to their surroundings and into the culture of the organization. Outside of having an air of being an outsider it would be rather difficult to detect if someone is "up to something" or planning any nefarious or malicious behavior if they are adept at covering their tracks within an organization, institution, company, or government agency. Insider-threats are more difficult to detect because co-workers do not always report suspicious behavior of their family, friends, co-workers, or contractors. It becomes easier to "explain away" the suspicious behavior than reporting the behavior because no one desires to be wrong as a result of possible retaliation, change in reputation, repercussions of being wrong about the allegations, or simply filing of the claim. Insider-threats try to cover their tracks by being deceitful in their actions, their access to data or information, and in their communications/intentions with others.

Currently it is virtually impossible to find someone who is not familiar with computer code and coding to some degree. However finding the right person with the right skill set who can identify information that is proprietary to a company, to a research topic, or who can identify information that is of a specialized nature is less common than one would be lead to believe. In order to commit espionage or cyber-espionage many aspects of the individual's background are necessary for infiltrating an organization's network. This is not an easy task as it requires skill and technique to infiltrate the system in question and if the access is constant then one must remain hidden and undetected as well as have the necessary access/level of skill to remain undetected while retrieving the information of importance. As a regular employee who does not have access to every project, and is not familiar with the particular projects, copying and transporting large amounts of information on any project would be very noticeable and would not go undetected. However, an individual who has access to projects of interest would be able to copy, transmit, and retain access to data that is of importance. Insider-threat assessments would be necessary to ascertain the identity, motives, capabilities, and damage done by such individuals if a threat is detected. Some examples of positions that would have the largest impact on security include employees who have the title of Data Scientist, Penetration Tester, or Data Analyst as they would have a diverse skill set that would allow them to be privy to the data, results, and clinical information of a study, and it would allow the scientists to be able to evaluate the information for value, accuracy, and for directions or possible avenues of discovery and research.

Initially, one would ask *what are data scientists, penetration testers, and data analysts, and what skills are needed to become one?* Data Scientist would have a mix of skills that does not just include a list of computing and programming abilities but also a diverse set of cultivated interests in other subject areas that allows them to be able to communicate and interact with others in various research and scientific fields. Without these diverse skills a data scientist would only be able to conduct one type of analysis and perform tasks in one generalized field. A Bioinformatician without the background in Biology would only be a computer scientist who is great at programming and scripting, but would not be able to accomplish many tasks in the way of analysis of biological data. Although it would be possible for the Bioinformatician to program types of analyses for biological data, in terms of interpreting it and making meaningful sense of the information, it would only look like letters on a screen (*i.e.*, code from *The Matrix*). Similarly, how effective would a Statistical Geneticist be in understanding genetics when they do not know the genetic code or know what the Central Dogma means? It is possible for the statistical geneticist to understand the number of people affected and what the person possessing the trait would have with regard to the complex traits, but it would be virtually impossible for them to understand the difference in the trait and what affect it would have on the individual physically. Their experience would leave them able to accomplish the task at hand, but knowing what the trait would mean and how it would display in humans would be lacking in regards to the statistician's skills.

Penetration Testers is a new position that has developed over the past five years within the cyber security field. Essentially, a penetration tester is a hacker who works for a company or agency to assist in the identification of vulnerabilities within a computing system and, therefore, detects their vulnerabilities. Penetration testers usually work with different software applications, different computing operating systems, and an abundance of programs/tools to help in the identification of software flaws, vulnerabilities of networks, and vectors that adversaries can potentially use to gain access to any system within the organization, institution, company, or governmental agency. As a penetration tester, analysis of the software and networks that the organization, institution, company, or governmental agency uses is assessed, and weaknesses are determined that can be used for potential exploitation. The educational background of a penetration tester can range from being self-taught in the use of various scripting and programming languages to being certified in the use of the software that allows the penetration tester to reverse engineer a solution. This type of training goes beyond the education provided on the Bachelor's degree level.

In order to be an effective analyst, the analyst would usually have the ability to make sense of information and see connections that others do not based on their background, information that they are given, and experience given the subject matter. Being able to see what may come and being able to predict the potential outcome is necessary when conducting an analysis of the information that is given to anyone; however, not having the proper abilities, background, experience, and thoughts that would come to an experienced analyst would mean that the analyst is only as good as the work that they are presented as they would lack the necessary skill set to provide a proper analysis. Although experience plays a large part in the process, experience and exposure helps to cultivate the interests that the analyst possess, and this in turn would lead to a better understanding and analysis that could only enhance their skill set and abilities.

RECONNAISSANCE, SCANNING, AND EXPLOITATION

Cyber-attacks can be initiated in various ways, from various locations, and using different methods depending on whether it is via an external network, initiated as a result of an insider-threat that is using the internal network, or a physical attack from an insider-threat that is directly connected to the computer/server. In many ways we can think about attacks as being conducted via the internet or internal network as the number of in-person physical attacks is fewer than ones that occur via networks. These types of attacks usually include the use of tools in the form of software programs and scripts that can be gathered from commercial systems that are common place within the company/industry, tools that have been personally coded and tested on other systems, tools that are available in the hackers arsenal, programs and scripts that have been acquired from the dark-net, or tools that are proprietary to companies that specialize and/or perform penetration testing/processes for clients. Regardless of the tools that one uses to infiltrate a system, the system that is vulnerable can or may be penetrated based on the services, access, type of users, or routes of exposure.

With any form of cyber-attack that is a result of corporate or cyber-espionage, three major steps are used in assessing a system prior to the attack on a system:

1. Reconnaissance
2. Scanning
3. Exploitation

With each step specific information is gathered and used in the cyber-attack. Information used for the attack that usually occurs from a remote site happens within minutes of accessing the system. Corporations tend to make themselves the target of attacks by releasing information to the public, to developers, and to contractors of their systems regarding the system's capabilities. Corporations tend to write and produce white papers that allow users of their systems to have an idea of the capabilities of their systems, what is available on the system, and the performance of new systems. Although this is used as a marketing tool, it can be used to give anyone conducting reconnaissance of the intended target information on the targeted system, or one that is scanning a system a chance to identify the capabilities of a system.

Scanning a system can give a wealth of information and can include various pieces of information that many companies would not know exist. Scanning a system can include identifying the services that are used on the system, the ports that are available for entry into the system, information such as which host network the system resides on – if the information is not known, the type of operating system that is employed by the system, and the number of barriers between the targeted system and the information of importance, as well as the initial gateway onto the system.

After the open sources and resources have been used to gain access, the system will be exploited. Any information that is taken from the system can be tracked but it remains unclear exactly how much information is taken, and once the system has been exploited it becomes the job of the system administrator, the security administrator, the forensic analyst, and the incident analyst to assess the damage and determine various aspects of the system that were compromised. In addition to system administrators looking for the information that has been taken from the systems, it is necessary that system administrators look for scripts, code, and programs that were created, produced, or left behind during the periods of intrusion. During these intrusions it is possible that information in the form of scripts and code may have been left behind on systems for later re-entry or to gain access or control of a system via a different method.

If information is taken as a result of espionage or cyber-espionage, one of the things that must be determined is if it occurred as a result of an insider in the organization, institution, company or government agency, or did it occur from an external intrusion. If it is determined that it was as a result of someone internal to the organization, institution, company or government agency then a review of the types of skills and access needed to conduct such an act is needed.

In an effort to detect and determine the insider-threat, it is necessary to analyze the abilities of the individuals who had access to the system and the importance of the data that was taken. When analyzing the data that may be of importance to anyone, it is essential to note that the information must have made sense to the person that may have taken it. Therefore, their perception of knowing the value of the data must be taken into account. When an organization, institution, company or government agency is being targeted via an insider-threat or via cyber-espionage it is of great importance to know what information is being targeted and what it resembles in appearance. Therefore, it is best to review the types of skills needed for an insider-threat. Take for instance three positions in particular for which many organizations, institutions, companies and government agencies are currently hiring: data scientist, penetration tester, and data analyst.

For the sake of this example, if a data scientist, penetration tester, or data analyst was considered to be the insider-threat, then the skill set of the scientist or programmer must be evaluated along with the level of access and the projects that were compromised. It is understood that data scientists and data analysts will analyze data from different sources, as they have different points of views and different skill sets based on their educational level, experience, research experience, assignment focus, and level of interest to the projects that they have contributed to in the past. A list of the skill sets that many data scientists and data analysts will have and are required to have differs by the project, educational level, experience, and the desired outcome of the project for which they may have been hired to contribute to in the organization, institution, company and/or government agency. However, they must be able to recognize different data types; otherwise, it would only mean acquiring data and information that may prove to be worthless and non-directional in terms of the organization, institution, company and/or government agency's plans and direction for research and capabilities.

Penetration testers can have an educational background that can range from being self-taught in programming and scripting to having documented education on all levels of the education spectrum. The skill set would be more diverse based on the interest of the project and the type of background needed to penetrate the system that is placed before them and the knowledge of the system. In many cases the computing system of the organization, institution, company and/or government agency could pose a challenge based on the tester's skill set; therefore, the need for additional assistance may be necessary based on their level of education and experience with the aforementioned system. A list of the skill sets that many penetration testers will have and are required to have differs by the project type and experience, educational level, and the desired outcome of the challenge that they may have been hired to report on once the assessment is complete.

Because the skill sets may be different across the three fields, it is understood that data scientists, penetration testers, and data analysts will have different educational backgrounds and experience as two individuals will never experience the same thing in the same manner. Therefore, it is necessary to illustrate a list of skills that data scientists, penetration testers, and data analysts may have and how they can differ based on the projects they may work on and how they can contribute to other projects. Listed in Figure 1 are a list of some suggested skills that 10 leading data scientist suggests are needed for a basic data scientist position (Eric, 2013). This list does not include additional skill sets that can assist across disciplines such as computational chemistry, genomic analysis, economic/commerce, and business analytics. With the skills listed in Figure 1, this means a data scientist that will have a lot of programming skills and analytical abilities; however, the data scientist does not have much diversity within the skill sets needed to authenticate and verify other forms of data that may be of a scientific nature. Therefore, an expanded list of skills and additional training with suggested topics and research areas have been constructed and displayed in Figure 2.

Listed in Figure 2 are the suggested skills that a data scientist or data analyst should possess to make them an effective data scientist and/or data analyst. Based on current estimates this would allow anyone to have a broad perspective of qualifications and diversity within their education and background, but additional skills may be necessary based on what the assignment may require. The skill set of a penetration tester can include a range of skills that would include programming, scripting, software engineering, and database development. However, one of the major skills that is needed but cannot be easily taught is the identification of underlying flaws within a system. For each of the educational backgrounds listed in Figure 2, a number of examples can be described to give an idea of the potential application of the skills set and diversity of the profession. However, for illustration purposes, an individual with an educational background in economic and finance may be necessary to understand and predict different ways that the global economy may be affected based on the changes in stock, stock prices, or agricultural responses to natural disasters in various geographical regions.

With an idea of the skills, experience, background, an insider-threat would probably possess, several questions remain unanswered. Now that the insider-threat has the data/information in their possession the questions that must be answered should include:

- *What will someone do with the information?*
- *What value is the information to someone else?*

Figure 1. Top Data Science skills and related areas (Evans, 2013)

Skill Set
Data Mining
Machine Learning
Analytics
Big Data
Predictive Analytics
Data Analysis
Predictive Modeling
Hadoop
Text Mining
Statistics
Natural Language Processing
Start-Ups
Algorithms
Distributed Systems
MapReduce
Data Warehousing
Business Intelligence
SQL
R
Scalability

- *What value is the information to another organization, institution, company and/or government agency?*
- *What value is the information to someone if they do not know how to make sense of the data or information that was taken?*
- *When committing cyber-espionage, how do you transport the large amounts of information to another organization, institution, company and/or government agency?*

When trying to determine any of the answers to the questions posed, this part of the process can become difficult based on the resources, experience, and background of the individuals involved in the analysis of the data that was acquired. Any number of possibilities exists with regard to the intentions of the individual and the potential outcomes of the information once that information has left the secured system/network. When asked, *what will someone do with the information*? The answer would have to

Figure 2. Data Science skills, knowledge/training, and capabilities

Skill Set	Knowledge/Training	Additional Skill Sets		Capabilities	
Data Mining Machine Learning Analytics	Programming/Networking	C/C++ Perl Python	MongoDB IT Java/Javascript	Algorithms Cyber-Security Data Forensics	Penetration Testing Cyber-Intelligence
Big Data Predictive Analytics Data Analysis	Science	Genetics Biology	Epidemiology Chemistry	Genetic Algorithms Disease Modeling	Personalized Medicine Genetic Database Development
Predictive Modeling Hadoop Text Mining Statistics	Economics	Global Finance Financial Infrastructure Trades/Agreements	Macroeconomics Microeconomics	Policy/Trade Agreements Global Economics	Economic Policy Development Financial Forecasting
Natural Language Processing Start-Ups Algorithms	Mathematics	Differential Equations Operations Research	Actuarial Science	Encryption	Data Compression Analysis
Distributed Systems MapReduce Data Warehousing	Statistics	Longitudinal Analysis Predictive Analytics	Probability and Statistics Stata/SAS	SEM of Economic Systems	Discrete Event Simulation
Business Intelligence SQL R Scalability	Public Policy Public Administration	Criminal Justice Quantitative Analysis	Qualitative Analysis Organizational Development	Profiling	Organization Science

include the statement that *understanding or predicting what an insider-threat will do with the information can be difficult or almost impossible.* It is not impossible to note that the information can be leaked on various websites, to different news media outlets, or even sold to different organizations, institutions, companies, and/or governments or government agencies.

When asked, *what value is the information to someone else*? The answer to the question is not straightforward as the information has an internal value as well as an external value. The internal value is dependent on the value that it holds to the person who acquired the information and what the person who acquired it will determine it is worth to them; however, the external value of the information is determined by the person that is willing to purchase or acquire the information from the person that acquired it from the system.

To answer the question, *what value is the information to another organization, institution, company and/or government agency?* This depends on the information, the type of information, the volume of information, and what form the information is in when it was acquired. If the information is of value then what one organization, institution, company, and/or government or government agency may be willing to pay for the information will be determined by what the organization, institution, company, and/or government or government agency in which the information was taken from may be willing to pay for the information not to be leaked on various websites, to different news media outlets, or to be sold.

Many individuals may not be able to answer the question, *what value is the information to someone if they do not know how to make sense of the data or information that was taken?* This is not uncommon as the person acquiring the information may not be the person using the information. Therefore, the information may not be of value to the person acquiring the information but the information will increase in value when it has been presented to interested individuals that wish to acquire the information. If the person acquiring the information is a data analyst, and they are working as an analyst in a vacuum this action would only hinder and hamper the process of analyzing the data as the insights that the analyst would have with regard to the data is limited by the person, their experience, and their background. However, with additional individuals assigned to the analysis of the data, one would have more options and skill sets added to the analysis of the data. This would move the process of analyzing the data that has been acquired along quicker and in different ways than what was originally intended. For instance, if someone hacked the servers of a pharmaceutical company for an experimental drug that has yet to be released onto the market it would not be easily identified by a data scientist with a background in purely scripting and coding (programming). They would have to be more useful and have the ability to identify computational data, medicinal chemistry, and clinical data of a compound that is of value. This is not the same as being able to read data from a Word document and an Excel spreadsheet.

Finally *when committing cyber-espionage, how do you transport the large amounts of information to another organization, institution, company and/or government agency?* Penetrating a secured network form a home computer with a normal internet speed is possible; however, computer limitations and internet speeds will limit connections and information retrieval (e.g., using a dial-up modem versus a T1 connection). Therefore, large amounts of information can only be transported by large networks and data systems that allow for transport of large amounts of information. Web based systems that can be accessed remotely from external systems can be penetrated from a distance and the information can be acquired by multiple cyber-attacks that are conducted from various locations if it is undetected. In order to reduce the possibility that the information would be of value to others, better encryption methods are necessary to deter the use of the information that was acquired via the cyber-attack.

Information that is encrypted can be more difficult to determine its value if the information is properly secured and encrypted via advanced encryption methods. Encryption methods that have been proposed and conducted on information can include a layered searchable data method, a hybrid defense network, as well as an authentication method that allows anonymity. Luo et al. (2014) suggested the use of searchable encryption techniques that enable the user to search through their secured data on the computer servers within a Cloud based system as well as on secured servers using query languages. The encrypted information residing on the server would be available in database format and reported in simple query reporting fashion. In a hybrid defense network, Cho and Pan (2014) suggest that development of a distributed network security measure that would allow for the development of a hybrid firewall, intrusion detection methods, virtual honeynet projects, and connectivity and interactive components that would connect and work in unison with each other as a protective measure. Finally Lee and Paik (2014) suggested authentication methods that would allow user on mobile devices that are on foreign networks to authenticate their access in an anonymous manner. Oh et al. (2010) moved the idea of using the Advanced Encryption Standard (AES) in a different direction with the implementation of a selective encryption algorithm. The process would use the AES procedure to build efficient, robust, secure encryption modes in addition the AES model. Meux's (1994) suggestion of using Record Linkage Numbers for the encryption to reduce the leakage of Social Security Numbers to the public and using it as a reference seems to be one standard that is still employed in the field. Brinkman et al. (2009) used a 128-bit encryption method for the protection of patient information and data that "incorporates lossless data compression using range encoded difference with a 32-bit cyclically redundant checksum to ensure data integrity." Each of these encryption methods are possible, and they would provide some layer of security. However, each of these suggested methods would have flaws and allow access by their virtual nature of being web based, Cloud based, or access via network providers that cannot be authenticated or verified. With the proper education, training, background and familiarity of any of these systems, a data scientist, penetration tester, and/or data analyst would be able to gain access to the information that they desire if they knew the flaws that are intrinsic to the systems.

It goes without saying the education, experience, and interests will be a motivator for retrieving information from a secured network, when trying to penetrate a secured system in the form of an insider-threat, or external threat. Previously within the publication *Cases on Research Based Teaching Methods in Science Education: Studies in Multidisciplinary Research* an understanding of the different skills that would be needed for other fields or professions was presented. Two chapters showed how a diverse background within the fields of science, genetics, and programming can be beneficial to a scientist who is considering a career within the fields of data scientist, penetrating testing, and data analytics.

SOLUTIONS AND RECOMMENDATIONS

Within any organization, institution, company, or governmental agency, security should be a priority and should be enhanced on a daily basis. We recommend that these instillations possess state-of-the art security systems where possible and have security staff in place to assist in the monitoring of their computer systems. Such security staff should include system administrators, cyber-security administrators, forensic analyst, computer incident analyst, a programmer/developer, a penetration tester, and at least one physical security personnel. These individuals should be able to assist in the encryption of data; the constant monitoring of areas where data is kept (*e.g.,* servers, buildings, and data centers); the constant review of changes to the material/data on the servers; the monitoring of people accessing the system, building, and data center(s); the monitoring of remote services and ports that are open to the outside world that can be used to access systems; and the monitoring of users that have access to their systems.

Whether in an organization, academic institution, company, or governmental agency, users of the system should be required to verify their access or supply a verifiable reason to access the information as a security procedure or as a means of authentication. When granting access to projects, the access to information should be limited to the projects that individuals are placed on, and their access should be narrowed based on their skill set and capabilities of their position. This would reduce the chances that an insider-threat would be able to access all the information within any organization. With any member of a research team the skill set of the team should be diverse for the task at hand, but no one person should have unfettered access to all parts of data on a server or project data that is accessible (see Figure 1 and 2).

FUTURE RESEARCH DIRECTIONS

Research in this field would require polling and surveying members of the data science and data analyst community to identify key components within their educational backgrounds, interests in their future endeavors, and project tasks to determine the correct mixture of necessary skills that can develop a well-rounded data scientist, penetration tester, and/or data analyst. Although this is possible, it is likely that skills in particular would only be identified as useful to have to help with the necessary tasks, and not within the educational background of every individual of the team. Based on the lists of skills suggested by Evans (2013) in Figure 1 and the ones suggested in Figure 2, it would seem that an enhancement on traditional algorithm techniques for improving pattern recognition and analysis would be crucial to working in the National Security field. In addition, data scientists, penetration testers, and data analysts would have to be able to collect, analyze, process, and disseminate results/data while making assessments on the policies and how they would be affected based on their recommendations. Although some of the skills needed may be acquired through training, others would have to be acquired over time as each task and situation is different and the skill set would only limit the individual making the decisions.

In order to conduct research in this field, certain questions must be asked and hopefully answered prior to and during the gathering of the research data. Research questions that can be explored could include:

- *Where would someone get the necessary reliable, trusted data to analyze for the studies that they would like to conduct?*
- *Would the government and companies be very forthcoming about the information that was taken, how it was taken, and/or by whom?*
- *Would these companies and agencies be able to identify exactly who took the material, how they were hacked, and when they were accessed?*
- *How have the companies and agencies been damaged and how are they still vulnerable?*
- *Which research methods would be best to use to see the cause and effect of the hack?*

Over the past five years the number of cyber-attacks that involve cyber-espionage have increased on many levels, and cyber-terrorism has become problematic and financially costly to companies. Therefore, the thought of constructing a hypothesis to research cyber-attacks, cyber-terrorism, or cyber-espionage and its relationship to National Security does not seem as straightforward as one may presume, and the research methods that one would use may not be the best method or approach to use. In many ways, a quantitative methodology or a qualitative methodology can be proposed, but the questions and the background of the person performing the study would be limited by their thoughts and training in the field. In Figure 2 we discussed what a professional in public policy and public administration with a background in criminal justice would be able to do in terms of research, and also what areas to this topic would be appropriate from a research standpoint.

It is generally believed that threats to National Security will only increase with the advancements in technology and capabilities that allow criminals to act from a distance allowed by computers and wireless systems. With our increased dependence on cyber-technology and its capabilities, it is not surprising that our susceptibility to cyber-attacks and the number of cyber-attacks as a result of cyber-espionage have also increased. With this in mind, different questions must be asked to measure and quantify the relationship between the number of cyber-attacks, the increase in cyber-terrorism, and the amount of cyber-espionage that occurs as a result of the activities of the targets that been hacked, or organizations that have been targeted. It is our belief that the relationship that can be determined would show a clear connection or correlation to the activities of the company, agencies, or people within the company or organization with regard to issues that are of concern by other companies, agencies, or people. Therefore, it would be imperative to systematically quantify and identify the number of cyber-attacks, then identify whether the information was gained via cyber-espionage and/or how it relates to corporate security and/or National Security. Although the results of the study may, or may not, change the National Security measures we have in place, it would be interesting to see how companies, academic institutions, organizations, and government agencies have changed how they conduct security measures in general.

CONCLUSION

National Security will always be in jeopardy of being breached as long as someone disagrees with a government. Whether these individuals are external to the government agency or a part of the agency the issue of an insider-threat is only compounded by their access to information within the organization or agency. It is understood that individuals who work for an organization, institution, company, or governmental agency may desire to harm the organization for whatever reason. In many ways we normally would not think about co-workers and other employees as an insider-threat nor would we desire to think about how we would have to go about detecting them in our midst. However we must think about what would happen to our National Security, our economy, and our national infrastructure if something was to occur as a result of an insider-threat that can affect our National Security, our economy, and other aspects of our way of life such as our financial industry.

With the increase in our dependency on cyber technology and the Internet, it is not surprising that there is an increase in susceptibility to cyber-attacks and an increase in cyber-espionage as a result of an insider-threat. Within this chapter the author explored how to assess the skill set of an insider-threat that would possess the skill set of a data analyst, penetration tester, and data scientist. Even though the experience, the background, and the level of access that the data scientist, penetration tester, and data analyst have would play an important role in their attempts to hurt or harm the organization, institution, company, or government agency, it is not to say that the only individuals who would try to harm the organization are going to be in the position of a data scientist, penetration tester, or data analyst. This chapter just looked at the development of the skill set the data scientist, penetration tester, and data analysts have and how they could stand out as an insider-threat. Therefore, at times one must look at our security protocols to see if it is possible to detect an insider-threat based on his actions and other behavior, in addition to skill set, education, and data access.

Although methods are in place to try to reduce the chances that these individuals would be able to cause harm to the organization it can still occur. Organizations go to great lengths to prevent the hiring such individuals with background checks or psychological evaluations; however, it is still possible that they can infiltrate the organization as an employee. Therefore, periodic monitoring and review of the employee's access to projects and information should occur. This can assist in exposing such individual's actions and intentions prior to any information being removed from systems or harm being done to the systems. This means that limited access to information would be necessary. Many things can be done to try to reduce the number of insider-threats and the access that they have; however, any organization, institutions, company, or governmental agency is only limited by their detection methods.

REFERENCES

Brinkmann, B. H., Bower, M. R., Stengel, K. A., Worrell, G. A., & Stead, M. (2009). Large-scale electrophysiology: Acquisition, compression, encryption, and storage of big data. *Journal of Neuroscience Methods*, *180*(1), 185–192. doi:10.1016/j.jneumeth.2009.03.022 PMID:19427545

Cho, Y. C., & Pan, J. Y. (2014). Hybrid Network Defense Model Based on Fuzzy Evaluation. *TheScientificWorldJournal*, *2014*, 1–12. doi:10.1155/2014/178937 PMID:24574870

Lee, Y., & Paik, J. (2014). Security Analysis and Improvement of an Anonymous Authentication Scheme for Roaming Services. *Scientific World Journal*, 2014. doi:10.1155/2014/687879

Luo, G. C., Peng, N. D., Qin, K., & Chen, A. G. (2014). A Layered Searchable Encryption Scheme with Functional Components Independent of Encryption Methods. *Scientific World Journal , 2014*. doi:10.1155/2014/153791

Meux, E. (1994). Encrypting Personal Identifiers. *Health Services Research*, *29*(2), 247–256. PMID:8005792

Oh, J. Y., Yang, D. I., & Chon, K. H. (2010). A Selective Encryption Algorithm Based on AES for Medical Information. *Healthc Inform Res*, *16*(1), 22–29. doi:10.4258/hir.2010.16.1.22 PMID:21818420

ADDITIONAL READING

Fan, L. J., Wang, Y. Z., Jin, X. L., Li, J. Y., Cheng, X. Q., & Jin, S. Y. (2013). Comprehensive Quantitative Analysis on Privacy Leak Behavior. *Plos One, 8*(9). doi:10.1371/journal.pone.0073410

Gil, S., Kott, A., & Barabasi, A. L. (2014). A genetic epidemiology approach to cyber-security. *Scientific Reports*, *4*, 5659. doi:10.1038/srep05659 PMID:25028059

Kim, J., Lee, D., Jeon, W., Lee, Y., & Won, D. (2014). Security Analysis and Improvements of Two-Factor Mutual Authentication with Key Agreement in Wireless Sensor Networks. *Sensors (Basel, Switzerland)*, *14*(4), 6443–6462. doi:10.3390/s140406443 PMID:24721764

Peng, N. D., Luo, G. C., Qin, K., & Chen, A. G. (2013). Query-Biased Preview over Outsourced and Encrypted Data. *Scientific World Journal*, 2013. doi:10.1155/2013/860621

Wright, A., & Sittig, D. F. (2007). Encryption characteristics of two USB-based personal health record devices. *Journal of the American Medical Informatics Association*, *14*(4), 397–399. doi:10.1197/jamia.M2352 PMID:17460132

Zhang, W. P., Chen, W. Y., Tang, J., Xu, P., Li, Y. B., & Li, S. Y. (2009). The Development of a Portable Hard Disk Encryption/Decryption System with a MEMS Coded Lock. *Sensors (Basel, Switzerland)*, *9*(11), 9300–9331. doi:10.3390/s91109300 PMID:22291566

Zhou, Q., Yang, G., & He, L. W. (2014). A Secure-Enhanced Data Aggregation Based on ECC in Wireless Sensor Networks. *Sensors (Basel, Switzerland)*, *14*(4), 6701–6721. doi:10.3390/s140406701 PMID:24732099

KEY TERMS AND DEFINITIONS

Coding: The process of assigning a code to something for classification or identification.

Cyber-Espionage: The use of computer networks to gain illicit access to confidential information, typically information that is held by a government or other organization.

Data-Mining: The practice of examining large volumes of data and pre-existing databases in order to generate new information.

Encryption: In cryptography, encryption is the process of encoding messages or information in such a way that only authorized parties can read it. Encryption does not of itself prevent interception, but denies the message content to the interceptor.

Exploitation: The action of making use of and benefiting from resources and features of an object.

Infiltrate: To pass into a territory or organization clandestinely and with hostile or subversive intent.

Intrusion: The act of intruding or invading privacy.

Pattern Recognition: Pattern recognition is a branch of machine learning that focuses on the recognition of patterns and regularities in data. This recognition can range from small to large depending on the pattern type.

Reconnaissance: Preliminary surveying or research to locate an enemy or ascertain strategic features.

Scanning: Looking at all the parts of something carefully in order to detect some features of the object.

Visualization: The formation of mental visual images, and the act or process of interpreting in visual terms or of putting information into visible form.

Chapter 5
Teaching New Dogs Old Tricks: The Basics of Espionage Transcend Time

Neal Duckworth
American Military University, USA

Eugenie de Silva
University of Leicester, UK

ABSTRACT

This chapter discusses how the basics of espionage have remained the same, even in the digital age. The pendulum of espionage--and protection from it--has swung wide over the past century. Different public and private sectors have renewed focus on not only cyber protections, but on increased physical protection of critical assets and ensuring trusted personnel in the workforce. Within this chapter, the authors review the basics of protecting critical assets to ensure that changes in espionage can be mitigated at an early stage. While the techniques of espionage have many variables, especially in a digital age, the authors have established that the use of a risk assessment that focuses on identifying the threats, the specific variables or methods of espionage, and developing and implementing mitigation measures is of the utmost importance.

DOI: 10.4018/978-1-4666-9661-7.ch005

INTRODUCTION

To look to the past for answers to the questions of the present and the future could be deemed an entirely idealistic notion. However, it is this analysis of the past that can lead to the discovery of beneficial tactics and strategies to protect critical assets from theft, compromise, or destruction. There is no question that the art of espionage has changed since the stealing of secrets began, but one basic premise has remained consistent throughout global conflicts, the Cold War, and now in the digital age: the secrets that were stolen, compromised, destroyed, or disclosed were not properly safeguarded. Consider a few well-known personalities: the Federal Bureau of Investigation Special Agent Robert Hanssen, U.S. Army Private Bradley Manning, and National Security Agency Contractor Edward Snowden. Scholars of national security issues recognize these names as those persons responsible for overwhelming losses of classified information and damaging U.S. national security and diplomatic relationships. However, what about Boeing engineer Dongfan "Greg" Chung and Mo Hailong? Chung worked for 30 years for Boeing and passed trade secrets back to China on military planes and capabilities; he was convicted "of six counts of economic espionage and other federal charges for storing 300,000 pages of sensitive papers in his Southern California home" (Flaccus, 2010). Hailong was allegedly conspiring to steal trade secrets from U.S. organizations; and Hailong's case even led the U.S. attorney for the Southern District of Iowa to state that, "[t]he information that was stolen in this case has an estimated value of five to eight years' worth of research time [...] [a]nd a minimum of $30 to $40 million" (Martin, 2014). Along these lines, it is imperative to recognize that not all cases of espionage involve the Intelligence Community (IC); other cases of espionage may focus on economic information, intellectual property, and other ways to increase a competitor's advantage.

Today's international media often reports the loss of information as a result of cyber-crimes and cyber espionage, with the "usual suspects" being unknown computer hackers or possibly an organized effort being orchestrated by a foreign nation. According to one report, it is even common for allies to suspect one another of economic espionage, which further exemplifies that "countries can be partners in traditional security matters yet competitors in business and trade" (Office of National Counterintelligence Executive, 2011). However, the traditional threat of espionage, which utilizes trusted employees to steal secrets, has not been eliminated with the expansion of cyber-crimes and cyber espionage. As public and private organizations respond to the expanded cyber threats, the most likely shift in tactics will be to return to the traditional method of coercing an organizational employee to gain access to facilities and information. It is important for organizations that invest so heavily on the prevention of cyber-crime and cyber espionage to not lose focus on mitigating the basic threats and vulnerabilities that could result in political, economic, and possibly even social havoc.

In the U.S. government, the identification and elimination of these threats is the responsibility of both counterintelligence and security officers. Counterintelligence serves as a more active approach that utilizes investigations, operations, collection, and analyses to both identify the foreign intelligence threat from outside and the possible corrupted trusted employees or insider threat(s). Security officers possess a much more agnostic approach to protection, and utilize an integrated protection plan which includes personnel, physical, information, and other types of security; it is often less important who or where the specific threat is from, whether it is a foreign intelligence service or a criminal.

While counterintelligence is primarily thought of as means to identify, neutralize, and exploit foreign intelligence organizations, such a strict interpretation leaves gaps based on different threats. State and local law enforcement agencies, private sector corporations, and even smaller federal agencies may face threats not just from foreign intelligence services, but also from transnational criminal organizations and non-state actors, such as terrorist groups. Accordingly, utilizing the best practices of the Departments of Defense and Justice, the Intelligence Community, federal, state, and local departments and agencies, as well as the private sector, organizations can renew focus on the protection of their critical assets.

Overall, this chapter addresses the critical need to analyze the unique threats and vulnerabilities, and develop mitigation measures that organizations can employ to increase the protection of critical assets from both cyber and traditional espionage threats. This chapter also identifies the need to utilize a continuous five-step cycle to assess and mitigate risk.

BACKGROUND

In recent years, there has been a wide array of academic articles devoted to illuminating the current and rising threats. In 2012, Director of National Intelligence James Clapper submitted a statement for the Worldwide Threat Assessment wherein he identified a plethora of possible attacks aimed at the U.S., such as the remote possibility of a major cyber-attack aimed at the U.S. critical infrastructure systems. "Cybercriminals also threaten US economic interests. They are selling tools, via a growing black market, that might enable access to critical infrastructure systems or get into the hands of state and nonstate actors" (Clapper, 2013, p. 3). Accordingly, it is necessary to note that the multitude of threats will continue as more and more persons, organizations, and/or nations seek to achieve economic, military or decision advantage, and accordingly, a concerted effort must be made by all organizations to identify and counter these threats.

Threats posed to the U.S. do not merely stem from outside factors, but also are partly due to internal failures or mistakes. For example, in the 2014 U.S. Intelligence Community Worldwide Threat Assessment, it was also further determined that, "Trusted insiders with the intent to do harm can exploit their access to compromise vast amounts of sensitive and classified information as part of a personal ideology or at the direction of a foreign government" (Clapper, 2014, p. 3). This, as is described in this chapter, is the reason why complacency should not be acceptable in the field. Global political actions can affect people in many different positive and negative ways. Today's accidental bombing of innocent civilians in a combat zone can turn trustworthy employees into spies, thieves, and saboteurs. A risk management approach, utilizing a continuous assessment of threats, vulnerabilities, and the ever-changing environment are an organization's best defense in developing and implementing risk mitigation measures.

Federal agencies and corporations are often the target of directed espionage to steal both classified intelligence and economic information. Take for instance the well-known case of Edward Snowden, the former National Security Agency (NSA) contractor, who stole classified intelligence data and released it to the public in 2013. Snowden's ability to both gain access to the information and exfiltrate the data, demonstrates the harsh consequences of a failure to effectively secure intelligence systems. Albeit the NSA systems were quite secure, they were vulnerable to bad intentions of employees; for instance, it was established in a report to Congress that Snowden managed to access critical data by using the Public Key Infrastructure (PKI) certificate of a co-worker, and then clandestinely captured the co-worker's password to later access a plethora of information (National Security Agency, 2014). This strategic plan that Snowden adopted to access classified information further elucidates the extent to which an insider threat can take seemingly inconspicuous actions that actually threaten an entity's infrastructure.

Snowden's case was profoundly highlighted in the media as revolutionary, due to the information that he managed to leak to the public; nonetheless, the action of leaking classified and sensitive information has not been uncommon in the past. In fact, in 2006, Thomas Drake (a former NSA senior executive) released classified information to a Baltimore Sun reporter, while half a world away Australian Julian Assange established WikiLeaks, providing a website to allow a global leakers to host their stolen data. Losses of classified information can damage military operations, diplomatic relations, and eliminate economic advantage, which highlight the need to utilize extensive protection measures to protect sensitive information, not just in the federal government, but also in any public or private organization.

The U.S. government has not idly waited and remained complacent with the release of confidential intelligence information. Legal mandates and acts have been passed in order to make illegal and further explicate the extent to which the stealing, hacking, or modifying, etc. of specific intelligence, military, and government data is punishable. Although many U.S. government leakers claim to be "whistleblowers," the majority choose not to utilize the appropriate mechanisms for reporting complaints. A person's lack of attempt to report perceived wrongdoing through established government channels is the primary method through which agencies justify charges of espionage and treason.

The covert nature of government activities is not novel. Rather, secrecy in the United States can be traced back as far as the 1700s wherein the members of the First Continental Congress were formally required to ensure that the proceedings remained a secret (Maus, 1996). For example, the following was made explicitly clear, "Upon motion, resolved, that the doors be kept shut during the time of business, and that the members consider themselves under the strongest obligations of honor, to keep the proceedings secret, until the majority shall direct them to be made public" (U.S. Government Printing Office, 1905, p.22). Accordingly, secrecy and covert discussions are deeply rooted in U.S. history. Nonetheless, the norms of current day society and public expectations of the intelligence field becoming overt and entirely accessible have opened the door for many to scrutinize the common practices of secrecy.

One of the more controversial acts passed to ban and counter the stealing of sensitive information was the Espionage Act of 1917. Passed in June of 1917, two months after Congress made the official determination for the U.S. to enter World War I, the Act outlined the punishments for any individual who was officially convicted of stealing information or classified data with regard to U.S. national defense and security "in order to harm the United States" (Galison, 2010, 944). The Act barred many activities that were deemed possibly detrimental to the national security of the country (Galison, 2010, 943). The intent of the Act, when it was first implemented, was to explicitly detail punishments for those who may be involved in espionage during the wartime, yet since this time, the Act has been updated several times over the course of many years; for instance, one year after its inception, in 1918, it was amended (Tedford & Herbeck, 2009). In addition, § 791 of the Act has since been repealed to more appropriately fit into the time period. § 791 pertained to "admiralty and maritime jurisdiction of the United States;" yet, it more appropriately fitted in the wartime when the act was first established ("United States Code," n.d.). Therefore, when this section no longer applied to the time period, and essentially made no sense, it was repealed. Other components of this Act, such as § 792 make illegal the aid or harboring of an individual who is known to have violated any provisions of the Act, whereas § 795 prohibits taking photographs, sketches, drawings, pictures, etc. of vital military installments without first receiving permission from the commanding officer ("United States Code"). Thus, while there are several individuals who do argue that this act is ambiguous and should not continue to be utilized, the Act does specifically make clear the ways in which an individual can and will be prosecuted for threatening the stability of the national security of the U.S. for conducting any activities that are listed within the provisions of the Act itself.

On another note, those in the intelligence field have been notified of the protections offered to personnel who would like to voice their concerns about specific intelligence or operational practices through the establishment of Presidential Policy Directive – 19 (PPD-19). This Directive outlines protection against retaliation or reprisal for employees of the IC ("Presidential Policy," 2012). Debates have continued with regard to the lack of explicit protection for IC contractors, yet the Directive nonetheless does establish a strong foundation for IC employees to make their concerns known without fear of harm or retaliation as a result.

It may also be important to note that it is the covert nature that provides individuals with the opportunity to carry out activities without compromising the life or lives of those who are involved in the field. Of course, this widespread secrecy could result in the abuse of power for those within the field; hence, this is the reason why intelligence agencies have oversight figures.

DEFINITIONS

To ensure that readers have an understanding of the way in which several terms are used within the context of this chapter, the following compilation of definitions has been presented. Within the intelligence field, many terms can be quite ambiguous; for instance, even the word "terrorism" has no universal definition. Thus, this presented work has utilized the following definitions of terms as the basis for all analyses.

- **Adversary:** An "individual, group, organization, or government that conducts or has the intent and capability to conduct activities detrimental to the US Government or its assets" ("Terms," 2011, 4).
- **Classified Information:** Any information/data that has been purposefully recognized and designated as to be protected against unauthorized disclosures ("Terms," 2011, 18).
- **Counterintelligence:** Intelligence activities concerned with identifying and countering the threat to security posed by hostile intelligence organizations or by individuals engaged in espionage or sabotage or subversion or terrorism ("Terms," 2011, 31).
- **Critical Asset:** A specific entity that is of such extraordinary importance that its incapacitation or destruction would have a very serious, debilitating effect on the ability of a nation to continue to function effectively ("Terms," 2011, 47).
- **Espionage:** Intelligence activities that are "directed towards the acquisition of information through clandestine means" ("Terms," 2011, 69).
- **Insider Threat:** An individual who uses their authorized access to government facilities and resources to harm the security of the United States "through espionage, terrorism, unauthorized disclosure of information, or through the loss or degradation of departmental resources or capabilities" ("Terms," 2011, 91).
- **Risk Assessment:** A systematic examination of risk using disciplined processes, methods, and tools. A risk assessment provides an environment for decision makers to evaluate and prioritize risks continuously and to recommend strategies to remediate or mitigate those risks ("Terms," 2011, 149).

- **Risk Management:** The process of identifying, assessing, and controlling, risks arising from operational factors and making decisions that balance risk cost with mission benefits ("Terms," 2011, 149).
- **Whistleblower:** An individual within an organization who exposes any actual, or alleged, wrongdoing to internal or external enforcement officers.

MAIN FOCUS OF THE CHAPTER

Issues, Controversies, and Problems

In the U.S. government, numerous laws and presidential executive orders support the protection of critical assets. Theft is a criminal act, and laws may be applied specifically to thefts or unauthorized disclosure of classified information to foreign entities, which are then utilized to ensure prosecution. As can be derived from popular cases of espionage that are broadcast in the media, such as the Snowden, Drake, and Manning cases, individuals involved in the theft of classified information make an effort to justify their actions by arguing a lack of other options to make concerns known. However, U.S. laws that safeguard critical assets and establish necessary security provisions work alongside whistleblower protection acts and other legal mandates to protect individuals and provide safe, legal alternatives for those in the field to shed light on possible violations of moral or legal principles.

Those who have leaked data, such as Snowden, Drake, and Manning, have faced severe consequences for taking what they considered to be socially just actions. In response, these individuals have raised arguments with regard to the actual extent to which the U.S. government has provided intelligence personnel and contract employees with reliable, legal routes to express their concerns as whistleblowers. Nevertheless, the arguments raised by these individuals would essentially require an entire reform of the U.S. intelligence system, which does not seem to be a viable option at the current time.

Failures in intelligence and counterintelligence, as well as a lack of effective safeguarding critical assets, have led to the need for increased priority being placed on risk assessments. However, risk assessments must be continuous to provide an actual basis on which mitigation measures can be established and adjusted. There appears to be a continuous pattern of remaining complacent with infrastructure and security procedures until an adversarial attack is successful or there is an intelligence failure; it is at this point that, many times, public outrage or public controversy leads to the public call for reform within the government and intelligence community. Complacency with security standards, and failures to predict and prevent major breaches of security cannot be the norm if progress is to be made. The continuous use of risk assessments can and will provide a strong underlying foundation for those in the field to identify vulnerabilities, which will ultimately provide the opportunity to strengthen systems from within.

Information derived from risk assessments must be adequately shared amongst those with the appropriate security clearances to prevent "stove-piping" of information and ensure proper analysis and mitigation. The September 11th attacks of 2001 acted as a major impetus for a reform of the intelligence community, as the lack of priority that was placed on information sharing quite certainly led to the failure to predict, and then prevent the attacks. Thus, if risk assessments are conducted, yet the results are not appropriately shared with the correct personnel, then the efforts would be futile.

Espionage is not limited to national security secrets to have an impact on a nation or organization. The Federal Bureau of Investigation (FBI) believes that 90% of the focus of foreign espionage is not aimed at classified military or intelligence secrets, but industrial and trade secrets which will increase their economic or even military advantage. FBI Special Agent David Thomas stated in a 2014 interview, that "The top secret, government, political secrets, all that top secret stuff that you kind of think about spies, [is] probably less than 10% of what they are trying to go after" (Dice, 2014). In 2011, the discovery of two men removing plant seeds from a Dupont research farm triggered an FBI investigation. Just two years later, the Department of Justice announced the indictment of "six Chinese nationals for conspiracy to steal trade secrets from U.S. seed companies" ("Six Chinese Nationals," 2013). This indictment gained wide media attention and raised awareness of both the foreign threat and the vulnerability of research farms, the plants of which must be grown and tested in the outdoors. Seed production would not, at first glance, appear to be a high target of espionage; however, years of research and development required to create a faster growing, higher-yielding, or nutritionally enhanced seed for rice or corn are necessary. In fact, in 2013, the Justice Department news release declared that "This "inbred" or "parent" line of seed constitutes valuable intellectual property of a seed producer [...] the estimated loss on an inbred line of seed is approximately five to eight years of research and a minimum of 30 to 40 million dollars" (VanderSchel, 2013).

The example above shows the importance of utilizing a risk management approach and implementing measures to prevent exploitation of identified vulnerabilities. These measures are not restricted to governments, although they will nearly always have more accurate information to use in assessing threats and vulnerabilities. Any organization has the capability to collect and analyze information specifically focused on protection of its critical assets.

Furthermore, by conducting risk assessments, security can be heightened and integration can be strengthened. The necessity of an integrated government has been amidst vital discussions in the intelligence field since the 9/11 attacks of 2001. More recently, the Department of Homeland Security (DHS) released a report to Congressional requesters wherein it was noted that a priority needed to be placed on integration and the coordination of vulnerability assessments (2014). It was also reported that "developing and implementing ways that data can be shared, as appropriate, and coordination facilitated across DHS could also help minimize duplication or gaps in assessment coverage" (U.S. Department of Homeland Security, Government Accountability Office, 2014). These types of reports further support the ways in which integration and risk management can go hand-in-hand. If more appropriate risk assessments are conducted, it may be further possible to maintain the integrity and integration of the organizations and companies.

Moving forward, risk assessments should provide insight to the threats and vulnerabilities, while giving security officials the necessary information to either confirm or disprove any suspicions or hypotheses. Risk management requires a unique blend of thinking—analyzing both and internal and external views toward threats and vulnerabilities. Linear thinking with regard to risk management should be blended with hints of non-linear thinking. It is a non-linear approach that will ultimately establish a culture of creativity within the field, whereas linear thinking will allow for successful risk management only in specific instances. Linear thinking, in this context, refers to the analysis, observation, and assessment of risks wherein individuals derive conclusions that are logical and rational based on an essential "line" of thinking. For instance, linear thinking will establish that if road 1 leads to road 2 and road 2 leads to road 3, then road 1 will lead to road 3 by virtue of rational deduction. However, non-linear thinking in this instance would not be constrained to logical deductions, since it would involve a higher form of creativity by possibly interpreting the scenario of roads 1, 2, and 3 as circular rather than straight lines. Both of these thinking patterns would reveal similar information about the same scenario, yet the two

Figure 1. An example of a common linear thinking process. The linear thinking shows the connection between 1, 2, and 3 as a straight line

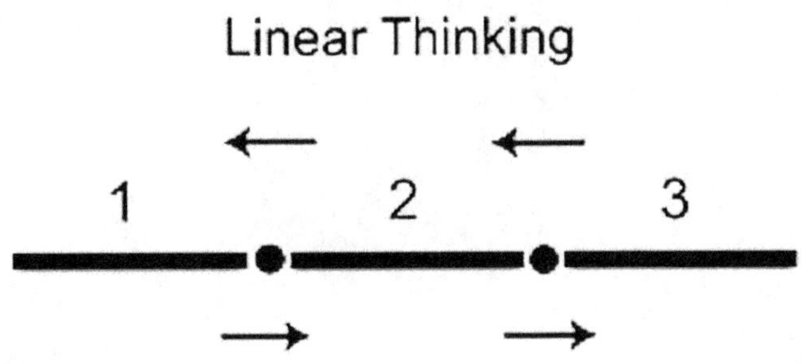

Figure 2. An example of a common non-linear thinking process. The non-linear thinking shows a possible connection between 1, 2, and 3 as a circle

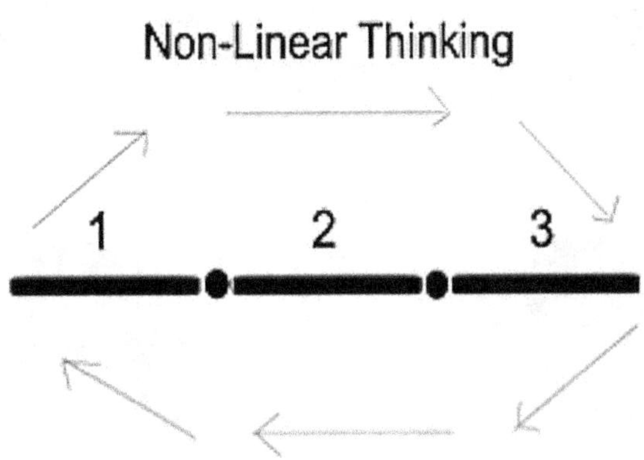

thinking styles will cause the analyses to take different paths to understand the presented information (see Figure 1 and 2).

Linear thinking will be the rock that firmly establishes the risk assessment cycle and any plain, logical deductions. Furthermore, the expansion of solely linear thinking with a blend of non-linear will further be useful in the establishment of a more thorough risk assessment as is exemplified within the following component of this chapter. Utilizing both linear and non-linear thinking will allow risk management to take into consideration a wider array of information, and therefore understand the full spectrum of threats and vulnerabilities, leading to more informed and effective mitigation measures.

Risk Management Overview

Lessons learned from the loss or unauthorized disclosure of classified intelligence information during and after the Cold War brought about much change in the U.S. government in the areas of personnel, physical information, and operational security. Successful foreign espionage operations were able to bypass these security procedures and pushed organizations to conduct risk assessments on the protection of their critical assets, which included intelligence information. The primary model for a basic risk assessment is Threat X Vulnerability X Impact = Risk. By simply looking at this model, one would notice

Figure 3. A five-step risk management model

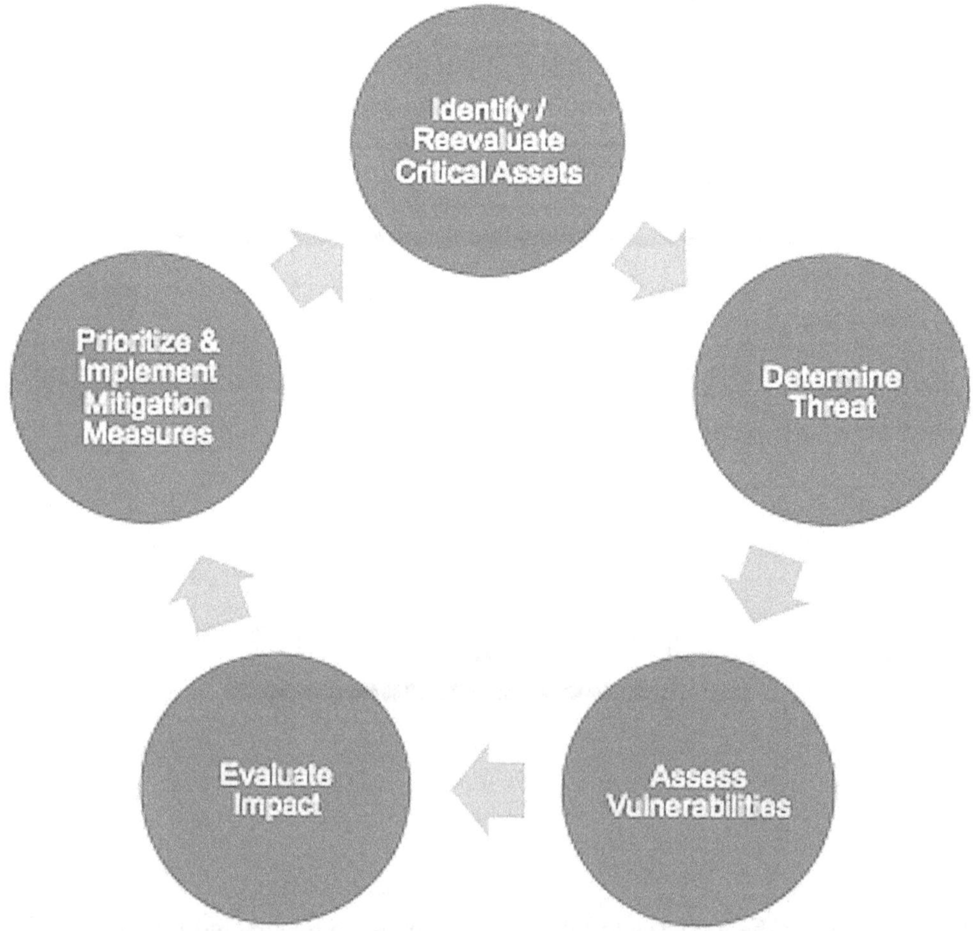

the linear and non-linear nature as previously explained, but also that it does loop back to continually assess the threats and vulnerabilities.

As displayed in the figure below, there is a necessity to repeat risk assessments beyond the initial assessment of risk and implementation of mitigation measures. Repetition can be time-consuming, yet it is fundamentally imperative that the different steps of risk assessments are conducted continually. Along these lines, the results of risk assessments must be viewed as the guiding factors that should shape the steps that are taken to minimize identified vulnerabilities and threats. Upon review of each of the noted stages in the figure above, it is unambiguous that they are immensely correlated and interdependent and it is thus the "repeat" stage that provides for seamless transitions and improvements (see Figure 3).

The recognition of countermeasures ultimately allows those involved in the operations to apply the learned information derived from the risk assessment. Through the identification of critical assets, those in the intelligence field are provided with the opportunity to establish the basis upon which threats can be determined and vulnerabilities may be assessed. If each of these stages is correctly conducted, with attention paid to detail, then the evaluation of impact and the prioritization and implementation of mitigation measures should be fairly easy. These stages should involve systematic analysis of resources.

Although the intelligence field is generally fast-paced, this process should not be rushed, as the failure to consider what may be deemed a minute detail, could potentially lead to major problems in the future.

Identify and Revaluate Critical Assets

The identification and designation of the "crown jewels" of an organization is paramount to their successful protection. Protection is not done for the sake of protection, but to ensure that an organization's primary mission is conducted without compromise. The loss or compromise of specific items, information, or even personnel, which would cause the loss or degradation of capability in an organization, should most likely be classified as a critical asset.

Critical assets can be defined in different ways. For a government agency, critical assets may be linked to its ability to function and complete assigned missions. For a manufacturing company, a critical asset may be the ability to deliver an uncompromised, high-quality product. However, in a research and development firm, critical assets must be free from compromise to economic competitors. In a national government, most critical assets are labeled with classification, which ensures special handling with personnel, physical, and information security safeguards. Every company, organization, and agency must determine what critical assets must be protected. Scientific companies need to protect research and development; nuclear power plants must safeguard access to the reactor; and law enforcement agencies must protect the names of its confidential informants.

With the aim of defining critical infrastructure and assets, John Moteff and Paul Parfomak published their 2004 work that provided an in-depth discussion of this topic. These researchers touched upon an assortment of legal acts and statutes in the U.S. that alluded to or defined critical assets and infrastructure. This research aided in the recognition of the specific, yet, many times, seemingly ambiguous nature of defining critical assets and infrastructure. For instance, Executive Order 13228, which was signed under President Bush's administration in 2001 in order to implement further critical infrastructure protection, established the "Office of Homeland Security and the Homeland Security Council" (Moteff and Parfomak, 2004, p.6). The Office and Council, in addition to other duties, were assigned the explicit orders of protecting "telecommunications […] special events of national significance […] airports and civilian aircraft […] [and] public and privately owned information systems" (Moteff and Parfomak, 2004, p. 6). The Executive Order further listed other assets that were to be protected; however, in the same year this Order was issued, the Uniting and Strengthening America by Providing Appropriate Tools Required to Intercept and Obstruct Terrorism Act of 2001 (USA PATRIOT ACT) was initiated wherein an apparently straightforward definition of critical infrastructure was provided.

The USA PATRIOT ACT defined critical infrastructure as, "systems and assets, whether physical or virtual, so vital to the United States that the incapacity or destruction of such systems and assets would have a debilitating impact on security, national economic security, national public health or safety, or any combination of those matters". This definition was also used in the Homeland Security Act of 2002 in which the notion of "key resources" was also instituted. This concept was defined as, "publicly or privately controlled resources essential to the minimal operations of the economy and government;" however, the act did not specifically outline the resources (Moteff & Parfomak, 2004, p.7).

Prior to 2001, there were comprehensive definitions of critical infrastructure, yet the absolutely broad and diverse nature of the field and activities related to national security seemingly made it difficult to determine each and every resource or asset that would fall under the definition of a critical infrastructure.

A year later, in 2002, the National Strategy for Homeland Security revisited this issue and provided another list of critical infrastructure, a detailed discussion of the critical infrastructure, and also introduced the term "critical assets." The critical infrastructure list now included, "Agriculture, Food, Water, Public Health, Emergency Services, Government, Defense Industrial Base, Information and Telecommunications, Energy, Transportation, Banking and Finance, Chemical Industry, [and] Postal and Shipping" (Moteff & Parfomak, 2004, p.8). This list broadly covered much infrastructure, yet new technology was rapidly emerging during this time; thus, the Strategy also made clear that there were distinctions between physical and cyber infrastructure and the protection offered. Moteff & Parfomak further explained critical infrastructure as,

[...] individual targets whose destruction would not endanger vital systems, but could create local disaster or profoundly damage our Nation's morale or confidence. Key assets include symbols or historical attractions, such as prominent national, state, or local monuments and icons. In some cases, these include quasi-public symbols that are identified strongly with the United States as a Nation.... Key assets also include individual or localized facilities that deserve special protection because of their destructive potential or their value to the local community. (2004, p.8)

Identifying critical assets can be both difficult and easy. For an intelligence agency, the identification of its personnel and the foreign assets that provide information would definitely be critical assets. Similarly, the list of what information policy makers are interested in would also require safeguarding. The definition of critical assets became much clearer following the 2002 and 2004 US publications; however, there still remained difficulty for non-US government organizations. One way to look at this is to consider what information, assets, or material, an organization would not want its adversaries or corporate competitors to obtain. Maybe it is the secret sauce at a restaurant; the research and development of a new mobile phone; or even the merger or acquisition of key industrial companies. What about an organization's brand or reputation? Could that be a critical asset? The above-mentioned definition of critical assets also noted individual and/or localized facilities that deserved special protection due to their potential for destruction or value to a local community; albeit, the strategy could have articulated the aim in a more lucid manner without any ambiguities.

If foreign intelligence agencies repeatedly planted misinformation into the US intelligence apparatus that was later learned to be false, would not the loss of confidence in US intelligence be a possible degradation of capability? In 2003, the US-led coalition invaded Iraq to prevent the development, and transfer to terrorists, of weapons of mass destruction. Operation Iraqi Freedom, or Operation Telic as it is known in the United Kingdom, was conducted on the basis of false information—misinformation provided by an Iraqi defector who now reportedly lied as a way to have outside countries topple his dictator, Saddam Hussein (Owen, 2012). The intelligence from Rafid Ahmed Alwan al-Janabi, code-named Curveball, was routed through German intelligence officers to other members of the coalition who were never allowed to speak directly to the source. Upon revelation that entire nations went to war based on misinformation was a direct blow to the US and UK intelligence agencies.

By taking a stance that objectively assesses situations without priority on stereotypical or commonly recognized "threats" or "vulnerabilities," one is able to more appropriately recognize the wider array of presented issues. Accordingly, intelligence officers and law enforcement personnel should be trained to identify vulnerabilities and do so with the complete understanding that threats may evolve over years or within days.

Determine Threats

Once an organization has identified its critical assets, a determination of the threat is required. Oftentimes, organizations know exactly where the threat comes from (e.g. a corporate competitor or foreign intelligence service), but specific research and analysis must be conducted to confirm and evaluate any threats.

Most government agencies have a well-known capability to conduct intelligence collection and analysis. However, any public or private organization can conduct its own "collection" and analysis. Collection--or research--into threats will predominantly focus on three areas to obtain information: employee reporting, open source (internet) research of publicly available information, and liaison with key counterparts or government agencies. It is through detailed research and analysis of small pieces of data that knowledge can be obtained.

During many espionage investigations, co-workers reveal that there was suspicious behavior that they discounted and did not report to supervisors or security officers. To establish a successful employee reporting program organizations must: 1) educate employees on what is important to the organization (identifying the actual critical assets may not be recommended for security purposes); 2) educate employees on what suspicious activity and co-worker behavior is important to report; 3) establish a method for employees to report suspicious activity or behavior of both employees and external activities; and 4) establish procedures to ensure that employees understand that any information reported will be held in strict confidence.

The second opportunity to research threats is through publicly available information, including Internet research, Freedom of Information Act (FOIA) requests of U.S. government agencies, and through the review of media comments and press releases. Research on social media can also be used to maintain awareness of current, new, and emerging corporate competitors, known economic threats, and even disgruntled current or former employees. With what is known about espionage, the use of open-source resources may even provide vital information that could be used to reevaluate current security practices. For instance, it has been reported, "Divided loyalties to another country or cause besides the United States have replaced money as the most common motive for espionage by Americans in the recent period" (Herbig, 2008, p.70). In addition, it was even established that disgruntlement was the third most common motive for Americans to commit espionage (Herbig, 2008, p.ix). Therefore, by utilizing a wide array of easily accessible sources, security personnel can appropriately monitor individuals and possibly detect signs of disgruntlement or espionage at early stages.

A third capability to gather information is through liaison with partner organizations, local law enforcement, and U.S. federal agencies, such as the FBI, Office of the National Counterintelligence Executive (ONCIX), or Defense Security Service. Government agencies such as the aforementioned have specific requirements to support and assist U.S. companies in protecting themselves from theft, sabotage, and compromise of economic and national security information. Fusion centers, accordingly, are also useful tools in heightening security.

While these three types of information gathering strategies can provide information to analyze and assess threats, it is not perfect. There are subjective decisions that must be made by decision-makers as they prioritize the threats to each critical asset based on the vulnerabilities that are identified. However, understanding the full-spectrum of possible threats and the capabilities of each threat provides an organization with information to better determine the vulnerabilities which these threats might exploit—all leading to better mitigation plans.

Assess Vulnerabilities and Evaluate Impact

After an organization determines what its critical assets are and what the potential threats to these assets are, efforts must focus on identifying the vulnerabilities that would lead to the loss, compromise or destruction of the critical assets. Each critical asset may have unique vulnerabilities. Some organizations may need to export critical assets, rely on intellectual property, out-source parts of a production cycle, or utilize sub-contractors to safeguard the critical assets. Each of these could represent a vulnerability, which must be analyzed to develop proper mitigation measures.

To highlight the numerous vulnerabilities that an organization may face, consider a mid-sized police department located on the southeastern U.S border. A police department's critical assets would include a database of undercover operations, and then shared department-wide network, which is used to access the database. Using this example, likely actors that would benefit from gaining this information include local criminals and non-state actors, such as the Mexican drug cartels who could use this information to identify and neutralize law enforcement penetrations into its operations and organizations.

There are many possible vulnerabilities, but consider how this information may be accessed. Physical access within the police department is most likely required; however, some personnel may have remote access to allow work from home. An employee of the police department with authorized access could abuse this trust and steal the data. Equally problematic, an employee with or without access could be coerced to introduce a computer program to seek out and penetrate encrypted files and exfiltrate or copy the files to an employee controlled storage device or printer. An authorized employee who does not secure his or her computer or office properly may also provide unwitting access to a coerced employee. Additionally, there may be hard copies printed off for administrative purposes; papers may not be shredded or otherwise destroyed; or there may be something as non-uniform wearing personnel who look to be on official business entering the rear of the police station and trying not to be noticed. There are multiple vulnerabilities that must be sought, thought through, and then mitigated. The high multitude of possibilities makes it an undeniable necessity that the identification of mitigation measures is not conducted in a thorough and timely manner.

The results that not properly mitigating the threat to organizational vulnerabilities can have a great impact. In the case of Curveball, the vulnerability of the western intelligence agencies and their analysis was that they never had direct access to him and were therefore completely reliant upon the Germans to ascertain his veracity. Furthermore, the Curveball debacle also was inundated with confusion and misinformation that explicates the ways in which a lack of integration within a community can lead to dire consequences. For instance, it was reported that MI6 had cabled the CIA to make known their doubts about Curveball and the discrepancies in his statements, yet it was further noted that "[Colin] Powell said that George J. Tenet, then the director of central intelligence, and his top deputies personally assured him before his U.N. speech that U.S. intelligence on the mobile labs was 'solid'"(Drogin &Goetz, 2005, p.2). The impact was that Curveball's disinformation resulted in the US-led coalition's invasion of Iraq and the deaths of thousands of personnel. On a lesser scale, but extremely important to the security of the southwest border, is the impact of having compromised access to law enforcement operations. Undercover police officers, informants, or their families could be killed, or they could be left in place and provided misinformation or information against competitors. Understanding the myriad of vulnerabilities and the need to implement mitigation measures is paramount to successful asset protection and management of risk.

Prioritize and Implement Mitigation Measures

Mitigation measures need to be comprehensive and also prioritized, as most organizations have resource strains. However, mitigation measures may include the introduction of strict access and need-to-know for access to the critical asset of undercover operations. Personnel with access could be subject to enhanced background investigations, polygraphs, and annual updates. Computers with access could "time out" and lock very quickly; be located in secure areas; and have their ports disabled to prevent copying information to an external drive or printing. Communications security could be annually upgraded and undercover officers prevented from coming to police stations. While this one example is very specific, it is representational of one small facet of an organization's activities, which could be of value to an opposing organization (in this example, a cartel), and the myriad of vulnerabilities present just around the data in a computer.

SOLUTIONS AND RECOMMENDATIONS

It is extremely likely that, as public and private organizations respond to the expanded cyber threat, there will be a return to the traditional methods of coercing an organizational employee to gain access to facilities and information. Furthermore, as insider threats become more prominent and critical infrastructure and adversaries target key assets, a priority must be placed on risk management, better integration of public and private sectors, and the protection of critical assets.

The twenty-first century essentially revolves around technology; hence, the rapid advances in technology will lead to a greater reliance on cyber systems to conduct espionage and carry out digital attacks. However, protection from the external attacks may lead organizations to reduce efforts to protect systems from within, which the authors in this chapter have highlighted as a key concern. In addition to making information more accessible and attacks easier to carry out, technological improvements also lead to greater vulnerabilities and will continue to evolve through the digital age. In the past, experts looked to the notion of Moore's law, which was the result of Gordon Moore's work in 1965, which states that the "number of transistors that can be fit on a computer chip will double every two years, resulting in periodic increases in computing power" (Peckham, 2012). With such immense technological increases in power, it would seem undeniable that change was impending every few years. However, according to one theoretical physicist Michio Kaku, Moore's law is no longer applicable and is essentially collapsing (Peckham, 2012). For instance, Kaku said that, "In about ten years or so, we will see the collapse of Moore's Law. In fact, already, we see a slowing down of Moore's Law. Computer power simply cannot maintain its rapid exponential rise using standard silicon technology. Intel Corporation has admitted this;" additionally, other experts in the field also supported these statements (Peckham, 2012). Hence, it is clear that current society is so unique in terms of technological advances that even previously, widely-accepted digital laws are being abandoned. Along these lines, it is important that security personnel recognize the distinct nature of the twenty-first century that will undoubtedly affect the entire globe, politically, socially, and even economically. Society is no longer evolving in the ways in which experts had predicted; society is actually rapidly evolving in ways that were previously unknown to experts.

Additionally, increased speed of adversarial cyber-attacks may soon no longer be an issue with identifying and blocking the theft of data. With an "even playing field" of computer speeds, there will likely be a reversion to traditional espionage techniques to identify and exploit vulnerabilities in organizational protection efforts, which may be more focused on external attacks.

FUTURE RESEARCH DIRECTIONS

Throughout this chapter the authors discussed both the relevance of historical lessons learned and the impact of current sabotage, espionage, and compromise efforts by corporate competitors or foreign intelligence services. The risk management model proposed in this paper is easily transferrable to future threats and vulnerabilities. However, while future adversarial efforts will evolve with technology, a primary challenge for protecting assets will relate to properly identifying the threat and implementing appropriate mitigation measures.

The identification of threats can always be categorized as external or internal. While protecting against external threats can nearly always be incorporated into organizational protection methods, when the threat is internally driven (e.g. a trusted employee) the protection of organizational assets becomes more complicated. Employees of an organization in most countries have specific rights as they pertain to privacy.

Future research should address could address three primary efforts:

1. **Transparency:** There is a need for transparency in hierarchical organizations, such as the public sector, and the laws on privacy that provide protection to employees while also restricting investigations. Take for an example the U.S. response to Edward Snowden's theft and disclosure of national security information to the Wikileaks website. Should a government be able to monitor anyone who accesses the WikiLeaks website? Or who subscribes to the Twitter feed of Julian Assange or others deemed as a possible "threat" to governments?
2. **Automation:** Another possible topic to research is the automation of risk assessments and mitigation measures to establish priority of effort. While this is done by many large organizations, analysis of different techniques and development of a unique process may streamline efforts.
3. **Economic Loss:** As noted above, there was an estimated loss of 30-40 million US dollars only related to the theft of research and development related to seed production. Theft of trade secrets, intellectual property, and research and development results, must result in an astronomically large amount of money, which should be properly researched and reported.

CONCLUSION

One argument which this chapter has desired to prove is that even in a digital age, the threats and vulnerabilities to an organization's critical assets are not only cyber-related. A holistic approach must be developed, implemented, and continuously refined to ensure the highest level of protection of critical assets, not only for government agencies, but also for any organization that needs to protect an asset.

The occurrences of sabotage, espionage, and compromise, referenced in this chapter, highlight the loss of assets in several different ways. However, the one constant is that these assets were critical to an organization's function or economic profit and there were gaps in their protection. Threats change, vulnerabilities change, and the effect of organizational protection and mitigation measures change, which is the basis for the need to continually assess risk and response. As the pendulum swings more toward the cyber threats and vulnerabilities, more gaps may be created in the protection against traditional threats. Continual assessment of all risks and vulnerabilities, and also the effect of the implemented mitigations measures must be requested and reviewed by organizational leaders. Accordingly, it has also been established through this chapter that researchers, in addition to practitioners must place a priority on the continuous improvement of security measures.

REFERENCES

Dice, M. (2014), *FBI Citizens Academy: Counterintelligence.* Retrieved from http://www.counton2.com/story/26181957/fbi-citizens-academy-counterintelligence

Drogin, B., & Goetz, J. (2005). *How U.S. Fell Under the Spell of Curveball.* Retrieved from http://downloadswww.leadingtowar.com/PDFsources_claims_nomobile/2000_2001_Jan_Sept_comndrms.pdf

Federal Bureau of Investigation. (2013). *Six Chinese Nationals Indicted for Conspiring to Steal Trade Secrets from U.S. Seed Companies.* Retrieved from http://www.fbi.gov/omaha/press-releases/2013/six-chinese-nationals-indicted-for-conspiring-to-steal-trade-secrets-from-u.s.-seed-companies

Flaccus, G. (2010). *Dongfan "Greg" Chung, Chinese Spy, Gets More Than 15 Years in Prison.* Retrieved from http://www.huffingtonpost.com/2010/02/08/dongfan-greg-chung-chines_n_454107.html

Government Digital Service. (2014). *Whistleblowing.* Retrieved from https://www.gov.uk/whistleblowing/overview

Herbig, K. (2008). *Changes in Espionage by Americans: 1947-2007.* Retrieved from http://fas.org/sgp/library/changes.pdf

LoisLaw. (n. d.). *United States Code. Chapter 37. Espionage and Censorship.* Retrieved from http://www.loislaw.com.ezproxy1.apus.edu/snp/fpopwind.htm

Martin, D. (2014). Watch: Unraveling the great Chinese corn seed spy ring. *Al Jazeera.* Retrieved from http://america.aljazeera.com/watch/shows/america-tonight/articles/2014/10/6/unraveling-the-greatchinesecornseedspyring.html

Moteff, J., & Parfomek, P. (2004). *Critical Infrastructure and Key Assets: Definition and Identification. CRS Report for Congress.* Retrieved from http://www.google.com/url?sa=t&rct=j&q=&esrc=s&source=web&cd=2&ved=0CCkQFjAB&url=http%3A%2F%2Fwww.dtic.mil%2Fcgi-bin%2FGetTRDoc%3FAD%3DADA454016&ei=Jgl6VMKSCrG0sAS8wYCgCw&usg=AFQjCNGnIi42ksabku3cy8G47VZd-cQRtGQ

National Security Agency. (2014). Memorandum for Staff Director and Minority Staff Director, House Committee on the Judiciary. Retrieved from http://msnbcmedia.msn.com/i/MSNBC/Sections/NEWS/nsa-snowden.pdf

Office of National Counterintelligence Executive. (2011). Foreign Spies Stealing US Economic Secrets in Cyberspace: report to Congress on Foreign Economic Collection and Industrial Espionage. Retrieved from http://www.ncix.gov/publications/reports/fecie_all/Foreign_Economic_Collection_2011.pdf

Owen, J. (2012). Man whose WMD lies led to 100,000 deaths confesses all. *Independent.* Retrieved from http://www.independent.co.uk/news/world/politics/man-whose-wmd-lies-led-to-100000-deaths-confesses-all-7606236.html

Rodriguez, G. (2013). *Edward Snowden Interview Transcript Full Text.* Retrieved from http://mic.com/articles/47355/edward-snowden-interview-transcript-full-text-read-the-guardian-s-entire-interview-with-the-man-who-leaked-prism

Tedford, T., & Herbeck, D. (2009). *Amendment to the Espionage Act of 1917.* Retrieved from http://www.bc.edu/bc_org/avp/cas/comm/free_speech/espionageactof1917.html

Terms and Definitions of Interest for DoD Counterintelligence Professionals. (2011). Retrieved from http://fas.org/irp/eprint/ci-glossary.pdf

U.S. Department of Homeland Security, Government Accountability Office. (2014). Critical Infrastructure Protection. DHS Actions Needed to Enhance Integration and Coordination of Vulnerability Assessment Efforts: report to Congressional Requesters. Retrieved from http://www.gao.gov/assets/670/665788.pdf

U.S. Government Printing Office. (1905). *Journals of the Continental Congress.* Washington, USA: Government Printing Office, Library of Congress.

VandenBos, G., Knapp, S., & Doe, J. (2001). *Role of reference elements in the selection of resources by psychology undergraduates*. Retrieved from http://jbr.org/articles.html

VanderSchel, K. (2013). *Chinese National Arrested for Conspiring to Steal Trade Secrets.* Retrieved from http://www.justice.gov/usao/ias/news/2013/Hailong%20-%20Arrest%2012-12-2013.html

KEY TERMS AND DEFINITIONS

Adversary: An individual, group, organization, or government that conducts or has the intent and capability to conduct activities detrimental to the US Government or its assets ("Terms," 2011, 4).

Classified Information: Any information/data that has been purposefully recognized and designated as to be protected against unauthorized disclosures ("Terms," 2011, 18).

Counterintelligence: Intelligence activities concerned with identifying and countering the threat to security posed by hostile intelligence organizations or by individuals engaged in espionage or sabotage or subversion or terrorism ("Terms," 2011, 31).

Critical Asset: A specific entity that is of such extraordinary importance that its incapacitation or destruction would have a very serious, debilitating effect on the ability of a nation to continue to function effectively ("Terms," 2011, 47).

Espionage: Intelligence activities that are "directed towards the acquisition of information through clandestine means" ("Terms," 2011, 69).

Insider Threat: An individual who uses their authorized access to government facilities and resources to harm the security of the United States "through espionage, terrorism, unauthorized disclosure of information, or through the loss or degradation of departmental resources or capabilities" ("Terms," 2011, 91).

Risk Assessment: A systematic examination of risk using disciplined processes, methods, and tools. A risk assessment provides an environment for decision makers to evaluate and prioritize risks continuously and to recommend strategies to remediate or mitigate those risks ("Terms," 2011, 149).

Risk Management: The process of identifying, assessing, and controlling, risks arising from operational factors and making decisions that balance risk cost with mission benefits ("Terms," 2011, 149).

Whistleblower: An individual within an organization who exposes any actual, or alleged, wrongdoing to internal or external enforcement officers.

Section 2
Understanding the Field

Chapter 6
Understanding Digital Intelligence:
A British View

David Omand
King's College, UK

ABSTRACT

This chapter examines digital intelligence and international views on its future regulation and reform. The chapter summarizes the lead up to the Snowden revelations in terms of how digital intelligence grew in response to changing demands and was enabled by private sector innovation and mediated through legal, Parliamentary and executive regulation. A common set of ethical principles based on human rights considerations to govern modern intelligence activity (both domestic and external) is proposed in the chapter. A three-layer model of security activity on the Internet is used: securing the use of the Internet for everyday economic and social life and for political and military affairs; the activity of law enforcement attempting to manage criminal threats on the Internet; and the work of secret intelligence and security agencies exploiting the Internet to gain information on their targets, including in support of law enforcement.

DOI: 10.4018/978-1-4666-9661-7.ch006

INTRODUCTION

"It is not the strongest species that survives, nor the most intelligent that survives. It is the one that is the most adaptable to change." Charles Darwin was describing what happens when rapid changes take place to the specialized niche in which a species has become comfortable, challenging its very survival. Coincidentally, the last twenty years have seen three revolutionary changes in the environment of Western intelligence agencies.

Rapid change certainly describes the new intelligence requirements after the end of the Cold War, the dissolution of the Warsaw Pact and the integration of central Europe into the Western community of nations. Even more so, after the al-Qaeda attacks on Washington and New York on 9/11 2001, the urgency of the demands for intelligence to counter international terrorism and instability created huge pressure on intelligence communities around the world.

Over the same period, however, all intelligence agencies have simultaneously had to try to adapt their activity to the profound changes wrought by the digital revolution in their technological environment. The popularity of the Internet as a means of communication, the invention of the World Wide Web and the ability cheaply to store digital data transformed the opportunities for obtaining intelligence and the opportunities have not stopped growing since.

The third set of changes concerns the legal and political structures within which most security and intelligence agencies in the democracies now operate, with their existence avowed, their activities subject to law, and with web sites explaining their purpose and recruiting the next generation of staff.

By the end of the first decade of the 21st century, the most advanced intelligence communities at least had adapted to these changes. The signals intelligence agencies in particular had begun to settle comfortably into a highly productive new niche, actively exploiting unprecedented access to digital information to deliver to their military and law enforcement customers much highly valued intelligence on their targets, often in near-real time and with little if any serious public controversy over their powers and reach.

The Snowden revelations have, however, exposed to unprecedented and uncomfortable national and international gaze the very success of the United States agencies and those of its close intelligence allies, including the United Kingdom, in adapting to the digital world. The protection of personal information from unlawful exploitation, and the legality, proportionality and adequacy of regulation of digital intelligence access and intelligence sharing have become major international political issues. The adequacy of the previous changes in legal powers and governance arrangements are seriously challenged.

Many governments are reappraising their reliance on major US Internet companies (and also their reliance on Chinese information technology suppliers as the UK Parliamentary Intelligence and Security Committee (ISC, 2013) has reported) as some of the methods of digital intelligence become more generally known. The US Internet and technology companies themselves are busy reassuring their customers that their data will be made invulnerable to the bad guys – and by that they include the intelligence agencies of their own government. Behind their stance lies the commercial reality that although approximately 40% of world population has access to the Internet most are in the developed world and the expected future growth in business will be in China and elsewhere in Asia and South Asia, South America and Africa, where there is a suspicion of the dominance of the US information and technology companies and their links to government as well as a natural wish to see the development of indigenous capability. At the same time, most intelligence and security agencies around the world are no doubt trying to work out how to close an apparent capability gap with the United States. Meanwhile Western law enforcement complains that they are no longer able to gather evidence as before and that risks to the public are rising (ISC, 2014).

The digital intelligence niche has therefore turned out to be not as easy to adapt to as the authors of some of the rather self-congratulatory PowerPoint slides stolen by the US contractor Edward Snowden from the US National Security Agency (NSA) and its close partner the UK Government Communications Headquarters (GCHQ) and then exposed by the media might at first have thought it would be. In addition therefore to the challenges of meeting pressing demands for intelligence and exploiting the potential supply from digital sources must be added a pressing third challenge: how to retain public confidence that these intelligence capabilities are not being misused.

This chapter examines this world of digital intelligence and the many ramifications of its exposure to public gaze, and the consequent wide polarisation of views internationally as to how the Snowden material should affect thinking about future regulation and reform. The chapter starts by briefly summarizing the events that led up to the unprecedented series of media articles, starting in early June 2013, revealing much about US and UK communications and Internet intelligence activity. It then examines how that activity grew in terms of the response to the changing demands for intelligence on al-Qaeda and its associates and was enabled by the parallel private sector digital revolution in Internet technology, both involving issues that predate Snowden. The importance of mediating through legal, Parliamentary and executive regulation the interaction between demands for and supply of digital intelligence will be seen to be at the heart of current international and domestic debates about the proper limits and governance of digital intelligence activity. A common set of ethical principles based on human rights considerations to govern modern intelligence activity (both domestic and external) is proposed in the chapter. In order to illuminate the resulting issues a three-layer model of security activity on the Internet is used: securing the use of the Internet for everyday economic and social life and for political and military affairs; the activity of law enforcement attempting to manage criminal threats on the Internet; and the work of secret intelligence and security agencies exploiting the Internet to gain information on their targets, including in support of law enforcement.

BACKGROUND

The Snowden Affair and International Responses to It

The issues around personal privacy in the digital age discussed in this chapter would probably sooner or later have become a focus for public policy debate, no doubt aided by the patient work over many years of investigative journalists and academics involved in studying the development of intelligence and security agencies, notably in the Anglophone world (Aid, 2012, Bamford, 1983). The flood of disclosures in 2013 and 2014 set in train by Edward Snowden, however, immediately set a new international agenda. Almost overnight the scale and reach of modern digital intelligence became household knowledge. The alleged range of targets of US intelligence included the Chancellor of Germany and the President of Brazil and set off firestorms of diplomatic protests led by those nations, and the disclosures relating to GCHQ put the longstanding Five-Eyes (US/UK/Canada/Australia/New Zealand) partnership in signals intelligence under unparalleled scrutiny and became an issue in the New Zealand general election.

The debate in the European Union over personal privacy in a data rich world in which the private sector harvests significant amounts of personal information was already complex, with discussion of a new draft European Union Regulation on Data Protection, and a specific new Data Protection Directive for law enforcement, but the Snowden revelations have made this debate intense and at times toxic. The European Parliament, for example, has called for suspension of the 'safe harbor' transatlantic code of practice of voluntary data protection standards for non-EU companies transferring EU citizens' personal data to the US and the suspension of the US/EU Terrorist Finance Tracking Programme that had generated significant intelligence helping to detect terrorist plots and trace their authors.

A number of caveats are, however, in order at the outset. Snowden was employed as a skilled systems security administrator by contractors working for the National Security Agency and would have had access to the networks carrying information about technical access programmes (his sources for the material he leaked). But he was not an intelligence analyst generating end product and seems to have had limited knowledge of how far the activity and techniques he has exposed were used in practice to generate actual intelligence and for what purposes. Nor had he been trained, as an analyst has to be, in the legal and regulatory framework surrounding intelligence requirements and warranting processes, intelligence assessment and reporting or oversight arrangements. In the case of the UK it would be fair to say that he had no knowledge of how intelligence activity is actually regulated and overseen and how the differences with the US legal framework are managed by British analysts so as to remain at all times within UK law. The journalists interpreting his material likewise have (understandably) written up the most obviously newsworthy items but have mostly lacked the perspective from which to interpret the wider significance of individual disclosures. Nevertheless, the revelations of what a modern digitally minded intelligence agency actually may have to do to fulfill its missions, and the subsequent campaigning by civil rights groups, bring together left and right of the political spectrum, and have provoked both US and UK governments into themselves making or authorising greater openness about their activities, material on which this chapter draws.

The young (age 23) Edward Snowden's first major contact with the world of secret intelligence appears to have been his training by CIA as a computer specialist followed by his two year assignment to Geneva as part of the US Mission to the UN to manage computer network security for them. Disagreements with his employers led to his resignation and subsequent employment by Dell Computers, under a cyber security contract at an NSA facility in Japan (NSA do not appear to have been fully aware that their contractors were hiring this young individual with a rather troubled back history with CIA).

Edward Snowden's outlook on life seems to have been an uneasy combination of that of the self-reliant American individualist (supporter of the right wing Tea Party Movement, anti-gun control and distrustful of Federal government) and of the Internet generation (with their belief that the authorities have no place in cyberspace and that innovation is best when government is absent). The modern equivalent of the frontiersman's necessary self-reliance and right to bear arms to defend himself being the Internet generation's right to strong encryption to provide absolute security for their activity on-line. It seems to be have been when working at Dell as a contractor for NSA that Edward Snowden became aware of the scale and reach of the NSA's gathering of data on the communications of US citizens, activity that he believed was a disproportionate and thus unlawful interference with the constitutional right (under the 4th Amendment to the US Constitution) of US citizens to protection of from unreasonable searches and seizures. It was when working for Dell that he began covertly downloading and removing copies of large numbers of very highly classified US intelligence documents (variously estimated as between 50,000 and 200,000 items).

He tried and initially failed to reach out securely to Glen Greenwald, an investigative journalist with a track record of exposing government secrets but did succeed in making contact in January 2013 with Laura Poitras, an American film maker living in Berlin, again with a track record in exposing previously undisclosed US military activity, and she finally connected him to Greenwald. It was whilst in contact with her that Snowden deliberately changed jobs in March 2013 to work for Booz Allen under an NSA contract, at their facility in Hawaii, because he felt that would give him better access to documentary material on secret programmes of global surveillance.

Snowden's access, and his ability to persuade (or bluff, against the rules) colleagues to give him even greater access, allowed him to examine – and it is assumed download - a vast cache of top secret material covering much of the digital intelligence work being conducted by NSA, including work in support of the US Armed Forces. Additionally, he was able to access and download a copy of a GCHQ internal web that had been mirrored to NSA to allow UK personnel working there and a few cleared NSA personnel to keep up to date with GCHQ activity. A copy of that latter cache, some 58,000 documents, was subsequently intercepted by the police at Heathrow Airport along with a large number of NSA documents being carried from Laura Poitras in Berlin to Glenn Greenwald in Brazil by hand of Greenwald's partner David Miranda (Robbins, 2013). It is claimed that Edward Snowden also passed over to journalists some 12,000 Australian intelligence documents.

The exposures have mostly focused on the large scale interception, storage and subsequent filtering of communications data and digital flows with programmes such as the US PRISM, and the UK TEMPORA. But the material has also revealed much about so-called 'close access' operations where special measures such as software or hardware implants are taken with a suspect's computer or other device to make its activity more accessible to the intelligence agency. The result, as earlier noted, has been intense scrutiny of NSA and GCHQ, questioning the legality of their actions in cyberspace, the effectiveness of oversight of the agencies, and the adequacy of the existing legislation itself to regulate digital intelligence.

The story of Snowden's flight to Hong Kong on May 20 2013 with copies of these documents, his release of material to journalists, in particular to the UK Guardian, Washington Post, New York Times, Le Monde and Der Spiegel, has been well recounted by those involved (Harding, 2014). Less well documented is his interaction with the assistant to Julian Assange, founder of Wikileaks, Sarah Harrison, his meetings in Hong Kong with her and Russian consular (and probably intelligence) officials and his flight to Moscow with Sarah Harrison. Following Russia's granting to him of leave to remain Snowden has stayed in Moscow and has continued to make public statements from there justifying as whistleblowing his decision to expose US and UK intelligence secrets. He left to the selected journalists to whom he gave the NSA and GCHQ material the task of sifting through the huge number of documents and to redact for obvious risks such as not putting in jeopardy individual intelligence officers named in the documents. The journalists, and their media outlets, did in the end publish detailed stories based on the documents timed and written to cause the maximum embarrassment to the US and UK authorities (or from their point of view to gain maximum publicity to bring the scale and nature of digital intelligence activity to public attention). The arguments that have ensued over the level of real damage by the revelations are considered later in the chapter. Further revelations are expected as the large number of stolen documents are trawled through by journalists and further stories about digital intelligence pieced together.

Snowden at least succeeded in one objective he had manifest, which was to expose the Federal Government's collection (and long term storage in the US) by the NSA of the digital call data of US citizens' telephone use, secretly authorised under s.215 of the US Patriot Act signed into law by President Bush on 26 October 2001 in response to the 9/11. This is a collection programme that Snowden believed was unconstitutional in the scale of intrusion into the constitutionally protected privacy of US persons. Snowden has referred to the impact on his attitude when he learned that at an open Congressional hearing in March 2013 when specifically asked about such activity the Director of National Intelligence, Jim Clapper had given a potentially misleading public answer (subsequently if somewhat belatedly corrected in a letter to the chair of the Committee). President Obama was obliged to admit to the existence of the programme and restrict its use; and Congress has considered but so far rejected (most recently in November 2014) legislation to regulate it by statute. The urgent need for intelligence on the ISIL jihadists responsible for the grisly beheading of US citizens and others in Syria and Iraq, and the fear of further jihadist inspired attacks in the US itself, seem to have driven the Republican majority in the Senate to filibuster the Bill out on the grounds that these were dangerous times to add constraints on the NSA.

Snowden is nevertheless widely regarded by civil rights activists as a legitimate US whistleblower. It can be argued that he did not exhaust his remedies, such as privately approaching the Senate Oversight Committee, before going public. The scale of his leaking also appears grossly disproportionate to his stated cause of wishing to expose domestic surveillance. As will be considered later in the chapter, the exposure by the journalists of so much detail about digital intelligence sources and methods has done, and will continue to, do significant damage to US and allied national security not least in relation to protecting cyberspace, supporting the armed forces on operations and hindering the prevention and detection of serious crime. That is something Edward Snowden himself has consistently claimed, as a self-proclaimed patriot, not to have wanted to do.

In the UK, the revelations have led to accusations by a section of the media and by civil liberties groups of unlawful intelligence gathering by GCHQ as the partner agency to NSA. It has also been alleged that UK intelligence analysts were able to use their close relationship with the US to get round UK legal restrictions on interception. Subsequent authoritative and independent examination (as will be considered later in the chapter) of these accusations have shown them to be based on misreading of the (admittedly complex) UK legislation together with exaggerated worst case fears about the actual conduct of UK intelligence activity that had no foundation in reality. Nevertheless, Edward Snowden's actions certainly crystallised genuine concerns on the part of some Parliamentarians, civil liberties and human rights organisations about the ease with which intrusions into privacy can be undertaking in the digital era, by intelligence agencies, by law enforcement and by the private sector for marketing purposes. His actions also precipitated concerns about whether legislation governing intrusive investigation had kept pace with the digital communications revolution, and doubts about whether the existing methods of oversight could provide sufficient assurance against misuse of these powerful tools of the intelligence agencies by any future government were it so inclined.

As a result of this pressure from civil rights organisations following Snowden, governments including the US and the UK are rightly taking care to re-examine processes and legal frameworks for intelligence activity and seeking to improve oversight mechanisms. In the UK, Parliamentary oversight is conducted by a Committee (the ISC) drawn from both lower and upper houses. The ISC is now conducting a major review of where the balance between security and privacy should be struck in the light of the Snowden material. A separate independent review into interception is under way by the think tank, the Royal United Services Institute (RUSI), at the request of the Deputy Prime Minister. The UK Government has also set up a statutory review of the law by David Anderson QC, the independent reviewer of terrorism legislation, to look at the capabilities and powers required by law enforcement and the security intelligence agencies, and the regulatory framework within which those capabilities and powers should be exercised. Civil liberties groups in the United Kingdom have in parallel mounted a full-scale legal challenge to GCHQ operations which is being heard in the specialist UK Court, the Investigative Powers Tribunal, set up by the 1994 Intelligence Services Act that first put GCHQ onto a statutory footing.

Perhaps the most damaging loss of trust has come from the common but unwarranted assumption that access in bulk to large volumes of digital communications (the 'haystack') in order to find the communications of intelligence targets (the wanted 'needles') is evidence of mass surveillance of the population, which it is not. The contrast in that respect between the accusations that have followed the reporting of the material stolen by Edward Snowden and the reassurance from the UK legal Commissioners and Parliamentary overseers could not be starker.

The statutory UK Interception Commissioner is a senior retired judge. The present Commissioner Sir Anthony May was President of a Division of the High Court, one of the most senior judges in the UK, and he has the power to visit the interception agency, GCHQ, talk to staff both senior and junior, and examine any of the records including the warrants authorizing interception. In his 2013 annual report to Parliament he has reported in the light of the Snowden revelations that everything GCHQ does is properly authorized, and legally properly justified including under Article 8 of the European Human Rights convention regarding personal privacy. He said categorically in his report that GCHQ does not conduct mass surveillance and that furthermore any such activity would be comprehensively unlawful. His description of the staff was in fact that they work lawfully, conscientiously, and effectively in the national interest. Furthermore he has confirmed that there is no jurisdiction shopping to get others such as their US partners to do what UK intelligence officers legally cannot. GCHQ does have bulk access by computer to the Internet, but that is for the purpose of carefully targeted, highly discriminating, selection of the communications of the targets where there are RIPA warrants authorizing interception with certificates attached authorizing the targets whose communications are being sought.

That is not to say that there are not issues for future oversight that deserve deeper examination, including whether the law itself should be amended to take account of the developments in the technology, whether present systems of Parliamentary and judicial oversight would be sufficient to prevent any future government from misusing these powerful intelligence tools and how much greater transparency can be secured for the citizen to understand the scope and the limitations on both public and private sector use of information that the individual may reasonably regard as personal. The outcomes of these British reviews will probably come together after the British general election in 2015 when it is likely there will be new legislation to replace or amend the existing legislation that governs the use by the intelligence agencies and law enforcement of intrusive investigative powers, the Regulation of Investigative Powers Act 2000 (RIPA 2000).

In order to examine the implications of the Snowden revelations the European Parliament is conducting an inquiry into the alleged electronic mass surveillance of European citizens. The German Bundestag has set up a special committee for broadly the same purpose. The German Government has also announced that it will transfer its government e-services from the US carrier Verizon to the domestic provider, Deutsche Telekom, ostensibly for reasons of protecting the privacy of German citizens and fears of US intelligence access via US providers. The French Government rapidly legislated in 2014 to provide statutory legal authority for its ongoing interception activity under the *loi de programmation militaire* (LPM) adopted on 10 December 2013 by the French Senate. This law enables the French secret services to intercept any electronic communication, under the direct authorisation of the French Prime Minister or President.

After the first round of revelations the US President was forced to order an immediate 'blue ribbon' inquiry into the conduct of NSA and subsequently to make a major public statement and publish for the first time the Directive to the NSA to govern signals intelligence collection (White House, 2014A). As earlier noted, Congress has continued to debate reforms in the relevant intelligence legislation, but the outcome is uncertain.

Whether the result of all this controversy and debate will be consistent, coherent, and effective reform, or will even be in the interests of the citizens concerned, very much remains to be seen. The outcome of the different strands of investigation, inquiry and political debate following the Snowden affair may well be changes to tighten up the way many democratic nations regulate intrusive intelligence activity and legislate to protect personal data. For many nations the exposure of advanced digital intelligence techniques will spur an effort to try to catch up, with a net increase in global digital surveillance including the monitoring of use by domestic publics of social media. And, of course, there are major nations such as Russia and China that remain highly secretive about their national intelligence activity, and where it must be assumed that many of the techniques of intelligence access exposed by Edward Snowden are and must be assumed will be in the future in regular use without the independent legal and Parliamentary oversight mechanisms that are becoming common across the democracies.

Even if the present utility of digital intelligence techniques as exposed by Edward Snowden is in the end accepted by the democracies, there will need to be answers to consequential questions about the adequacy of safeguards in place, through warranting intrusive activity and legal and Parliamentary oversight, that would prevent any possibility of future misuse. The potential supply of information from Internet usage by individuals may need detailed regulation, and the consumer may need additional protection for misuse of their personal data that they make available on social media and other applications, for example through the activity of data integrators or brokers who combine multiple sources of information about individuals or organisations for sale to the loans and insurance market based on inferences about their likely risk profile or buying propensities.

There are also issues being probed by these inquiries around the effectiveness of measures of redress for the citizen when mistakes are made or State or private sector authorities over-reach themselves. At a minimum, a mechanism for independent investigation is needed together with the authority to set matters right after mistakes have been made, for example by removing an individual from a watch-list or no-fly list.

Issues of a more philosophical nature are also being raised in the debates now taking place between civil rights groups and supporters of digital intelligence activity. For example, the legitimacy of attempting a trade-off within the basket of human rights between security for the general public and privacy for an individual under suspicion, noting that neither security nor privacy can be an absolute right. It can be argued that without at least a basic level of security it is unlikely that privacy or any other rights can be protected. It is also apparent that human rights are recognised universally in the democracies precisely to avoid the risk that the interests of the majority will be used to justify abuse of the minority.

A further set of hard questions concerns the claims of some that the individual must have the right to anonymity in cyberspace. That assertion is in turn challenged by those who oppose the right to anonymity when the individual is committing crimes or harming society, since a right to anonymity was never accepted in the pre-digital world of three dimensions. And the assertion of anonymity has also to be reconciled with the right to justice, to have the law upheld and to public safety.

Similarly, personal privacy for communications and personal information transmitted or held in cyberspace is seen by some campaigners as an unqualified right, along the lines of the claims made by the original Internet pioneers that cyberspace was a new realm where the old regime and its mores was not welcome. On the other hand, the widespread and growing use of social media has led others to the opposite conclusion, that such traditional expectations of personal privacy for material committed digitally to social media are outmoded.

A fundamentally important issue for all the inquiries following Snowden is defining what actually constitutes an intrusion into personal privacy when all our digital communications pass through complex computer systems. The computers are not sentient and have no understanding. Does the intrusion then take place when the information comes to the notice of a sentient being, the police officer or intelligence analyst? Our communications do all already pass through many computers in the course of their delivery, just as all our financial transactions by debit or credit card pass through the banks' audit systems. Computers are not conscious and that these intimate details are subjected to the security algorithms should not be a concern. Only if a potential security threat is discovered will the material be examined by a human being – in the interests of fraud prevention. Should the public mind that a computer of an intelligence agency is also capable of accessing personal data in bulk, when duly warranted, in the interests of public security? Within a sound legal framework for intelligence, it can be argued that there is no ethical difference between a legally authorised GCHQ computer scanning through a chunk of the Internet to find the communications of a suspect, and exactly the same material passing through an ISP computer, when we know that the ISP will legally have to deliver from its computer the suspect's communications on production of a warrant.

The security and intelligence concerns raised by the Snowden affair, considered in this chapter, also feed in to a wider global debate about Internet governance and the perceived dominance of the US government and the major US Internet companies. That American influence is so great is entirely understandable given the origins of the Internet and the sources of investment and innovation that have driven it thus far. The US Administration declared, however, in March 2014 that in the light of this international feeling it would be prepared to relinquish the role that hitherto the US Department of Commerce (the National Telecommunications and Information Administration – NTIA) has played in coordinating and funding essential Internet functions such as the domain names system. The Administration has, however, made this conditional on a workable transition plan being prepared to a new multi-stakeholder form of governance, involving the industry and civil society as well as governments. The International Telecommunications Union (ITU) for example is not acceptable since it is a United Nations body and thus accountable only to governments. As Melissa Hathaway has expressed it 'Modern societies are in the middle of a strategic, multidimensional competition for money power, and control over all aspects of the Internet and the Internet economy' (Hathaway, 2014). The reactions of the political class around the world to the Snowden revelations has to be seen through that lens. The former Swedish Prime Minister Carl Bildt is chairing an International Commission into Global Internet Governance that will explore the policy implications of such Internet governance issues, and will have to deal with the largely hostile world reaction to the Snowden revelations and the role of the US Internet giants.

MAIN FOCUS OF THE CHAPTER: ISSUES, CONTROVERSIES, AND PROBLEMS

Examining Critically the Demands for Intelligence

An essential part of understanding the background to the Snowden revelations lies in the changing nature of the demands for secret intelligence since the end of the Cold War, and most notably since 9/11. What is sought by government and law enforcement is intelligence on what might broadly be described as international threats to public safety and security, above all terrorism but also notably serious international criminality (including cyber-crime and intellectual property theft) and illegal arms and WMD proliferation networks often stemming from ungoverned regions or countries at risk of instability.

Put another way, the challenges of demand arise from the widespread reinterpretation by governments of what they now mean by national security in a world in which the authorities have to manage day to day simultaneous risks, many of which impact upon the individual citizen whether at home or working or travelling abroad without in most cases being able to eliminate those risks. That challenge in many ways erodes traditional distinctions between managing domestic threats and managing those emanating from overseas given the unprecedented global interactions between the two with cheap international travel and near-instant global communications. An offensive cartoon is published in a domestic newspaper and a hostage is seized overseas or an embassy burns on the other side of the globe. A jihadist beheading video from Syria may stimulate a 'lone wolf' terrorist attack at home. The Internet itself challenges the concept of sovereignty and national boundaries.

From that perspective, national security – the prime justification for intelligence activity over the years - can best thought of today as a state of confidence on the part of the public – and the international finance and capital markets – that the major risks facing the nation and its interests are being anticipated and managed such that normal life can continue. The test of success in maintaining security is normality: one indicator of success, for example, is whether there is investment in the future in the confident expectation that economic and social life will continue, without the public having had to sacrifice essential liberties, and able to demonstrate the nation is at peace. Whilst direct elimination of most risks through government action is infeasible, in the case of terrorism and serious crime anticipation of threats using pre-emptive intelligence is certainly possible, to disrupt plots and bring to justice at least some of those intending harm and to guide actions to reduce societal vulnerability and build national resilience.

That challenge of supporting national security over the last decade has thus changed the nature of the demands for secret intelligence. Senior police officers, operational staff in such areas as immigration and border control, revenue and customs and airport security and government policy makers working on counter-terrorism and counter-criminality strategies can all benefit in their work from pre-emptive intelligence. There are many insistent demands from law enforcement for leads, for example, that may allow evidence gathering to be planned leading to the arrest or at least disruption of terrorist plots. Often the public can be protected by preventing such risks crystalising if intelligence is available on those who pose the threat. Intelligence priorities today also must certainly include throwing light on the rapidly growing threats to cyber security and intellectual property theft and thus to economic prosperity in a global trading world.

Military commanders too need pre-emptive intelligence both to support their mission and for force protection. A range of different types of intelligence is needed to support modern military operations, often in near-real time, including for the purposes of target location and identification. This chapter highlights a key issue, which is that the capabilities and techniques to acquire and process the intelligence for support for military operations, as well as to secure defence communications and weapons systems, is likely to rely upon the same type of digital capabilities and techniques as for tracking terrorists and serious criminals. The use of mobile devices and of communications using the Internet Protocols is now near universal in military as well as civil life, as evidenced by all the current and recent campaigns by British Armed Forces in Afghanistan, Iraq, and Libya. Another example would be the exploitation by intelligence agencies of security flaws in software or hardware or network design for collecting intelligence on a wide range of military as well as terrorist and criminal targets. The knowledge thus gained is also invaluable in advising the armed forces on the security of their own systems from compromise.

More often than not nowadays a common feature of the demands placed upon an intelligence community by the armed forces and law enforcement alike are for actionable intelligence about *people* – the dictators committing or threatening to carry out war crimes, terrorists, insurgents, hackers, cyber- and narco-criminal gangs, people traffickers and paedophile networks. For these so-called non-State actors what is likely to be sought as of most value are their identities (a non-trivial issue given digital anonymity), associations, location, movements, financing and intentions. Often large issues of public policy rest on the outcome. Trying to establish whether there are Russian paramilitaries in Eastern Ukraine, for example, on which UNSC and European Council sanctions decisions may rest. Or whether ISIL jihadists in Iraq and Syria, responsible for the appalling executions of hostages, will bring their campaign to domestic streets in Europe. Of course, there are still demands from government for intelligence on the activities of some traditional States and their intentions where these may bear on key national security interests – but even in such cases the communications of interest are likely to be carried on virtual private networks on the Internet.

Not all intelligence requirements are, however, of equal importance or urgency. The limited budgets for intelligence activity at a time of general austerity in public expenditure (at least in the UK) should force prioritization. Most of the top priorities will be obvious, in supporting the armed forces on operations and in providing leads for counter-terrorist operations to protect the public, or where there are important diplomatic decisions to be taken as with the negotiations with Iran over its nuclear enrichment programmes and over sanctions on Russia in relation to its actions in Ukraine, especially Crimea.

Intelligence agencies also have the task of providing strategic warning of new threats not yet on the policy-makers' radar, and leeway has to be allowed in authorizing intelligence collection operations accordingly. There are nevertheless important principles of proportionality and necessity that should, as discussed below, apply to legislation governing the intelligence agencies, so those inside the agencies also have a legal duty to satisfy themselves that the degree of intrusion or moral hazard likely to be occurred is in proportion to the harm to national security or public safety that is to be prevented or the benefit to be gained. Additionally the operation must be necessary to help achieve the approved purpose, and must be one whose purpose could not reasonably be achieved in another way that did not have to involve secret intelligence. Not everything that technically can be done, should be done.

Examining the Potential Sources of Digital Intelligence

A second set of challenges - and opportunities - facing the intelligence community relates to the supply side: how the varied demands for intelligence just described, especially on non-State actors operating globally, can possibly even partially be met. An important part of the answer has come over the last few years from two advances: the arrival of the digital age that has girdled the globe with the packet-switched high-speed networks that comprise the Internet and carry the World Wide Web; and the availability of cheap data storage to make it possible for even the most intimate aspects of our life to be stored digitally by governments and private companies for our lifetimes and beyond.

The scientific discoveries of the 1960s and 1970s around solid state physics and the behavior of material at the quantum level, and around quantum electrodynamics and the behavior of light enabled the development of the laser (and thus the ability to write and read digital data at scale and speed), of the fibre-optic cable that allowed the transmission of such digital information long distances at close to the speed of light, and of the microprocessor that powered the logic circuits to make it all happen. Mathematical techniques for compressing data meant that microwave circuits and even traditional copper cables could carry multiple parallel channels of digital information, greatly expanding the capacity of existing networks. The first dial-up Internet service provider started in 1989, and in 1991 the first GSM digital mobile network was launched in Finland, with the first UK SMS text message being sent a year later. The potential of the Internet as a vehicle for commercial activity began to be properly realized with the invention of the Word Wide Web in the early 1990s, and interpersonal communication quickly followed. By 1996, Hotmail was started as an email service (bought by Microsoft a year later for no less than $400m).

By the 1990s therefore signals intelligence agencies were facing multiple challenges in obtaining their raw material, including coping with the switchover from analogue mobile phones to digital networks. By 1999 the first fully Internet capable mobile phone was on sale in Japan. In the UK's GCHQ this digital revolution had been predicted and seen as a major intelligence opportunity as well as a technical challenge. In the mid-1990s re-engineering by GCHQ was under way of its Cold War legacy systems to cope through its SINEWS Sigint New Systems programme (Aldrich, 2012). By the turn of the century the digital age was well and truly launched.

Two technical developments in particular, had brought the digital Internet revolution to maturity: the adoption of open Internet and network protocols (for example, the Domain Names System, Internet Protocol, Border Gateway Protocol, and formatting protocols such as those of the World Wide Web) that brought innovation and competition bringing costs down to levels that small and medium size enterprises and the general public could begin to afford and the discovery and development of public key encryption that made on-line monetary transactions feasible (first discovered by GCHQ mathematicians Ellis and Cocks but kept secret, and later rediscovered and patented by Diffie and Hellman). Now electronic services are widespread under the headings variously of e-commerce, e-payment, e-banking, e-government and e-learning. These technological changes continue and are still profoundly altering the possible ways in which intelligence about people can be supplied by accessing digital communications and the digital traces and records people leave behind.

The volumes of communications have continued to grow geometrically, and are now almost beyond comprehension. One leading company, Microsoft, has over a billion users of its Cloud services with 1.3 billion email addresses sending 4 billion emails a day and uploading 1.5 billion photographs a month. Skype calls via the Internet are taking up 2 billion minutes per day. The techniques of the pre-digital age cannot be used to find the suspects' communications let alone examine them. The emphasis has to be on computerized selection and discrimination so as not to overwhelm the human analyst, although even then only a tiny sample of global communications could conceivably come within the reach of an intelligence agency. Even then digital steganography makes it possible for those with messages to hide to incorporate them into photographs, videos, slides and text in an almost infinite number of ways.

The main driving forces here have been the innovations funded and introduced by the private not the public sector. The public is only now beginning to recognize – stimulated by the controversy over digital privacy that the Snowden affair has generated - the business model that makes the Internet economically viable, and cheap to the user, indeed largely free at the point of use. Personal information of users can be collected and monetized and sold for marketing and other purposes. This complex metadata ecosystem has driven the massive take-up of easily available software applications (now universally just called 'apps') for mobile devices and the rapid adoption of social media (of which there are thousands of different variants available worldwide). Such developments have transformed the ease and variety of ways of interacting digitally between individuals and within groups, and has made multi-media ubiquitous – video, photograph, graphic and text all combined. A further relevant development has been the provision of Cloud services, not just for easily accessible data storage but also to enable mobile devices to access very powerful software programmes too large to fit on individual devices, such as search and inference engines able to recognize context and thus be faster and more efficient, translation to and from multiple languages and voice activated inquiries.

Private enterprise harvests and exploits information about people and their everyday activities linked back to their mobile platforms such as phones, tablets, and laptops and in future to a range of other household and business devices. No doubt, in the near future, digital 'wearables' will also be popularized as consumer goods (an example is the bracelet that takes pulse and heart rate measurements and links to the owner's mobile phone – and in the future possibly direct to the doctor's surgery to warn of impending trouble). In the future, the Internet will be connected to a very wide range of other devices (the so-called 'Internet of things' or more recently 'the Internet of Everything – IoE), again increasing the stock of information that is relatable to an individual and from which useful intelligence might be derived.

Communications data – who called whom, where, when and how – has for many years proved an invaluable tool for uncovering networks of association between a suspect and other individuals. UK law (RIPA, 2000) specifically recognizes this and provides for the authorities to obtain it, and to pay for companies to retain it for a specified period and make it available on production of lawful authority. Most recently, the term 'metadata' has been used to describe a wider category of information obtainable from an individual's Internet use such as obtaining their Internet browsing history. Such metadata is of great value to the private sector for marketing purposes and to target advertising to the current interests of an individual consumer. It can also be correspondingly attractive to the intelligence agencies, when legally authorized, as a source of information on a suspect. The power of such information in breaching individual privacy was recognized by civil liberties organisations when the UK interception legislation (RIPA 2000), was being debated and the UK government accepted as a result that the definition of communications data in the Act would be based on the old fashioned 'who called whom, for how long and from where'. Accessing the broader metadata that digital communications enables on a domestic suspect (their complete browsing history, for example, or their digital address book) is therefore for British analysts equivalent in law to accessing the 'content' of a communication and they would have to have the relevant domestic warrant personally signed by a Secretary of State.

Often an essential part of the benefit to the user of an app comes from geo-location (from such techniques as triangulation of mobile cell tower signals or directly from GPS receivers now built into devices) that provides an instant map or location of where they are and of the nearest café, restaurant or retail outlet for whatever service is sought, or the location of friends nearby. The opportunity offered by mobile phone geo-location has been quickly taken up by police services, for example to test alibis, to eliminate suspects from an inquiry and to help track possible witnesses after a serious crime such as a sexual assault by helping identify who was in the neighborhood of the crime when it was committed. The power of keeping track over a period of the location of a mobile device (and what other mobile phones or devices might have been in the close vicinity of that device) is clearly of interest to the police, but is potentially very intrusive as has been recognized by Parliamentarians and civil liberties organisations.

At the same time as the rapid expansion of digital communications, Governments, banks and companies alike, driven by the need for efficiencies and cost cutting, have globally digitized back offices and put customer services and record keeping on-line providing yet more potential sources of information about suspects. Tracing individuals through rapid look-ups of immigration and passport databases, or their movements through advance passenger information from the airlines, or through credit and debit card transactions or through the bank and interbank payments systems are examples. These are traditional means for meeting the demands of detectives investigating a criminal case, for which warranted access is provided for in all jurisdictions. In the digital age, however, what has attracted critical attention is the speed with which such demands can be met, and the low cost of enquiries in comparison with the traditional 'shoe leather' methods. The potential for excessive use of such access when digital has become an issue.

This digital information ecosystem is therefore capable, when the request is duly authorized, to *supply* intelligence to the authorities about people and their location as never before, from data in motion travelling around the global packet switched communications networks, and data at rest in many hundreds of millions of databases ranging from vehicle registration to the address books on a suspect's mobile device. This ability of both government and the private sector to generate relevant information has naturally attracted the close attention of the law enforcement and intelligence authorities faced with the increasing demands for information about their suspects and targets as described earlier.

A good example is to be found in social media intelligence (SOCMINT) (Omand, Bartlett & Miller, 2012). In August 2011, a series of riots and instances of looting took place in a number of English towns and cities. Over the period, messages between rioters indicating criminal intent, including tactical intelligence on the location of police patrols, were sent in huge numbers through both open source social networking, such as Twitter, and closed system networks, such as the BlackBerry Messaging Service and closed groups such as chat forums. Similarly, huge numbers of Internet messages appeared trying to provide information from the law abiding public to the police, either about an outbreak of disorder or the identities of the people behind it. Since then, the British Government has embraced this medium of information and communication. The Metropolitan Police, for example, established a social media monitoring hub, in time for the London Olympics. A number of police forces in the UK and elsewhere are believed to be trialling various types of automated social media collection and analysis to collect information to help criminal investigations and gauge the 'temperature' of communities they are working with. The so-called Arab Spring, popular uprisings in 2010 and 2011 across North Africa, likewise have prompted many governments around the world to acquire the capability to collect and analyse information from digital social media including computerized sentiment analysis to help judge whether protests are likely to turn violent.

There is a debate to be had in due course by the historians whether the demands for intelligence on people were the primary driver encouraging intelligence agencies to become ever more ingenious in finding ways of accessing digital personal data (something that the Snowden material certainly demonstrates); or whether it has simply been the potential for supply of such everyday information, driven by the universal need to drive down costs by digitizing business processes and the private sector's ability to monetize our personal data, for marketing purposes, that has created its own demand from law enforcement and intelligence agencies. Certainly the customers for intelligence and their targets around the world must now be aware that their agencies may be able to answer complex questions that previously would have been regarded as hopelessly intractable.

The truth is probably both that demand calls forth supply, and that availability of supply stimulates new demands. It must be expected that supply and demand will continue to interact dynamically as new applications and devices arrive. We must also expect the barriers to entry into this international intelligence market to fall as its value is recognized and the understanding of how to go about some exploits, such as at least the simpler forms of social media monitoring, become commonplace globally, including unfortunately in those countries that are pre-occupied with monitoring their population for signs of violent opposition to the regime.

The Democratic Constraints of Ethics and Law

At this point the third set of challenges for the world of secret intelligence in the democracies becomes very apparent. In addition to the dynamic interaction described between the new demands for secret intelligence, and the new digital means of supplying them (and in the process the creation of new demands that previously it would not have been feasible to meet), there is a growing issue over public acceptability of the methods of digital intelligence given their power for abuse in the wrong hands..

Once these powerful tools started to be used for the purposes of public safety and protection of the domestic population it was inevitable that, for example through the prosecution of criminals, public awareness would increase. Investigative journalism had already focused over the years on the work of the US National Security Agency and exposed some key tools. The Snowden revelations took this process many steps further forward, with details being published of a range of major digital intelligence programmes.

Security and intelligence authorities have always had to face moral hazard as an inevitable consequence of seeking secret intelligence. At its most fundamental, intelligence helps to improve the quality of decision- making, whether by police officers, military commanders or policy makers, by reducing ignorance about the threats that face us. It is a legitimate function of government. Obstinately, however, there remains vital information that the enemies of a free society - the dictators, terrorists, insurgents, cyber- and narco-criminal gangs and others - do their best to prevent the authorities from knowing. It is the purpose of *secret* intelligence to overcome the will of these others and to supply to police officers, military commanders, and policymakers at least an insight into the threats they pose so that they can detect and where possible prevent these threats and when necessary acquire evidence to put before a Court. To overcome the will of that other inevitably risks moral hazard.

If human sources are recruited then they and their families and friends may be placed at risk. If technical means are used then there will not only be calculated intrusion into the privacy of the suspect but potentially also collateral intrusion into innocent family members or innocent contacts of the individuals under suspicion. Another example of the moral hazard is the risk that there will be collateral invasion of the privacy of those not under investigation but whose communications have to be intercepted and filtered to find those of the suspects. All detection of serious crime will involve examination of the innocent in order to eliminate them from the investigation, and that inevitably involves intrusion upon their privacy, at least for a time. Such risks should of course be minimised by intelligence processes and procedures but if no such risks can be run then secret intelligence will never be obtained and the security of society placed at risk.

As some of the documents stolen by Edward Snowden and now published reveal, the very existence of Internet and cyber technology has created powerful new opportunities to acquire intelligence on legitimate targets (including providing locational data, other metadata and social media intelligence). In parallel, as this chapter has outlined, in the private sector a comparable interaction between new information demands and new means of supply is taking place, creating commercial benefit from 'big data' knowledge about potential customers.

If - and it is a risk – nations are over-zealous in response to Edward Snowden in constraining digital intelligence gathering capability and data sharing then the interests of the public will be failed since governments will not be able to manage the risks from terrorism, cybercrime and other criminality, nor will they have the intelligence on which sound policy decisions can be made.

If on the other hand nations fail to be seen internationally to exercise sufficient restraint on the use of the powerful digital tools in the hands of their intelligence agencies then the resulting unease on the part of a vocal section of national publics and in such bodies as the European Parliament will destabilize the very intelligence communities whose work is essential in the collective interest to manage 21st century risks.

The approach taken by the British government to these matters since the 1980's provides an example of how considerations such as those held by the European Court of Human Rights can be used to set up a sound legal framework within which all security and intelligence operations can be constrained so as to be compatible with the European convention on human rights (ECHR). The UK intelligence community has thus been able, with GCHQ in the lead, to adapt its methods to modern digital technology to enable new forms of intelligence gathering in ways that respect human rights.

This third challenge, of behaving ethically and lawfully faces not just the agencies in the democracies but their governments and societies. Matters must be so arranged in order that the agencies can legally obtain the intelligence to meet the legitimate demands of law enforcement, the armed forces and government, whilst behaving ethically in accordance with fundamental principles of international human rights adopted by the General Assembly of the United Nations on 12 December 1948, including the right to life, liberty and security of person (Article 3) as well as protection from arbitrary interference with privacy, family, home or correspondence (Article 12).

In the exercise of individual rights and freedoms, the Universal Declaration of Human Rights recognises that there are circumstances where nations may limit privacy. The Declaration states that such rights shall be subject only to such limitations as are determined by law solely for the purpose of securing due recognition and respect for the rights and freedoms of others and of meeting the just requirements of morality, public order and the general welfare in a democratic society (Article 29). In the case of the UK and other EU member states the agencies must also behave in accordance with the equivalent provisions of the European Convention of Human Rights and the rights enshrined in the Treaty of European Union. Thus in the later (1953) formulation of the European Convention on Human Rights, it is stated that 'Everyone has the right to respect for his private and family life, his home and his correspondence. There shall be no interference by a public authority with the exercise of this right except such as is in accordance with the law and is necessary in a democratic society in the interests of national security, public safety or the economic wellbeing of the country, for the prevention of disorder or crime, for the protection of health or morals, or for the protection of the rights and freedoms of others'. Furthermore, not only must all these standards be secured in reality but they must be clearly seen to be secured in the eyes of the public if confidence is to be maintained. The UK incorporated the ECHR into domestic law in the Human Rights Act 1998, so these provisions very directly bind all UK security, intelligence and law enforcement activity without exception.

Thus the domestic legal framework of regulation and oversight within which intelligence activity has to be conducted will – and should - inevitably constrain the free interplay of demand for and potential supply of intelligence, not least derived from digital sources. That constraint also inevitably involves the public avowal of intelligence activity, and the according of legal status to the agencies that collect and analyse secret intelligence, as well as the provision of at least enough information outside the secret circles of agency activity to enable confidence in their activity to be justified publicly. It is not enough, as is the case in the UK today, for the insiders to be confident that there are very effective safeguards. It is also essential for the democracies that the interaction between demand and supply for digital information is *seen* to be regulated effectively by applying safeguards that are recognized will give assurance of ethical behaviour, in accordance with modern views of human rights, including respect for personal privacy in accordance with Article 8 of the European Convention or its equivalent.

There is a compelling precedent in the 'just war' thinking that has led over a long period to the codification of the principles that should govern armed violence. *Jus ad bellum* sets down the necessary conditions for entry into armed conflict to be justified and *jus in bello* governs the use of violence in conflict. The well known principles of necessity and proportionality and limiting collateral damage have emerged from this tradition. These principles, recognising the just application of force to protect the innocent and the interests of society from those who would do them damage, can be translated into comparable *jus in intelligentiam* to govern the purposes for which allows intelligence agencies to operate and invest in powerful and intrusive capabilities and *jus in intelligentio* to govern their authorisation and use in specific circumstances. The author has derived six principles of just intelligence from this approach (Omand, 2010). In brief, as applied to digital intelligence these are:

1. There must be sufficient sustainable cause.

There needs to be a check on any tendency for the secret world to expand into areas unjustified by the scale of potential harm to national interests, so the purposes of intelligence should be limited by statute. It is not an authorized purpose for the NSA or GCHQ for example to collect information to afford a competitive advantage to companies and business sectors.

2. There must be integrity of motive.

Integrity is needed throughout the whole system, from collection through to the analysis, assessment and use of the resulting intelligence.

3. The methods to be used must be proportionate.

The likely impact and intrusion into privacy of the proposed intelligence collection operation, taking account of the methods to be used, must be in proportion to the harm that it is sought to prevent.

4. There must be right authority.

There must be a sufficiently senior authorisation of intrusive operations and accountability up a recognised chain of command to permit effective oversight. Right authority too has to be lawful.

5. There must be reasonable prospect of success.

Even if the purpose is valid (guideline 1) and the methods to be used are proportionate to the issue (guideline 3) there needs to be discrimination and selectivity (no fishing expeditions) with a hard-headed assessment of risk of collateral intrusion on others.

6. Recourse to secret intelligence collection should not be used if there are open sources that can provide the information sought.

Bringing all these perspectives together can provide the basis for an ethically defensible position:

- The security and intelligence authorities are charged with the protection of the public. They have a duty to seek and use information, including digital intelligence, to help manage threats to public and national security.
- Secret intelligence, because it involves overcoming the efforts of others to prevent acquire it, inevitably involves running moral hazard such as intrusion upon privacy.
- Society can nevertheless constrain intelligence activity by an ethical code that is based on well understood and tested principles and that respects the right to privacy.
- The effectiveness of secret intelligence rests on sources and methods that must remain hidden otherwise the targets know how to avoid detection. Oversight has therefore to be by proxy: by senior judges and Parliamentarians who can on society's behalf be trusted to enter the 'ring of secrecy' and to give confidence that these ethical standards are being maintained.

Manifesting such principles and demonstrating that the intelligence agencies abide by them will go a long way to meet the challenge that intelligence agencies in the democracies are also to be *seen* to behave consistently in ways that the public will consider ethically sound.

Assessing the Damage Done by Edward Snowden's Actions

The newspapers and media outlets responsible for disseminating Snowden's material have naturally wished to emphasise the care with which they have screened published material to minimise the risk of harm to national security as they see it and to the individuals involved, for example by redacting the names of intelligence officers from the material. Evidence to the House of Commons by the heads of the UK intelligence agencies, supporting comment by informed insiders in the US, has emphasised that intelligence gathering has already been affected adversely. It is not possible from information released publicly to provide a full assessment of damage, but some observations are possible including the effect that the publication of these documents may have on the political and social context within which intelligence agencies are situated.

The first and most obvious problem is the general increase in awareness of the likely targets for warranted surveillance by the authorities of how their communications may be used to identify and locate them and identify their associates. Whilst mention of individual techniques can be found in the cyber security literature, and at times even in popular fiction, it is the cumulative impact of so many stories on the front pages that will cause the terrorists and criminals (and others) to sit up and take notice. Of course, all law enforcement and intelligence work around the world will find it harder and will lose from the Snowden revelations, even the Russians who are harbouring Edward Snowden and no doubt counting upon making the most in propaganda terms of his revelations about the US.

A further level of difficulty arises from the publicity attached to certain techniques, including those of network attack, close access and hardware implants. It is clear that exposure of US and UK successes in the Snowden material adds specific point to the general increase in awareness by friend and potential adversary alike of the nature of modern intelligence activity, including awareness of the steps they can take to reduce the chances of being intercepted.

It is, however, likely to be the international and commercial pressures arising from the revelations that may turn out to be more important in the long term. The public debate that arose after the publication of the Snowden material has highlighted the relationship between governments, their publics and other Internet stakeholders. The manner in which intelligence agencies access digital information on their legitimate targets often requires cooperation from the communications and Internet industry. This is often framed by civil liberties lobbies in terms of commercial organisations failing to safeguard their users' private information and thus 'betraying' their users to governments. This is a problem for intelligence agencies as it produces pressure on the communications and Internet industry not to cooperate with Western governments for fear that their commercial reputation in other markets will suffer. Interception of warranted material that might have been available previously may not be possible for much longer without active industry cooperation, as the Director of GCHQ, Robert Hannigan observed in the Financial Times on 13 November 2014.

The Internet companies are now at pains to distance themselves from any perception of cooperating with government and are investing heavily in strong encryption to shut out interception, whether by criminals or the NSA. The advanced techniques revealed in the Snowden material have also triggered an intelligence arms race as beneath the surface nations large and small recognize they have a capability gap in comparison with the US and seek in private to close it, as well more publicly advocating stronger defences for their own national systems and the personal information of their own citizens.

Preserving the multi-stakeholder character of the Internet is therefore doubly important, in no small part because some stakeholders have the ability to seriously reduce the ability of intelligence agencies to function. As a result of the Snowden revelations, there is huge pressure to introduce end-to-end hard encryption in all major communications bearers and between the major Internet service providers. Such developments will make it harder to achieve the kind of bulk access needed to locate the communications being sought and will drive intelligence agencies to seek access closer to their targets, producing it is claimed a more discriminating approach, but also one that is potentially more intrusive on the suspect and those around him.

Living with Multi-Layered Security Activity on the Internet

The Snowden revelations reveal security interactions between three levels of human activity that take place on the Internet: at the top level our everyday social and economic transactions; at the second level below, the work of law enforcement to ensure that we can live our digital lives safely at the top level; and far beneath, the secret world of intelligence agencies. Managing the challenges of global digital intelligence in the future will depend upon a better understanding of what has to be achieved at each level if nations are to realise the economic and social benefits of the Internet whilst maintaining public safety and security in ways consistent with democratic values and human rights.

The Security of Everyday Activity

The first top layer is where our everyday activity on the Internet takes place. Communicating, sharing, entertaining, and trading. Retaining confidence in the Internet and its financial systems and transactions is fundamental for global economic well-being. This was recognized by the OECD in 2011 when it published a recommended set of principles for Internet policy making, including promoting and protecting the global free flow of information; promoting the open, distributed and interconnected nature of the Internet; promoting investment and competition in high-speed networks and services; and promoting and enabling the cross-border delivery of services.

Nations such as the UK have realized the importance of confidence in the Internet and are devoting considerable resources to improving cyber security. We do need very secure encryption in everyday communications to protect our private information and financial transactions and defeat the global cyber criminals. It has nevertheless been alleged as part of the Snowden revelations although denied by the authorities that measures taken to help NSA and GCHQ acquire access to digital data have themselves weakened the Internet (Jackson, 2013). When flaws are detected in software systems (as they are all the time, given the staggering complexity of modern software and the interactions of applications, operating systems and communications) there is a potential tension with (as inferred from some of the Snowden material) the value to intelligence agencies of exploiting such flaws and exploits. The US White House has however made clear that when it is a choice of keeping a vulnerability for future covert use or disclosing it to bolster cyber defence, and it is a close call, the defence should always win. This is for the sound military reasoning that a defence being breached is much more serious than losing the hypothetical value of a future tool.

The principal threat to Internet confidence in fact comes from the rapid increase being seen in malware on the Internet designed for the most part for criminal gain. Cyber-crime of all types is the most rapidly growing form of crime. Some of this crime exploits the characteristics of software directly. Some could be characterized as simply traditional forms of crime (theft for example) that can be perpetrated digitally at much lower risk than old-fashioned analogues such as robbing banks. Some traditional illegal trading made possible at scale by the existence of the 'dark net' component of the Internet (such as Silk Road and similar illegal marketplaces selling drugs and counterfeit items, accessible only by using anonymising software such as Tor). The scale of Internet criminal enterprise itself spawns criminal marketplaces for false identities, credit card details and malware exploits that can be used for criminal purposes. The increasing dependence on the Internet of everyday life, and of the critical national infrastructure on which we rely, introduces new vulnerabilities into society. Even where systems are air-gapped from the Internet, such as the control systems for nuclear plants, the potential exists for breaches of such security through the access required for visiting contractors or the staff of the facility themselves.

Everyday Internet use is also the level at which Data Protection legislation, both national and international (for example the European Union Data Protection Directives embodied in UK law in the Data Protection Act 1998), kicks in to protect our personal data from unlawful use. Such data protection is based on identifying and protecting personal (as against other data) by insisting upon the consent of the subject, and under the latest proposals giving the subject the 'right to be forgotten' and thus the legal power to compel the deletion of personal data.

As noted earlier, the Internet is neutral and carries both legitimate and illegitimate traffic round the packet-switched global networks. Criminals of all types use the same range of mobile devices and applications as everyone else. Sitting below the everyday level therefore is a layer of law enforcement activity, police, customs, immigration, and other enforcement authorities attempting to control the worst excesses of criminality and to uphold the law.

The Law Enforcement Layer and Its Problems

In most jurisdiction law enforcement has the right to seek warrants to obtain the communications of suspects, terrorists and criminals of all sorts and information about their activities such as laundering criminal gains. As explained in this chapter in the context of the demand for intelligence, much of the required information to pursue criminal suspects (and to eliminate the innocent from police enquiries) now comes from digital sources, under conditions that society legislates for and oversees. There is inevitable tension between these two levels: the privacy needed for healthy everyday life and the intrusions that law enforcement must impose to uphold the law, but it is not an irresolvable conflict between them since, as discussed earlier in the chapter, security and the protection of rights go together in a democracy.

At the law enforcement level, there is regulated international cooperation, for example through advance passenger information and watch list data exchanges and liaison through Interpol and Europol. Such exchanges recognize the international nature of organized criminal activity on the Internet. Major Internet service providers will normally respond to lawful requests from law enforcement to remove material that encourages terrorism or serious criminality such as child abuse. But there are growing and serious problems for law enforcement in the digital era. Examples from the UK perspective include:

- The rapidity of the growth of crime on the Internet is running well ahead of the number of trained cyber capable police officers
- The tools or exploits for cyber-crime can be bought from hacking specialists so those conducting cyber-crime do not need any longer to be software hackers themselves.
- The most serious cyber criminals are based in jurisdictions overseas where Mutual Legal Assistance requests and European arrest warrants may not be respected.
- The advent of digital technology is making the task for law enforcers of obtaining communications data and warranted communications much harder. Even where they wish to cooperate, the traditional telecomms and cable companies are increasingly physically unable to respond to legal warrants and provide the information to which the authorities are legally entitled since they have no business need to collect or retain information about their customers' use of digital services that are free at the point of use and are covered by the flat rate subscription.
- Many of the modern Internet Service Providers (ISPs) that do have the data are located overseas and may be subject to conflicting requirements from different legal jurisdictions.
- Another area of difficulty is gaining access to encrypted material on suspects' computers and mobile devices on which vital evidence may lie, for example in prosecuting members of paedophile networks. Mobile device software is becoming so secure that the manufacturers cannot unlock mobile devices protected with a full password.

Increasingly therefore the police have looked to the intelligence community for support in tackling terrorism and serious crime, by looking to a third layer of security activity on the Internet which is the work of national intelligence agencies.

The Intelligence Layer and Its Problems

Police and intelligence services have not always been ready to cooperate with each other. But several legislatures have made express provision to allow intelligence agencies to assist law enforcement, including to try to overcome the problems of access to Internet communications data (in the case of the UK, the 1989 Security Service Act and the 1994 Intelligence Services Act make the detection and prevention of serious crime a legitimate function for the security and intelligence agencies).

There is, therefore, a third layer of activity beneath that is able to support law enforcement, and thus help uphold the law and ensure the security of the public, which is the work of national intelligence agencies, something as noted above for which the UK Parliament made express provision in legislating for the intelligence and security agencies. The main role for these agencies is on national security issues, such as supporting the armed forces and diplomacy and most recently uncovering State sponsored cyber-attacks, but they do have an important and legitimate role helping law enforcement and one that is increasingly important in the digital age.

Unlike the law enforcement level international intelligence cooperation is mostly bilateral and episodic, based on perceptions of mutual advantage at the time, with the notable exceptions of the 5-eyes community, NATO members' cooperation on military intelligence to support its operations and the EU's sharing of strategic intelligence assessments to support collective actions.

There is no international law regulating espionage, and never will be since all nations engage in it but there is no agreed definition of what it is and few will admit fully to it. Traditionally, therefore, the intelligence level was hidden by nations, unavowed to their publics and largely nationally unregulated. In some European traditions individual intelligence services or security police services were the fiefdom of individual Ministers such as those of Defence or the Interior and used for political ends. Remarkably, the UK in advance of most European partners, decided over twenty years ago under Margaret Thatcher to legislate for the domestic Security Service, MI5, and then in 1994 under her successor John Major for the other UK intelligence agencies the Secret Intelligence Service, MI6, and GCHQ and impose on them the same basic regime for intrusive investigative activity as for law enforcement through RIPA 2000.

As already explained, UK intelligence activity, including in digital data access, is regulated by law. The Snowden revelations nevertheless came as a surprise to the general public (and the public seems similarly surprised at the extent to which the private sector is harvesting and monetizing their personal data). Government could have done more over the last few years to explain that meeting legitimate demands for digital intelligence for law enforcement, as well as for national security, is enabled by access to the Internet. And that whatever the scale of computerized access, the human analyst is only is allowed to see what legal authority allows her or him to see.

Sometimes it is the intentions of some within a friendly state that are the subject of the requirements for intelligence. One of the striking aspects of the post 9/11 world is the rapid expansion of intelligence liaison relationships to enable terrorist cases to be pursued cooperatively. Not even the United States can meet its intelligence requirements for national security on its own. But it must be recognized that, just occasionally, such cooperation may not be forthcoming or not adequate to the situation. There is also the phenomenon of what has been called 'frenemies' (a word that has now reached the Oxford English Dictionary) with whom friendly relations may be maintained despite fierce rivalries.

For some nations, their wish now to nationalize their Internet clouds risks distracting from their own economic and social needs for an open Internet and an effective law enforcement level. Such thinking encourages those authoritarian nations that wish to fragment the Internet so as to facilitate censorship and social control. Requirements on how data is routed on the Internet are also often proposed in the name of improving security. Their implementation can have the effect of establishing cartels or reinforcing market power in the international trade of communication services.

After the criticism of the US for apparently intercepting the mobile phone of German Chancellor Angela Merkel, President Obama gave a classic response: 'I have made clear to the intelligence community that unless there is a compelling national security purpose, we will not monitor the communications of heads of state and government of our close friends and allies' (White House, 2014B). That is as much as governments overseas can expect. Attempts to negotiate standing bilateral or multilateral 'no spy' agreements in the abstract with no national security get-out clauses are bound to fail.

The best that can be hoped for by way of an international norm for the authorization of intelligence activity is that, in the democracies but not alas elsewhere, processes should be in place to ensure that the requisite legal authority (in accordance with the national legal framework governing the agency and its activity) is secured, and that the wider domestic and political implications are properly considered. Ethics come into play here, as do strategic considerations. Not everything that might be legally justifiable may be sensible in terms of progress towards long-term goals. The potential impact on international and domestic public opinion should operations go wrong or be exposed provides some check on rash decisions or failure of the intelligence agencies to seek up to date authorisation. That political factor will be more influential if the politician most responsible for the conduct of a nations's external relations is in the decision loop. In the case of the United Kingdom the British Foreign Secretary has personally to sign off on all sensitive overseas operations, and the Home Secretary likewise on intrusive domestic operations, a system that exposes the work of the secret agencies to a high degree of political understanding and scrutiny. It will also help if there are time limits placed on Ministerial authorisations of intelligence operations forcing agencies to re-seek and re-justify approval. A former US Director of Central Intelligence, Stansfield Turner, coined a test for those authorizing intelligence decisions, in effect do not authorize an operation if, were it to become public knowledge, you would be ashamed to stand up and defend it. That captures the essence of the political risk decision that ought in a well-regulated intelligence community always to accompany the necessary legal and regulatory considerations.

CONCLUSION

Like some elementary experiment in mechanics the three forces described in this chapter – of demand for actionable intelligence, of the supply of digital data to meet those demands, and of public attitudes to the methods used – will act on a national intelligence community in different ways in each country; the path through the digital future for intelligence will depend upon their resultant.

The threats outlined amply justify putting powerful digital tools in the hands of our intelligence community, not least to support law enforcement. The issue for current inquiries is less the powerful tools themselves but how the public can be reassured that under any future government those tools will only be used in lawful ways - as is undoubtedly the case today - that do not infringe beyond reasonable necessity our right to privacy for personal and family life.

REFERENCES

Aid, M. (2012). *The Secret Sentry*. London: Bloomsbury.

Aldrich, R. (2006). *GCHQ*. London: Heinemann.

Bamford, J. (1983). *The Puzzle Palace*. London: Penguin Books.

Harding, L. (2014). *The Snowden Files*. London: Faber and Faber.

Hathaway, M. (2014). Connected Choices: How the Internet is Changing Sovereign Decisions. *American Foreign Policy Interests*, *36*(5), 300–313. doi:10.1080/10803920.2014.969178

ISC. (2013). *Intelligence and Security Committee*. Inquiry into Huawei.

ISC. (2014). Intelligence and Security Committee, Report on the Intelligence Relating to the Murder of Fusilier Lee Rigby.

Jackson, J. (2013). NIST Denies Tampering with Encryption Standards. *PCWorld*, *10*(Sept), 13.

Omand, D. (2010). *Securing the State, London*. Hurst, New York: Oxford University Press.

Omand, D., Bartlett, J., & Miller, C. (2012). Introducing Social Media Intelligence (SOCMINT). *Intelligence and National Security*, *27*(6), 801–823. doi:10.1080/02684527.2012.716965

RIPA. (2000). Regulation of Investigative Powers Act.

Robbins, O. (2013, August 27). Cabinet Office witness statement of Oliver Robbins to the High Court.

White House. (2014A, January 17). PPD-28, Presidential Policy Directive.

White House. (2014B, January 17). President Obama's speech at the Department of Justice.

KEY TERMS AND DEFINITIONS

Digital: This describes electronic technology that generates, stores and processes data in terms of two states, zero and one, as compared with the earlier analogue technology.

Intelligence Ethics: A social, religious, or civil code of behaviour considered correct, in relation to the activity of secret intelligence agencies and the use made of intelligence by their customers.

Intelligence Governance: This covers the establishment of policies, and continuous monitoring of their proper implementation, to regulate secret intelligence activity by a combination of executive, judicial and Parliamentary bodies.

Internet: This describes the network of communications networks that carries global digital communications and operates to common protocols.

Law Enforcement: This is the organized upholding of the law, including the detection and prevention of crime, by national and local police, revenue and customs, border and other state agencies.

Privacy: The freedom from unauthorized intrusion into private behavior and unauthorized access to personal information.

Secret Intelligence: This is information acquired by intelligence agencies where the holder of the information does not wish it to be obtained, and the acquiring agency does not usually want it revealed that it has access to it or how that access was achieved.

Snowden: Edward Snowden was a US contractor working for the National Security Agency responsible for leaking to journalists large numbers of top secret documents describing the sources and methods of digital intelligence gathering.

Chapter 7
Surveillance and Resistance:
Online Radicalization and the Political Response

David Martin Jones
University of Queensland, Australia

ABSTRACT

This chapter provides readers with an overview and discussion of the manner in which the Internet and social media has facilitated movements, ranging from Aryan Nations and the various European Defence Leagues, to the Global Jihadist Movement and anarchist groups. As the phenomenon of netwar and online recruitment evolved after 9/11, extremist movements motivated by illiberal and apocalyptic ideologies have found the Internet a congenial space for organization, dissemination, education and radicalization. This chapter examines the difficulty liberal political democracies have in censoring these groups and the ideas they promote. Civil rights organizations immediately condemn state electronic surveillance as an invasion of civil liberties, and present the liberal democrat with an acute moral and political dilemma. This chapter finally considers the tactics democratic states might prudently adopt in order to preserve the national interest.

DOI: 10.4018/978-1-4666-9661-7.ch007

INTRODUCTION

The security of a nation relies not only on officials who maintain the physical protection of assets, but also on the ways in which personnel protect the nation from harmful mindsets that seek to cause havoc or destruction. Voegelin, the Austrian philosopher who fled the Third Reich in the wake of the *Anschluss* (1938) argued that the ideological fanaticism of the Nazis was not only a moral and political mistake, but also a spiritual perversion. More precisely, so far as the political religions of the twentieth century, fascism, Stalinism, Maoism and more recently the Salafism of the Global Jihadist Movement (GJM) are concerned, the meaning or substance of religious phenomena moved from a spiritual concern with transcending the mundane world towards the realisation of imaginary fantasies of immanent apocalypse and the fashioning of this worldly utopias. These fantasies, as Barry Cooper observes, are not "always recognized for what they are because the image of an earthly condition of perfected humanity" was, in Europe, before 1990, expressed in scientific, or, more accurately, "scientistic" language (1999, p.4). This was not, of course, the case with revolutionary Islamic thought, but it remains the case with other ideological social movements of both left and right that have evolved since 9/11, whose animating political religions focus upon the renunciation of God. This is the case with both race based and anti-capitalist social movements, which, like al-Qaeda also pursue, what Ernest Sternberg terms, "world purificationism" (2010, p.64). We will briefly discuss the commonalities between these evolving political religions and Islamism before examining the western state response and its implications both for future war and the future of western, secular, liberal democracy.

BACKGROUND

The Extremist Right After 9/11: Cultural Nationalism and Political Activism

As Emilio Gentile, following both Hannah Arendt and Eric Voegelin argues, totalitarian ideologies, whether of a Marxist-Leninist or a national socialist provenance, attribute 'sacred status to an earthly concept' whether that concept is the race, the nation, the proletariat or, in more recent green left thought, the planet itself (2000, pp.18-19). This sacralisation of the political provides the space for an apocalyptic clash between the world waiting to be born and the doomed quotidian order that resists it. Such an ideological perspective, as Hannah Arendt classically explained, reveals a decadent past about to perish, a present that reveals the opportunity for radical change and the potential for realizing an ideal future (1951, pp. 472-479). Those who possess the ideological key to history, moreover, accept the necessity of violence to bring about the new order. In fact, the politically religious mind considers violence both clarifying and purifying. This is a view embraced by all modern revolutionary creeds whatever their nationalist, fascist, Marxist-Leninist, Maoist or Islamist provenance, since the nineteenth century.

The concept of three ages that informs such politically religious thought: a corrupt past, the divided present, and the purified third age waiting to be born, ultimately revives, in a modern guise, a tradition of hermetic and gnostic speculation that dates from the millenial speculations of Cistercian monks like Joachim of Fiora (1145-1202) and subsequently elaborated in the chiliastic practice of Anabaptist and radical sectarian "saints" in sixteenth and seventeenth century Europe who sought to realize the ideal of the age of perfection (Voegelin, 1974, p.268 & Cohn, 1969). An analogous process of perfectionism and purification occurred in the salafist and Wahabbist interpretations of Islam in the course of the nineteenth century that culminated in Sayyid Qutb's apocalyptic politically religious reinterpretation of the message that Mohammad had received in seventh century Mecca.

In contrast to religiously focused ideologies, race based ones emphasise the *palingenesis* or rebirth of the nation or race through a purgative process of ethnic cleansing. Classically exemplified in Third Reich ideology and practice, Roger Griffin contends that all fascist ideology shares the sense of living at an imminent turning point in contemporary history when the dominance of the allegedly bankrupt forces of conservatism, individualistic liberalism and materialist socialism finally give way to a new era where an activist nationalism triumphantly reasserts itself (1991, p.32). From this perspective violence is necessary to overcome national degeneracy and eliminate parasitical elites who have betrayed the nation and aborted its rebirth. This apocalyptic nationalist vision informs the white supremacist thought that has exercised an extremist, but minority presence in western democracies since the early days of the Cold War, the era of European decolonization and the US fear of international communism. Post 9/11, racist or fascist ideology, that social scientists and historians once treated as an aberrant moment in European history, has proved both resilient and increasingly attractive to an alienated, working class, white demographic in both Europe and the USA. This has been particularly evident as the period of post war social democratic consensus in the west gave way to an era of speculative millennial capital. In this context, extremist ideologies appeal to a new, emerging class, the precariat, in low paid, semi-skilled work on short term contracts. This class emerged with the decline of traditional, blue-collar industries as multinational corporations moved offshore and reshaped the global economy after 1990. This new class in developed western democracies, existing somewhere between welfare dependency and unskilled employment, became more conspicuous as the western financial crisis deepened after 2008. As unemployment levels, especially amongst young, male worker in Europe and the US reached historic highs, the white precariat class offered a fertile breeding ground for right wing extremism (Standing, 2011, pp. 1-5).

Networks, movements and parties committed to this white nationalist or white supremacist ideology hold that the cosmopolitan, liberal, ruling elites have abandoned their national cultures and the white race in favour of international or regional arrangements like the United Nations or the European Union. At the same time, this transnational business and political elite exploit supranational and state bureaucracies, constitutions and courts to exercise a tyranny over once free peoples.

In the US, this alienation took the form of movements like the Ku Klux Klan (KKK), whose origins date from the era of reconstruction in the Southern United States after 1865, but whose clan organizational structure revived in the 1960s to oppose the movement for civil rights. KKK members often shared links with the Aryan Nations Church of Jesus Christ Christian that felt that the government "no longer represents the White Race in this Nation" ("Church of Jesus Christ," n.d.). RAND Corporation described the Aryan Nations churches of the 1990s as 'the first truly nationwide terrorist organization' in the United States (START University of Maryland, 2008) The 1960s also witnessed, the foundation of Lincoln Rockwell's American Nazi Party. After Rockwell's assassination in 1967, the party mutated into the National Socialist White People's Party, before settling on its current title, the National Alliance in 1974.

Alongside such clearly racist groups there emerged in the 1980s various state based militia movements associated with the right wing Posse Comitatus that saw attempts to restrict gun ownership and the imposition of federal law at the expense of state rights as part of an international conspiracy against the values of the American Revolution. Prior to 9/11, a visceral anti-Semitism characterized these movements. Indeed, they termed the tyranny they confronted the Zionist Occupied Government (ZOG). It was the role of the various state militias to resist this creeping federally imposed, Zionist, tyranny. Militias adopted both a libertarian and a Christian, white, fundamentalist rhetoric and were prepared to organize and train for the prospect of an imminent racial Armageddon. National Alliance leader, William Luther Pierce outlined the terms of a future apocalyptic race war in his fiction, *The Turner Diaries* (1978). Set in 2099, the Diaries recount Earl Turner's guerilla insurgency to overthrow the US federal government and wage a brutal race war to exterminate inferior races first in America and subsequently globally. In 1993, the Southern Poverty Law Center described it as "the bible of the racist right" (Macdonald, 1978). The work inspired Robert Jay Mathews to form The Order or Silent Brotherhood, which undertook a series of robberies and bombings between 1983-4 culminating in the murder of talk show host Alan Berg. Mathews died in a shootout with the FBI in December 1984. Somewhat later, Pierce wrote *Hunter* (1989) that provided a fictional account of a developing terrorist character, the lone wolf, Oscar Yeager.

The toxic mixture of parochialism and paranoia that informed US Right Wing Extremism (RWE) ensured that white supremacist and militia groups interpreted the FBIs siege of Christian Identity survivalist Randy Weaver and his family's farm at Ruby Ridge, North Idaho in 1992, followed by the siege of David Korresh's Branch Dravidian compound in Waco, Texas between February and April 1993 which culminated in the death of 76 sect members, as further proof of ZOG's tyranny. To counter it, white supremacy activists, maintained, demanded a strategy of leaderless resistance and lone wolf attacks on federal agencies.

By the mid-1980s, Louis Beam, a former Vietnam veteran, had emerged as the leading strategic thinker of US RWE. He served as both a state leader of David Duke's Knights of the Ku Klux Klan and as the Aryan Nations Ambassador at Large. His thinking influenced the formation of The Order and the acts of lone wolf terrorists, like Timothy McVeigh, a veteran of the first Iraq war. It was Beam who linked these asymmetric actors to a wider terror strategy. Beam considered his "concept of leaderless resistance a fundamental departure in theories of organization" (1995, pp. 5-15). It was based upon the guerrilla cell organization:

...but does not have any central control or direction... Utilizing the Leaderless Resistance concept, all individuals and groups operate independently of each other, and never report to a central headquarters or single leader for direction or instruction, as would those who belong to a typical pyramid organization. (Beam, 1995, pp. 5-15)

Such thinking inspired Timothy McVeigh to bomb the Alfred. P. Murrah Federal Building in Oklahoma City in 1995. McVeigh's bomb claimed 165 lives. It was the most serious terrorist attack on US soil prior to 9/11. McVeigh and his accomplices sympathized with the militia and patriot movements, but acted outside any formal structure. Police found pages from *The Turner Diaries* amongst McVeigh's effects.

In the course of the 1990s websites like stormfront.org promulgated the ideology, racist mythology, and the strategic thinking of the US white right to an international audience. Started by Klan leader, David Duke in 1990, by 2000 it was the most visited hate site on the Internet. Significantly, the internet serves as a vital medium not only for promulgating leaderless jihad, it has also facilitated the post 9/11 proliferation of white supremacist ideas and the phantom cell structure of leaderless resistance both in the US and across Europe and Australia.

Although identity and race based nationalism never died out in Western Europe after 1945, right wing nationalist and neo-fascist social movements have attracted growing popular support in both the UK and Western Europe since the mid-1990s. Thus Germany, Austria and Italy, states that experienced fascist, totalitarian regimes between the 1920s and 1940s, have since the 1990s witnessed the reemergence of extreme nationalist political parties informed by racist myths of Aryan supremacy. Whilst the German *Strafgesetzbuch* (criminal code) forbids neo-Nazi material and the 'use of symbol of unconstitutional organizations' this has not prevented the emergence of the extreme right Nationalist Party (NPD) which captured 9.2% of the vote in the Saxony state elections in 2004. Attempts to ban the party have thus far failed. Meanwhile, Germany has also witnessed the emergence of an illegal neo Nazi movement, the National Socialist Underground (NSU), allegedly responsible for a number of unsolved assaults upon and murders of migrant workers and gay men since the mid-1990s (http://www.spiegel.de/international/topic/right_wing_extremism/).

The period from the end of the Cold War also saw growing electoral support for RWE political parties in Austria. In the 1999 general election the late Jorge Heider's Austrian Freedom Party (FPO) captured 27% of the vote and briefly shared government with the Conservative People's Party. Similarly in Italy, far right parties have never been absent from the political scene since the fall of Beneto Mussolini's Fascist regime in 1944. The neo fascist Italian Social Movement (MSI) dates from 1946. Constitutional change after 1995 saw the formation of parties openly nostalgic for a return to Mussolini era activist politics. These included the Northern Alliance (*Lega Nord per l'independenzia di Padania*) formed in 1991, the National Alliance formed in 1995, and the *Forca Nuova* or New Force party, which began in 1997. After 1995, these faction prone parties have periodically joined, formed alliances, and participated in coalition governments of the right with Silvio Berlusconi's *Forza Italia* and, after 2008, with Berlusconi's People of Freedom Party (*Il Popolo della Liberta*). Indeed, Mussolini's granddaughter, Alessandra, sits in the Italian parliament as a PdL representative, whilst Northern Alliance leader Gianfranco Fini served as President or Speaker of the Chamber of Deputies between 2008-2011.

Elsewhere in Europe, Jean Marie Le Pen's *Front National* (National Front) dates from 1972 and emerged from a number of militant right wing groups opposed to the decolonization of Algeria and the inauguration of the Fifth Republic (1958). Le Pen's party initially attracted former Poujadists, the Ordre Nouveau (ON), and alienated former servicemen with links to the right wing terror group the OAS (*Organisation de 'l'Armee Secret*) that attempted to assassinate President De Gaulle in 1965. Over time, however, Le Pen's anti- immigration and anti-European Union policies proved popular electorally. By the 1990s, the FN emerged as the third force in French politics and under the leadership of daughter, Marine le Pen, from 2012, the FN commanded more popular support than the two mainstream parties in French politics (http://blogs.telegraph.co.uk/news/douglascarswellmp/100242451/the-front-national-is-the-most-popular-party-in-france-are-you-happy-now-eurocrats/). Similarly in Greece, the anti –immigration, national socialist, Golden Dawn party has achieved growing political prominence as the European financial crisis devastated the Greek economy. In elections in 2012 Gold Dawn gained 7% of the popular vote and 21 parliamentary seats. The party has a violent paramilitary wing, the *stormarbeitung*, responsible for attacks on migrants and synagogues. It also has links with the French National Front, the Italian *Forca Nuova* and the German NDP.

In a similar vein, RWE political parties have achieved an electoral presence and political representation in Sweden, the Netherlands, Norway, Denmark and Finland. In the Netherlands anti-immigration parties, like Pim Fortuyn's List briefly shared government in 2002, whilst Geert Wilder's anti-Islamic and anti-immigration, Freedom Party commands 17% of the popular vote and, since elections in 2012, holds 18 parliamentary seats. Elsewhere, in Finland the True Finn party, like the FN in France, now has more popular support than mainstream parties according to polls conducted in December 2013.

Meanwhile, in the UK the British National Party (BNP), a party with links to the US National Alliance, whose policies have an affinity with the French National Front, also saw its electoral appeal improve during the 1990s. Formed in 1982 as the white extremist National Front party factionalised and declined, the BNP attracted alienated, young, white, working class voters, especially in areas of high Asian migration both in London and in Northern cities like Rochdale and Bradford. The aftermath of 9/11 and the London bombings of 2005 saw a further surge in support amongst the emerging white precariat class. Under the leadership of Nick Griffin the BNP won 6.2% of the vote and two seats in the European parliament elections in 2009. Although it formally eschews violence, the party's stance attracts a violent fringe. The neo-Nazi lone wolf, David Copeland, who carried out 3 nail bomb attacks in London in 1999, belonged to both the BNP and the National Socialist Movement. In 2009, the BNP joined the French National Front and the Hungarian extreme nationalist Jobbik party to form an Alliance of European National Movements (Hitchens & Brun, 2013, p.3).

All these parties share an ideology of ethnic nationalism and promote a political message of protectionism, hostility to mass migration and open borders. They all seek the dissolution of the EU and oppose the elitism and political disengagement that characterise the mainstream European conservative and social democrat political parties that support further European integration. RWE parties all support programmes of either repatriation or coercive integration for legal migrants from non-European, or Muslim backgrounds. The political credibility of these movements received a powerful boost from the European financial crisis after 2009 and the austerity measures unelected European Commissioners imposed upon national economies that created very high levels of unemployment across the Eurozone apart from Germany. This has further exacerbated the precariat class' consciousness of its political and economic marginalization.

Historically, as with the US white supremacist movements, these right wing parties share a visceral anti-Semitism that reflects their national socialist ideological origins. Jean Marie Le Pen, for example, is a holocaust denier and Zionism constituted the focus of both RWE conspiracy theories and political violence prior to 9/11. The more extreme elements of these movements also share a race mythology and a perception of oppression and national decadence that only violence and an apocalyptic race war can solve.

However, after 9/11, RWE thought increasingly substituted Islam for Zionism as the main protagonist in the Manichean struggle for race supremacy. Somewhat incoherently, in some versions of these racially extremist political religions, both Zionism and Islam represent the cancer incubated within the decaying national body politic that requires surgical removal. In fact, the growing appeal of right wing nationalist parties correlates directly with the emergence of leaderless jihadist resistance across Europe. Indeed, it was only as this threat became increasingly home grown after 9/11 that these extremist groups opportunistically targeted Islam, rather than Zionism, as the source of national decline. Interestingly, the Syrian born, but formerly European based, Spanish citizen and jihadist Abu Musab al Suri (aka Mustafa Nasar) promulgated a specific strategy of cultivating leaderless and lone wolf attacks across Europe after 2001 with the object of fomenting violent division within liberal, multicultural western cities.

Al Suri is the architect of the jihadists' post-9/11strategy and the author of the jihadist treatise, *Dawat al-Muqawamah al-Islamiyyah al-Alamiyyah* (*The Call to Global Islamic Resistance*), a 1,600-page tome published on the web in 2005. *The Call* proposes a strategy of decentralized jihad, rather than one that depends on clandestine hierarchical organization. Evidently influenced by Louis Beam and the thinking of US white supremacists, al Suri, who is sought by Spanish authorities for links to the Madrid bombings

(2004), proposed a wave of "individual jihad" in the West. The CIA arrested al-Suri in Pakistan in 2005 and handed him over to the Syrian authorities. He was released in 2012 and the whereabouts of what CNN termed 'the most important jihadist you have never heard of' are currently unknown (Samuels 2012, see also Hitchens, 2015 pp.250-75).Subsequently, Ayman al Awlaki of al Qaeda in the Arab Peninsula, an American born Yemeni salafist rendered the *Call* into a more palatable form for western consumption through his glossy online magazine *Inspire* (Hitchens, 2015). The social media strategy of al Suri and al Awlaki formed the basis for Islamic State's social media strategy after 2014 and proved extremely successful in its recruitment of foreign fighters and inspiring lone actor attacks (see Samuels, 2012).

After 9/11, therefore, the appeal of leaderless resistance and defence against leaderless jihadism directly influenced the ideology and strategic thinking of the violent fringes of European right wing extremism. It also facilitated the development within white RWE of a European counter jihad movement (ECJM) comprised of English, Dutch, Norwegian, Danish and Swedish Defence Leagues. After 2009, the leagues shared a commitment to an overarching nationalism combined with a willingness for street combat. Following the phantom cell structure, also advocated by al Suri for leaderless jihad, the ECJM 'is a loosely organized, decentralised network of sympathetic groups' (Hitchens & Brun, 2013, p.3). The internet plays a crucial role in maintaining this structure and facilitating a pan western network to Stop the Islamisation of Nations (SION) which links similarly minded groups in the US, Australia and New Zealand.

In this context, the English Defence League (EDL) has no formal membership, but evolved out of white Luton Town football supporters opposed to the recruitment activities of *al- Muhajiroun* in downtown Luton. The EDL founder Tommy Robinson (aka Stephen Yaxley-Lennon) had belonged to the BNP. At various street protests organized between 2009-13, Robinson argued that 'I am a hundred per cent certain that there will be civil wars within Europe between Muslims and non-Muslims'. This is a position Robinson shared with his fellows in the ECJM as well as with supporters from Islamophobic websites like Robert Spencer's *Jihad Watch* and Pamela Geller's *Atlas Shrugged*. As Alexander Mellagrou-Hitchens and Hans Brun explain in their study of the ECJM:

The ECJM's activism is inspired by an ideology which presents the current jihadist terrorist threat to the West as part of a centuries-long effort by Muslims to dominate Western civilisation. The ideology also insists on the existence of a conspiracy to "Islamise" Europe through the stealthy implementation of Islamic Sharia, and holds that many of Europe's Muslims are actively engaged in this conspiracy in various ways. The actions of Muslims in the West are viewed almost solely through this frame, and evidence of "Islamisation" is seen everywhere, in everything from the availability of halal meat in the West, to incidents of rape of non-Muslim Western women by Muslim men. The other main protagonists in this conspiracy, according to the Islamisation narrative, are found within a European liberal elite that refuses to resist the attack (Hitchens & Brun, pp. 3-4).

From this totalizing perspective, all European Muslims are engaged in an assault on European cultural identity and a campaign for European Islamization. Thus, Niccolai Sennels' influential blog, *The Gates of Vienna*, that takes its name from the Ottoman siege of 1683, contends that 'Islamization is a phenomenon that has existed since the Muslim prophet Mohammed lived 1,400 years ago'. As the website continues, 'we are now in a phase of a very old war'. In a similar vein, Bat Ye'or in *Eurabia* (2005) promoted an influential conspiracy theory that demonstrated how European political elites accommodated Middle Eastern states and Islamic leaders after the 1973 oil crisis facilitating both the Arab world's desire to eliminate Israel and mount a cultural conquest of Europe. Contemporary Muslim migrants to Europe, Bat Ye'or explains, represent the latest phase in a historical mission dating from the seventh century to eliminate Europe and subsume it into the greater caliphate. On the basis of such reasoning, the ECJM believes that Europe is on the brink of a civil war to be fought between indigenous Europeans and Muslim migrants. This is, the ECJM contends, the only logical outcome of the EU and the European political classes betrayal of national interests, witnessed in the increase in the Muslim population of Europe and the fact that Islam is a religion immune to reform and secularization.

In March 2012, the various defence leagues from Norway, Denmark, Sweden, Finland, Germany and the UK met in Copenhagen, where Mimosa Koiranen of the Finnish Defence League condemned the creeping Islamization of Europe and stated that 'sharia teaching should be an offence'. The EDL similarly considers Islam an existential threat to European national identities and responds with violent street demonstrations to examples of leaderless jihad in the UK. Thus when home grown jihadists Michael Adebolajo and Michael Adebowale murdered Lee Rigby in May 2013, the EDL and BNP organized protest marches in Woolwich and Whitehall. Elements connected to these groups were also responsible for a dramatic increase in attacks on Islamic Mosques and culture centres in the weeks following the murder (*Daily Telegraph* 23 May 2013; *The Independent* 28 May 2013).

Most emblematically, the case of Norwegian white supremacist and Norwegian Defence League member, Anders Breivik demonstrates the growing attraction of ideologically motivated lone wolves to leaderless and unpredictable violence. Breivik's July 2011 attack on Oslo and a youth league camp on the island of Utoya resulted in 77 deaths. Breivik later stated that the ostensible purpose of his killing spree was to draw attention to his rambling 1500 page compendium, *2083 A European Declaration of Independence*. The work alludes to the EDL and was published online under the pseudonym Andrew Berwick, Justiciar Knight Commander for Knights Templar Europe and the pan European Patriotic Resistance. The Knights Templar, of course, were a medieval, European crusading order (1129-1312). Breivik, like the ECJM more generally, presents his modern crusade in terms of a historic and religious civilizational clash (Berwick, 2013, pp.595-645). He thus presented his attack as an action in the patriotic insurgency against European Islamization, a civil war that, he believes, has already started in France and England. His worldview is Islamophobic, and anti-feminist, but interestingly supports far right Zionism. Breivick planned his attack over nine years and his actions were symptomatic of a determined and self-radicalised, lone wolf.

RWE leaderless resistance animated by white precariat insecurity and the fear of home grown Islamist violence represents a growing concern for European and US liberal democracies. Like al Qaeda, RWE inhabits a gnostic and apocalyptic worldview. The white racial account of world history anticipates a final conflict to resolve the divided and miscegenated present leading to *palingenesis* or the rebirth of a racially purified order. Like al Qaeda too, right wing extremism finds mainstream, secular, democratic politics corrupt, treacherous and tyrannical. In the European case, RWE exploits the weakness of the European Union and the alienation of an emerging western precariat. Here the EUs failure to deliver higher living standards, the economic recession it has caused by locking different European economies into a single currency, together with its open borders policy has fuelled the xenophobia upon which extremist politics thrives. Interestingly, like al Qaeda, white right extremists find the phantom cell organizational structure, and leaderless resistance that Louis Beam initially propounded and which Abu Musab al Suri and Ayman al Awlaki adapted and projected onto a global canvas, strategically appealing.

By a curious irony, a similarly apocalyptic political religion also informs the anti-capitalist movement of hard left, post democratic radicals like Anonymous and internet linked anarchist groups as well as extreme environmental activists like the Animal Liberation Front. It also informs the world view of more moderate, but globalization resistant, social movements for peace, justice and emancipation. We shall, therefore, briefly consider what Bernard-Henri Levy termed, the new barbarism of the anti-capitalist Zombie left (Levy 2008) before finally turning to why western political democracies have struggled to address the burgeoning ideological threats to political order and political freedom.

The Zombie Left and World Purificationism Post 9/11

Interestingly, an anti-anti Islamism characterizes new post 9/11, left thinking about terrorism and insurgency. Since the 1990s, leading western university departments developed often abstruse and unfalsifiable constructivist and critical theories about world politics that afford theoretical support to media, non-governmental organisations (NGOs) and legal elites that question the politics of fear that they contend western democratic governments and their security agencies promote. These opinion forming elites share a common suspicion of western government responses to al-Qaeda and the Global Jihadist Movement (GJM) both at home and abroad.

They prefer instead transnational structures and global forums that, while deploring the violence of non- state actors like al-Qaeda, empathise with their alienation and condemn global capitalism and western liberal democratic states for perpetuating the global injustice that induces such ‘resistance’. Academic international relations departments of a critical disposition, evince an elective affinity with the critical thinking and the political analysis of ostensibly non-violent Islamist groups like Hizb ut-Tahrir (see Jones & Smith, 2014, chapter 6).

This ideological critique of the west in general and the US and Israel in particular has, in other words, extended beyond the murky archipelago of academic speculation to inform an emerging global movement against capitalism, globalization and the western imposed state security order. This ‘transnational progressive movement’, as John Fonte terms it, increasingly assumes the form of a political religion (Fonte, 2002, pp.1-14). Like the rise of RWE, transnational progressivism emerged from the end of the Cold War and a radical democratic critique of liberal market states, combined with an enthusiasm for what Jurgen Habermas termed ‘post national constellations’ like the United Nations and the EU. Since 2001, this progressive, radical critical thinking presents transnational redemptive social movements and transnational NGOs (TNGOs) in a Manichean conflict with global capitalism and the U.S. inspired Neoliberal ‘Empire’ that sustains it (Sternberg, 2010, p.61). Drawing upon a range of often contradictory, but suitably arcane, critical, anarchist, radical feminist, environmentalist, Frankfurt school, post-colonial and deconstructionist theories, to give it academic plausibility, its more prominent anarchist and post Marxist ideologues like Noam Chomsky and Hardt and Negri view TNGOs and global social movements functioning as the revolutionary antithesis to global capitalism. Just as Marxist Leninist thought recognized in the international proletariat a revolutionary class that exposed the contradictions in industrial capitalism, so social movements, like the World Social Forum, play an analogous role in revealing the contradictions of global capitalism (Chomsky, 2004; Hardt & Negri 2010; Del Valle, 2010).

Critics of this totalizing new Left vision, like Bernard Henri Levy, sees this movement replacing the post 1968 libertarian left with a new barbarism that assumes we are living in dark times of conflict where an exploitative, Neoliberal capitalist order serves as a prophylactic against a just global society waiting to be born. This new left political religion identifies a world controlling state-military-corporate-legal-educational-media complex that enforces a globally unjust order (Levy, 2008, 24; Sternberg, 2010, p.63). Since this makes for a somewhat amorphous enemy, Levy further argues that the new ideology requires the United States and its allies to function as the concrete imperial enemy, whilst Israel plays a special role as its particularly demonic accomplice (Levy, pp.28-30).

In a similar vein, Nick Cohen argues that this evolving activist style experienced with the Iraq war (2003) a 'dark liberation', that inspired its adherents to 'spread the theories of Jewish-Zionist world conspiracy…and excuse even the most brutal theocratic-fascist regime, as long as they opposed the United States and the capitalist status quo' (Cohen, 2007, pp.4-14).

This new left constitutes an inchoate 'non-religious chiliastic movement which preaches global human renewal and predicts apocalypse as its alternative' (Ibid. p.61). As with political religions of the past, this new left 'purificationism', as Ernest Sternberg terms it, contrasts the degenerate present with a utopian future. As Sternberg explains:

The world system that perpetuates oppression is known as Empire. It exercises domination through corporate tentacles, media manipulation, state power and military prowess. It is selfish, greedy, ruthless, racist and exploitative and heedlessly pollutes the earth.... Under the thrall of Neoliberal Empire, people live in poverty, food is contaminated, products are artificial, wasteful consumption is compelled, indigenous groups are dispossessed and nature itself is subverted. (Sternberg, p.74)

By contrast the anti-globalization or *alter* globalization movements, that paradoxically consist of transnational networks of NGOs, sympathetic academics, radical pacifists and grass root global justice, indigenous peoples and environmental activists seek to expose and overthrow this imperial system. In the early twenty first century, as John Fonte and Bernard- Henri Levy argue, these activists have moved from the political fringes to shape mainstream, international, political debate. (Fonte, p.1; Levy, pp.137-45).

Indeed, by 2011 those committed to this anti-capitalist worldview, 'lead hundreds of activist groups and NGOs, conduct seminars and hold marches at international conferences, receive support from governments and eleemosynary institutions, enjoy various despots as their cheerleaders, are woven into the workings of the UN and the EU… and subscribe to a coherent though not uniform doctrine' (Sternberg 2010 p.66).

In order to overthrow the Neoliberal order requires those who share the vision of what the World Social Forum terms 'a better world' to exploit local conditions of oppression and form 'bunds' or affinities with like-minded groups networking across communities, borders and cultures (http://www.forumsocialmundial.org.br/noticias_1.php?cd_news=2556&cd_language=2).

This transnational network of purified victims seeks to instantiate an environmentally clean, culturally harmonious, politically just and sustainable world, run on alternative energy. The purified new order will be liberated from toxicity, capitalism and carbon. In this Manichean view the various networks and movements struggle for an international regime of peace and justice against the selfish national interests of western democracies. From this perspective, international rules will replace the 'chauvinist laws bounded by nationality (and)…climate and energy flows will come under transnational management' (Sternberg, 2010, p.76). As the nation state order weakens, a transnational cadre of NGOs will replace it and serve as the globe's humanitarian enforcers and equalizers. As Fonte observes, the movement's ideology is 'post democratic' and dismisses mainstream political parties and representative democratic institutions as corrupt, hypocritical and oppressive (Fonte, p.2). *Soi disant* radical democrats favours in its place a form of direct, participatory democracy where grass roots activists raise the consciousness of the alienated and expose the toxicity of the liberal capitalist order. In these local forums, dominated by the radical visionaries, activist facilitators will create conditions for the rectification of false consciousness, leading to the enforcement of global justice and non–instrumental reason. This purified order, both locally and globally, will replace the partial will of self-interested states and create a transnational, therapeutic, participatory absolutism. This utopian vision thus posits a world on the cusp of a globally just cosmopolitanism achieved through the effort of communities of like-minded idealists. Ultimately the gnostics who anticipate the new order waiting to be born possess the recondite knowledge to act as guides to social and political transformation and emancipation.

From this perspective, the global evil that the US led liberal capitalist system perpetuates, justifies resistance to it. Thus although social activists, in this loosely structured but evolving movement of redemption, embrace pacifism and denounce the warfare state, they nevertheless, as we have seen, empathise with the global resistance of the weak and oppressed. In other words, although not defending violence, they broadly condone global resistance of the al-Qaeda inspired leaderless variety. 'Resistance', as opposed to the more pejorative term 'violence' functions euphemistically to legitimate, for example, the insurgency in Iraq after 2003. Thus at the European Social Forum held in London, (2003), the audience enthusiastically welcomed speakers praising Iraqi resistance, but, as Nick Cohen observed, no one raised embarrassing questions about decapitations and suicide bombings (Cohen, p.301). This constant demonization of western influence, whether it is actively engaged in Afghanistan or Iraq, or passively indifferent to inter-tribal and sectarian civil war in Syria, and North Africa serves ultimately to fuel the grievances of those already aggrieved in ghettoised minority communities and prepared to countenance violence for the purposes of clarification and purification.

Yet, at the same time as the new radicals denounce western perfidy and hypocrisy they equally minimize the mass crimes that occur in regimes that the ideology considers subordinate or subaltern. This neglect and historical distortion not only gives succour to non-western despotisms it also serves 'to annihilate whole chapters of contemporary history, killing one more time, millions of men and women, whose whole crime was being born and whose second was in dying the wrong way'(Levy,pp.137-45). This disregard for historical accuracy, a worrying feature of recent academic critical studies, facilitates what Orwell described as the corruption of political language. The language of such critical and emancipatory discourse appears 'designed to make lies sound truthful and murder respectable' (Orwell, 1946). As thought corrupts language, language corrupts thought. In the context of the new radicalism, humanitarian terms become weapons to attack the flaws of liberal democracies 'while self-professed humanitarians excuse the pervasive crimes of despots' (Sternberg, p.83).

Since 2008, the global financial crisis, that exposed major flaws in the western financial system, gave further credence to this evolving radical critique of liberal democracy and, its institutions. At the end of the Cold War, it appeared too many commentators that the liberal market state order would benignly reshape the globe through its soft cultural and commercial power. Twenty years on, and as a consequence of the long war waged on terror internally and externally and a global economic crisis of western regulatory fashioning, Neoliberal Empire appears increasingly under siege. Government bail outs of banks too big to fail while small businesses went to the wall and defaulting mortgage holders lost their homes revealed the limitations of the rational market as well as the hubris of investment bankers. The crisis legitimated loose congeries of anarchist inspired direct action groups, like Anonymous, that promoted the non-violent, but highly visible and disruptive Occupy movement that disrupted Wall Street in September 2011 and eventually spread to 951 cities in 82 countries. The leaderless movement, organized through social media, exposed how the US and UK governments had facilitated the concentration of wealth in 1 per cent of the population. The movement claimed, 'We are the99 per cent' and called for radical economic redistribution and a new financial order.[1] Anonymous, the loosely associated international collective of anarchist inspired activist and hacktivist entities, facilitated the spread of this leaderless, anti-capitalist resistance.

Anonymous originated in 2003 as a virtual anarchist network that conducts denial of service attacks on government, religious and corporate web sites it deems antithetical to its ideals. In particular, Anonymous has conducted cyber-attacks in support of whistle blowers like Edward Snowden, Bradley Manning and Julian Assange's Wiki leaks. In the Anonymous world view Assange, Manning and Snowden are 'heroes' of radical progressivism for exposing the US government's covert and tyrannical surveillance powers. In July 2013, Anonymous launched its operation to support Edward Snowden for revealing the 'dirty secrets' of the US government's covert surveillance activities (http://www.youtube.com/watch?v=AcDnjFemPuc). Its You Tube videos declare, somewhat threateningly, 'We are Anonymous, We are legion. We do not forgive. We do not forget. We are coming. Expect us'(http://www.youtube.com/watch?v=AcDnjFemPuc). In its 2014 apocalyptic challenge to the 'so called' global capitalist elite, Anonymous informed its fellow 'citizens of the world' that they spread the message of 'true love, peace and compassion' against the 'unsustainable' toxic order based on 'murder, hate, oppression and disorder' that was 'killing the surface of the planet'. 'We are the 99 per cent' they declared, 'we are the new world order' (http://www.youtube.com/watch?v=o74sMCU_kPQ).

As Alexander del Valle has observed, there is a curious symmetry between the red (extreme left), brown (extreme right) and green (the latter colour representing both Islamist and environmentalist) movements, the totalitarian paths they follow and the politically religious certitudes they embrace and promote through phantom cells, social media and leaderless resistance (del Valle, 2010, p.25). The different components of this axis, with varying degrees of commitment, share a common belief in a decadent and corrupt past, a prevailing failed and hypocritical western political order and the need for resistance and violence to engender a rebirth and bring about a harmonious and inexorable new order or third age. How we might finally consider has the secular, political, democratic state order responded?

Pluralism, Democracy and Deracination

The political philosopher, Leo Strauss, presciently observed in the 1950s, that the first half of the troubled twentieth century had undermined faith in the secular, liberal, democratic Enlightenment project. He considered that:

The crisis of the West consists in the West having become uncertain of its purpose. The West was once certain of its purpose – of a purpose in which all men could be united and hence it had a clear vision of its future... We do no longer have that certainty and that clarity. Some among us even despair of the future, and this despair explains many forms of Western degradation. (Strauss, 1964, p.11)

A society accustomed to understanding itself in terms of a liberal, universal and progressive purpose cannot lose faith in that purpose without becoming utterly bewildered. This bewilderment and its implications for the liberal democratic or political appreciation of the threat of political violence from non-state actors has only further crystalised this sense of bewilderment.

Although we have focused in this work on the Islamist take on political religion, it is evident that, since the end of the Cold War, the pursuit of political and spiritual purification and an apocalyptic transformation of a corrupt world order is by no means confined to Islamist jihadis. Al-Qaeda only presents the most evident manifestation of this burgeoning activist style. The challenge it poses is just the latest in a line of revolutionary assaults on the political systems of modern, European democratic states since the late nineteenth century.

Those attracted to this style of thinking and the utopian and apocalyptic solutions they provide to local and global problems pose a complex challenge for political rule and the western, secular order. At the core of the west's difficulty is a need both to take utopian ideologies seriously, whatever their provenance, whilst reaffirming the idea of politics as a distinct form of activity practiced within a territorial unit of rule.

Problematically, western governments, their militaries, their media and their eleemosynary institutions have underestimated the role that political religion of an Islamist provenance plays in both recruitment to Islamism and the passage to the violent act, which its dogmatic teaching sacralises. Instead, a progressive commentariat, itself a product of western self-loathing, discountenances the rhetoric of Islamist purity, redescribing it instead as a response to social and economic exclusion which, to some extent, legitimates its resistance to western capitalism and global injustice. Somewhat paradoxically, democratic governments and their media and academic elites only see right wing extremism for the totalitarian threat it poses to politically pluralist societies.

Yet, in what used to be standard introductions to politics written during the Cold War, by *inter alia* Bernard Crick, Robert Dahl, Kenneth Minogue, Hannah Arendt, Leo Strauss or Michael Oakeshott the western European and North American experience of political democracy sustained, with difficulty, a 'common world in which we may talk to each other' (Minogue, 1995, p.vii; see also Crick, 1962; Oakeshott, 1962; Arendt, 1954 and 2005; Strauss and Cropsey, 1984). For Leo Strauss, political philosophy was synonymous with the ancient Greek polis. As we noted in chapter 7, the diversity of the city state sustained the political condition. The Greeks considered the tribe incapable of high civilization and large, imperial societies could never experience the freedom of ruling and being ruled by law (Strauss and Cropsey, p.3). Indeed, as one leading conservative essayist of the 1970s when asked what he had learnt as an undergraduate at Cambridge, he replied, 'that the rule of law is more important than the vote' (Gale, in Johnson, 1990, p.22).

Central to politics, therefore, is a limited government that accepts the separation of the public from the private realm. It is the fact of recognising such a separation that 'distinguishes politics-we may loosely identify it with freedom and democracy-from despotism'. Indeed, 'the western political tradition rested on the rejection of despotism' (Minogue, p.4). The overarching public world of the state further maintains a structure of law appropriate to a self-determining association to sustain this civil life.

By contrast, the despot considers everything in society his private property. The politically religious and the politically correct modern versions of despotism see everything in society and on the planet for that matter, material for intervention and regulation. Postmodern ideological despotism further assumes, as we have seen, the achievement of a post democratic state of perfection via resistance, regulation and purification.

Politics by contrast accepts the human condition for what it is and this condition is never perfect. As Bernard Crick observed, politics is 'not religion, ethics, law, science history, or economics. It neither solves everything nor is present everywhere' (Crick, p.23). Crucially, as Aristotle first recognized, it is about the acceptance of difference rather than the despotic imposition of unity. 'There is a point', Aristotle noted,

...at which a polis by advancing in unity will cease to be a polis: there is another point short of that at which it may still remain a polis, but will none the less come close to losing its essence and will become

a worse polis. It is as if you were to turn a harmony into mere unison or reduce a theme to a single beat, the truth is that the polis is an aggregate of many members. (Aristotle 1946, 2.5, p.14)

Ultimately, politics can only occur in organized units of rule or states whose members or citizens recognizing a condition of mutual equality, nevertheless, recognize themselves to be an aggregate of many members and not a single tribe, religion, interest or tradition. It necessarily recognizes a plurality of contending interests as its foundational feature. As a consequence, politics in the west became a plausible response to the problem of governing a complex modern state. Political freedom, rather than an abstract liberation, is a further consequence of this recognition because political democracy tolerates the articulation of different interests and does not propose an ideal, utopian or transnational solution to the problem of rule. Politics becomes the public activity of free citizens and freedom is the privacy of citizens from public action. A further feature of political rule is that it offers only one solution to the problem of order, despotism, oligarchy and even democracy in the sense of a tyranny of the majority or in its grassroots activist version an enlightened minority of activists are anti-political forms of rule.

A particular order sustains the practice of political freedom and political rights. The authority to make a common law made through representative institutions and apply it equally to all citizens requires as Thomas Hobbes first observed a Leviathan state. As Steven Pinker has recently demonstrated, with a wealth of statistics, not available to the author of *Leviathan* (1651), the '*Leviathan*, a state and a judiciary with a monopoly on the legitimate use of force can …inhibit the impulse for revenge, and circumvent the self –serving biases that make all parties believe they are on the side of the angels' (Pinker, 2011, pp.682-3). Indeed, one of the tasks of political science, as opposed to political religion, is to explain the processes by which political society evolved from tribe and clan 'to the power-units whose rise and decline constitute the drama of history'. Along with elucidating this process, 'we can also trace', Eric Voeglin contended, 'the attempts to rationalize the shelter-function of the *cosmion* the little world of order, by what are commonly called political ideas' (Voegelin in Cooper, 1999, p.39). In other words, political thinking from Aristotle to Pinker, seeks to rationalize the territorially bounded shelter that gives meaning to human life against the external forces of 'disintegration and chaos, a shelter in the end that is maintained by force' (Pinker, p.39).

Ultimately, the order that enables political activity, commerce, and cosmopolitanism to thrive is national, or more accurately confined within a state that has a monopoly on the legitimate use of violence to sustain itself. It is not, in other words, transnational, multilateral, regional or international. Although a sovereign political democracy may participate in such arrangements, it cannot have its lawful authority subject to supranational guidance or international or regional courts of law and human rights. Consequently, how a politically democratic state conducts foreign relations will be very different from its internal ordering.

Politics in this view, then, requires the constitutionally limited authority of the state for its practice. Therefore maintaining its borders and the terms of membership is a matter of necessity and prudence rather than abstract or global justice. As early modern theorists of the state from Machiavelli to Jean Bodin and John Milton acknowledged the *res publica* (the public thing) has the right and reason to maintain itself. As J.H. Hexter explained, the English phrase 'reason of state' is an inadequate translation of the French *raison* and Italian *ragioni*. Inadequate, because it obscures the fact that, in French and Italian, the phrase implies a guiding concern with the actual *right* of the state (Hexter, 197, p.168). This right means that the protection of a political democracy is a matter not of justice, but necessity. This right, moreover, may be expressed in terms of both the right of the state's survival as well as the conditions for preserving and developing civilization or, in the language of Miltonic republicanism, maintaining liberty and virtue.

To sustain the political condition in the present context might, therefore, require the state as a matter of prudence to engage in surveillance, define the terms of its membership and engage in external conflict to sustain its security and integrity. Somewhat problematically, however, as a number of perceptive commentators have shown, the political classes in both Europe and to a lesser extent Australia and North America have abandoned politics, properly understood, together with a prudential statecraft in pursuit of post national or transnational abstractions and utopian projects of rational modernization.

More particularly, catch-all political parties, that, during the first wave of modern mass representative democracy, served as the political vehicle for marshaling a collocation of social and political interests and organizing citizens for political engagement, have given way to cartel parties. The modern cartel party uses the resources of the state to maintain its position within the political system. As Richard Katz and Peter Mair argued, since the end of the Cold War, mainstream political parties, 'adopt themselves to declining levels of participation and involvement in party activities by not only turning to resources provided by the state but by doing so in a collusive manner'. Somewhat differently, Anthony Barnett observed that in the post Cold War era democratically elected governments increasingly function like 'a large media corporation' (Barnett, 2000, p.3). This fusion of the media and political domains has produced, Peter Oborne contends, a new system of government, where 'techniques of manipulation, deception, smear and constitutional capture have taken power away from the ordinary voter and placed it in the hands of the (new) political class' (Oborne, 2007, p.xvii).

This manipulative corporatism (Barnett, p.3) fractured the relationship between this political class and the people has led to a hollowing out of mainstream parties and the democratic political process in the west. Peter Mair even contends that:

The age of democracy has passed. Although the parties themselves remain, they have become so disconnected from the wider society, and pursue a form of competition that is so lacking in meaning, that they no longer seem capable of sustaining democracy in its present form. (Mair, 2013, p.1)

The changing character of modern western political parties has affected their standing, legitimacy and effectiveness and as a consequence the legitimacy and effectiveness of modern democracy. Problematically, political leaders and the parties they serve no longer represent ordinary people, but function as emissaries of a central bureaucracy. This is particularly case in Europe, where mainstream party elites have turned the EU into a 'protected sphere, safe from the demands of voters and their representatives' (Ibid, p.125). As a consequence a technocratic and democratically unaccountable European directorate has progressively taken decision making away from national parliaments. Indeed, from the currency and the economy, to counter-terrorism and immigration, decisions are made elsewhere. Somewhat disturbingly, politicians encouraged this process, as they sought 'to divest themselves of responsibility for potentially unpopular policy decisions and so cushion themselves against possible voter discontent' (Ibid., p.130 see also Katz & Mair 1995). This means that in Europe and to a lesser extent in Washington and Canberra, decisions 'which viscerally affect the lives of voters are now taken by anonymous bureaucrats rather than politicians responsible to their voters' (Oborne, 2014, p.20). Consequently, Peter Mair argues, parties are failing because 'the zone of engagement- the traditional world of party democracy where citizens interacted with and felt a sense of attachment to their political leaders- is being evacuated' (Mair, p.16). This abandonment has led both to a burgeoning popular indifference to politics and democracy and created a climate conducive to extremist and anti-political enthusiasms. Politics and politicians appear increasingly remote and irrelevant to the quotidian concerns of citizens they nominally represent. The rhetoric of manipulative populism reinforced this perception. Leaders like Tony Blair in the UK, Barack Obama in the US and Kevin Rudd in Australia presented themselves as above politics. At the same time, the academic literature on policymaking, institutional reform and governance reflected a similar anti-political sentiment. Consequently,

Citizens withdraw from parties and a conventional politics that no longer seem to be part of their own world: traditional politics is seen less and less as something that belongs to citizens or to the society, more and more as something done by politicians. There is a world of the citizens –or a host of particular worlds of the citizens- and the world of the politicians and the parties and the interaction between them steadily diminishes (Mair, p.98).

As a consequence of this new alignment, the European elites have come very close to the abolition of 'what we have been brought up to regard as politics and have replaced it with rule by bureaucrats, bankers and various kind of unelected expert'(Oborne 2014, p.1).

Nor are things much better the other side of the Atlantic. As David Runciman argues, during the financial crisis that overwhelmed the US economy after September 2008, 'no one could doubt that democracy was deeply implicated' (Runciman, 2013, p.265). Subsequently, institutional inertia and budget gridlock on Capitol Hill between 2009-2013 only reinforced the sense of popular alienation from the US political class. The fact that Obama presented himself as a post partisan and post political redeemer only heightened the sense of democratic malaise.

At the same time the failure of the long wars in Iraq and Afghanistan only seemed to confirm the fact that democracies have not learned how 'to avoid unwinnable wars' (Ibid p.306). Even more worryingly democratic politicians and their militaries had lost sight of strategic objectives and 'bungled' their war aims (Strachan, 2014, p.3).

It is, of course, no surprise that the period after 1990 that witnessed the rise of manipulative populism and the hollowing out of western democracy coincided with the rise of political religions that sought the solution to the disenchantment and hollowing out of democracy in either Islamist, right wing populist or transnationally progressive post political soteriologies. These versions of this worldly Salvationism offer shelter from the disintegration of the practice of politics properly understood in ways that the political classes have failed to appreciate. As Anthony Barnett, noted, New Labour's manipulative populism was 'bound to come to grief on the variegated realities of modern Ukania' (Barnett, p.1). More precisely, as former Liberal Democrat leader, Lord Ashdown, observed 'if this is the age of the collapse of (democratic) beliefs, the dissolution of institutions, then what you are going to find is people who find an appeal in answers that are simplistic'. These simplistic answers range from a recourse to Islamist inspired jihadism and the white supremacist reaction, to communities in the UK, 'born under other skies (and) …from other cultures who would prefer to police themselves' (*The Guardian* 19 January, 2014). When minority communities 'take the law into their own hands', as Tom Winsor, the Chief Inspector of Her Majesty's constabulary alleged in January 2014, the rule of law, integral to the maintenance of political democracy dissolves (Ibid).

CONCLUSION

To address the problem of sacred violence and the political religion that welcomes it requires, therefore mainstream political parties to recover the practice political democracy, where politicians make hard choices in the national interest. However, although a crisis of politics, exemplified by the rise of political religions, threatens western democracy, it has survived equally severe crises in the course of the twentieth century. As David Runciman shows, the history of democracy in the modern age is both cumulative and cyclical. 'The experience of crisis builds up over time, no crisis is quite like the one before, because the one before is always there to serve as a warning and a temptation' (Runciman p.296). Yet the 'repeated sequence of democratic crises over the past hundred years also describes a single overarching narrative', namely that twentieth century democracy was a success story. At the end of that short century (1914-1990) western democracies emerged as the richest and most powerful states the world has ever seen. 'They had defeated their enemies and enabled their citizens to prosper. But success on that scale comes at a price' (Ibid). It has Runciman contends, 'blinded democracies to the enduring threats they face'. Paradoxically, 'the cumulative success of democracy has created the conditions for systemic failure' (Ibid). The elite abandonment of the idea of politics clearly contributes to the potential for such a failure. Democracies however have a way of stumbling through crises and it is perhaps this capacity over time that gives them an edge over their ideological autocratic and politically religious rivals.

MAIN FOCUS OF THE CHAPTER

Issues, Controversies, and Problems

The key issues address here are the rise of right and left wing extremism both in the United States and in Europe as a result of the emergence of the internet and social media that facilitates the communication of radical ideologies and as a basis for recruitment and radicalization. The paper identifies the anti-political messages that both right and left extremism promulgates together with the promotion of an anti-pluralist, transnational identity politics. The chapter argues that the social media has facilitated ideological understandings that present a serious and neglected threat to the political order and the nation states of the west that have sustained a modern, secular, political democratic understanding. It further contends that political parties and national governments have to promote more forcefully, both online and through state education the value of secular politics and the pluralist and secular basis of all successful and stable political states in a world of fragmented identity and insecurity.

Solutions and Recommendations

The main recommendation of the chapter is the need to reboot representative government and institutions and more vigorously promote through eleemosynary institutions and state media the utility and value of commitments to the secular, pluralist democratic basis of political order in the West.

Future Research Directions

Future research should explore how and in what manner groups recruit online to promote both narrow ethnic or religious identities that create opportunities and motivations for radicalization and violence. Future research will also address if and how social media might be controlled, the problem of more intrusive government surveillance and its impact on the condition of liberty.

Conclusion

To address the problem of sacred or purifying violence and the ideologies that welcome it requires mainstream political parties to recover the practice political democracy, where politicians make hard choices in the national interest. However, although a crisis of politics, exemplified by the rise of political extremism, threatens western democracy, it has survived equally severe crises in the course of the twentieth century. Yet the history of democracy in the modern age is both cumulative and cyclical. The experience of crisis builds up over time, no crisis is quite like the one before, because the one before is always there to serve as a warning. However, the repeated sequence of democratic crises over the past hundred years also describes a single overarching narrative, namely that twentieth century democracy was a success story. At the end of that short century (1914-1990) western democracies emerged as the richest and most powerful states the world has ever seen. They had defeated their enemies and enabled their citizens to prosper. But success on this scale came at a price. The price was complacency that blinded democracies to the enduring threats they face. Paradoxically, the cumulative success of democracy has created the conditions for systemic failure. The elite abandonment of the idea of politics and its ever growing recourse to managerialism clearly contributes to the potential for such a failure. Democracies however have a way of stumbling through crises and it is perhaps this capacity that gives them an edge over their ideological, autocratic and fundamentalist rivals.

REFERENCES

Anonymous. (n. d.). We are Anonymous [YouTube Video] Retrieved 20 April 2014 from http://www.youtube.com/watch?v=AcDnjFemPuc

Anonymous (n. d.). We are the ninety nine per cent [YouTube Video]. Retrieved 21 April 2014 from http://www.youtube.com/watch?v=o74sMCU_kPQ

Arendt, H. (1954). *Between Past and Future*. London: Penguin.

Arendt, H. (2005). *The Promise of Politics New York: Random House Hannah Arendt, (1951) The Origins of Totalitarianism*. New York: Houghton Mifflin Harcourt.

Aristotle, . (1946). *The Politics Oxford*. Clarendon Press.

Barnett, A. (2000). Corporate Populism and Partyless Democracy. *New Left Review*, (May-June): 1–8.

Beam, L. (1992, January). Leaderless Resistance. *The Seditionist*, *12*, 1–5.

Berwick, A. (2013). 2083 A European Declaration of Independence. London: self-published

Carswell, D. (2013, October 22). The Front national is the most popular party in France. The Telegraph. Retrieved from http://blogs.telegraph.co.uk/news/douglascarswellmp/100242451/the-front-national-is-the-most-popular-party-in-france-are-you-happy-now-eurocrats/

Chomsky, N. (2004). *Hegemony and Survival, America's Quest for Global Dominance London*. Penguin.

Church of Jesus Christ Christian Aryan Nations Converse. (n. d.). Retrieved from https://www.aryan-nations.org

Coates, S. (2014, January). Voters' trust in society is collapsing, says Ashdown. *The Times*.

Cohen, N. (2007). *What's Left? How the Left lost it's way*. London: Harper.

Cohn, N. (1969). *The Pursuit of the Millennium*. London: Paladin.

Cooper, B. (1999). *Eric Voegelin and the Foundations of Modern Political Science* Columbia: University of Missouri Press Bernard Crick (1962, 2005). In *Defence of Politics*. London: Continuum.

RAND Corp. (2008). Terrorist Organizations Profile Aryan Nations. Retrieved from http://www.start.umd.edu/tops/

del Valle, A. (2010) I Rossi Neri, Verdi: la convergenza degli Estremi opposti. Islamismo, comunismo, neonazismo, Torino: Lindau

Fonte, J. (2002). Liberal Democracy versus Transnational Progressivism: The future of the ideological civil war within the West. *Orbis*, Summer, 1–14.

Gentile, E. M. R., & Mallett, R. (2000). The Sacralization of Politics: Definitions, Interpretations and Reflections on the Question of Secular Religion and Totalitarianism. *Totalitarian Movements and Political Religions*, *1*(1), 20–37. doi:10.1080/14690760008406923

German Right wing extremism. (n. d.). Retrieved from http://www.spiegel.de/international/topic/right_wing_extremism/

Griffin, R. (1991). *The Nature of Fascism*. London: Pinter.

Hardt, M., & Negri, A. (2001). *Empire*. Cambridge, Mass: Harvard University Press.

Hexter, J. H. (1973). *The Vision of Politics on the Eve of the Reformation*. New York: Basic Books.

Johnson, P. (1990). A Gale for all seasons'. *Spectator (London, England)*, *10*(November), 21–22.

Jones, D. M. (2005, Spring). Peace Through Conversation. *National Interest*, *79*, 1.

Jones, D. M., & Smith, M. L. R. (2014). *Sacred Violence Political Religion in a Secular Age*. London: Plagrave.

Katz, R. S., & Mair, P. (1995). Richard S Katz and Peter Mair, Changing Models of Party Organization and Party Democracy: The emergence of the cartel party. *Party Politics*, *1*(1), 5–31. doi:10.1177/1354068895001001001

Levy, B.-H. (2008). *Left in Dark Times: A stand against the new barbarism*. New York: Random House.

Macdonald, A. (aka William Luther Pierce) (1978). The Turner Diaries. Hillsboro, West Virginia: National Vanguard Books.

Mair, P. (2013). *Ruling the Void: The hollowing out of Western Democracy*. London: Verso.

Mellagrou-Hitchens, A. (2015) *The Global Jihad Movement in the West* [Unpublished PhD thesis]. King's College, University of London, London.

Mellagrou-Hitchens, A., & Brun, H. (2013). *A Neo-Nationalist Network: The English Defence League and the European Counter Jihad Movement*. International Centre for the.

Michael, G. (1995). *Lone Wolf Terror and the Rise of Leaderless Resistance, Nashville Ten*. Vanderbilt University Press.

Minogue, K. R. (1995). *Politics A very short introduction*. Oxford: Oxford University Press.

Oakeshott, M. (1962). *Rationalism in Politics and Other Essays*. London: Methuen.

Oborne, P. (2007). *The Triumph of the Political Class*. London: Pocket Books.

Oborne, P. (2014, January 1). Europe is slowly strangling the life out of national democracy. *The Daily Telegraph*.

Oborne, P. (2014, January 1). Europe is slowly strangling the life out of national democracy. *The Daily Telegraph*.

Orwell, G. (1946). Politics and the English Language. Retrieved from http://www.orwell.ru/library/essays/politics/english/e_polit

Pinker, S. (2011). *The Better Angels of our Nature, Why Violence has Declined London*. Penguin.

Runciman, D. (2013). *The Confidence Trap A History of Democracy in Crisis from World War 1 to the Present*. Princeton: Princeton University Press.

Samuels, D. (2012, April 6). The new mastermind of jihad. *The Wall Street Journal.* Retrieved from http://online.wsj.com/news/articles/SB10001424052702303299604577323750859163544

Southern Poverty Law Center. (n. d.). Louis Beam. Retrieved from www.spl.org

Standing, G. (2011). *The Precariat: the new dangerous class*. London: Bloomsbury.

Sternberg, E. (2010, Winter). Purifying the World what the new radical ideology stands for. *Orbis*, 60–75.

Strachan, H. (2014). *The Direction of War Contemporary Strategy in Historical Perspective*. Cambridge: Cambridge University Press.

Strauss, L. (1964). *The City and Man*. Chicago: Rand McNally.

Strauss, L., & Cropsey, J. (1986). History of Political Philosophy. Chicago, IL: Chicago University Press.

Study of Radicalisation and Political Violence. (n. d.). King's College, London.

The Daily Telegraph. (2013, May 23). Murder of Lee Rigby provokes anti-Muslim attacks.

The Guardian. (2014, January 19). Communities 'taking law into their own hands', says police chief inspector.

The Independent. (2013, May 28). Islamaphobia attacks rise dramatically after the murder of Lee Rigby.

Voegelin, E. (1974). Political Religions, and The Ecumenic Age (Vol. 4). In Order and History (Vols. 1–5). Baton Rouge, Louisiana: Louisiana University Press.

KEY TERMS AND DEFINITIONS

Apocalyptic: Pertaining to the revealed future of the world, founded on the vision granted to Saint John of Patmos and the book of the New Testament relating to it.

Chiliasm: The doctrine of the millennium and the physical reappearance of Christ to rule on earth for a thousand years.

Ethnocentric: A belief that one's own culture is superior to other cultures.

Leaderless Resistance: Aryan Nations theorist, Louis Beam's concept that instead of the traditional cell structure of proscribed radical or revolutionary groups, the electronic media could instead be used for purposes of radicalization and organization rendering terrorism more protean and unpredictable.

Lone Wolf: White extremists, Alex Curtis and Tom Metzger actually coined the term 'lone wolf' in the mid-1990s for the type of lone actor radical mobilized through leaderless resistance.

Palingenesis: The ideal of racial purification.

Precariat: The new class of young, white and non-white males who lack a coherent identity and find themselves in precarious and unstable short term contract employment in the post global financial crisis world.

Purificationism: The ideal common to both left and eight extremism that the deficiencies of capitalism, the market and the democratic order can be overcome through the pursuit and implementation of an abstract model based on a version of identity politics.

Soteriological: A doctrine pertaining to salvation.

ENDNOTES

1 The slogan appeared on the Tumblr blog page in August 2011

Chapter 8
Developing Discourse and Tools for Alternative Content to Prevent Terror

Marina Shorer-Zeltser
Institute of Identity Research IDmap, Israel

Galit Margalit Ben-Israel
Beit-Berl Academic College, Israel

ABSTRACT

Within context of multiculturalism and openness in Western countries, the work of terrorist activity recruiters can become easier and simple. In this framework, it's important to analyze techniques used by terrorists to manipulate support and good intentions of people inclined to sustain justice and peace into the radicalization and terrorist actions using interpersonal communication and Internet content. This article provides an overview on the Muslim minority in Western Europe, religious discourse and radicalization techniques used to incline religious content into terms of actions. It also suggests usage of inclusive cultural and religious policy to start an intra-community dialog and broaden de-radicalization.

DOI: 10.4018/978-1-4666-9661-7.ch008

INTRODUCTION

The inclination of certain parts of Muslim European population towards devastating terror rhetoric propagated by Al-Qaeda and ISIS and its affiliates requires a close look as to the origins of the inclination and the ways this rhetoric can be dismissed or at least put into contest with more balanced explanations of the reality. As Bernard Lewis states in his fundamental analysis regarding Muslim-Western cataclysm, "Most Muslims are not fundamentalists, and most fundamentalists are not terrorists, but most present-day terrorists are Muslims and proudly identify themselves as such" (Louis, 2003, p. 117).

The origins of the 20th and 21st Century religious-ethnic tension between House of Islam and Christianity clearly stem from the daily confrontation between ways of life and traditions of both groups living side by side in Europe and other Western countries. Indeed, Europe enjoyed decades of economic revival after the WWII inviting millions of Muslims to the European countries in an attempt to rebuild its infrastructures. The idea was that after several years of work the singles would return back to their families in the source countries. The history showed that the idea was wrong. Most of the gastarbeiters would definitely prefer to stay in the new countries, striving to copy their home lifestyle in the new state house.

Being a minority, most of the first, second and third-generation European Muslims proudly keep their religious affiliation and adhere to the laws of the countries of residence, including those of public appearance and clothing. It is a small minority; mainly of people who have a psychological inclination to non-conformist and abnormal behavior, which would actually look for terrorist activity, while some will just sympathize it. Lewis goes forward and says that,

the response of many Arabs and Muslims to the attack of the World Trade Center was one of shock and horror at the terrible destruction and carnage, together with shame and anger that this was being done in their name and in the name of their faith. This was the response of many – but not all. There were reports and even pictures of rejoicing in the streets in Arab and other Muslim cities at the news from New York. In part, the reaction was one of envy – a sentiment that was also widespread, in a more muted form, in Europe. Among the poor and wretched there was a measure of satisfaction – for some indeed of delight – in seeing the rich and self-indulgent Americans being taught a lesson. (Ibid, p.132)

First generations of immigrants generally experienced life conditions improvements compared with previous standards, which supposedly determined the choice of migrating to wealthier social contexts like EU area and North America. Contrarily, following younger generations could impact social exclusion and/or other hard disadvantages not benefiting from new privileges. As such, *the most important factor in Muslim Diaspora communities 'radicalization [is] the failure of successful Muslim integration and absence of institutionalization of Islam in many European countries* (Anspaha 2008).

Furthermore, Neuman & Rogers suggest that the radicalization became possible and comes into expression into religious discourse because,

one of the most powerful triggers in the European context are experiences of exclusion and discrimination in Western society. European Muslims, especially the second and third generation, often feel that – despite governments inclusive rhetoric – Western societies have not offered them the full respect and equality they believe they deserve. Violent extremists have long realized that this sense of alienation and social frustration can be capitalized upon in order to attract recruits. (Neuman & Rogers, 2007)

Determining which factors have been influencing the most the religious radicalization can be a result of large-scale statistic multi-variate analysis. All the more, since most part of the Muslim immigrant population is concentrated in big cities, municipalities and local institutions are in a favorable position to observe and examine some factors bolstering radicalization and leading to violent behaviors. Most of the effective policies for de-radicalization were implemented on street-neighborhood level. As Peter Neuman has argued: *the process of joining the jihad is more of a bottom-up than a top-down activity, with individuals actively seeking out opportunities to be recruited rather than being 'brainwashed' or 'manipulated' into joining up* (Neumann 2008, 7). Therefore, the identification of stressful and critical situation of a person can be done in a better plausibility at the local intimate level, while successful treatment can prevent joining extremist lines.

An additional factor, which can cause a radicalization outcome, is the Internet environment. However, the moderating effect of the Internet discussion does not fully defuses potential dangers of the purposeful intimidation by extremists (Eickelman & Piscatori, 1990; Castells 1997). Eickelman describes links between Islamic groups, as well as the nature of relationships within the groups themselves, as dispersed, multiple, fluid and subject to disjointing at short notice (Eickelman 1998). In this respect, this study addresses familiar characteristics of both extremists and common Internet users: they both are mostly young and male. In addition, facts show contradiction with the well-established thinking of terrorists as non-rational emotional people brought to the circle of terrorism by poverty and hard life-conditions. Analyses concerning suicide terrorists in the Middle East reveal that the potential suicide terrorists come from religiously surrounded, middle-class families with a college education background (Kimhi & Even, 2004). Therefore, here exist some empirical sustains of the claim of Crenshaw that new shifts of the terrorist activity to religious ground had begun. Regarding discussions on Internet Muslim sites, Jacques Waardenburg points to the growing trend (especially among young people) for discarding national or regional traditions and focusing upon the Qur'an and Sunna in order to distinguish what is truly Islamic - that is, normative - from what is secondary (Waardenburg 1998).

But the Internet is not the only source. New tools also appear to be emerging, such as an alleged plot described by the Guardian as aiming to *'overthrow' teachers and governors in secular state schools in the city and run them on strict Islamic principles* (Pidd 2014a). The allegations come as the result of the discovery early in March of the so-called "Operation Trojan Horse" (Gilligan 2014) dossier, which the *Guardian says offers a five-step plan to take over schools in communities with large Muslim populations with the help of what it calls 'hardline' parents who follow the strict Salafi branch of Islam* (Pidd 2014b) More than 25 schools are said to be involved.

Though some have called the Salafist-led "Operation Trojan Horse" a hoax, most believe the situation is quite real – and evidence of a deeper problem. As Charles Moore pointed out in the *Telegraph, The schools in question are mainstream, secular, taxpayer-funded state schools, but even asking about them provokes outrage. It is alleged, for instance, that at Park View, speeches in favour of the now-dead al-Qaeda ideologue of terrorism, Anwar al-Awlaki, have been made. Yet there is tremendous institutional resistance to investigating (Moore 2014).* It is striking that these events come in the wake of recent efforts to clamp down on homeschooling in the UK, after evidence emerged; many Muslim children were being radicalized at home. That discovery last month led London Mayor Boris Johnson to describe radicalization as *a form of child abuse*, (Johnson 2014) and to call for the children of radical Muslims to be placed in State care.

While perhaps not an ideal suggestion, the proposal highlights the challenges that Europe's lawmakers now face: as the threats and means of radicalization in the West become clearer, solutions remain elusive. In the Netherlands, for instance, youth considered likely to travel to Syria have had their requests for passports (or passport renewals) denied. But the truth is that it's easy enough to enter Turkey (and from there, cross into Syria) with a standard European ID card, and many of these youth have Turkish or Moroccan passports, anyway (Esman 2014).

As such, the recruitment process into terror is long and gradual. It is not only the desire of the future terrorist to take an action which plays a role but rather the ability of the terrorist network to act and execute an action, providing tools and weapons and synchronizing actions with other members of the network. Radicalization of a person is a continuing process sometimes occurring under the proper guidance of imam and mufti and sometimes is a self-deductive process by its own. In any case, the terrorist actions are the climax of the long and broad process occurring under the ground. As Ulph describes,

we have been confronting and intercepting fully formed jihadists, but these are merely at the end of a long-term ideological training process that produces them. We have yet to tackle this production process, which means that they will continue to replace themselves at a rate faster than we can intercept them. We have underestimated the ideological training, which is of the magnitude of an entire education and indoctrination system, and we fail to understand its purpose. We have failed to take the Jihadists seriously, intellectually and culturally, and as a result their corrosive influence is progressing unopposed. It is, I think you will agree, simply unbelievable that we are now in our sixth year after the attacks on September 11th and still without a coherent map of the enemy, of their cause and their ideological methodology. (Ulph 2007)

It can be interesting to chase the development of the mobilization message throughout all the Internet content yet the usefulness of this method is quit questionable. According to Omar Ashour, *As opposed to its effects on radicalization, the Internet can play a vital role in promoting a counter-narrative and in facilitating counter-radicalization and de-radicalization efforts* (Ashour 2010). That is, numbers of those who became more fanatic or extreme driven after continuous exposure to the malicious content are fascinating by their own for scientific and practical purposes. However, this approach does not bring the empirical knowledge any closer to the understanding of the ability of the mobilized subject to create substantial damage on the Net or execute a terrorist act using Internet tools. Therefore, additional strategy of de-radicalization in the broad sense, which is presenting alternative content, can be considered a better solution for the issues of Internet mobilization and terror.

MAIN FOCUS OF THE CHAPTER

It is not self-obvious what de-radicalization means for different audiences. Is it an actual participation in terroristic activity or just a quite support of one? By the common sense, de-radicalization policy and techniques would look to reverse and blur radicalization processes and help people and groups who already involved in that activity to find their way out. Most of the de-radicalization programs are targeted to individuals rather than groups, as it is generally perceived to be a personal choice of people to join certain activities. Moreover, in the working paper submitted by the Institute for Strategic Dialogue (ISD) on behalf of the European Policy Planners Network on Countering Radicalization and Polarization (PPN 2010), it is stressed that,

It is important to distinguish between the cognitive and behavioral aspects of de-radicalization; in other words, de-radicalization that seeks to change views versus disengagement which aims to alter behavior. It is often assumed that one necessarily leads to the other, but research shows that this is not always the case. (PPN 2010, 3)

THE METHODOLOGY

Among the various divergent religious groups, the Muslim Diasporic groups, i.e. geographically dispersed away from their national Homeland, are paid growing attention lately, since most of the terrorist acts were associated with extremists coming from some of these communities. Mandaville found evidence to suggest that the Internet is most often appropriated for political purposes by the Diasporic Muslims of the Western world. He also admits that, for the overwhelming majority of Muslims who seek Islam online, the Internet provides a forum to conduct politics within their religion. In the absence of sanctioned information from recognized institutions, Muslims are increasingly taking religion into their own hands. Through various popular newsgroups and e-mail discussion lists, Muslims can solicit information about what Islam says about any particular problem (Mandaville 1999). Sacad al-Faqih, whose research on the Internet revealed a moderating effect on Islamist discourse and believes that in these new arenas of communication one sees a greater convergence in the center of the Islamist political spectrum and a weakening of its extremes. A need for a positive association with large and powerful community often prompts young people to join so-called 'fundamentalist' movements (Schiffauer 1999).

As for June 2014 a search engine brings 96,400,000 million results for the term "Islam" on English; 128,000,000 million results for this term on Arabic; 22,000,000 million results on Hindu and 29,700,000 million results on Persian. In that ocean of information, letters, articles, opinions, sharing of experiences and of fatwas an average site has an opportunity window of 3-5 seconds to present the most relevant information for the visitor and grab his/her attention. If the site presents no relevant information, the visitor will just continue looking further on the web.

Therefore, Internet mobilization and recruitment for terrorist activity is not an easy task. Presenting Internet content in an attractive way is complicated and, in the recent years, it became more and more sophisticated and belongs to the realm of the professionals of the highest level. The content presented should be *broad* to provide emotional involvement so most of the visitors can find at least few keywords to associate with. It also should be *engaging,* as a visitor should feel that the content opens a real discussion and opinion sharing. Finally, the materials of the site should be *short* and *reflective* from the explanatory point of view and yet full and *comprehensive* as the comments presented should be as professional as they could be.

The Internet content is no more a naïve and spontaneous gathering of some interesting information but a well-planned and analyzable textual constructions aiming to achieve multiple aims like publicity, sharing of information, fundraising or commercial profit and even mobilization for political legal or illegal actions. Since the devastating attacks of Al Qaeda and other terrorist cells, the outstanding potential of the Internet medium to serve as a mobilization tool became obvious both to the field practitioners and to the researchers in the discipline of creating and analyzing of the Internet content. The usage of the code words and techniques by the mobilizers is not a spontaneous deed nor a sudden outcome, but rather a planned and systematic effort. Contrary to the believe of FBI assistant director, Louis Reigel, that stated that Al Qaeda and related terrorist networks are presently incapable of mounting cyber-attacks that could damage US critical infrastructure, we do believe that they are gaining proficiency and knowledge of how to use Internet for cyber-attacks (Louis 2003).

Correspondingly, Steve Coll and Susan Glasser describe Al Qaeda as the first *guerrilla movement in history to migrate from physical space to cyber space* (Coll & Glasser, 2005), using modern communications and information technologies to (re)create online the operational bases they once possessed in the physical world in sanctuaries such as post-2001 Afghanistan. Coll and Glasser further on that the 'global Jihad movement', sometimes led by Al Qaeda but increasingly made up of diverse groups and ad hoc cells with less direct links, has become a 'web-directed' phenomenon, allowing for a virtual community, guided indirectly through association of belief, to come alive (Coll & Glasser, 2005).

Moreover, Roy identifies the characteristics of European Islamic terrorists and suggests ways to understand and tackle this problem. It highlights special attributes of Islamic terrorists with respect to their integration, background and radicalization and reviews approaches to Muslim immigration and integration. Subsequently, the paper suggests steps to push toward a Western Islam. The author finds no clear-cut sociological profile of the radicals or anything that could link them to a given socio-economic situation (Roy, 2007).

The Internet mobilizers not only validate site content against its ability to draw attention of the visitors, they also take more direct approach of gathering details of the visitors by implementing cookies, sign-in forms and readings for download to create specific direct contacts with their visitors. Thus, according to Nordeste & Carment,

terrorists use modern software to capture Internet user demographics (and those of their affiliates and front organizations) to identify those who may be sympathetic to a related cause or issue. These people are then individually contacted by email and asked to make a donation to an organization with no direct ties to the terrorist organization. (The Canadian Centre for Intelligence and Security Studies, 2006)

Moreover, according to the authors, this process of capturing information and profiles of the users who browse their websites is also used for the related activities of recruitment and mobilization. Users who seem most interested or well suited to carrying out an organization's because are contacted much in the same manner as those solicited for donations. The increasing ability to interact personally online has offered terrorist groups and recruiters the option of being more proactive in their recruitment drive. Recruiters roam online chat rooms and cybercafés, post messages on online bulletin boards, looking for receptive individuals, and particularly vulnerable youth, who, through grooming and encouragement in a private online setting, can encourage joining the ranks of a terrorist group (The Canadian Centre for Intelligence and Security Studies 2006).

Furthermore, once identified, Nordeste & Carment states that the potential recruits are bombarded with religious decrees, propaganda, and training manuals on how to become a part of the 'global Jihad movement'. Those who become ensnared either by rhetoric or curiosity are then guided through an online maze of secret chat rooms or instructed to download software, which enables users to speak to each other on the internet without fear of being monitored, at which point the personal online indoctrination begins (The Canadian Centre for Intelligence and Security Studies 2006).

WAYS OF RADICALIZATION

Muslim Diasporic communities allow for its members intimate connection with the tradition and religion, support in daily life and spiritual guidance for those who struggle to find own identity in the remote society. Communities serve as an efficient channel to communicate, transfer knowledge and information and tips to first-, second and even third- generation members. And yet, it is within the community that the terrorist finds a possible route to communicate and mobilize new recruits into their activity through frequent impersonal and closed circles.

The methodology of recruitment is incremental yet it can be traced within one case into another, during the analysis of recruitment procedures. Mark Sageman claims that there is no new terrorist born into the terrorist activity, yet it is a gradual shift into a new perception:

Over time, there is a general shift in values: from the secular to the religious; from the material to the spiritual; from short-term opportunity to long-term vision; from individual concerns to communitarian sacrifice; from apathy to active engagement; from traditional morality to specific group morality; and from worldly gains to otherworldly rewards. This transformation is possible only within intense small group face-to-face interactions. The values and fellowship of these groups not only forge intense bonds of loyalty and a collective identity but also give a glimpse of what a righteous Islamist society could be like. The small size of these cliques and the mutual dedication of their members allow them to spontaneously resolve their problems among themselves. The quality of these small and dense networks promotes in-group love, transforming self-interest into self-sacrifice for the cause and comrades. The militants' experience in these groups deludes them into believing that social problems would also be spontaneously resolved in a righteous Islamist society, accounting for their curious lack of concern about what this ideal society would actually look like or how it might function politically or economically. (Sageman, 2005)

Magnus continues the discussion with his explanation that:

The distinction between the faithful and those standing outside the group is reinforced in the daily discourse of the clerics of these terrorist groups. The clerics' language and phraseology shapes the followers' reality, reinforcing the loyalty and social obligation of the members to the group and reminding them of the sacrifices already made, as well as the direction of the struggle. In this task, many religious terrorist groups draw heavily upon religious symbolism and rituals to reinforce the sense of collectiveness. Examples of this emphasis on collectivity include the local reputation of the fighters of the underground military wing of Hamas, famous for never surrendering to arrest, the growth of Hamas martyrology, which lionizes martyrs with songs, poems and shrines, and the frequent symbolic burning and descant desecration of Israeli and American flags by several Islamic groups across the Middle East. This collectiveness is also reinforced by the fact that any deviation or compromise amounts to treachery and a surrender of the principles of the religious faith are often punishable by death. (Ranstorp, 1996)

The usage of the Internet can serve a great help for the mobilizers, availing upload of videos and pictures that stress and arose hatred among the viewers. As for Bukay: *Beginning in August 1996, [Bin Laden] used verses from the Qur'an and the Hadith to argue that Jihad was compulsory to expel non-Muslims and Westerners from Saudi Arabia.* On February 23, 1998, though, he expanded his Jihad when, with Zawahiri at his side, he announced the creation of the International Islamic Front for Jihad against the Jews and Crusaders (Bukay 2006).

Few samples of recent terror mobilization activities: Earlier this month, German authorities arrested two men, one Turkish and one German, on suspicion that they were connected to ISIL, also known as ISIS. A woman with German-Polish dual-nationality was also arrested for allegedly paying €4,800 to ISIL to facilitate their work. According to *Die Welte*, police also searched the homes of several other Germans believed to have joined or be planning to join the terrorist group (Die Welte 2014). On Wednesday, Dutch authorities reported that two men with Netherlands passports had committed suicide attacks in recent weeks – one in Iraq, the other in Syria. Reportedly, a third Dutch Muslim was caught by the Syrian Secret Service (Van der Laan 2014). They are not alone. Among Western Muslims who have gone to Syria to fight, roughly two-thirds have joined ISIL or the al-Qaida-affiliated Al Nusra Front, according to a report by the International Centre for the Study of Radicalization in London (Esman 2014). In fact, Al-Monitor estimates that *European jihadists in Syria are more numerous than official statistics indicate. Indeed, they point to the existence of entire French-speaking and German-speaking brigades in the Aleppo region* (Rosenthal 2014). Others, like the Dutch suicide bombers, venture elsewhere – mostly to Somalia and Iraq.

More are likely to follow: throughout Europe, officials are again sounding alarms about radicalization among Muslim youth. As has long been the case, many of them are radicalizing through the Internet, thanks to various extremist web sites and YouTube videos, several featuring U.S. and European preachers. Others are being led by imams at their local mosques, and, in the UK, by schools (Esman 2014).

WAYS OF DE-RADICALIZATION

De-radicalization discourse inside the Muslim community is based on two main features: the authority of the imam to issue fatwas and the implementation of the fatwas into daily life by the enquirer. As such Sisler points that,

An increasing number of Muslims living in Islamic countries and abroad are at the present time approaching scholars and counselors via the internet. Oftentimes they are seeking answers to pressing topical social questions; namely how to behave in compliance with the religious laws in the modern world. There are hundreds of internet sites where committees of major Islamic scholars - or sometimes just enthusiastic individuals - give legal opinions that range from questions of personal behavior to theoretical political dilemmas. (Sisler 2006)

Sisler proceeded into in-depth analysis of virtual fatwas by 3 Muslim sites and found out that sites, which were directed to Diasporic Muslims offer a less restrictive interpretation of the Quran and Hadith. For example,

The ... muftis live in Western countries and know local laws and customs. Qaradawi has stated that in the case of contradicting fatwas a Muslim must follow the one that his true conscience believes is closer to the truth. The approach of Islam-Online towards sensitive issues is significantly different from the strict legalism of Fatwa-Online. This could be seen also in the revision of traditional Islamic legal dichotomy between Dār al-Harb and Dār al-Islām (literally 'The House of War' and 'The House of Islam'). The European Council for Fatwa and Research proposed that Western countries should be classified as Dār al-Da'wa - The House of Invitation. (Sisler 2006)

On the contrary, on the site www.fatwa-online.com the question of the judgment between the Muslims the mufti answers that, *It is obligatory for the Muslims to appoint a judge to pass judgment between them according to Islamic law (...) It is not permitted for (them) to request a legal decision from anyone who does not judge according to the Book of Allah and the Sunnah of His Messenger* (Caeiro 2003, 11).

There are indeed numerous efforts by European governmental organizations and NGOs to present alternative content to the members of the Muslim communities, which can be mentioned regarding their de-radicalization prominence. The Contextualizing Islam in Britain project, in which Cambridge University lead an established group of academics and scholars in a debate about Islam in the country. The content of these discussions will be disseminated to a wider audience, helping to strengthen young people's understanding of their faith. The Radical Middle Way Roadshows, which create an intellectual space to engage on issues that are confusing and challenging to young people through the use of prominent domestic and international Islamic scholars. They take place at a number of locations around the country, through cooperation with local partners. Young Muslims Advisory Group (YMAG is a group of 23 young Muslims, aged 17-26, from across England with a broad range of backgrounds and experiences which reflect the ethnic and denominational diversity of Muslim communities in the UK.

For all the initiatives, the de-radicalization process can be furthered and deepened both by internal effort of the Muslim community and religious authorities to provide a balanced view of the complex issues of the daily routine and by the effort of authorities to enable representation of cultures and different traditions into mainstream discourse. As such the Institute for the Near East Policy suggested that:

As countries in the Middle East and Europe have begun to better understand the radicalization process and what feeds it, many countries have begun to create programs to combat it. These programs are designed specifically to intervene early in the radicalization process to prevent it from taking place or to reverse radicalization in cases where it has already occurred. European countries are developing independent approaches to preventing radicalization, though some coordination is beginning to take place. (The Washington Institute for the Near East Policy 2009)

According to the Institute there are three main approaches dominating currently the policy of transition of Muslim values into European society: French, British and Dutch. The French strategy, according to the Institute, differs greatly from the British and Dutch approach in that France sees radicalization as a problem of social integration rather than a religious issue. As such, it maintains a strong police and intelligence presence, rather than cooperating with local imams to create a connection between them and the local community (The Washington Institute for the Near East Policy 2009). According to Mirahmadi & Farooq,

In the past twenty years, the French government has invested in an approach which relies heavily on law enforcement agency interventions. For example, when the Muslim terrorist threat reached its height during the Algerian civil war, France used its intelligence agencies to disrupt terrorist networks. Today, the state continues to maintain a strong sense of police and intelligence presence through the Central Directorate of Interior Intelligence which monitors individuals with suspected ties to radical groups. A great deal of the intelligence work is carried out by undercover agents who have the capacity to "incite" one or several suspects to break the law. Suspects with even the smallest or remote connection to a terrorist plot can be apprehended and imprisoned. (Mirahmadi & Farooq, 2010)

While France is confident that this approach is highly effective, there is more widespread support for the Dutch method. This approach involves greater community engagement and the use of tools — imams, teachers, and social workers — already existing within the community network. In Holland, the city of Amsterdam has developed a particularly innovative approach to countering radicalization at the local level. Amsterdam created an information house which has developed networks in the local communities, and to whom people can turn regarding concerns about specific individuals. This information house is designed to resolve and address concerns about radicalization versus merely increased religiosity, for example. The information house works closely with law enforcement, which is only involved if a given person is deemed to pose an immediate danger. Otherwise, the information house itself will try to intervene and defuse the situation.

According to Mirahmadi & Farooq:

[The British] PREVENT program is a good model because it works with a broad spectrum of Muslim voices, opens the marketplace of ideas, and empowers local organizations. Unfortunately this has also been the program's greatest weakness. Since a wide range of organizations were encouraged to seek partnerships with the government, few benchmarks for partnerships based on shared values were imposed. The government did not adequately differentiate between moderate, mainstream Muslims and hardline Islamist groups. As a result, some groups that worked against state interests, desired an Islamist state in the UK, and supported violent Jihad were empowered.46 It was not until four years after PREVENT was initiated, that the government published updated guidelines that stipulated Organizations funded under PREVENT need to demonstrate a commitment to our shared values. (Mirahmadi & Farooq, 2010)

Unfortunately, even this new policy has not stopped the UK government from working with unsavory groups. For those already in jails British government implemented the de-radicalization center, main features of which had been separation of extremist prisoners according to groups and ideology in order to slow the spread and exchange of jihadist ideology; Special staff overseeing each unit (Brandon, 2009).

It could be argued, then, that extremist movements succeed in offering potential recruits identities empowering them through the construction of their sense of self-confidence. Interestingly, this document stresses on a European Strategy on violent radicalization including a focus on employment, social exclusion and integration issues, equal opportunities and non-discrimination and inter-cultural dialogue as well as broadcast media, the Internet, education and youth engagement. This EC Communication argues that the failure to integrate provides "fertile ground for violent radicalization to develop". Furthermore, alienation from both the country of origin and the host country can make it more likely for a person to look for a sense of identity and belonging elsewhere such as in a powerful extremist ideology (Kerwin & Stock 2007).

In June 2009, the report of the EU Counter Terrorism Coordinator discussing the revision to the Radicalization and Recruitment Action Plan proposed action in six key areas, including mapping the current situation across EU Member States on Imam training to be led by Spain, and work on the role of local authorities in preventing radicalization led by the Netherlands. Swedish authorities took the lead for examining the role of police officers in recognizing and countering radicalization aiming at raising attention on the need of community policing. With regard to youth immigrants concerns, the November 2009 EC Counter Terrorism Discussion Paper reported that

Denmark is in the lead on disengagement and de-radicalization, particularly among young people. In addition to being a lead country, Denmark is currently implementing an EU-financed project on targeted intervention in relation to de-radicalization, which is headed by the Danish Ministry of refugee, Immigration and Integration Affairs and also involves the Danish Security and Intelligence Service and selected municipalities. Both projects are based on the Danish national action plan to prevent extremist views and radicalization among young people, which aims at strengthening democratic cohesion. (Fink & Hearne, 2008)

Though recently speared across Europe, the radicalization of Muslim groups is not a unique European phenomenon. It rather crosses the ocean towards other Western countries, as an Australian sad news cover. After a deadly attack of Haron Monis, which held several people hostage in the Lindt Chocolate Cafe [Australian] Authorities were concerned about a minority of Australia's small Muslim community. They have said that about 70 Australians are fighting with extremist groups in Syria and northern Iraq. Another 20 have returned to Australia after fighting in those places. Spy chief David Irvine, the director general of the Australian Security Intelligence Organization, said in August that about 15 Australians had been killed so far in these conflicts, including two suicide bombers. He also said 100 or more people within Australia were "actively supporting" militant groups by recruiting new fighters, grooming suicide-bombing candidates, and providing funds and equipment to militants (BBC NEWS AUSTRALIA, 2014).

SOLUTIONS AND RECOMMENDATIONS

In general, it can be concluded that regional and international security problems can be understood in more profound way if the research takes into account the relationship between terrorism and new media technologies. If the civilians are exposed to the information and technological revolution, it is logical to assume that terrorist groups share the same benefits and advantages. The terrorists endeavor to mobilize local and international groups, trying to gain advantage by activating loyal civilians who are exposed to the cultural and technological resources of their targets. In this respect, special interest can be brought to the issue of religious communities on the Internet.

FUTURE RESEARCH DIRECTIONS

The future research on the radicalization and de-racialization techniques and policy cannot be taken apart from the research on media, in this case of Internet media. Goetinck (2013) asks how can this issue of increasing radicalization be tackled and how do we prevent more youngsters from running off? Reflections on possible repressive or preventive measures has caused a lot of ink to flow: administrative or legal approach, discourage youngsters to fight in Syria through social media, to take away identity cards, counter-radicalization programs, prevention leaflets, online counter-discourse for radicalized youngsters.

The question of how Europe can prevent radical Muslims to head out in the future is thought-provoking, since these youngsters are gripped by the Jihadi ideology and do not dread prison sentences nor bullets. Moreover the EU authorities face the huge challenge of identifying the "would-be terrorists" among the fighters who returned from Syria. Though we need to contain the influence of these extremists, it is obvious that not all of these youngsters come back as terrorists by definition. Finally, the fuss about the foreign fighters should not be playing into the hands of those who believe that each pious Muslim is a potential threat for society (Goetinck, 2013). The research phase should not only indicate what are the current home issues facing security agencies in their fight of the terror threats, but also take into account international developments, threats and solutions.

CONCLUSION

It is clear that the way it takes long time to create a negative atmosphere to advance radicalization, the same if not longer time would it take to de-radicalize tensions. On the full specter of solutions and policy approaches from strict prohibition of any extremist activity and till the encouragement of the participation by all of the groups, including those whose loyalty is doubted, the final decision should be made when considering the characteristics of the group, support for the extremist voices and the individuals involved. Our research shows that among the tools for preventing of further radicalization and de-radicalization of the groups the *mentoring* and *"role modeling"* is suggested to be one of the most successful ones. Since, a substantial group of the youngsters involved in the terroristic activity look for social approve and sense of belonging, a person who been considered a terrorist and could show them the way out would serve as a powerful counter-effect.

Brandon suggests that 'de-radicalization' includes certain Islamist or Jihadist individual undergoes a number of experiences and realizations. These comprise of growing doubts about efficacy of Jihadist tactics and the morality of Jihadist attacks; increasing doubts about theological legitimacy of both Jihadism and wider Islamist ideology; realization that holding Jihadist beliefs is harming one's own personal interests – and a realization that such suffering is neither noble, glorious nor respected or appreciated by others; increased willingness to compromise initially on some minor aspects of Islamist ideology in order to improve quality of life in prison. They add that one of the important ways to restrain radicalization processes would be growing estrangement from other Jihadists at a social and personal level and growing tolerance for other ways of life and interpretations of Islam (Brandon, 2009).

A realization that non-Muslims are not intrinsically hostile to Islam and Muslims is crucial for successful de-radicalization process. The de-radicalization ideas are not always welcomed and sometimes are perceived in the negative light by the target audience. For example, the think tank Quilliam had been addressed in the following way by the Islamist forum:

I don´t know much about the "Quilliam Foundation" (because I´m not from the UK)... but two days ago I saw a video, where Maajid Nawaz (director of Quilliam Foundation) spoke... and the things that he said were full of Kufr.... and he always used words like "extremists", "fundamentalists" etc. ... Allahul Mustazan!! I just looked at their Website.... and seems to me, as if they are promoting a completely other...Deen!!...May ALLAH swt destroy the Quilliam Foundation and their Dhala! (Quilliam 2009)

Presenting alternative content and promoting shift in the discourse is an important task both for the Western countries and Muslim communities living within. Probably this is the reason why more and more sound Muslim scholars try to provide non-violent commentaries and even issue fatwas, which are aimed to reduce terroristic activities within the communities. An example for the development of this shift can be the "Anti-terrorism fatwa" launched in London on March 2nd, 2010. The fatwa was launched by the renowned, mainstream Muslim scholar Shaikh Dr Tahir ul-Qadri who issued a comprehensive fatwa prohibiting terrorism and suicide bombing at a press conference in Westminster, London. Founder of the international Minhaj-ul-Quran movement, his fatwa was significant because Minhaj-ul-Quran is a major grass-roots organization with hundreds of thousands of followers in South Asia and the UK. Its special significance is due to the fact that Shaikh Dr Tahir ul-Qadri is a widely recognized and respected authority on Islamic jurisprudence. Moreover, the fatwa condemns suicide bombers as destined for hell, which helps remove extremists' certainty of earning paradise after death. Finally, the 600-page fatwa is arguably the most comprehensive theological refutation of Islamist terrorism to date and thus Dr Tahir ul-Qadri's fatwa will set an important precedent and will allow other scholars to similarly condemn the ideas behind terrorism (SAJA FORUM 2010).

It can be concluded, that the actual work by the governments should underline a real shift in values by the terrorist and extremist activities recruits which can be achieved by few steps: a successful work on the community level, where they ought to offer a real partnership for the Muslim community members. The next step would be the development of the competitive coherent messages both in terms of interest and relevance to the audience. This can contest with the extremist solutions and interpretations of the terror recruiters and mobilizers and putting forward a more positive and peaceful alternatives. It is however should be done within carious strategy as Ashour mentions that: "Since the 1960s, empirical data have consistently shown that sophisticated counterarguments to the ideologies of violent extremists without conveyance by credible messengers can have only limited success (Ashour 2010).

REFERENCES

A Framework for Understanding Terrorist Use of the Internet. (2006). *ITAC, 2*, The Canadian Centre for Intelligence and Security Studies, The Norman Paterson School of International Affairs, Carleton University. Retrieved from http://www4.carleton.ca/cifp/app/serve.php/1121.pdf

Anspaha, K. (2008, September 25). The Integration of Islam in Europe: Preventing the radicalization of Muslim Diasporas and counterterrorism policy. *Paper presented at the ECPR 4TH Pan-European conference on EU Politics*. Retrieved from http://www.jhubc.it/ecpr-riga/virtualpaperroom/026.pdf

Ashour, O. (2010). Online De-Radicalization? Countering Violent Extremist Narratives: Message, Messenger and Media Strategy, *Perspectives on Terrorism, 4*(6). Retrieved from http://www.terrorismanalysts.com/pt/index.php/pot/article/view/128/html

Brandon, J. (2009). *Unlocking Al-Qaeda - Islamist Extremism in British Prisons*. London: Quilliam.

Bukay, D. (2006, Fall). The Religious Foundations of Suicide Bombings Islamist Ideology. *Middle East Quarterly, 13*(4), 27–36. Retrieved from http://www.meforum.org/1003/the-religious-foundations-of-suicide-bombings

Caeiro, A. (2003, March 19-23). The European Council for Fatwa and Research. Proceedings of the *Fourth Mediterranean Social and Political Research Meeting*, European University Institute, Florence.

Carter, J. A., Maher, S., & Neumann, P. R. (2014). #Greenbirds: Measuring Importance and Influence in Syrian Foreign Fighter Networks. *ICSR* report. King's College, London. Retrieved from http://icsr.info/wp-content/uploads/2014/04/ICSR-Report-Greenbirds-Measuring-Importance-and-Infleunce-in-Syrian-Foreign-Fighter-Networks.pdf

Castells, M. (1997). *The Power of Identity: The Information Age, Economy, Society, and Culture* (Vol. 2). Oxford: Blackwell Publishers.

Coll, S., & Glasser, S. B. (2005, August 7). Terrorists turn to the Web as base of operations, *The Washington Post*, A1.

Eickelman, D. F. (1998, Winter). Inside the Islamic Reformation. *The Wilson Quarterly, 22*(1), 80–89.

Eickelman, D. F., & Piscatori, J. (Eds.), (1990). *Muslim Travellers: Piegrimage, Migration and the Religious Imagination*. Berkeley: University of California Press.

Esman, A. R. (2014, April 25). Experts Warn More European Muslim Youth Are Radicalizing. *IPT News*. Retrieved from http://www.investigativeproject.org/4362/experts-warn-more-european-muslim-youth-are#

Fink, N. C., & Hearne, E. B. (2008, October). Beyond Terrorism: Deradicalization and Disengagement from Violent Extremism. IPI Publications & International Peace Institute Report. Retrieved from http://www.ipinst.org/media/pdf/publications/beter.pdf

German authorities arrest three people for alleged ties to Syrian radical group. (2014 March 31). *Deutsche Welle*. Retrieved from http://www.dw.de/german-authorities-arrest-three-people-for-alleged-ties-to-syrian-radical-group/a-17533472

Gilligan, A. (2014, April 20). 'Trojan Horse' schools: the leaked inspectors report. *The Telegraph*. Retrieved from http://blogs.telegraph.co.uk/news/andrewgilligan/100268346/trojan-horse-schools-the-leaked-inspectors-report/

Goetinck, M. (2013, October 25). Syria: a magnet for European Radicalised Muslim Youngsters. *MEDEA Institute*. Retrieved from http://www.medea.be/2013/10/syria-a-magnet-for-european-radicalised-muslim-youngsters/

Institute for Strategic Dialogue. (n. d.). The Role of Civil Society in counter-Radicalisation and De-Radicalisation, *PPN Working Paper*. Retrieved from http://www.strategicdialogue.org/allnewmats/idandsc2010/PPNPaper-CommunityEngagement.pdf

Islam: Anti-terrorism fatwa launch in London. (2010, March 2). *SAJA FORUM*. Retrieved from http://www.sajaforum.org/2010/03/islam-antiterrorism-fatwa-to-be-issued-in-london.html

Johnson, B. (2014, March 2). The children taught at home about murder and bombings. *The Telegraph*. Retrieved from http://www.telegraph.co.uk/news/politics/10671841/The-children-taught-at-home-about-murder-and-bombings.html

Kerwin, D., & Stock, M. D. (2007, Fall). National Security and Immigration Policy: Reclaiming Terms, Measuring Success, and Setting Priorities. *The Homeland Security Review*, *1* (3), 1-56. Retrieved from http://www.teachingterror.net/HS/National_Security_and_Immigration_Policy.pdf

Kimhi, S. & Even, S. (2004, November). Who are the Palestinian Suicide Bombers?, *Jaffe Institute for Strategic studies, Memo 73*, Ramat Aviv, Tel Aviv University.

Louis, B. (2003). The Crisis of Islam – Holy War and Unholy Terror (p. 117; p, 132). New York: Random House.

Mandaville, P. (1999, March). Digital Islam: Changing the boundaries of religious knowledge? *Newsletter 2*, 23. Retrieved from https://openaccess.leidenuniv.nl/bitstream/handle/1887/17137/ISIM_2_Digital_Islam-Changing_the_Boundaries_of_Religious_Knowledge.pdf?sequence=1

Mirahmadi, H., & Farooq, M. (2010, December). A Community Based Approach to Countering Radicalization - A Partnership for America, *World Organization for Resource, Development and Education (WORDE)*. Retrieved from http://www.worde.org/wp-content/uploads/2010/12/WORDE-Counter-Radicalization-Report-Final.pdf

Moore, C. (2014, April 18). A weak establishment is letting Islamists threaten British freedoms, *The Telegraph*. Retrieved from http://www.telegraph.co.uk/news/uknews/terrorism-in-the-uk/10775118/A-weak-establishment-is-letting-Islamists-threaten-British-freedoms.html

Neumann, P. R. (2008). *Joining al-Qaeda: Jihadist Recruitment in Europe* (p. 7). New York: Routledge.

Neumann, P. R., & Rogers, B. (2007). *Recruitment and mobilization for the Islamist militant movement in Europe, A study carried out by King's College London, the 4th European Commission King's College*. London: University of London.

Pidd, H. (2014a, March 7). Alleged plot to 'take over' and run schools on strict Islamic principles. *The Guardian*. Retrieved from http://www.theguardian.com/uk-news/2014/mar/07/alleged-plot-birmingham-schools-islamic-principles

Pidd, H. (2014b, April 14). *Twenty-five Birmingham schools inspected over Islamist 'takeover plot.' The Guardian*. Retrieved from http://www.theguardian.com/uk-news/2014/apr/14/birmingham-schools-investigated-over-islamist-takeover-allegations

Ranstorp, M. (1996, Summer). Terrorism in the name of religion. *Journal of International Affairs*, *50*(1).

Rewriting the Narrative - An Integrated Strategy for Counter-radicalization. (2009, March). Presidential Study Group Reports. *The Washington Institute for the Near East Policy*. Retrieved from http://www.washingtoninstitute.org/templateC04.php?CID=311

Rosenthal, J. (2014, April 9). European jihadists form ISIS brigades in Syria, *ALMONITOR*. Retrieved from http://www.al-monitor.com/pulse/originals/2014/04/europe-jihadist-isis-syria-qaeda-terror-france-germany.html#

Roy, O. (2007). Islamic Terrorist Radicalisation in Europe. *Centre for European Policy Studies (CEPS)*. Retrieved from http://www.isn.ethz.ch/Digital-Library/Publications/Detail/?ots591=0c54e3b3-1e9c-be1e-2c24-a6a8c7060233&lng=en&id=45688

Sageman, M. (2005, Spring). The Normality of Global Jihadi Terrorism. *The Journal of International Security Affairs*, *8*, 1–10.

Schiffauer, W. (1999). Islamism in the Diaspora: The Fascination of Political Islam among Second Generation German Turks, *Transnational Communities Program Working Paper*, Oxford. Retrieved from http://www.transcomm.ox.ac.uk/working%20papers/Schiffauer_Islamism.PDF

Sisler, V. (2006). Islamic Jurisprudence in Cyberspace: Construction of Interpretative Authority in Muslim Diaspora. In R. Polcak, et. al. (Eds.), *Proceedings of Cyberspace 2005 conference*, Brno, Masaryk University (pp. 43–50). Retrieved from http://www.digitalislam.eu/article.do?articleId=1420

Ulph, S. (2007, May 24). The Salafist and Islamist framework for Jihadism, Manifesto Experts. *Testimony to the Open Hearing of the Senate Select Committee on Intelligence*. Retrieved from http://intelligence.senate.gov/070612/ulph.pdf

Unlocking Al-Qaeda: Islamist extremism in British prisons. (2009, February). *Quilliam, British de-radicalisation centre*. Retrieved from http://www.sunniforum.com/forum/showthread.php?52941-British-de-radicalisation-centre

Van der Laan, D. S. (2014, April 23). AIVD: twee Nederlandse jihadisten pleegden zelfmoordaanslag, *ELSEVIER*. Retrieved from http://www.elsevier.nl/Nederland/nieuws/2014/4/AIVD-twee-Nederlandse-jihadisten-pleegden-zelfmoordaanslagen-1508028W/?cmpid=NLC%7Celsevier_dagelijks%7C2014-04-23%7CAIVD:_twee_Nederlandse_jihadisten_pleegden_zelfmoordaanslag

Vatis, M. (2001). Cyber Terrorism and Information Warfare: Government Perspectives. In Y. Alexander & M. S. Swetnam (Eds.), *Cyber Terrorism and Information Warfare*. New York: Transnational Publishers Inc.

Waardenburg, J. (1998). *Islam et Science des Religions*. Paris: Les Belles Lettres.

Who are Australia's radicalised Muslims? (2014, December 16). *BBC NEWS AUSTRALIA*. Retrieved from http://www.bbc.com/news/world-asia-29249462

KEY TERMS AND DEFINITIONS

Community: A social, religious, occupational, or other group sharing common characteristics or interests and perceived or perceiving itself as distinct in some respect from the larger society within which it exists.

De-Radicalisation Factors: Include a range of activities to reduce radicalization and tense. Usually include civil society and cultural awareness initiatives.

European Muslims: Total number of people creeding Islam in European Union, not including Turkey.

Internet Content: Written content specifically designed to appear in websites.

Internet Terror: The use of Internet in terrorist activities, including acts of deliberate, large-scale manipulation, falsification, propagation and mobilisation to seed terror and fear.

Manipulation: Psychological manipulation is a type of social influence that aims to change the perception or behavior of others through underhanded, deceptive, or even abusive tactics.

Mobilization: Act of marshaling and organizing and making ready for use or action.

Radicalisation: Radicalization (or radicalisation) is a process by which an individual or group comes to adopt increasingly extreme political, social, or religious ideals and aspirations that (1) reject or undermine the status quo or (2) reject and/or undermine contemporary ideas and expressions of freedom of choice.

Recruitment: The action of finding new people to join an organization or support a cause.

Religious Discourse: Usually refers to religious language in the major world faiths from various viewpoints and reflects on how it is situated within wider intellectual and cultural contexts.

Religious Inclination: Characteristic disposition or tendency to act in a religion guided way; a propensity to follow religious guidance.

Terror Prevention: The attempt to reduce deter terror and terrorists.

Chapter 9
The Value of Personal Information

K.Y Williams
Walden University, USA

Dana-Marie Thomas
Walden University, USA

Latoya N. Johnson
Walden University, USA

ABSTRACT

Many cyber-attacks that result in data loss can be prevented if the target of the cyber-attack is properly prepared, has the necessary and latest defenses in place, and is constantly monitoring for attacks and intrusions. Whether those cyber-attacks occur as a result of user error; network issues (password files being created and distributed to a list of people); direct assaults (direct intrusion via a designed hack, system flaw, or exploitation of a known network/software issue); or due to an insider-threat (giving a password to a trusted co-worker who then uses it for other means) one aspect of prevention that must be addressed is the need for better security and additional layers of protection on the data that resides on the servers and in computing systems. With up-to-date protocols, reduced access to the system, and compartmentalization of information, it is possible to reduce the amount and type of data that is lost in many cyber-attacks. This chapter explores five types of information that are targeted during cyber-attacks, and discuss why this information is of importance.

DOI: 10.4018/978-1-4666-9661-7.ch009

INTRODUCTION

With each cyber-attack the amount and type of data that hackers are retrieving is increasing with more vicious, blunt force, direct attacks, and in the accuracy and efficiency of the attacks. Government agencies have noticed that during the past decade the increase in the information targeted by hackers has grown from what was only information found on servers in government agencies to now include information from servers of financial systems and corporate entities. With this increase of cyber-attacks, the nature of the stolen information has increased to include more specific, personal information.

In the past many individuals, organizations, academic institutions, companies, and government agencies generally thought that one individual alone was usually responsible for as attack, and in the past this may have been the case. However, it is no longer plausible to think that a sole individual is responsible for the substantial number of hacks that occurred over the past decade. In fact, it is far more reasonable to think that larger groups of individuals numbering from three to ten (at least) are responsible for the attacks that have occurred on the different companies, financial entities, and government agencies, and depending on the sophistication and complexity of the system, the number of people involved only grows. Interestingly more direct well-coordinated cyber-attacks targeted towards an individual, organization, academic institution, company, and government agency are no longer scarce, and they are becoming commonplace.

With the increase in the number of cyber-attacks, it seems that hackers may have obtained and secured diverse funding sources to support the cyber-attacks. With renewed funding, computational resources, networking, and multimedia/storage resources, hackers are able to achieve the goal(s) of their attacks with more accuracy and efficiency than in previous years. By utilizing the underlying nature and blind spots within digital systems and having a familiarity with the encryptions used within digital systems, advanced coding, and general knowledge of the flaws within operating systems and servers, hackers are finding it easier and easier to access the targeted systems. This makes the timing and type of attack increase with more efficiency, and with each attack it leaves many of the targets even more vulnerable than expected.

As the number of security breaches increase, hackers not only are able to explore systems with each attack, but also may leave ways to get back into a system for future use. With each intrusion into the system, the information that hackers target range from personal to financial to intellectual in nature. Because the type of information obtained during an attack can vary, it is important to keep in mind that the intent of the attack may be based on the motivation of the person or organization who intends to use the information obtained by the hackers, and not necessarily the hackers themselves if it is done for the benefit of a third party. Private information such as Personal Identifying Information (PII), Personal Health Information (PHI), and private data is valuable in a very particular market and to select groups of people/buyers. Financial Information, Credit Information, and Credit History Information will have a different market, such as others who may have a desire of to gain financially, in the immediate future, or the long term. However, intellectual property and discovery information have a very different value and interest to the right company, buyer, or agency. Additionally cyber-attacks and security breaches that target these types of information hold value if the right combination of information is placed together to create a profile or idea of a particular person, or if the goal is to gain financially from a security breach. This chapter explores these types of information, discusses how the information can be used to compromise individuals, organizations, academic institutions, companies, government agencies, and then explores how financial institutions can be affected by such intrusions.

BACKGROUND

Intrusions into Personal, Private, and Professional Lives

Nothing is impenetrable. If someone designed or built a computer system or network, then it is possible for someone else to penetrate, circumvent, cripple, dismantle, or occupy the system. No one in the computer industry, information storage industry, or technology development industry wants to think of cyber-attacks, unwanted intrusions, or security breaches occurring as it will become a nightmare to investigate, report, and analyze the breached systems when these attacks do occur. However when they occur various checks must occur to ensure that the potential for them to occur in the future is reduced. Cyber-attacks on individuals, organizations, corporations, government agencies, financial institutions, and academic institutions occur and recent events within the last decade would give anyone the impression that those attacks occur on a daily basis, or that they are becoming more and more common place. These data breaches have increased in number and frequency as a result of the improvements in technology, the innovations and strides made within technology and wireless communication, and with the increased capabilities of remote and wireless networks. With each new capability and system access, such innovations make it easier for hackers to gain access to more secure systems. Having personal and private computers, smartphones, home security systems, and televisions that have wireless connections connected to the internet through a private network does not mean that it is secure even though it is on a private network. It only means that they are networked to the same system and convenient to the owner. Therefore, it is not surprising that these advances have also affected corporate security.

At the time of writing of this manuscript, two highly publicized and very detailed cyber-attacks occurred on Sony Pictures Entertainment and Sony Gaming System affecting their servers and data networks. With these types of cyber-attacks, Sony Pictures Entertainment security systems were breached and approximately 100 TBs of data/information was taken from their servers (Robb, 2014). Information in the form of unreleased motion pictures, incomes of the executive employees, PII, and detailed financial information of the company was placed on the Internet by a group called Guardians of Peace (Robb, 2014). In addition to the leaked movies from Sony Pictures Entertainment, the group responsible for the hack also released employee data/information and warned employees that their "family will be in danger." This also was accompanied with additional demands in regards to not releasing a movie that portrayed the Democratic People's Republic of Korea leader Kim Jong-un in a negative light (Robb, 2014). This is just one example of how the goal of the intrusion is related to the type of the information stolen when a system is hacked.

Private networks are not only vulnerable to cyberattacks, but they have also been hacked to allow intruders to enter into private systems where they have been able to take control of an automobile (CBS, 2014), air traffic control systems (Cooper, 2015), and nuclear power plants (Kwaak, 2015). Such incidents are not a representation of the normal home systems, but with each system coming online as a result of wireless connections to any network, it allows for additional ways for intruders to enter and penetrate our levels of privacy to include our cars, homes, finances, and personal communication devices. Recent hacks of several manufactures of webcams by a Russian group showed that many users of the different systems and services use the manufactures' passwords to not only setup up the system, but also they retained the manufactures' default password after installing the system. This made it easy for the group to gain access to private systems and then exploit them based on the information. The group then showed the world how users are not making themselves safe or safer based on the use of manufacturers' passwords and their inability to change basic features and system passwords (Kottasova, 2014).

A further explanation into the types of commonly hacked information and how they are related to the goal of the hacker (or the hacker's client) may help the system and network engineers better equip their infrastructures to thwart cyber-attacks.

MAIN FOCUS OF CHAPTER

Intrusions into Personal, Private Lives

Private information includes Personal Identifying Information (PII), Personal Health Information (PHI), and private data and holds value for different reasons. Eleanor Meux (1994) stated that data that includes PII such as "demographic (e.g., race, gender, age) and clinical (e.g., diagnoses, procedure)" data that can be linked to financial information should be considered confidential as it becomes of value. This information becomes of value not only to the person whose information is contained within the documents, but also to individuals that could benefit from knowing about said data within the documentation. Most documents that contain such information usually include social security numbers and dates of birth.

Research published on the use of PII and the use of the information when acquired via cyber-attacks revealed that it can be used to create a false identity and to commit fraud only under the disguise of another individual (i.e., identity theft). Additionally these results have shown that PII is valuable in a very particular market and to select groups of people/buyers. From this research several other things have become apparent in terms of risks. Research into the use and acquisition of PHI exposed that information containing personal health information has been used to deny individuals health insurance or coverage based on pre-existing, and could be used in gaining treatment for illnesses based on the information of a person with health insurance. Within the software and web community many times programmers and developers do not take security into consideration at every step and stage of the development process, therefore many issues can arise after the deployment of a website or a software suite of programs. However security of medical and clinical data (Chen, et. al. 2009) and personal information (Landi & Rao, 2003) is necessary at each stage of development of software, websites, and web applications. Neame (2013) reiterated that sharing of health records can be done effectively and in a private manner, and goes on to share how "a method of verifying authenticity, integrity, and authorships is required, which can be provided using a public key infrastructure (PHI) for crytopgraphy" a sentiment previously stated by Steinbrook (2008).

Financial Information

Credit Information and Credit History Information is another form of information targeted during cyber-attacks. This can have a lasting effect on individuals when issues are not resolved immediately and in the proper manner. The three credit agencies that monitor the actions of individuals usually rely on information submitted from companies that have accounts associated with individuals by demographic information (name, age, and income) and social security numbers. Because this type of PII can be acquired via cyber-attack it becomes easier for someone to assume the identity of an individual and make purchases in another person's name. If only demographic and social security information is used by the credit agencies then it becomes impossible for a person to correct the errors or purchases if they are not made immediately aware of the issues. Similar to financial institutions, credit institutions offer constant credit monitoring as an option (and usually after credit incidents have occurred); therefore credit incidents can go unnoticed until an individual applies for credit or obtains a copy of his or her credit report.

This type of information usually has a different market and interest to others who may have an idea of wanting to gain financially via larger purchases that can go unnoticed or undiscovered. When information of this type is captured it is easily identifiable and usable in different systems and in the establishment of other identities. Information in the form or emails, text messages, photos (Sang, Ling, & Alam, 2012) and credit card information can be easily captured by hackers via cyber-attack and card skimmers. Sang, et al., (2012) outlined how security measures can be used to encrypt this information and also how information within text format can be encrypted and hidden with double-random phase encoding.

Value attributed to financial information has also shown that the right information can be used to instantly affect the bank accounts and credit accounts of individuals from various financial institutions. With constant monitoring of debit/credit activity being an option for bank accounts as opposed to the standard package of a bank account, this lapse in security makes it easier for a hacker with the proper financial information to recreate a debit card or credit card containing stolen credit/bank information. This type of financial gain can be traced to various locations and purchases without giving the actual identity of the individual or group who stole the information, but it should generate information on who may have used the information and in what manner.

Intrusions into Professional Lives

Intellectual Property in the way of innovation, invention, software and application (Apps) development has the potential for increased financial gain. Regardless of who developed the information, having information or the discovery of information can be of value to any interested individual, corporation, agency, or institution – if they are the right company, buyer, or agency. In many cases, the gain of the type of information may be proprietary, and this type of information may be accessed via different means than the normal cyber-attack or in addition to a cyber-attack. Intellectual property and discovery information may be acquired via cyber-espionage or corporate espionage (see other manuscript). The loss of such information due to a cyber-attack becomes costly to the company, individual, agency, or institution in terms of legal fees, court time, and trade agreements. However by encrypting the information with the use of double-random phase encoding methods (Sang, et al., 2012) it is possible to add an additional layer of security onto the information that will allow for more security on systems where proprietary information resides.

With all of the information that can be gained and the value that is contained within each form of information, there are various ways that someone can use the information for present and future gain. Therefore one must ask the questions: *Once information is in hand, what can be done with it?* Additional questions include: *Will someone be able to construct an identity or re-construction an identity based on the information? Is it possible to falsify information or reproduce records for another individual?*

When faced with the following two questions, *will someone be able to construct an identity or re-construction an identity based on the information,* and *is it possible to falsify information or reproduce records for another individual,* one must think about the value of the information to others, not to themselves. Once hackers have personal information in hand, any number of things can occur and can be done with the information. The limits are only at the whims of the person who is using the information and his or her intentions. If a hacker sells the information to someone who is looking to conduct any fraudulent actions then the use of the person's demographic information, SSN, and salary can be used to recreate an identity and begin to purchase items based on the person's identity and credit information. Opening additional credit accounts and making purchases using a person's identity can go undetected if the person is not aware of the actions for at least one week; however, the actions can be stopped by paying attention to ones credit on a routine bases. If a hacker sold the personal health information of someone who has a very good health insurance plan to someone who needs medical attention, then the recipient would be able to receive medical treatment and healthcare for personal medical illnesses that they normally would not have been able to be treated for based on their own health insurance.

Reconstruction of an identity is not as difficult as one would assume mainly because various electronic entities do not communicate with each other, and different data systems and databases do not have access to information that other systems may have, (*i.e.,* banking and financial institutions usually do not have access to medical records). Therefore a person who lives in Washington, D.C. may be able to have their personal health information duplicated and used by someone in Birmingham, AL in an effort for the person to obtain medical treatment for an illness, but a financial institution would not be aware of the intrusion. However if the person used the stolen personal financial and personal health information to duplicate an identity, debit or credit card, and try to obtain medical treatment for an illness, then the financial institution would be aware of the duplication. The financial institution would alert the person that someone may have tried to use a debit or credit card with their information in another location that where they normally use their debit or credit card, but it does not mean that the financial institution would alert other authorities or health care providers or insurance companies that a potential breach is occurring or have occurred.

Value in Each Type of Information

Different forms of risks exist: intrusions into personal privacy, loss/acquisition of PII and/or PHI, financial loss, loss of credit/changes in credit, denial of service, data reduction, data duplication, data loss, loss of physical and intellectual property, and/or breaches of personal and network security. However, these security risks can be reduced by having improved security measures, reducing activity and access to private networks, establishing password update and reminder measures, adding additional authentication methods, and improving on identification and authentication methods.

The thought that hackers do not exist or that the average person is not a target is slim in regards to the amount of information that is leaked and how it can affect an individual. Within any security or law enforcement agency that provides protection for each of these agencies/systems – police, government, intelligence, or industry – members of the security field usually have a clear idea of the type of person(s) that are responsible for the incidents based on digital signatures, known identity/aliases, language structure/coding style, or confirmation of identity for known offenses. Many agencies have information on prior offenses and people that have hacked their systems in the past. For instance, the FBI's list of 10 most wanted cyber criminals (as of December 14, 2014) (Pagliery, 2014) included:

- Nicolae Popescu
- Dumitru Daniel Bosogioiu

- Evgeniy Mikhailovich Bogachev
- The Chinese Army Five
- Alexsey Belan
- Peteris Sahurovs
- Artem Semenov
- Alexandr Sergeyevich Bobnev
- Carlos Enrique Perez-Melara, and
- Noor Aziz Uddin

Each of these individuals and/or group is wanted for various crimes and carries rewards ranging from no reward to $1 Million USD. Each of the named cyber criminals allegedly committed crimes that ranged from writing malicious spyware that affected consumers on public websites such as personal and private information on dating sites, to defrauding government agencies, companies or everyday customers of bank information, payments, or PIN (personal identification numbers) for ATM transactions. The type of crime does not simply reflect large crimes that affect only one type of entity or large organizations or companies, but it also ranged to affecting the everyday costumer of companies such as Loews, Walmart, Home Depot, J.C. Penney, and Sears.

Hackers who have perpetuated such crimes began with simply learning how to code, and the ability to code (or writing in code), which can be gained by proper education, being self-taught or instinctually. Coding can be outsourced to private companies, individuals, or as a recently as December 5, 2014 even convicted criminals (Fink & Segall, 2014). Fink and Segall (2014) states that convicted criminals with no direct computer access are being taught and trained to code while thy complete their incarceration periods. For example the inmates of San Quentin State Prison are being trained to code as a means of trying to prepare them for a life outside of prison, these prisoners are being trained with the hopes of allowing them to gain a set of skills that should help them reduce recidivism and give the prisoners a hope for a better life and job prospects outside of prison. Recidivism rates for convicted felons are particularly high for repeat offenders. However, equipping a convicted felon with a set of skills that can affect a large number of people's personal information, personal health information, and credit information can be seen as a potential hazard and risk. The convicted felon may be considered a risk for individuals and companies who would employ the individuals once they are released from prison as other members of society would see the individuals as having a larger propensity for using the skills gained to create more sophisticated crimes in the future, especially given the value in each of the types of information that can be obtained during a cyber-attack.

PII

Personal Identifying Information (PII) holds a wealth of information. PII such as demographic information (age, race, income, ethnicity, address, SSN, and salary) allows for many data managers and data manipulators to be able to reconstruct or duplicate the identity of a person if they possessed the right sequence and type of information. Research shows this type of information is valuable and necessary for identity theft and identity reconstruction. Meux (1994) suggested that information available in discharge records and discharge databases that contain SSN should be encrypted as it contains personal identifiers. The researcher developed a Record Linkage Number encryption algorithm that would allow the encryption of SSN so that databases could be released to the necessary agencies that require records of discharge information without releasing the SSN. It is not unheard of that systems are compromised for various types of information, as this information can easily assist criminals in creating false identities. However, other forms of information are just as valuable as PII. When this information is coupled with financial information then identity reconstruction becomes possible, and at that point only physical/health information complete with biometric data would be a means for correctly identifying individuals when disputes arise over proper identification. Systems and services have reported how such information as PHI and PII can be invaluable for the use of identity duplication and identity reconstruction.

PHI

Personal Health Information (PHI) is invaluable when used as a means to identify an individual, as a way to get medical treatment for an ailment, or when used to extort money from an individual that would otherwise wish to keep certain health information private. PHI can be used to properly identify an individual who may have been assaulted, murdered, or may be living under an assumed identity. Having the medical and health information of the individual can rule out individuals or properly identify the individual that is using the information. Individuals who may not have medical/health insurance or wish to be treated for an ailment may assume the identity of an individual who does have the same ailment and is being treated for the same ailment. In this case, having the PII and PHI of the individual can assist a person in getting the necessary treatment for the ailment. In many instances physicians do not retain photographs of individuals or transmit identifiable information along with records from one medical facility to another; therefore, it becomes easier for a person to assume the identity of someone when they have the necessary information for identity theft. Many individuals wish to keep certain information private as the stigma associated with various diseases tend to cause others to wonder about the potential for the individual to accomplish a task or question their ability to perform the duties of a position. The need to keep information private increase when it can result in the loss of a position, the loss of wages as a result of illnesses, or potentially a change in career as a result of various types of diagnoses. Therefore, it becomes imperative that an individuals' health information should remain private.

Guan, Zhang, and Ji (2013) maintains that privacy of medical data can and should be made secure and private as early as preschool in order to protect and students' privacy and to remove stigmas associated with certain ailments. Therefore, they developed an algorithm that protects PHI of preschoolers' privacy as it is "unnecessary for education authorities to know the identities of the children." They suggest the use of a public key cryptosystem to secure the medical health data.

Financial Information

In terms of financial information, it is not unheard of for a financial institution to have information removed from a system; however, the layers of authentication needed to get to the financial information makes it more difficult to infiltrate than to receive the information from a different source. Take for instance some of the most publically known data hacks that occurred with regard to information from customers that has affected and implicated financial institutions. Such hacks included the penetration of Home Depot, Target, Sony, TJX, and Heartland – five of the biggest ever credit card hacks compiled and reported by Jose Pagliery and Julianne Pepitone of CNNTech (Pagliery & Pepitone, 2014), include:

1. Home Depot had to investigate whether customer data in the form of debit and credit cards were lost as a result of a hack to their payment/electronic charge system. It is estimated that more than 40 million customers' information was lost. This can lead to a reduction in many aspects of the corporation in the way of customer trust, store foot-traffic, revenue, and stock prices.
2. Heartland Payment Systems (Heartland) was hacked in 2008 and reported data loss for 130 million customers. Heartland processes credit card payments for companies that use VISA, MasterCard, and American Express. This type of data loss is one of the largest in history due to the number of people affected and the companies it affected.
3. In 2005, TJX, which includes stores such as T.J. Maxx and Marshalls, lost the data of 94 million customers to a data breach that went unnoticed. Within this breach, customer credit card information was also retrieved and stolen from the company computer system. The exact nature of the breach was not clear to the customers that were affected.
4. Although Sony has had several public breaches in the past five years, two of the most well-known occurred in 2011 and 2014. In 2011, Sony PlayStation Network use of the media streaming service Qriocity investigated an "external intrusion" that put customers' information at risk. Later Sony Online Entertainment placed personal information at risk not credit card information which affected 77 million customers. The 2014 hack of the aforementioned system suggested that there was North Korea Regime involvement, which resulted in a 100TB of information being leaked to the public.
5. During the 2013 holiday season Target was targeted and infiltrated. This theft included data for 40 million cards that were used between November 27, 2013 and December 15, 2013. Within this theft numerous safeguards and alarms within their system were reported to have been triggered but ignored.

Timing of conflicts and intrusion within any system is very important and costly with any system. Whether that intrusion is in the form of a data breach, a reduction in services, a denial of services, an unwanted intrusion, an access of the system, or data leak, the use of the system and having access to the system after an attack leaves the institutions vulnerable. Use of the system and timing of the system intrusion can result in loss of the system for future use. Axelrod and Iliev (2014) discuss the timing of cyber conflicts and how resources and use of resources can be timed to determine when resources should be used and how they can be exploited.

If one was to review the data breach of Target 2013 it is possible to see how using this information could have been optimized based on the mathematical modeling of Axelrod and Iliev. Because of the holiday period a massive amount of information could have been gathered and taken between the days of Black Friday and Christmas Eve of 2013. Using information and sale data available within the company reports and normally reported during the holiday period should and could show spending patterns of the customers that can be used in planning and implementing a targeted attack. With proper planning and targeting, a well targeted attack could have impacted the system more than what was intended based on the reports of the cyber-attack. This type of data loss is expanded upon in the companion chapter located within this volume, titled: *Cyber-Threat Detection in Corporate and Cyber-Espionage*.

University of Maryland Economics graduate student Calvin Wang, states that 2015 will be a year of increased cyber-attacks simply from the trends within the global market. With an eye and ear for Macroeconomics and Policies governing trade agreements, Wang expects a large increase in cyber-attacks that will start to target the trade industry. Additionally he hypothesizes that more hacks will focus on privacy violations and global prosperity and loss of intellectual property and financial hacks. It is common belief that in a time of crisis, it seems that it becomes plausible for a company and individuals to steal rather than to conceive their own brilliant idea.

Ideally one considers economic and social trends that would be affected based on an increase in cyberterrorism. However it is necessary to think about the effect on the micro and macro scales as well. National Security within every country will play a part in how the economy will be affected, not only locally, but also internationally as other nations are also entangled and intertwined. This could lead to a larger effect than one could imagine, especially as it relates to trade, finance, and industrial finance in the form of lending, banking, savings, and networks that are linked to affected targets.

No doubt, it becomes clear how an increase in cyber-attacks would have an effect on the system, and it would become problematic for victims and markets that are the target of the cyber-attacks. Unfortunately, the cyber-attacks will get worse with the constant networking and connections that use and rely upon advanced technology and wireless connections. The heady dependence on wireless access and networking for convenience makes it easier for hackers to have access to private computers, personal information that is in public domains, general consumer information that resides in purchasable databases, spending/purchasing habits and information within the infrastructure of places of employment.

Credit Information

Credit Information and PII are necessary for identity reconstruction and identity theft. In these instances it is necessary to have an idea of the person's credit history and credit information when assuming the identity of an individual. With a person's PII any criminal can obtain a copy of a credit report of the intended target. This information can be used to establish credit at another location and also compromise the credit of an individual in the future based on purchases, credit cards, and bank information that the perpetrator may have at his (or her) disposal. However, this is not limited to just assuming an identity and making purchases but also to reproducing the credit history of another individual as one's own. Therefore one must ask, *"How long before the credit agencies become the target?"*

With the right intrusion method, credit agencies and their methods for thwarting threats to their system can become a target for hackers that wish to insert identities based on the information obtained by others. Many times for identity thief to be successful one identity is duplicated for the personal use of another; however, in the case of identity insertion a false identity can be created and placed into a system when using information that may be realistic in nature. Credit companies can become the target of cyber-attacks for other reasons. With major credit agencies the information that is contained within the agency is not consistent across other credit agencies; therefore, the information may not be duplicated accurately across agencies. The leading credit agency may be the target and information loss could or would not be the only outcome. In addition to information loss and duplication, the outcome could be the insertion of information into the system. Credit ratings and credit score alterations could affect the future of an individual for years if undetected.

Private Data/Information

It is not surprising that various laws have been passed pertaining to the exposure and release of private information such as pictures, emails, letters, videos, contact lists, and personal information as these types of information can be (and usually are) invaluable to the right buyer. Having private information that many people do not know and usually would not share can be detrimental to a person's career, reputation, company portfolio, or finances. Using these types of data, encryption can play a large role in how this data is reduced in value due to the amounts of computer power that would be needed to break the encryption.

Data encryption of emails has been used by government agencies for years within the US and in other countries; however, the encryption of photos is not a practice that personal handheld devices or smartphones use when storing information or when sending photos or information to others. The use of encryption algorithms that are user specific and smartphone specific can be an additional feature that is used in the establishment of the operating system of the phone and in the communication network. Current personal computers use security and encryption algorithms to lock and protect computers, but once someone have access to the computer they have access to all of its contents unless there are password protected. This is similar to the passwords and protections on smartphones and handheld devices. Although the user has the ability to encrypt the material on the systems, not every user wishes to use passwords for each area of their phone as it would be inconvenient and time consuming to the user.

Intellectual Property

Inspiration and innovation does not always happen at a desk, in a company or research lab during the hours of 9 AM – 5PM. True inspiration and innovation happens when someone least expects it and in a manner when they are not prepared for it to occur. The use of ideas and theories that come from the inspiration and the innovation leads to intellectual development and planning that becomes of value to employers, research groups, and companies that find it useful and of interest. This innovation leads to intellectual property for the individual and becomes the property of the company if the person is employed to create such innovation in the course of their position.

Within the current digital and data driven age, wireless communications, computer systems, and application development are all important areas for intellectual property and idea development. Such development can be done within an individual's home on a personal computer or laboratory computer and continued within the workplace with the help of others. Such innovation usually means that someone has information in a less secured area than what was originally intended as development of the idea may have begun in a personal and not a professional area. Therefore, the intellectual property of the individual can be acquired from cyber-attacks of the personal accounts of individual computers of people within the various research and scientific fields.

Once the Intellectual Property or corporate information is found and it is determined to be of value, its use can assist in financial gain by an individual or organization with very little effort on the part of the hacker. In order for the hacker to understand the information and determine that they have the correct information, they would have to have inside information on what information they are looking for or to gain access to the entire contents of the computer or server where the information is stored, and then copy the entire data system. Once the information has been retrieved it would become of value back to the owner/developer and also to others that would like to acquire the information. This information can be used to leverage financial information, existing information from the developer or the researcher, or to achieve an end that was not originally intended by the developer as they may be forced to assist in other endeavors based on their knowledge and experience.

Acquisition of the new information can be sold or licensed for usage to other companies or agencies based on the type of information. The companies of interest or parties involved in the hack would benefit from the information and then gain based on the information retrieved and acquired from the cyber-attack. The result of the cyber-attack could be to gain help to advance research that may be already underway within the area, only it may have stalled or seemed impossible to achieve based on the knowledge of the parties involved in the development. Having a different perspective on the area or information on the area can improve and move the research goals in the field forward in the area. Thus, the prospective from an individual within the field and their innovative ideas and inspiration in the field would allow one area of research and innovation to progress that would not have progressed without the additional information.

When acquiring information that comes from a cyber-attack, the acquisition, collection, compression, encryption, transport, and storage of large data that can be found on company servers is not be an easy task to accomplish. Although it is possible to store information from a personal computer on a small system, the storage of information from a larger system requires additional storage space that is not as simple as an external hard drive. In order to acquire, collect, compress, encrypt, transport, and store the information, the complete task requires that the information be processed and secured via a tested mechanism that will ensure that the data is retrievable after the process and that it is unharmed during the processing. However testing these processes requires having large data sets for this process to be perfected. Researchers like Brinkman et al. (2009) used large scale electrophysiology data to illustrate this process and encryption to show how medical data would undergo this process. This process shows that the acquisition, collection, compression, encryption, transport, and storage of information as a result of a cyber-attack of a personal and corporate system would allow the most informed and astute hacker to be able to penetrate the networking system of a company, acquire the information of value, and move it as needed to buyers or parties of interest.

SOLUTIONS AND RECOMMENDATIONS

Having the right protections in places for sensitive information is important and necessary when one compares the result of a data loss and what can happen with the information to the cost of that will be attributed to the company's negligence in security measures.

Recommendations Based on Information Currently Available

Individuals, organizations, academic institutions, companies, and government agencies that have access to individuals PII, PHI, financial information, intellectual property, and other sensitive material should have better security on the servers that contain the information. Protections, safeguards, detection methods, and constant surveillance should be standard with each system and within the security department. Each of the entities and companies that have access to personal information of consumers should have better means of communication between agencies and to the media in regards to what was taken, as well as alerts that include information tracking and automated communications used for alerting security officers of unwanted intrusions. Breaches of a personal computer or a personal network are a means of direct targeting of an individual that can be for any number of reasons; however, when individuals are targeted for personal or intellectual property it becomes difficult to determine if the information taken belonged to a particular person or to a company. In the case of information that belongs to a company, the company's security measures should be in place to establish what occurred, when it occurred, how much information was taken, and what are the potential ramifications for the breach.

Constant review of the triggers and surveillance methods that are already in place and used within the security departments of companies that have access to consumers' personal and financial information is necessary when companies have access to the personal data that is targeted for financial gain. This constant monitoring can reduce the likelihood that a breach can be successful and it can reduce the amount of information taken if a breach occurs. Constant monitoring of the systems can lead to a reduction in the time it takes to disable networks and systems when they are under attack, and it will also reduce the amount of information that would be stolen during an attack.

Constant credit monitoring should be a standard part of any financial institutions account features for all types of accounts. Usually in data breaches one of the major forms of support that companies offer to victims of data breaches is "free credit monitoring" for a pre-determined period of time. These services can range in price and level of service. Although this is effective in reducing the possibility of identity thief or identity duplication it is not 100% effective to safeguard against the complete duplication of the identity. Identity duplication can be reproduced simply by being in the physical presence of a person to make them the victim of identity thief. Additionally, financial institutions that rely on credit monitoring as a practice should also include verification of identity and cross-communications with agencies that can be affected by the breach of information and the hack that can and may have occurred.

Unfortunately, following these recommendations are only the beginning. Because of the type of information that can be obtained through cyber-attacks, trying to get the information necessary to fully analyze scenarios that have resulted in intrusions often comes with the possibility of having to access information that is protected under other confidentiality laws that would require multiple layers of consent. Furthermore, publishing information on research could provide potential hackers with the opportunity to circumvent recommendations before they can be implemented. Thus, with the constant evolution of technology and while trying to maintain the integrity and confidentiality of others involved, it is necessary to consider any other areas that may require improvement.

Areas of Improvement for Security

Evidence and research is needed on data security, newer means of protection on data systems and data networks, and the development of a knowledge repository inclusive of instructions and known methods that work to safeguard material and systems from intrusion. These ideas can lead to the development and dissemination of information that can assist individuals who are not the most technologically savvy to safeguard their personal computers against cyber-attacks that can potentially lead to data loss.

Means for evaluating how many people change passwords and what is done to remind individuals to change passwords on a regular basis. Examples of this is most commonly seen in universities, companies, and government agencies, as they try their best to constantly update Acceptable Use Agreements as it pertains to users of the computing systems. Moist organizations have users update their passwords on a regular basis based on the networking systems and the strategies that companies use to remind their users; consequently, users who do not follow these guidelines find it difficult to login, use, or navigate their company's systems as many systems will lock user accounts for non-compliance. This is quickly becoming a standard operating procedure for those who try to stay ahead of hackers attempting to penetrate the company computer systems, and networks; or trying to obtain the passwords that users may have been assigned based on insider information, because it becomes easier for a cyber-attack to occur if the users have not changed or updated their passwords on a regular basis. Therefore it is not uncommon that more systems are now requiring that users update their passwords on a regular basis to make it more difficult to obtain the passwords created by users.

Most systems that are in place now require users to have at least two forms of authentication, and various components when creating a password. Current requirements include: two capitalized letters, two numbers, two lower case letters, two special characters, at least ten letters in length, and not previously used within the last year. This is now becoming the normal method for password changes and part of the Acceptable Use Agreements as every person that is non-compliant or late in changing this information becomes a liability to the organization. Non-compliance with this process can inadvertently allow intruders to have access to the system.

Research into the private financial systems: (a) Financial/Banking Industry Intrusions and (b) Credit Agencies. Information has not been published in these areas as a result of privacy policies and banking/financial institutions privacy statements. However, since cyber-attacks may be able to cripple, dismantle, affect the infrastructure of a company, or potentially affect the infrastructure of our economy, these areas should be analyzed from various aspects – on the micro scale and; on the macro scale, both nationally; and globally. It is possible that financial institutions have already analyzed these types of scenarios on each of these scales and from various flashpoints that include an agricultural and cultural crisis; changes in the European Trade and Economic Market; volatility within the current Russian economy; different aspects of banking, lending, and stock exchanges that are located and housed on Wall Street; and individual banks collapsing on a micro/macro scale. Additional analysis and D-Day scenarios exist for various contingencies and economic fall-outs from these scenarios; nevertheless, this information would be considered proprietary and should never be made public, printed, disseminated, or acknowledged; however these theoretical instances should be studied. This is not uncommon or unexpected and the repercussions that can occur as a result of this information being made public could be disastrous for any individual, agency, company, country, or nation. However, prevention and safeguards must be in place for any type of economic/financial failure, otherwise a domino effect may occur as a result of a collapse of one (or several) economic systems. With the collapse of one system, it is possible to see how other foreign markets and businesses associated with the market would be affected and could lead to an economic and financial crisis for other agencies, companies, countries, or nations.

CONCLUSION

As previously stated, with each intrusion into the system, the information that hackers target ranges from personal to financial to intellectual in nature. Because the type of information obtained during an attack can vary, it is important to keep in mind that the intent of the attack may extend beyond the hacker's desire for financial gain and include the motivation of the person or organization who intends to use the information obtained by the hackers if it is done for the benefit of a third party. Once the different forms of information are in hand, what can be done with the information can range from:

A. Identity Construction/Re-construction
B. Falsification/Reproduction of vital and financial records
C. Financial Lost that can be immediate or in the future
D. Loss of Property that can occur on a private, personal, and/or intellectual level, or
E. Medical Fraud

Identity Construction/Reconstruction

With the right information, any number of things can occur in regards to identity construction and reconstruction. Individuals who are skilled in identity construction and reconstruction can use the information to create false identities of individuals that are deceased, create identities for older individuals from records of children, and even recreate the same identity of an individual in another state.

Falsification/Reproduction of Vital and Financial Records

Falsification of vital and financial records or the reproduction of vital and financial records is routinely done as a means to change the identity of an individual or to swap identities. Individuals who would desire to swap identities typically do so to deter law processes and procedures from occurring or not to be identified by law enforcement authorities.

Financial Lost

Any information that is taken from an individual in an attempt to committee fraud can and may result in financial lost to the individual if financial institutions are not constantly monitoring the transactions of their customers. With constant credit monitoring, bank alerts, and transaction verification implemented in financial institutions, it can be difficult for customers to have transactions occur without their notification.

Loss of Property that can occur on a private, personal, and/or intellectual level

Physical properties in the form of land, homes, of automobiles are usually tracked via hard copy documents that are not normally part of a cyber-attack. However, recent changes to procedures in some financial institutions has led to certain transactions that were traditionally performed through hard copies alone being transitioned to electronic systems, such as mortgage trading between banks, thereby leaving potential opportunities for cyber-attacks. Furthermore, intellectual property that is in form of digital records or data that is proprietary to a company that resides on personal or private networks and serves are able to be retrieved by cyberattacks. Showing ownership and tracking the location of this information once it has left the environment that it was conceived and developed is a difficult task and should security measures that track proprietary information should be possible.

Medical Fraud

Using the information of an individual who has medical insurance is not a new phenomenon. Individuals have been willing and knowingly used the medical and health insurance information of friends and family in the past to obtain medical care, prescription medicine, and medical treatment in the time of crisis. However, the use of such information is considered medical fraud and has become an increasing area of potential business for hackers who have clients that are interested in obtaining information on individuals with particular medical illnesses.

There are a number of outcomes that can be derived from these different pieces of valuable information that is listed and outlined within this chapter, and the manner in which the information is used will have an effect on an individual that can be lasting and goes well beyond the immediate instances that are listed above. These effects can have a rippling and crippling effect that depends of the level of severity of actions by the people that perpetrated the crime or cyber-attack, and the amount of information that the hackers acquired during the cyber-attack. Additionally the impact on the company systems should not be overlooked or disregarded as a result of the loss of information. Having access to information pertaining to an individual not only poses a personal risk to the individual but also to the personal credit, career, financial status, or credit history for years, and it can affect the person's employer – if additional information in the way of employer user accounts and passwords are also acquired. If the employer is a national agency or government entity, then the security implications can be gravely impacted. Each of these actions can be committed by any criminal, and can be committed with very little information.

REFERENCES

Axelrod, R., & Iliev, R. (2014). Timing of cyber conflict. *Proceedings of the National Academy of Sciences of the United States of America*, *111*(4), 1298–1303. doi:10.1073/pnas.1322638111 PMID:24474752

Brinkmann, B. H., Bower, M. R., Stengel, K. A., Worrell, G. A., & Stead, M. (2009). Large-scale electrophysiology: Acquisition, compression, encryption, and storage of big data. *Journal of Neuroscience Methods*, *180*(1), 185–192. doi:10.1016/j.jneumeth.2009.03.022 PMID:19427545

Chen, D. Q., Chen, W. B., Soong, M., Soong, S. J., & Orthner, H. F. (2009). Turning Access (TM) into a web-enabled secure information system for clinical trials. *Clinical Trials*, *6*(4), 378–385. doi:10.1177/1740774509338228 PMID:19625330

Cooper, A. (2015, March 2). *Air Traffic Control System Vulnerable to Cyberattack*. Retrieved from http://www.cnn.com/2015/03/02/politics/cyberattack-faa-air-traffic-control-hacking/

Egan, M. (2014, December 22). *Thank you Sony! Cybersecurity Stock Soar*. Retrieved from http://money.cnn.com/2014/12/22/investing/sony-cybersecurity-stocks/

Fan, L. J., Wang, Y. Z., Jin, X. L., Li, J. Y., Cheng, X. Q., & Jin, S. Y. (2013). Comprehensive Quantitative Analysis on Privacy Leak Behavior. *Plos One*, *8*(9). DOI:10.1371/journal.pone.0073410

Guan, S. P., Zhang, Y., & Ji, Y. (2013). Privacy-Preserving Health Data Collection for Preschool Children. *Computational and Mathematical Methods in Medicine*. Doi:10.1155/2013/501607

Interactive, C. B. S. (2015, February 6). *Car Hacked on 60 Minutes*. Retrieved from http://www.cbsnews.com/news/car-hacked-on-60-minutes/

Kottasova, I. (2014, November 20). *Russian Website Streams Thousands of Private Webcams*. Retrieved from http://money.cnn.com/2014/11/20/technology/security/hacked-web-cameras-russia/

Kwaak, J. S. (2015, March 17). *North Korea Blamed for Nuclear-Power Plan Hack*. Retrieved from http://www.wsj.com/articles/north-korea-blamed-for-nuclear-power-plant-hack-1426589324

Landi, W., & Rao, R. B. (2003). *Secure De-identification and Re-identification*. Proceedings of AMIA 2003 Symposium.

Meux, E. (1994). Encrypting Personal Identifiers. *Health Services Research*, *29*(2), 247–256. PMID:8005792

Neame, R. (2013). Effective sharing of health records, maintaining privacy: A practical schema. *Online Journal of Public Health Informatics*, *5*(2), 217. doi:10.5210/ojphi.v5i2.4344 PMID:23923101

Pagliery, J. (2014, November 18). *FBI's 10 Most Wanted Cyber Criminals*. Retrieved from http://money.cnn.com/gallery/technology/security/2014/11/18/fbi-cyber-most-wanted/

Pagliery, J., & Pepitone, J. (2014, September 5). *Five of the Biggest-Ever Credit Card Hacks*. Retrieved from http://money.cnn.com/gallery/technology/security/2014/09/05/biggest-hacks/

Robb, D. (2014, December 22). *Sony Hack: A Timeline*. Retrieved from http://deadline.com/2014/12/sony-hack-timeline-any-pascal-the-interview-north-korea-1201325501/

Rooney, B. (2014, December 5). *Hackers Threaten Sony Employees Families*. Retrieved from http://money.cnn.com/2014/12/05/news/sony-threatened-by-hackers/

Stelter, B. (2014, December 14). *Sony Lawyers tell Media to Stop Reporting on Material Stolen by Hackers*. Retrieved from http://money.cnn.com/2014/12/14/media/sony-hack-lawyer-media/

Wallace, G. (2015, February 15). *Hackers Stole from 100 banks and Rigged ATMS to Spew Cash*. Retrieved from http://money.cnn.com/2015/02/15/technology/security/kaspersky-bank-hacking/

ADDITIONAL READING

Baker, D. B., Masys, D. R., Jones, R. L., & Barnhart, R. M. (1999). Assurance: The power behind PCASSO security. *Journal of the American Medical Informatics Association*, 666–670. PMID:10566443

Breiger, R. L., Boorman, S. A., & Arabie, P. (1975). Algorithm for Clustering Relational Data with Applications to Social Network Analysis and Comparison with Multidimensional-Scaling. *Journal of Mathematical Psychology*, *12*(3), 328–383. doi:10.1016/0022-2496(75)90028-0

Cho, Y. C., & Pan, J. Y. (2014). Hybrid Network Defense Model Based on Fuzzy Evaluation. *Scientific World Journal*. Doi:10.1155/2014/178937

Cimino, J. J., Socratous, S. A., & Clayton, P. D. (1995). Internet as Clinical Information-System - Application Development Using the World-Wide-Web. *Journal of the American Medical Informatics Association*, *2*(5), 273–284. doi:10.1136/jamia.1995.96073829 PMID:7496876

Doreian, P. (1980). On the Evolution of Group and Network Structure. *Social Networks*, *2*(3), 235–252. doi:10.1016/0378-8733(79)90016-9

Fink, E., & Segall, L. (2014, December 5). *Hire a Coder Behind Bars*. Retrieved from http://money.cnn.com/2014/12/05/technology/coding-san-quentin/

Frank, O. (1978). Sampling and Estimation in Large Social Networks. *Social Networks*, *1*(1), 91–101. doi:10.1016/0378-8733(78)90015-1

Gil, S., Kott, A., & Barabasi, A. L. (2014). A genetic epidemiology approach to cyber-security. *Scientific Reports*, *4*, 5659. doi:10.1038/srep05659 PMID:25028059

Guo, X. F., Zhang, J. S., Khan, M. K., & Alghathbar, K. (2011). Secure Chaotic Map Based Block Cryptosystem with Application to Camera Sensor Networks. *Sensors (Basel, Switzerland)*, *11*(2), 1607–1619. doi:10.3390/s110201607 PMID:22319371

He, H., Fan, G. T., Ye, J. W., & Zhang, W. Z. (2013). A Topology Visualization Early Warning Distribution Algorithm for Large-Scale Network Security Incidents. *Scientific World Journal*. Doi:10.1155/2013/827376

Hripcsak, G., Cimino, J. J., & Sengupta, S. (1999). WebCIS: Large scale deployment of a Web-based clinical information system. *Journal of the American Medical Informatics Association*, 804–808. PMID:10566471

Kim, J., Lee, D., Jeon, W., Lee, Y., & Won, D. (2014). Security Analysis and Improvements of Two-Factor Mutual Authentication with Key Agreement in Wireless Sensor Networks. *Sensors (Basel, Switzerland)*, *14*(4), 6443–6462. doi:10.3390/s140406443 PMID:24721764

Lee, Y., & Paik, J. (2014). Security Analysis and Improvement of an Anonymous Authentication Scheme for Roaming Services. *Scientific World Journal*. Doi 10.1155/2014/687879

Luo, G. C., Peng, N. D., Qin, K., & Chen, A. G. (2014). A Layered Searchable Encryption Scheme with Functional Components Independent of Encryption Methods. *Scientific World Journal*. Doi:10.1155/2014/153791

Morse, R. E., Nadkarni, P., Schoenfeld, D. A., & Finkelstein, D. M. (2011). Web-browser encryption of personal health information. *Bmc Medical Informatics and Decision Making, 11*. Doi:10.1186/1472-6947-11-70

Oh, J. Y., Yang, D. I., & Chon, K. H. (2010). A Selective Encryption Algorithm Based on AES for Medical Information. *Healthcare Informatics Research*, *16*(1), 22–29. doi:10.4258/hir.2010.16.1.22 PMID:21818420

Peng, N. D., Luo, G. C., Qin, K., & Chen, A. G. (2013). Query-Biased Preview over Outsourced and Encrypted Data. *Scientific World Journal*. Doi:10.1155/2013/860621

Sang, J., Ling, S. G., & Alam, M. S. (2012). Efficient Text Encryption and Hiding with Double-Random Phase-Encoding. *Sensors (Basel, Switzerland)*, *12*(10), 13441–13457. doi:10.3390/s121013441 PMID:23202003

Wright, A., & Sittig, D. F. (2007). Encryption characteristics of two USB-based personal health record devices. *Journal of the American Medical Informatics Association*, *14*(4), 397–399. doi:10.1197/jamia.M2352 PMID:17460132

Zhang, W. P., Chen, W. Y., Tang, J., Xu, P., Li, Y. B., & Li, S. Y. (2009). The Development of a Portable Hard Disk Encryption/Decryption System with a MEMS Coded Lock. *Sensors (Basel, Switzerland)*, *9*(11), 9300–9331. doi:10.3390/s91109300 PMID:22291566

Zhou, Q., Yang, G., & He, L. W. (2014). A Secure-Enhanced Data Aggregation Based on ECC in Wireless Sensor Networks. *Sensors (Basel, Switzerland)*, *14*(4), 6701–6721. doi:10.3390/s140406701 PMID:24732099

KEY TERMS AND DEFINITIONS

Breach: The act of breaking or failing to observer a law, agreement, or code of conduct.

Credit History: An electronic or hardcopy record of a consumer's ability to repay their debts with a demonstrated responsibility in repaying debts in a timely fashion as determined by the creditor.

Credit Information: Information about a person, business, company, or institution to pay is creditors or suppliers.

Cyber-Attack: The use of electronics to attempt the intrusion, delay, damage, or destruction of a computer network or system.

Data Leak: The unauthorized transfer of classified information from a computer or datacenter to the outside world.

Data Loss: An error condition in information systems in which information is destroyed by failures or neglect in storage, transmission, or processing.

Financial Information: Records that outline the financial activities of a business, an individual or any other entity.

Intrusion: The act of intruding or the condition of being intruded upon; an inappropriate or unwelcomed addition.

Personal Health Information (PHI): Also referred to as protected health information, generally refers to demographic information, medical history, test and laboratory results, insurance information and other data that is collected by a health care professional to identify an individual and determine appropriate care.

Personal Identifiable Information (PII): Any data that could potentially identify a specific individual.

Prevention: The action of stopping something from happening or occurring.

Protection: The action of protecting, or the state of being protected.

Section 3

Novel Implementations and Forward Thinking

Chapter 10
Application of Mathematical Modeling for the Secure and Intelligent Energy Infrastructure

Tianxing Cai
Lamar University, USA

ABSTRACT

The unpredictable damage caused by potential attack and natural disaster may impact the operation of energy infrastructure, which is vital to local and national security. Thus, mathematical modeling based decision making tools become a must, because they can provide the scientific strategy to enhance the security and intelligence of energy infrastructure. In this chapter, the preliminary framework of a mathematical model is introduced. It includes the definition and characterization of energy network with the capability of self-recovery and the efficacy of the road map generation to handle the uncertainty of identified damage. The new methodology is the preliminary study for the future work in this field.

DOI: 10.4018/978-1-4666-9661-7.ch010

1. INTRODUCTION

According to Macmillan Dictionary, the definition of national security is "the protection or the safety of a country's secrets and its citizens" (Macmillan Dictionary, 2015). Therefore the purpose of national security is National security is to require the government and its parliaments to protect the state and its citizens against all kind of national crises. The common elements of national security are military security, political security, economic security, environmental security, security of energy and natural resources, cyber-security, empowerment of women (Romm, 1993; Paleri, 2008; Lippmann, 1943; Buzan, Wver & Wilde, 1997; Diamond, 2010; Rollins, John, & Henning, 2009; Lemmon, 2013; Devanny & Harris, 2014; Davis, 2010; Taylor, 1974; US NATO Military Terminology Group, 2010; Obama, 2010). Energy security is the combination between national security and the accessibility of natural resources for energy consumption. The development of the economical market and industrial operation are always requiring the utilization of cheap energy as much as possible. However, the unbalanced distribution of energy supplies in the regional and global wide has led to significant vulnerabilities.

The long-term solutions to enhance energy security have included the methods to reduce dependence on the energy source which is imported from the other countries, grow the supplier team, and exploit indigenous fossil fuel or renewable energy resources, and decrease the demand by energy conservation. The short-term solutions to enhance energy security are trying to satisfy the availability and consumption of petroleum, natural gas, nuclear power and renewable energy. Thus, the energy infrastructure is vital to local and national security. The potential attack and natural disaster may impact the energy security. Since the loss or damage quantity is very difficult to be predicted or even cannot be predicted, the following and corresponding rescue will be delayed and this will raise the public safety threats. Therefore qualitative and quantitative decision making tools, which rely on the historical expert system and the mathematical modeling, are becoming more and more necessary because they can provide the reasonable and scientific analysis and optimization in the energy security enhancement and energy infrastructure intelligence. In this chapter, the preliminary framework of mathematical model will be introduced. It will include the definition and characterization of energy network with the capability of self-recovery and the efficacy of the road map generation to handle the uncertainty of identified damage.

2. RESEARCH PROGRESS

The scholars and researchers from the government, universities and research institutes have proposed the potential mathematical models which can be used to simulate and achieve the target of the uninterrupted availability of energy sources at an affordable price". The models will consider long-term energy security (timely investments to supply energy for economic developments and environmental sustainability) and short-term energy security (the capacity and capability of the energy system to provide emergency response to sudden changes within the supply-demand balance).

Markandya and Pemberton provided a framework to analyze energy security in an expected utility framework (Markandya & Pemberton, 2010). Their contribution can be further applied to handle the risk of disruption of imported energy. Their analysis has disclosed that the importance of an energy tax as a tool in maximizing expected utility, and how the level of that tax should be manipulated based on the values of key system parameters such as risk aversion, probability of disruption, demand elasticity and cost of disruption.

Bazilian, Rogner, Howells, Hermann, Arent, Gielen, Stedutof, Muellerf, Komorg, Tolh and Yumkella (Bazilian, et.al., 2011) have looked at the potential concerns in the area of energy, water and food policy. These issues can involve the problems of not only ensuring access to services but also environmental impacts to price volatility. Their study has provided the identification of these interrelationships, which is important to help target synergies and avoid potential tensions. They have presented the description of some of the linkages at a high-level of aggregation, some promising directions for addressing the nexus, the attributes of a modeling framework that specifically addresses the nexus, and the supporting information for more effective national policies and regulations.

Clastres (Clastres, 2011) has stepped into the field of interdisciplinary research in the deployment of smart grids in electricity systems. The technology itself will help to promote competition, increase the safety of electricity systems and combat climate change. However, the authors have disclosed many raised economic questions during the boom in smart grids. Based on their study, the public policies should be adjusted in order to achieve several targets. The first target is to make stipend for the potential gains from smart grids and the related information flow; the second target is to regulate the new networks and a motivation for investors; the third target is to rely on the new competitive offerings and end-user pricing systems in order to improve the allocated and productive efficiency, with the minimal risk of market power; the fourth target is to apply the real-time data on output and consumption, generators and consumers in order to adapt to market conditions; the fifth target is to make the smart grids enhance the development of renewable energy sources and new technologies, by assisting their integration and optimal utilization.

Turton & Barreto (Turton & Barreto, 2006) have paid their attention to the security of energy supply and climate change for policy makers and important magnitudes of the long-term seek for a sustainable global energy system. Their research has examined the role of several policy instruments in managing energy security and climate risks and motivating technological change towards a more secure and climate-benign global energy system in the future. The study has been preceded with ERIS, a multi-regional energy-systems "bottom-up" optimization model with technology learning. Their corresponding analysis has provided some policy insights and identifies synergies and trade-offs relating to the potential for security of supply policies to support the uptake of new technologies, decrease the cost of pursuing climate change lessening policies, and assist a possible switch to a hydrogen economy.

Jansen & Seebregts (Jansen & Seebregts, 2010) have reviewed the recent approaches towards the measurement of long-term energy security and security externality valuation. Their attention has paid to two approaches (diversity-based indices and the Supply/Demand Index). They have also proposed the concept of energy services security with a focus in the demand point of view. Their study will really help the application of the comprehensive methodology to gauge the flexibility of a society to satisfy the requirements of its population for energy services in the long time period ahead from various inter-related perspectives.

Urban, Benders & Moll (Urban, Benders & Moll, 2007) have applied the mathematical modeling in the energy system of developing countries. With the continuous increase of energy consumption, the global climate change and global and regional energy settings should be closely connected for the investigation. Energy models will help to explore the future development in the industrialized countries and developing countries. The energy model will satisfy the new requirements of present-day energy models to adequately explore the developing countries' energy systems in the future. Their study has provided the assessment whether the main characteristics of developing countries can fit well into the currently available energy models. In their study, the main characteristics from the developing Asia have been put into a model comparison of 12 selected energy models in order to test their suitability for developing countries. Their research has disclosed that many models are biased towards industrialised countries and the main characteristics of developing countries have been neglected. They can be observed in the informal economy, supply shortages, poor performance of the power sector, structural economic change, electrification, traditional bio-fuels, urban–rural divide. The researchers have highlighted that energy models have to be adjusted and new models have to be built for the purpose to more adequately address the energy systems of developing countries. They have also presented the potential improvement opportunity for energy models to increase their suitability for developing countries and the advice on modeling techniques and data requirements.

3. PROPOSED METHODOLOGY

Ensuring energy security has been at the centre of the mission of the energy system management. The national and international organizations are continuing to work to improve energy security in the longer time period by the enhancement of energy policies. The result of short-time energy shortage under abnormal situations (earthquake, tsunami, and hurricane) will be able to raise local regions to suffer from postponed rescues, extensive electrical energy outages, terrific financial losses, and even public safety risks. The intelligent energy dispatching through an effective energy transportation network, targeting the minimum energy recovery time, should be a must for the energy security. The novel methodology has been developed for energy network dispatch optimization under emergency of local energy shortage [20]. The proposed methodology has included four stages of work. The first step is to characterize emergency-area-centered energy network including the information of the capacity, quantity, and availability of various energy sources are determined. The second step is to identify the energy initial situation under emergency conditions. The third step is to conduct the energy dispatch optimization based on a developed model. The last step is to proceed the sensitivity analysis for the relationship between the minimum dispatch time and uncertainty parameters. The methodology framework can be described by Figure 1. The energy dispatch optimization problem is modeled as an MILP or MINLP problem

3.1. Objective Function

The objective function of this energy dispatch model is to achieve the minimal recovery time which is necessarily to be used to satisfy every form of energy at each position. The method in the form of the discrete time is recommended to be used. This methodology will help to divides the concerned time period into many small time intervals. In addition, the logical binary variables are employed to indicate whether the energy dispatch has already met the requisite or not at the specific time instance.

3.2. Energy Balance Constraints

Energy balance should also be met at each position, which means the energy accumulation is equal to direct energy input from other positions in the energy network, plus converted energy from other forms of energy in this place, and energy supply outside the assumed energy system; minus direct energy output from this place, consumed energy quantity which has been converted to other forms of energy, and the energy consumption demand in this place.

Figure 1. General methodology framework (Cai, Zhao & Xu, 2012)

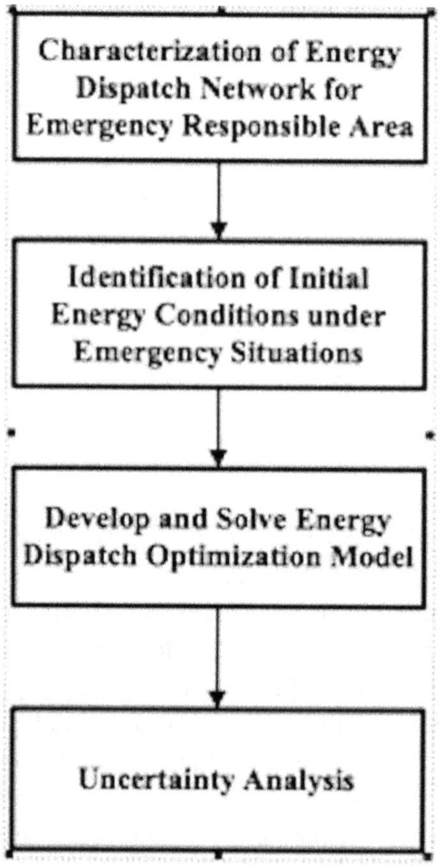

3.3. Energy Conversion and Transportation Constraints

The energy conversion and transportation items have special constraints that should be held in the optimization model. For example, the generated energy quantity is the product of available energy resource quantity and conversion efficiency. Furthermore, the available energy quantity should not be over the energy inventory quantity and the energy generation cannot be above its capacity limit. Another feature of energy transportation is the input energy quantity to one position should be equal to the output energy quantity from another position for a transportation from another position to the destination and there is a time delay between the departure and the arrival of such a transportation. This quantity is mainly determined by the distance between the above two positions, and the traffic conditions in that time period.

3.4. Energy Inventory, Consumption, Input, and Output Constraints

Energy inventory in each place should not be beyond its limit. Based on the energy inventory, the energy consumption at each node should also be restricted. The amount of demand energy for consumption is a proportion of the energy inventory quantity from the last time slot. Each type of energy fed to one position should satisfy not only the limit of each individual transportation capability, but also the total energy input limit from all the other positions and each type of energy output from i should satisfy not only the limit of each individual transportation capacity, but also the total energy output limit directed to all the other positions.

3.5. Logic Constraints

The logical binary variables have been used to represent whether the supply of specific energy type at the specific location at the specific time instance meets the requirement or not.

4. CONCLUSION AND FUTURE WORK

The above-introduced methodology is only the result of preliminary study to help the future work in this direction. The real management for suck kind of intelligent and secure energy infrastructure will focus on the comprehensive consideration of population distribution, roadway safety, the constraints of transportation routes, transportation capacity and capability for the optimal emergency response planning with the minimal potential impact to the community.

REFERENCES

Bazilian, M., Rogner, H., Howells, M., Hermann, S., Arent, D., Gielen, D., & Yumkella, K. K. et al. (2011). Considering the energy, water and food nexus: Towards an integrated modeling approach. *Energy Policy*, *39*(12), 7896–7906. doi:10.1016/j.enpol.2011.09.039

Buzan, B. (1998). *Ole Wver & Jaap De Wilde. Security: a new framework for analysis* (p. 239). Lynne Rienner Publishers.

Cai, T., Zhao, C., & Xu, Q. (2012). Energy network dispatch optimization under emergency of local energy shortage. *Energy*, *42*(1), 132–145. doi:10.1016/j.energy.2012.04.001

Clastres, C. (2011). Smart grids: Another step towards competition, energy security and climate change objectives. *Energy Policy*, *39*(9), 5399–5408. doi:10.1016/j.enpol.2011.05.024

Davis, R. T. (Ed.), (2010). U.S. Foreign Policy and National Security: Chronology and Index for the 20th Century (Praeger Security International Series Illustrated ed.) (pp. xiii–xiv). ABC-CLIO.

Devanny, J., & Harris, J. (2014). The National Security Council: national security at the centre of government. Institute for Government & King's College London.

Diamond, J. (2005). Malthus in Africa: Rwanda's Genocide. In Collapse: How societies choose to fail or succeed.

Jansen, J. C., & Seebregts, A. J. (2010). Long-term energy services security: What is it and how can it be measured and valued? *Energy Policy*, *38*(4), 1654–1664. doi:10.1016/j.enpol.2009.02.047

Lemmon, G. T. (2013, April 8). The Hillary Doctrine: Women's Rights Are a National Security Issue. The Atlantic. Macmillan Dictionary. (n. d.). Retrieved from http://www.macmillandictionary.com

Lippmann, W. (1943). *U.S. Foreign Policy: Shield of the Republic*. Boston: Little, Brown.

Markandya, A., & Pemberton, M. (2010). Energy security, energy modelling and uncertainty. *Energy Policy*, *38*(4), 1609–1613. doi:10.1016/j.enpol.2009.01.046

Office of the President of the United States. (2010, May). National Security Strategy. *The White House*.

Paleri, P. (2008). National Security: Imperatives And Challenges. New Delhi. Tata: McGraw-Hill; Retrieved 23 September 2010.

Rollins, J., & Henning, A. C. (2009). *Comprehensive National Cybersecurity Initiative Legal Authorities and Policy Considerations*. Washington, D.C.: Congressional Research Service.

Romm, J.J. (1993). Defining national security: the nonmilitary aspects. America's Task in a Changed World (Pew Project Series), Council on Foreign Relations.

Taylor, M. (1974). The Legitimate Claims of National Security. Foreign Affairs (Council on Foreign Relations, Inc.) 52 (Essay of 1974). doi:10.2307/20038070

Turton, H., & Barreto, L. (2006). Long-term security of energy supply and climate change. *Energy Policy*, *34*(15), 2232–2250. doi:10.1016/j.enpol.2005.03.016

Urban, F. R. M. J., Benders, R. M. J., & Moll, H. C. (2007). Modelling energy systems for developing countries. *Energy Policy*, *35*(6), 3473–3482. doi:10.1016/j.enpol.2006.12.025

US NATO Military Terminology Group. (2010). *1 (02) "Dictionary of Military and Associated Terms", 2001 (As amended through 31 July 2010). Pentagon, Washington: Joint Chiefs of Staff* (p. 361). JP: US Department of Defense.

KEY TERMS AND DEFINITIONS

Disaster Management (Emergency Management): Disaster management (or emergency management) is the creation of plans through which communities reduce vulnerability to hazards and cope with disasters. Disaster management does not avert or eliminate the threats, instead it focuses on creating plans to decrease the impact of disasters. Failure to create a plan could lead to damage to assets, human mortality, and lost revenue.

Energy: In physics, energy is a property of objects which can be transferred to other objects or converted into different forms, but cannot be created or destroyed.

Government: A government is the system by which a state or community is governed.

Infrastructure: Infrastructure refers to the fundamental facilities and systems serving a country, city, or area, including the services and facilities necessary for its economy to function. It typically characterize technical structures such as roads, bridges, tunnels, water supply, sewers, electrical grids, telecommunications, and so forth, and can be defined as "the physical components of interrelated systems providing commodities and services essential to enable, sustain, or enhance societal living conditions."

Mathematical Modeling: A mathematical model is a description of a system using mathematical concepts and language. The process of developing a mathematical model is termed mathematical modeling.

National Security: National security is a concept that a government, along with its parliament (s), should protect the state and its citizens against all kind of "national" crises through a variety of power projections, such as political power, diplomacy, economic power, military might, and so on.

Optimization: In mathematics, computer science, operations research, mathematical optimization (alternatively, optimization or mathematical programming) is the selection of a best element (with regard to some criteria) from some set of available alternatives.

Simulation: Simulation is the imitation of the operation of a real-world process or system over time.

Chapter 11
The Need for a National Data Breach Notification Law

Kirk Y Williams
Walden University, USA

ABSTRACT

Individuals, groups, organizations, companies, and foreign government agencies that threaten the National Security of other countries, not only threaten their National Security but also threaten the security of state agencies, and the security of the individuals, groups, organizations, academic institutions that are consumers of those companies. Therefore, a National Data Breach Notification Law that would inform consumers once unwanted intrusions in the form of a cyber-attack occurs that results in the disclosure of their personal and financial information is needed. In the requests for a National Data Breach Notification Law suggestions have been made on what the law should include, and how the information should be reported to the public and to the individuals affected by the cyber-attack. This chapter explores how a National Data Breach Notification Law should be produced that would require uniformity across all states with guidelines that relate to the compliance of the law as it can affect individuals, organizations, academic institutions, companies, and governmental agencies.

DOI: 10.4018/978-1-4666-9661-7.ch011

INTRODUCTION

Individuals, groups, organizations, academic institutions, companies, and governmental agencies have all instilled a sense of security within our daily lives based on our reliance and use of secured forms of technology. With this reliance on secured forms of technology and communication networks, technology users – consumers – have begun to delude themselves into thinking that companies have levels of security and safety that exists within their secured and trusted networks that can defend itself from all forms of cyber intrusions. In their daily lives, consumers rely on those secured and trusted networked systems to access private information on secure Internet sites, and to conduct various forms of business in a safe and secure manner; therefore, that access must be global to complete the tasks at hand, and secured to not allow for communication interception by third parties. However with the reliance on technology, communication networks, and the access that users desire and require, consumers also make themselves dependent on the security that is in place for each system that they access, only consumers never tend to think about how they leave themselves open to intruders who may also access those same secured networks. When intruders enter into these systems with unauthorized access, this leads to a security breach and can lead to a data loss or a data leak.

Each new security breach that leads to a data loss or a data leak can result in more companies being hacked and causes more consumer information to be released to the public. Each attack on a company not only compromises the security of the company, but also reduces the trust of the public in the individuals, organizations, academic institutions, companies, and governmental agencies that are in the business of providing security and protection to consumers that supposedly have safeguards in place to protect consumers and their information. When these safeguards fail, it leaves consumers wondering: *What where the safeguards that companies were using to protect the consumer(s) and their data/private information?* However, additional worries have increased with regard to protecting data from security breaches, and consumers have begun to ask: *Should more be done to safeguard consumer information? What additional items should be considered with regard to the state and federal laws and the reporting of security breaches, data loss, and data breaches*?

Although these are the typical questions that one would ask after a security breach that results in data loss occurs, it should be the forethought on everyone's mind when establishing public and private policies that govern data loss as a result of a security breach. Over the last five years, numerous individuals, organizations, academic institutions, companies, and members within the governmental agencies have called for a change in the reporting and openness of information that resulted in data loss, the reporting of security breaches that resulted in data loss. With these requests these individuals, organizations, academic institutions, companies, and members within the governmental agencies have requested reporting in the form of laws and policies to be established on the state and federal level to govern the reporting of the information and notification of the data breaches that resulted in a data loss. With these requests, these individuals, organizations, academic institutions, and companies feel that the US government should consider constructing and implementing federal policies that govern security breaches that result in a data loss. In their formation of such policies, it has been suggested that federal agencies consult with state officials on the laws that each state has in place, determine what the states would like to achieve with their laws, evaluate what they are doing to enforce the law, and review how the state established reporting from organizations, academic institutions, companies, and government agencies that have been breached.

Currently each individual state have some laws in places that comprise a patch work of laws that focus on data breaches, but each state is not consistent and the laws in place are not effective across the entire United States. Therefore the objective of this chapter is to inform others where they can find information on which states have policies and laws at the local and state level that pertains to notifications and security breaches, suggest how such policies can be enforced, suggest what can be done on the federal level in the way of developing a National Data Breach Notification Law, and discuss areas of the Data Security and Breach Notification Act of 2015.

THE NEED FOR A NATIONAL DATA BREACH NOTIFICATION LAW

With each new cyber-attack, security breach, data leak, or data loss, constantly evolving, different and inconsistent responses are reported to the consumer as described in blogs, media reports, and company reporting. The length of time and manner of reporting suggests that enforceable state and federal policies are not in place to govern the reporting of data loss as a result of a cyber-attack and/or security breaches that lead to data loss, how the reporting should be handled, how the information should be reported to the public, how customers affected by the data loss should be contacted, or what legal recourse the customer has with regard to their breach of privacy and security.

In preparing this manuscript it became apparent that many states do not have policies, regulations, or laws in place that would consider them to be a part of a national standard, and the states that do have data breach policies, regulations, and laws in place are not enforced. Also during the development of this manuscript the Data Security and Breach Notification Act of 2015 (Committee on Energy and Commerce, 2015) was presented and put into action. With these developments how the public and private sector will respond to this Act have not been analyzed or fully understood, but it leads to areas for potential research in various social and behavioral fields.

Some questions that were being asked prior to the Data Security and Breach Notification Act of 2015 included questions such as: *how long will it be before the government step in to enforce and regulate compliance? How long will it be before the government regulates the types of information than can be placed on the various computers that are connected to external networks?* Every company and agency has policies on how they handle connections to the network, data infrastructure, host-client systems, authentication, and protection from external hacks. However, these policies are not consistent across organizations, academic institutions, companies, and/or organizations that work with governmental agencies.

If one were to scan the Data Loss Database (www.datalossdb.org) it would be possible to see how many cyber-attacks that resulted in data loss have occurred over the previous years and statistics on the cyber-attacks, inclusive of what type of attack, the type of data that was loss, and whether it was an attack as a result of an internal or external threat. With this information one can see how often systems that belong to groups, organizations, academic institutions, companies, and/or governmental agencies have been penetrated and/or hacked, and how much information was lost in the cyber-attack. Additionally information in the way of how organizations, academic institutions, companies, and/or governmental agencies were affected and the number of parties involved in the cyber-attack, security breach, and data leak is also available within this database. This resource is reported here to illustrate the availability of information that exists on the number of cyber-attacks, the types and frequency of attacks, and the volumes of data that has been loss as a result of cyber-attacks that have occurred over the previous years.

At the time of development of this manuscript, a total of four states did not have Data Loss Notification Laws and a Centralized Data Loss Reporting system in place on the state level, while 35 states did not have a Data Loss Notification law. BakerHofters (2015) Data Breach Charts shows the susceptibility of many states and their broad range of on the definition on what is considered personal information. This table can be used to as a starting point for understanding how inconsistent states are in regard to their definition on information that is considered personal. Because of the inconsistency in definitions and the number/types of policies in each state, and the level of reporting, it is not surprising that individuals, groups, organizations, and local leaders have requested additional state and legislature laws should be met with regard to public and federal policies being developed in the form of a National Data Breach Law.

Some areas that have been suggested that can be used to focus the development of the state and federal policies have included:

A. Listing the type of information that was loss during the cyber-attack and/or security breach and the number of people that it affected.
B. Establishing offices within the organizations, academic institutions, companies and government agencies with an appropriate hotline for consumers who are requesting information about the cyber-attack that have affected them, and local and state government offices and agencies that consumers can contact to assist in determining if they were affected by the data loss.
C. Federal development of a national data breach notification law that keeps track of, lists, and documents which states are in compliance with all aspects of the Data Security and Breach Notification Act of 2015.
D. A standard support package that would be available to any individual that have been affected by a cyber-attack that is in accordance with the loss of private information from an organization, academic institution, company, or governmental agency.
E. More accurate and open reporting with regard to how, where, when and what methods were used in the security breaches that lead to the loss of data from the organization, academic institution, company, or governmental agency.

MAIN FOCUS OF THE CHAPTER

Local and state agencies, in conjunction with federal agencies should set a clear set of guidelines and policies for what organizations, academic institutions, companies, and government agencies should do when security breaches occur – especially when data loss occurs. These guidelines should be in accordance with the Data Security and Breach Notification Act of 2015 and should be easily adoptable based on the guidelines of the Act. With the request of the Act from individuals, group, agencies, companies, and even former congressmen Mary Bono (Bono, 2015), this Act will has very clear and direct information that will assist law makers, organizations, academic institutions, companies, and organizations that work with government agencies guidelines that will be achievable and enforceable. The requests and suggestions from these individuals who have called for a national data breach notification law is a result of requesting a standard approach that organizations, academic institutions, companies, and organizations that work with governmental agencies can comply to and follow as local, state, and federal government move towards establishing a consistent and transparent national data breach notification law. With the requests for a national data breach notification law a lot of guidelines have been suggested that the policy should include and how information should be handled on various levels of government and at the organizational level. Prior to development of the Data Security and Breach Notification Act of 2015, some of the areas that have been suggested that the National Data Breach Law should cover includes:

1. A federal measure with policies that governs the reporting of information that was loss as a result of a cyber-attack, security breach, or data leak. In the reporting of this information, the reports should be: clear, concise, identifiable in the types of information leaked or stolen, and objective via the media reporting mechanism.
2. Listing and documenting which states are in compliance with the Data Security and Breach Notification Act of 2015, and what is considered compliance on the federal and state level. Additionally, outlining what is necessary for governance of compliance and enforcement for non-compliant agencies on the local and state level.
3. Reporting should contain information on who initiated the cyber-attack, how the entity gained access to the system, who may be involved in the cyber-attack, and from what location(s). Initially this information may not be known; however, however the establishment of timelines, dates, and information should be identifies and stated as to when the information will be made available. Additionally, a coordinated response team complete with an investigation should be coordinated with the state and federal agencies in conjunction with the organization, academic institution, and company that was the target of the cyber-attack.
4. The policy should include what type of announcement should be made, when it should be made, how the company should work with the appropriate federal agency and local law enforcement officers to assist in capture and prosecution of the individuals, organizations, or company involved in the cyber-attack; the level and type of compensation to the victims (consumers affected by the cyber-attack); and penalties for future cyber-attacks based on lapses in security. Additionally, complete and accurate reporting to consumers to allow for complete understanding of the types of data that was leaked and what was loss once a complete review of the security systems have been completed. The compromised systems and data infrastructure of the computing system would then be reported to the appropriate state and federal offices to demonstrate compliance once new security measures and capabilities are met.

These requests come as a result of the increase in the range of targets, as the targets are more diverse and include retail companies, healthcare organizations, hotels and entertainment companies, and financial institutions. Each of these industries have been a victim of or seen the increase in the number of highly publicized, large-scale security data breaches that have left many consumers affected by the cyber-attacks. Additionally, the number of breaches that have been made public shows that the cyber-attacks have affected a large number of consumers.

Although many business owners and companies are aware of the how the cyber-attacks affect their financial standing within their organization, they may not be aware that a lot is at stake when the organization is breached and their loss is not just in terms of a direct financial loss of the corporate accounts; however cyber-attacks usually result in additional losses in terms of potential intellectual property and information on projects that may be in development as well as increased concerns in security from consumers and the potential loss of numerous consumers. This usually results in a costly and time-consuming litigation that affects many of resources and departments of the organization, academic institutions, company, and government agency. Then this includes the need for more government and regulatory investigations at the request of the consumer, and in turn this damages the confidence of the consumer in trusting the company's ability to protect personal, proprietary, and financial customer information via an online environment or whether the information is locked away on secure servers.

Every company has a Terms of Use Agreement that gives the company the right to employ data capture methods and data mining tools that most consumers are not aware of until a cyber-attack, security breach, or data leak occurs on a large scale that it affects a significant population or number of consumers. However with each update of the Terms of Use Agreement many customers increase the amount and type of data that can be collected from them and reduce their rights as a result of this agreement. These Terms of Use Agreements allows their information to be sold to a third party, and this allows for more data capture and personal data information usage than they originally thought or agreed upon. Therefore it is not surprising that companies and agencies who capture daily consumer data are able to predict, analyze, market and personalize the experience of the customers as their personal information allows the company to have more tailored experiences for the customer. Therefore the use of predictive analytics and statistical analysis techniques can give an overall picture of the consumer which is clear and concise. This in turn makes the information valuable to any company that is willing to tailor a customized experience to a particular type (or types) of consumer(s). With more purchases and information gathering on the consumer, the better and easier it becomes to market and predict a customer's needs, wants, spending habits, purchases, and lifestyle. Therefore more personalized and cultivated tools and information makes the information more valuable to the company as it relates to all of the purchases, payments, and financial history and transaction history of the customer. With companies as large as Target, Home Depot, or Sears it is impossible to image the amount, types, and size of data that resides on their secure servers and the pictures that such information would paint of the average consumer that frequents their establishments.

Inspection of the Data Loss database could assist policy makers of the severity of the cyber-attacks because many unanswered questions can be answered and used as a basis for the development of a state and local laws. Questions that can be asked and answered are:

1. Are individuals, companies, organizations, foreign agencies, or foreign countries initiating cyber-attacks, are they increasing in frequency, and are the targets diverse?
2. In what sector (public or private) have cyber-attacks occurred the most?
3. What number of consumers have the cyber-attacks affected, and in what areas of the country?
4. Based on national census information and the number of people that have been affected by cyber-attacks, how have companies responded to offering support based on the individual loss to the person?
5. What local and state policies have been adopted to assist the company and consumers affected by cyber-attacks and data loss; what forms of support to the consumer have been offered, and how has local, state, and federal agencies assisted in mediating support for companies and individuals affected by the cyber-attacks?
6. What states have Data Loss Laws in place, and what states have Data Reporting Centers in place to assist consumers that have been the victim of a data loss as a result of a cyber-attack? Are these companies in compliance with local and state laws? Where are they not compliant? What is considered compliant by the company? How and when are consumers alerted to the company's security breach and data loss?

7. Finally, have significant breaches within security occurred more in the corporate industry, in government agencies, or in the financial industry?

Future questions can be asked after a cyber-attack occurs that analyze the security measures, practices, software, and precautions that were in place as a result of previous cyber-attack, security breach, or data leak. Such questions can include:

1. How many cyber-attacks have been successful and resulted in a loss in consumer data in the past?
2. In regards to the information breaches, what individual, group, organization, academic institution, company, or foreign government agency initiated the attack, and how did the entity gain entrance to the system?

These questions and concerns are important because many aspects of the economy, consumer's daily life, transactions, communications, and daily livelihood depend on a consistently connected global market that is networked and updated in real-time. These markets and systems must be able to work in an environment that transmit different data types and data packets, establish and connect with different communication systems, and have space for additional resources in a very secure fashion as the information provided could be sensitive in nature and should not be made public. From a security perspective a cyber-attack on this type of system can be a nightmare if sensitive information is transmitted and intercepted, or if the information is compromised. Therefore the need for cyber-security that reduces or removes this worry is essential and necessary.

Cyber-attacks take place daily only many are not as successful and therefore go unmentioned. System Administrators see numerous attacks daily, only the attempts are usually thwarted by the systems and the safe guards that are in place to prevent any unwanted intrusions. However some systems can be compromised based on the means that hackers have used to gain access to the system, the flaws that exist within systems, and how previous intrusions into the systems have occurred. When systems are breached an assessment of what was done to prevent the attack; what was left behind after the attack; how long access was acquired to the system; what was taken or duplicated; if any information was leaked and how much information was leaked; and what were the entry points/ports that were accessed. All of these questions and means must be identified and answered. This does not mean that the coding structure and language of the code is not identified or analyzed (if any is left behind) but also additional access must be curtained and how the hackers penetrated the system must be evaluated for addition/future intrusions on the system. With each day the number and frequency of cyber-attacks are increasing; however delays exist with regard to how the cyber-attacks are being reported, where they occurred, where they are reported, and when the cyber-attacks have been reported to the consumers.

Many entities that have called for a National Data Breach Notification Law believe that some of the vulnerabilities within our security system exists as a result of our openness of information of our computing systems, testing and capabilities of the system, instillation of programs on secure systems, and known weaknesses and vulnerabilities of commonly used computer systems and software packages. Based on the number and types of cyber-attacks, information on the attacks have shown that several common themes are present that point to the vulnerabilities that exist as a result of different computing systems:

1. Openness on the types of computer systems used within the organization that was been breached
2. Testing and capabilities of the system

3. Non-proprietary programs placed on the computer systems
4. Private consumer information that is placed on the system that is also connected to the Internet
5. Weaknesses and vulnerabilities of known computing systems that are public knowledge

It has been suggested that organizations, academic institutions, companies, and governmental agencies should reduce their:

1. Openness of information that resides on their systems.
2. Increase their penetration testing and intrusion capabilities of their systems to the industry standards and then the standards set forth by their state and federal agencies.
3. Constantly maintain and monitor their security programs and protocols to protect the information that is on their system.
4. Consult with external companies to identify the weaknesses and vulnerabilities of their system on a regular basis.

By doing this every local and state agency would be able to hold organizations, academic institutions, and companies to a standard that would have a clear and achievable level of security that would be able to fit any additional policies that would be put in place at a later date. Such policies would handle connections to external networks, data infrastructure, host-client systems, authentication, for intrusion protection. These types of activities would form the basis for public and private policy compliance with local, state, and federal laws. Because current policies across local and states agencies, organizations, academic institutions, companies and governmental agencies are not consistent, it is imperative that a federal policy should be put in place for how organizations, academic institutions, companies and financial institutions react to the public and what information hold be disclosed when a cyber-attack that results in data or financial loss does occur. It is understood that better policies on the local, state, and federal level governing: communication, encryption, servers, and compliance with law and regulations that also state fines, penalties, and additional cost for pursuit and capture of perpetrators of cyber-attacks is needed. Additionally development and research in the area of cyber encryption and authentication is necessary to safeguard against future invasion of personal and financial privacy and consumer data loss, as information in the form of PHI, PII, and credit information is invaluable.

SOLUTIONS AND RECOMMENDATIONS

With any incidence and/or occurrence of a cyber-attack, a security breach, data leak, or data breach, hindsight will always suggest that more could have been done to prevent the attack, security breach, data leak, or data loss. In addition to this notion, it is our belief that more can be done to have local and state agencies to become uniform in their reporting of cyber-attacks, how the information is reported, how consumers affected by the security breach, cyber-attack, data leak, or data loss are notified, and the timing that information is reported to consumers that have been affected by the cyber-attack.

Information such as the policies and procedures that govern the listing and documentation on what states are compliant, who is in compliance, what is considered compliant based on the standards set forth by the Data Security and Breach Notification Act of 2015 should be the starting point for anyone interested in updating and changing their company policies and anyone who desire to change their policies on the state and/or local level. If each state meet the requirements set forth and established in the Data Security and Breach Notification Act of 2015 it would show consistency, transparency, and proper notification via creditable and reputable channels that can be accessed and available to the consumers that have been affected by cyber-attacks, security breaches, data leaks, and data loss. As a result of the Data Security and Breach Notification Act of 2015, companies would be required to report accurate information in a more timely fashion to its consumers, and assist customers, state and federal agencies, and law enforcement agencies with the identification and apprehension of the perpetrators of the cyber-attacks. Under this law, offices should be established to assist states and companies who are not in compliance with established federal or state policies and regulations, and offices would be able to assist them in becoming compliant with laws on the state and federal level. Additionally, individuals, groups, organizations, academic institutions, companies, and entities that work with state agencies should have to bear some of the cost and burdens in the apprehension and investigative costs that would be incurred on the federal level if they are not compliant with the established security standards, state and local polies and regulations, and federal policies and regulations, and areas of the Data Security and Breach Notification Act of 2015. With each new change, a standard for openness and transparency with regard to cyber-attacks, security breaches, data leaks, and data loss with regards to the policies that govern information, reporting, and notification should be updated and disseminated to state and local agencies to update them based on changes that can affect compliance on the federal level. This information can be easily displayed, reported, and communicated to the general public and federal agencies, and tracked within a data system that allows for accurate, timely reporting.

FUTURE RESEARCH DIRECTIONS

Research into the development of the Data Security and Breach Notification Act of 2105 and how parts of the act will affect the various individuals, groups, organizations, academic institutions, companies, and entities that work with state agencies should be the initial source of research areas. Future research can focus on the different parts of the development process, and how the policies that will be put into place will affect others, and the objectives of the policies were developed and how they will be exploited by others willing to circumvent the policies. Additionally, research in the area can focus on what issues existed with each state when constructing State Laws and how it will impact the various states when it begins to adopt the federal law(s) that are to come. Some general research questions that can be asked and explored could include:

1. What local, state, and federal policies are in place based on the state, and what events occurred do to cyber-attacks and cyber-espionage that resulted in the development of the policies that are in place?
2. What is considered compliance on the state and federal level with regard to the Data Security and Breach Notification Act of 2015, and what measures exist in regards to enforcing compliance with local and state agencies who are non-compliant?
3. What states are non-compliant and what is being done to become compliant based on the Data Security and Breach Notification Act of 2015?

Not all states have data breach laws, and many individuals, groups, organizations, academic institutions, companies, and entities that work with state agencies are concerned as a result of the lack of consistent state laws. Therefore requests have asked that law makers have uniform laws across states as uniformity is necessary on the state and federal level. Because of the lack of uniformity across states, it is not surprising that not all information reported in the media is unclear and not concrete on how reporting and notification of a data security and/or breach should occur. Therefore a general and special reporting system and a time for reporting became necessary on both the state and federal level. Since reporting was not uniform or governed by a federal law, measures that included an office for proper communication regarding the cyber-attacks in question, a reporting system, a notification system, and an office of compliance that regulates compliance and information is necessary for the proper notification to individuals that may be affected by data security and/or breaches that have occurred on the and can affect individuals, groups, organizations, academic institutions, companies, and entities that work with state agencies.

From an academic standpoint, it goes without saying that additional research is needed within this area to assess additional aspects of cyber-security, cyber-terrorism, and cyber-espionage especially as it relates to the social-economic impact on the individuals, organizations, academic institutions, companies, and governmental agencies. If research in these areas are conducted then the information would give researchers a better understanding of cyber activity and intrusion methods that have caused the requests for the Data Security and Breach Notification Act. This research would shed light on what has led to the increased cyber activity in the way of cyber-attacks, cyber-terrorism, and cyber-espionage and the attempts of breaching security on all levels and not just national security. When researchers look at the potential outcomes of the information that have led to the increase in cyber activity, it may be possible to see the changes in our security structure, and what impact it will have on how we: operate and have designed our defense systems, national defenses, national security, national cyber-security, and cyber-security, as it relates to groups, organizations, academic institutions, companies, and entities that work with state agencies. It would also be possible to analyze issues that relate directly to cyber-terrorism and what issues would still persist in how the Act would handle issues of cyber-terrorism. The Intelligence Community, individuals, groups, organizations, academic institutions, companies, and entities that work with state agencies have played a large role in our defense and cyber defense systems, and have helped to shape the digital age and the constant evolution of our global internet system. Therefore requesting their assistance and guidance would be essential in understanding and preparing preventive methods for any future cyber-attacks and/or system intrusions. With each cyber-attack, data breach, or security breach, a set of parameters should be applied to categorize and analyze the cyber-attack in order to assist in determining how access was gained by intruders, determining the susceptibility to cyber-attacks, analyzing the levels of complexity with regard to the cyber-attack and security systems that were circumvented, and the instillation of prevention methods to reduce future cyber-attacks, security breaches, and data breaches. Once categorized each cyber-attack should be analyzed even further for predictive means, and for an understanding of how others see and perceive the security infrastructure based on previous cyber-attacks and how they were coordinated over time. These areas could give students, researchers, and agencies a means for conducting research within the field in the upcoming future, and it would provide students, researchers, and agencies a means for understanding and analyzing how others perceive the national security and cyber-security of various government agencies. This type of research would give corporations within the United States and national security agencies a measure for increasing performance and capabilities as a result of the successful and failed attempts to cyber-attacks where individuals, groups, organizations, or countries have tried to circumvent their systems and to means to analyze how foreign entities have tried to gain access to different systems.

CONCLUSION

Outlined with this chapter are the most recent and published works on the Data Security and Breach Notification Act of 2015 that contains provisions that were expected and unexpected, requested and suggested, and advocated for by former congressmen, individuals, groups, organizations, academic institutions, companies, and members of the government. Based on previous requests and suggestions individuals, groups, organizations, academic institutions, companies, and members of the government requested a uniform notification process that occurs within a predetermined time period after the cyber-attack, communications with potential victims of the cyber-attack that occur in a clear and concise manner, and an established form of support for the consumers that have been affected by the cyber-attack.

Within this publication, numerous questions were stated as to why the need for a national data breach notification law was necessary and in many ways the Data Security and Breach Notification Act of 2015 addressed these issues and concerns and explored avenues as to what could happen in various situations. The need for this type of act grew as a result of the number, type, and amount of cyber-attacks and data breaches have increased over the previous years and it became imperative that safeguards must be in place against criminal cyber activity. With these safeguards, a priority should have been placed on notifying individuals that their personal information, personal health information, financial, and private data may have been exposed to the public as a result of a security breach, a data leak, or a cyber-attack.

However, prior to the Data Security and Breach Notification Act of 2015 no published material existed to suggest that a difference in the way that we handled notification to individuals existed, (*and nothing suggested that attempts to circumvent National Security system have been put into place but any agency, even though changes and updates have been applied daily*.) How we handle and have handled intrusions on servers and the methods that have been used to detect intrusions that occur on organizations, academic institutions, and companies' servers is very important as it has a huge impact on the customers' ability to continue to conduct business online. By analyzing the security system and the intrusion detection/defense systems in public and private sector and holding them accountable to uniform laws across the United States and on the state level, it will be possible to gain a clear idea of how information was safeguarded on the various organizations, academic institutions, and companies' servers. This information when accurately reported on based on uniform standards can give an idea of the data that was loss due to a security breach, a data leak, or a cyber-attack. With additional technological and data systems being brought online daily, additional safeguards and policies were needed to measure, manage, reduce, identity, and prevent the number of cyber-attacks; therefore, how we respond to the attacks should have been evaluated and enhanced.

In many ways it is not possible to retaliate in a cyber-attack unless the attacker is known and can be directly traced back to the source, but if the current policy is to defend against any cyber-attack, security intrusion, or to prevent a data leak, one must ask, *when do we strike back and how?* It has long been thought that intruders have invaded various organizations, academic institutions, and company servers and systems, and as these systems have already been compromised and infiltrated, the individual(s) and/or groups/organizations are committing cyber-espionage and are waiting to strike. If action is taken in response to a cyber-attack – what form of retaliation is possible if our system has intruders that are present and persistent without our knowledge? Also what type of harm or damage would come to our computing infrastructure as a result of retaliation? If this is true then on both sides one must be aware of the issues that could result from a cyber-attack and the resulting retaliation. Also how would we measure our success from a simultaneous cyber-attack? Would we measure it by the services that remain in place once both sides have attacked, and wouldn't that leave everyone vulnerable to other enemies (foreign and domestic)? Do we measure our success by the number of services that remain viable and stable after our individual attacks? Therefore a means is needed to understand how to remove the internal threats without increasing our vulnerability to outside threats while keeping our position intact in our own computing systems.

REFERENCES

BakerHostetter. (2015, May 23). *Data Breach Charts*. Retrieved from http://www.bakerlaw.com/files/Uploads/Documents/Data%20Breach%20documents/Data_Breach_Charts.pdf/

Bono, M. (2015, January 20). The need for a national data breach law. *The Hill*. Retrieved from http://thehill.com/blogs/pundits-blog/technology/229968-the-need-for-a-national-data-breach-notification-law/

Committee on Energy and Commerce. (2015). Data security and breach notification act of 2015. Retrieved from http://energycommerce.house.gov/sites/republicans.energycommerce.house.gov/files/analysis/20150312DataSecuritySummary.pdf

Korolov, M. (2015, January 13). Obama proposes new 30-day data breach notification law. Retrieved from http://www.csoonline.com/article/2868096/data-protection/obama-proposes-new-30-day-data-breach-notification-law.html

Peterson, A. (2015, April 15). Why this national data breach notification bill has privacy advocates worried. *The Washington Post*. Retrieved from http://www.washingtonpost.com/blogs/the-switch/wp/2015/04/15/why-this-national-data-breach-notification-bill-has-privacy-advocates-worried/

Peterson, A. (2015, April 15). Why this national data breach notification bill has privacy advocates worried. *The Washington Post*. Retrieved from http://www.washingtonpost.com/blogs/the-switch/wp/2015/04/15/why-this-national-data-breach-notification-bill-has-privacy-advocates-worried/

KEY TERMS AND DEFINITIONS

Cyber-Security: Is the body of technologies, processes and practices designed to protect networks, computers, programs and data from attack, damage or unauthorized access. In a computing context, the term security implies cybersecurity.

Data Leak: The unauthorized transfer of classified information from a computer or datacenter to the outside world. Data leakage can be accomplished by simply mentally remembering what was seen, by physical removal of tapes, disks and reports or by subtle means such as data hiding.

Data Leap Prevention: Is a strategy for making sure that end users do not send sensitive or critical information outside the corporate network. The term is also used to describe software products that help a network administrator control what data end users can transfer.

Detection: The action or process of identifying the presence of something concealed.

Intrusion Detection Measures: A type of security management system for computers and networks.

Security: The state of being free from danger or threat.

Server: A server is a software program, or the computer on which that program runs, that provides a specific kind of service to client software running on the same computer or other computers on a network.

Chapter 12
Combating Terrorism through Peace Education: Online Educational Perspective

Eugenie de Silva
University of Leicester, UK

Eugene de Silva
Virginia Research Institute, USA

Eriberta B. Nepomuceno
Bicol University, Philippines

ABSTRACT

This chapter focuses on peace education as a vital resource to combat terrorism. It is herein established that an everlasting solution to terrorism could only be reasonably expected if individuals' states of minds are altered. Accordingly, it is further determined that such changes are feasible through peace education, which will ultimately provide a firm basis for fact-based, non-violent, analyses of situations, and resolutions of issues. Furthermore, the authors of this chapter have further incorporated how peace education through online educational classrooms and courses will be extremely useful in the twenty-first century as more activities are conducted through cyber systems.

DOI: 10.4018/978-1-4666-9661-7.ch012

INTRODUCTION

"What is the point of learning this?" utters many students as they journey through their academic careers. Whilst a multidisciplinary approach to all subjects can answer students' individual questions about the necessity of learning specific information, a broader view of education can aid in the recognition of why and how education can, not only improve the knowledge and wisdom of students, but also can contribute to the combating of terrorism and the securing of nations. Universities and colleges are bastions and repositories of learning and culture. Accordingly, universities and colleges could also play an important role in combating terrorism and bringing about a culture of peace through re-education, re-training, and rehabilitation. This is another prime reason why governments and private entities support the work of education.

Primarily, individuals view education as a means by which to gain knowledge to benefit one's own academic and professional life. Whilst this is certainly true, education is a resource that can also benefit an entire society. Education not only teaches subject matter, but also promotes the adoption of a diverse, fact-based, accepting perspective to global issues. Whilst it may be difficult for students to develop an understanding of how education can provide benefits that are not immediately identifiable, it is imperative that they are not swayed against education as a result of their lack of comprehension. Therefore, while general education can be useful in the establishment of a non-violent mindset that aids in the recognition of the harmful effects of terrorism, peace education focuses on specifically designed curricula that more effectively prevents individuals from turning to terrorism. For instance, according to a 1999 UNICEF report, peace education is described as,

...the process of promoting the knowledge, skills, attitudes and values needed to bring about behavior changes that will enable children, youth and adults to prevent conflict and violence, both overt and structural; to resolve conflict peacefully; and to create the conditions conducive to peace, whether at an intrapersonal, interpersonal, intergroup, national or international level. (Fountain, p.1)

In general, peace education can enable one to alter their worldly view; thus, transforming their perspective of the world in a manner that focuses on conflict resolution through peaceful processes, especially through a reliance on education, training, and peaceful discussions. It may seem that peace education requires the standard brick and mortar classroom environments that provide a sense of strong guidance to pupils; however, as technology revolutionizes the twenty-first century, online education will surely provide the most convenient pathway for such peace education to be promoted, especially to those with limited educational centers. A reliance on online education will not only lessen costs related to peace education, but will provide students with novel opportunities to engage with curricula that effects a positive and necessary change. Moving forward, the University for Peace was "established in 1980 by the General Assembly of the United Nations, with the mandate to support the Peace and Security objectives of the United Nations through a world-wide programme of education for Peace" (University for Peace Accreditation, 2015). Accordingly, the University for Peace Distance Education (www.elearning.upeace.org) is an example of the shift in reliance from traditional educational processes to online and distance education to offer degree in peace education.

Therefore, the authors of this chapter have sought to provide a clear understanding of the reasons why peace education should be offered at all levels, especially though online courses and classrooms. This chapter provides an overview of how peace education will be useful as the world witnesses the rise of radical and terrorist organizations. The authors acknowledge the beneficial nature of traditional educational processes, yet, for the purposes of this research, have placed a focus on an online educational perspective to discuss the topic of peace education as a way to discourage individuals from turning to terrorism and encourage peaceful resolutions of issues.

BACKGROUND

As is the case with all topics and issues, there are diverse, varying opinions that do not align. The topic of peace education is that which welcomes wide-ranging discussions and analytical analyses. There are some individuals who would argue that peaceful resolutions are not, in their entirety, the most successful or plausible ways in which to handle all situations. Au contraire, there are certainly others who feel that peace education and peaceful resolutions should always be the initial response to major issues. Therefore, it would seem that the arguments generally stem from controversy over the use of violent versus non-violent approaches; thus, the effectiveness and usefulness of peace education could seemingly be overridden by the possibly politically motivated or biased discussions of violence versus non-violence to resolve issues. The researchers in this chapter maintain the notion that the safety of citizens of a nation is paramount; hence, while the researchers agree in uniformity that peaceful resolutions are a priority, the researchers also contend that military intervention or physical force may be necessary in cases of immediate, impending violence or threat to individuals.

In 1999, the UN General Assembly adopted the Declaration and Programme of Action on a Culture of Peace. Within the text, the Constitution of the United Nations Educational, Scientific and Cultural Organization was quoted to highlight that, "since wars begin in the minds of men, it is in the minds of men that the defenses of peace must be construed" ("Declaration and Programme," 1999). This is an underlying theme in the argument presented through this chapter. The notion of peace education should be viewed as a means by which individuals are taught and given opportunities to develop a paradigm wherein peaceful resolutions and peaceful discussions are the norm. Peace education should not be seen as a resource to be left on the backburner until an issue arises; rather, it should be an active, not passive, tool used to establish a revolutionary culture across the globe. Further, peace education should be recognized as a step beyond simply teaching students to learn about peace, but it should be viewed as a means by which instructors can instill peaceful messages and peaceful outlooks through education.

Article 1 of the Declaration and Programme of Action on a Culture of Peace provides a detailed list of the basic foundation for a culture of peace. This Article is important to this chapter, since it provides an opportunity to briefly assess the possible counterarguments for such beliefs pertaining to a culture of peace and peace education. Take for instance Article 1, section c that reads, "Full respect for and promotion of human rights and fundamental freedoms" ("Declaration and Programme," 1999). However, various cultures and religions can blur the lines of what is meant by human rights and fundamental freedoms, especially when individuals from different cultures and religions adopt subjective viewpoints to assess human rights and fundamental freedoms. In the United States of America (USA), the issues of human rights and fundamental freedoms have been primarily discussed in the media due to the legalization of same-sex marriage, and the current issues with gun laws and the ownership of guns. Therefore, when speaking about peace education and a culture of peace, broad statements about human rights and fundamental freedoms could result in technical issues that could blur the lines of what is necessary to establish peaceful progress. Regardless, these issues have already been taken into consideration and countered in 1993 at the Vienna World Conference on Human Rights when it was put forth that it was the "duty of States to promote and protect all human rights and fundamental freedoms, regardless of their political, economic and cultural systems," ("What Are," 2015). Therefore, the ideological standpoints of individuals should not have a bearing on the variation of human rights and fundamental freedoms. Listed below are the main human rights and fundamental freedoms as provided through the Convention for the Protection of Human Rights and Fundamental Freedoms and amended by Protocols No. 11 and No. 14 for the Council of Europe:

- Right to Life
- Prohibition of Torture
- Prohibition of Slavery or Forced Labor
- Right to Liberty and Security
- Right to a Fair Trial
- No Punishment without Law
- Right to Respect for Private and Family Life
- Freedom of Thought, Conscience, and Religion
- Freedom of Expression
- Freedom of Assembly Association
- Right to Marry
- Right to an Effective Remedy
- Prohibition of Discrimination
- Derogation in Time of Emergency
- Restrictions on Political Activity of Aliens
- Prohibition of Abuse of Rights
- Limitation on Use of Restriction on Rights

Moving forward, this chapter directly relates to Article 4 of the Declaration and Programme of Action on a Culture of Peace. Article 4 writes, "Education at all levels is one of the principal means to build a culture of peace. In this context, human rights education is of particular importance ("Declaration and Programme," 1999). Education at all levels has been generally viewed as that which requires a brick and mortar environment and strict guidance from instructors to train students to do well on standardized testing. In fact, in some areas of the world, such as the USA, school funding depends on how well students perform on their standardized tests; hence, this fosters an academic culture wherein instructors act as trainers for students to memorize information to simply pass tests. These environments will certainly not be useful in the active promotion of peace education, since they do not allow students to have creative freedom or flexibility to explore the field. This is not to disregard on-ground environments, but it is to place a focus on the unique freedom offered through online learning environments. A suitable environment is equally as important as high standard courses. Online education does not stipulate that a student only learn from online resources; rather, as online education has expanded, it has allowed students to access wide-ranging resources that complement the online, academic process. It is the online, accredited universities with a strong background in providing high standard education (based on novel research into the progressive ways in which education should be provided to students with diverse backgrounds) that will be effective in promoting peace education across the globe.

Additionally, some students who disassociate school and education from their daily lives will most probably be more inclined to do so when they feel that going to their traditional on-ground classes is a completely different environment than their general, home environments. Through online education, students are able to complete the same high-standard, academic assignments while in their own homes, which further enables them to realize how their education is not that which takes place only outside of one's home. Moreover, online instructors commonly realize that their students are not being offered the exact same opportunities as those in on-ground courses (e.g. there is a lack of physical interaction); hence, the instructors do generally include examples of how the course information can be linked to the students' daily lives and how they can apply the learned information on a daily basis. Many students also have limited time schedules, since they must juggle their personal and professional lives. Thus, online learning through asynchronous courses allows students to balance their lives without having to worry about how to complete their education and manage their lifestyles. Many online courses also include live, online lectures that can be accessed by the students, which reiterate main concepts within the courses and provide necessary interaction. The online discussion boards in online courses are also vital tools that are used to maintain daily interaction and promote active engagement to ensure that all students are able to take part in academically rigorous discussions of the subject-content.

MAIN FOCUS OF THE CHAPTER

Issues, Controversies, and Problems

In recent years, the globe has witnessed catastrophic events that have undermined years of peace-building discussions and law enforcement strategies. It was the Irish Republican Army (IRA) that declared, after failing to achieve their goal of taking the life of Margaret Thatcher, "Today we were unlucky, but remember we only have to be lucky once --- you will have to be lucky always" (Bingham, 2013). Law enforcement must not simply be lucky, they must be strategically formidable against the terror of the world; however, it does seem that while law enforcement of many countries have managed to detect and deter many possible attacks, terrorists and the criminals-alike have been lucky several times. In fact, it only took one day in June of 2015 to allow terrorists to simultaneously carry out attacks on three different continents (Botelho, 2015). If one is to go along with the notion that it was luck that allowed the criminal acts to occur, then these strokes of bad luck on the part of global law enforcement show the extent to which peace education and providing legitimate access to peace education to individuals across the globe is an inherent necessity, in addition to a stronger and more focused global law enforcement strategy.

Which Culture is Better?

The issue with the current culture is that the world is seemingly, hopelessly divided by the notion that various cultures are extremely different and certain cultures are better than others. These subjective arguments that typically rely on biased views of various cultures are based on individual determinations of the harshness of activities in specific cultures. For instance, in Sri Lanka, a primarily Buddhist country, it is quite typical that individuals will not eat beef, due to their Buddhist philosophical teachings. This culture in Sri Lanka would most probably view the USA culture of eating and/or selling beef in most restaurants across the country as inhumane. On the other hand, in the USA, a country founded on Christian principles, yet recognized for its diversity, marriage proposals would most likely come from an intimate partner with whom the involved parties have been in a relationship. This culture would most probably view the Sri Lankan culture (not currently widespread in the twenty-first century, yet still prevalent) of parents bringing marriage proposals to their children to find a suitable partner, as a restriction human rights to free choice. To take it one step further, if individuals from both of these cultures analyzed the culture of Saudi Arabia wherein a beheading is simply another form of legal punishment, it is most probable that the individuals would view this as inhumane and violation of human rights to an extent. Yet, individuals from Saudia Arabia, a country that aligns itself with Islamic teachings, would view the ways in which individuals from both Sri Lanka and the USA wear certain clothes, listen to certain music, and present themselves in general as vulgar and inappropriate. In each of these cases, there are fact-based discussions that could arise to resolve the issues; yet, each of the individual parties around the world, regardless of whether it is admitted or not, allow opinion-based arguments to be included into professional and legal discussions. The authors' analyses of this topic are included in the following section.

Access to Peace Education?

A failure to accept others, and a lack of a holistic view of the world is another issue that contributes to a lack of peace in the world. This issue can be directly resolved through peace education as a means of fostering a global culture of acceptance and peaceful resolutions. Yet, as can be realized by considering Malala Yousef's story, individuals around the globe do not always have access to educational facilities. For those in Western countries, it may be easy to take advantage of the ease by which individuals can step outside their homes and physically attend an educational institution. While education is imperative, the safety of individuals is also highly important; therefore, short-term and long-term solutions need to be set in place to overcome these hurdles. Even if individuals have strong passions for peace education, it may not always be possible for them to attend academic institutions and receive the necessary education to pursue a future in the field.

Terrorism and Lack of Education

In many areas of the world, terrorism is currently a major issue that has devastated the lives of many innocent civilians. In many cases, terrorism is largely religiously motivated. Many major instances of terrorism, such as the Islamic State of Syria and the Levant (ISIL), are the result of radical individuals working under the guise of religious abidance. Of course, not all terrorism is the result of religion, such as the Liberation Tigers of Tamil Eelam (LTTE) in Sri Lanka, which were racially, ideologically motivated. The motivating factor of terrorism always needs to be addressed in order to find the most appropriate solutions. Accordingly, it is necessary to also take into consideration that terrorism is preventable. The authors of this chapter stipulate that individuals embracing terrorism, however, is not preventable through the use of violent, military intervention. In fact, the authors of this chapter argue that the use of violent strategies can result in the growth of terrorism by those seeking retaliation for the violent Courses of Action (COA). For example, a religiously motivated terrorist organization is the result of an ideological issue not a physical problem. Therefore, how can one expect to entirely deter such a terrorist organization by using physical force when the issue is internal? It may be possible to eliminate individuals who have radical mindsets and work for terrorist organizations, yet by doing so we are not eliminating the root of the issue. Security operations must be strategic and tactical; the security personnel must not simply believe that killing a terrorist would eliminate the terrorism issue. In most cases, killing a terrorist simply will create another terrorist. Therefore, other COAs must be taken, in addition to eliminating terrorists, to ensure that terrorism would not be a continuous cycle.

When what is sought is acceptance and to be a member of a larger community, individuals may try anything to achieve it. Take for an instance a young adult who stems from a poverty-stricken background and has tried many times to be an active member of the community, yet a lack of education and financial means has prevented this individual from achieving his/her goals. When a terrorist organization advertises a prosperous life (a life around other individuals who would provide support and acceptance), it is not unusual or illogical for the aforementioned individual to join the organization. Individuals who join terrorist organizations do not necessarily have to be aligned with the terrorist organization's ideological standpoint; rather, the individual simply has to be disaffected with his/her current life and/or the individual must be seeking a radical change/retaliation. Terrorist organizations can take advantage of under-educated individuals who feel as though they have no other, realistic opportunities to be a member of a larger group of individuals. Additionally, those who are extremely intelligent can also easily be swayed to turn to extremism. The Unabomber was actually a former child prodigy who began his studies at Harvard University at sixteen years old, and even held a Ph.D. before the age of twenty-five. This individual, while not religiously or racially motivated, resorted to violence and radicalism in order to achieve his goals. High intellectual capabilities that are left unguided can have disastrous consequences as shown in the case of the Unabomber. This also proves that it is not simply any education that is the key, but a good education in an environment that is supportive of each learner and considers each student as more than simply a number in the system.

Through the use of propaganda, terrorist organizations can also subtly sway individuals to agree with the group's teachings. Hezbollah was a major terrorist organization known for plainly using propaganda through video games. For instance, in 2007, reports showed that Hezbollah was releasing another video game based on its "34-day conflict" ("Hezbollah Video," 2007). Hezbollah's video games normalized the killing of Israeli soldiers by ensuring that the players adopt the role of Hezbollah in the game. For younger players, this can have disastrous consequences, since the repetitious behavior of earning points and rewards for killing certain individuals and wreaking havoc can lead them to subconsciously believe that it is appropriate behavior in real-life circumstances. Propaganda does not always have to be directly aimed at making a point about an ideology; rather, propaganda for terrorist organizations can be successful if it requires individuals to reconsider their lives and even briefly consider how their lives could be improved by aligning with a terrorist organization's ideology. Even if the individuals do not immediately join the terrorist organization as a result of the propaganda, it is possible for such propaganda to plant a seed within the minds of individuals. This seed can then grow, and ultimately sprout without the terrorist organization having to take any more actions; the daily negativity on the parts of the individuals and the discontent with their lives can force them to recall the consideration of a better life by joining a terrorist organization.

SOLUTIONS AND RECOMMENDATIONS

Which Culture is Better? None?

Human rights and fundamental freedoms, in addition to the safety of citizens are some of the main issues that should be placed as a priority for security officials; therefore, a main issue that is currently faced is the fact that individuals from various cultures continue to refuse to believe that one culture may work in one area of the world, but that same culture cannot and should not be forced on others in various other parts of the world. It is not the entire culture that is the issue; rather, it is the specific acts within the culture that should be regulated to ensure peace. For example, it is not the following of Islam in the Middle East that is the sole issue; rather, it is the allowance of outdated Islamic practices to guide the legal arena that is the issue. Similarly, it is not the issue of Christian leaders in Western countries dominating the political arena; rather, it is the issue of allowing outdated Christian practices to guide legal framework that is the issue. Therefore, the authors of this chapter contend that while certain cultures may follow varying religions or hold varying ideologies, it is not the place of members of the international arena to regulate what the culture should be in a country, rather regulations should be in place to maintain uniformity with regard to the upholding of human rights and fundamental freedoms.

Access to Peace Education? Online Education

Online education can be a major step forward in countries wherein the lives of students are threatened when leaving their homes to earn an education, especially females. Although access to the Internet may be a separate hurdle, students can collaborate to work together to earn their education in the safety of their own homes, if at least one student is able to access the Internet. This is certainly a short-term solution, yet it also contributes to the long-term solution, which is educating a new generation and influencing the older generation. Education is a long-term solution, and it would be quite rare for education to act as an effective short-term strategy that will immediately result in a recognizable change of mind across the globe. Yet, as a long-term solution, education is a necessary way forward that allows individuals to be introduced to novel ways of thinking and assessing situations. In January of 2015, the Finance Minister for Pakistan, Mujtaba Shujaur Rehman, even clearly elaborated on the fact that "terrorism and unemployment could be eradicated by the promotion of quality education" ("Reforms and Initiatives," 2015). Individuals from around the globe staunchly support the promotion of education, yet the continuous discussion of education as a necessity can only help to the extent that the discussions are not simply used as political means of gaining support to further a political agenda. When one argues that education is necessary to prevent terrorism and crime, it is further necessary to provide real-life strategies to ensure that more individuals have access to appropriate educational opportunities. If individuals simply continue to discuss what is already known, then it will be illogical to hope that any real progress will be made. It is for this reason that the authors of this chapter believe that, in addition to the presented argument that education is necessary, online education will be a formidable tool to encourage education and provide access to more individuals in various countries.

The online arena provides students with equal opportunities to enroll in courses that would not otherwise be available to them through on-ground courses. Furthermore, the wide-ranging nature of online education would also provide novel opportunities to study under individualized experts in many fields of interests, which would be more academically stimulating than simply enrolling and taking part in the available on-ground courses that could limit their selection options. Furthermore, online learning through qualified institutions would also give opportunities for various student-learning styles. Upon a first glance, it may seem that online learning would not actually be welcoming or useful for students with specific learning styles that require hands-on learning; however, the continuous evolution of the online academic arena has made it possible for students with various learning styles to benefit. For instance, for students in the natural science fields, such as physics and chemistry, that typically require hands-on experience in laboratories, online academic institutions could provide lab-packs (which are physical lab packets that are sent to students' homes) and access to virtual laboratory simulations, in addition to uploading videos of the laboratory practices. Therefore, online learning has expanded and grown to take into consideration and resolve such issues.

Terrorism and Lack of Education

While propaganda can take many different forms, it is also necessary to realize that well-educated individuals who study at institutions that provide appropriate guidance, fact-based learning, and support will be less likely to fall victim to such propaganda. For example, in a study at the Harvard University Kennedy School of Government pertaining to the impact of radio propaganda in Rwanda, it was determined that "basic education may limit the persuasive power of a given propaganda," since it "enables citizens to access alternative news sources" (Yanagizawa-Drott, 2011, p.20). A more educated individual will always be in a better situation to handle issues and analyze situations, since they have a stronger foundation upon which to progress. Therefore, issues with terrorism can thus be limited and eventually eliminated by providing more educational opportunities. Yet, once again, the provision of more academic opportunities is essentially an idealistic notion without also relying on online education. If there is not enough funding to pay for instructors and teachers in certain areas of the world, an educational institution could even set up a partnership or collaboration with online universities and colleges to provide lectures via distance resources. This would cut down costs related to providing education and would also allow for greater flexibility to teach students.

Cultural Change in Perception: Time and Education

Through efficient peace education, it becomes possible to alter mindsets in a positive manner. By providing quality education to individuals across the globe, it further becomes possible to establish a culture of rigour and critical thinking that no longer depends on outdated assumptions, but rather depends on fact-based, scientific, and academic analyses of situations. Of course, in order to entirely eliminate terrorism, there must be a cultural change across the globe. Firstly, it should not be assumed that terrorists, alone, are the only ones contributing to the issues; individuals should take into consideration that those who allow individuals to become terrorists by isolating them or forcing them into a position that makes them feel unaccepted are also a major part of the problem. Individuals should not feel as though their only solution is to become a terrorist; furthermore, those who believe fighting terrorism is solely in the hands of law enforcement or security personnel are also a contributing factor to terrorism. Every individual can contribute to the elimination of terrorism; however, in order for every individual to effectively play a role in this quest, there must be a positive cultural change. By ensuring quality education to all individuals, one can establish a long-term paradigm shift that would enlighten those who are unaware of the indirect or direct ways in which they may be contributing to the instability of the security across the globe. By diversifying the academic arena to include peace education into many online, academic institutions, it would be possible to provide more individuals with the opportunity to learn about new perspectives and learn about the ways in which they can contribute to the safety of citizens; simply by offering new information to students, it will become possible to slowly, but steadily open the eyes of the population to a more accepting and diverse culture.

As times have evolved, activities that were considered a-typical in the past slowly have become widely accepted and considered to be normal. Take for instance the current cultural norms of the world that were not always accepted, such as stricter laws enforced in countries like Singapore, or even the recent shift in normality like the legalization of same-sex marriage in the USA. Each of these seemingly typical activities were not always the norm. At one point in history, individuals did not abide by these cultural norms; however, after legally making changes to rules and regulations and establishing a formal framework upon which to move forward, individuals became accustomed to these practices and now individuals generally live without questioning these general norms. Therefore, in the same manner, if changes are made to academic curricula, especially by implementing more peace education courses into online academic institutions, individuals would slowly become accustomed to the norm that is settling differences in a peaceful manner, accepting diverse cultures, and promoting academic opportunities that focus on peaceful resolutions of issues on a daily basis. It may be difficult for individuals to accept cultural changes at a fast pace; however, it is possible to establish a cultural change by first making the necessary legal changes, and then providing ample time to allow individuals to become comfortable with the new norm. Initially, those in positions with political power must make solid use of their power in order to establish strict regulations that make it possible for more individuals to earn education; this is not limited to countries that have issues with certain populations unable to attend schools, due to religious concerns, this also spans to Western countries, especially the USA, that allows private institutions to make it seem that if one pays more for a degree, they are more educated or more admirable. Education is a necessity and a right; it is illogical to force students to attend schools to graduate with debts that will take many years to resolve. Head officials should make education free and accessible to all individuals. Students should not feel that they must strive to pay the overwhelming academic tuition fees to attend private institutions with the hopes that potential employers will hire them for attending an expensive institution, and that the employers will help to pay off their debts they have acquired while bettering themselves to become contributing members of society. Although not all individuals will agree with such ideas, it is important that those who do agree take the time to rationally defend these arguments and ensure a universal change and improvement to ensure quality access to education, especially peace education.

Furthermore, as time changes and cultures evolve, educators and researchers must firmly devote their time to change the perception of the public to positively eliminate the current culture that allows for the biased judgment of individuals or groups, while also failing to consider how and why history repeats itself with regard to the development of terrorist organizations. The same way in which advocates stand up to ensure equal rights and anti-bullying campaigns, there should be active campaigns to support a judgment-free culture that does not isolate individuals or result in radicalization by forcing individuals to feel as though they have no other choices in life.

FUTURE RESEARCH DIRECTIONS

This chapter essentially acts as a general basis for other researchers to delve into the evolution of online education to focus on peace education. Researchers must take the initiative to focus on how online education may revolutionize academic opportunities for those in developing countries, and would allow for greater opportunities to prevent individuals from turning to terrorism. It is imperative that researchers adopt an unbiased and objective view of online education when evaluating it in relation to the possible prevention of terrorism. In reality, it is the focus on education that can alter individuals' mindsets to prevent joining a terrorist organization. As the online academic arena expands, it will undoubtedly be a formidable tool in the fight against terrorism; accordingly, researchers must devote time to evaluate the most useful ways in which to take advantage of online, academic expansions for the benefit of the security of the globe.

It would also be useful for researchers to delve into analyses of the rationally proven ways in which online peace education can provide more opportunities to under-developed areas of the world, especially areas wherein students have safety concerns in attending physical, academic institutions. The research could also elaborate on the expenses that would be incurred for students in such areas as they seek to complete their education via online institutions. It would be useful to weigh the costs of physical education versus the costs of online education; furthermore, these analyses could also investigate whether or not students in such areas would be less vulnerable to possible terrorist propaganda if they completed online educational programs.

CONCLUSION

In its entirety, peace education through online learning can be a step forward to aid in the deterrence of terrorism and the prevention of individuals turning to terrorism to fill voids or retaliate. The adaptive and flexible environment provided through online education allows students to maintain balanced professional, personal, and academic lives. When individuals turn to terrorism, law enforcement personnel are forced to strengthen defense mechanisms and systematically plan, predict, and prevent any possible harm to citizens around the globe. Thus, rather than turning to violent, military intervention to resolve issues that are generally internal (e.g. philosophical, religious, or psychological), the use of peace education through online education can result in peaceful progress and novel developments that allow for the changing of mindsets to prevent individuals from even considering terrorism as a possible choice in their lives.

Although the authors recognize that education is a long-term solution to terrorism, the authors also contend that it can result in effective short-term changes to mindsets that would further discourage individuals from turning to terrorism or falling victim to the propaganda of terrorist organizations. Peace education, in particular, as a long-term solution has been further argued as a necessity through online education to provide more opportunities to those who worry about their safety when attending physical academic institutions to earn their education. The revolutionary nature of online education will be useful in allowing students to specialize and learn more about distinct fields without the hassle of physically entering dangerous situations that put their lives at risk. Through this work, it is hoped that the readers understand that the usefulness of online education spans beyond busy, working adults who do not have time to physically attend classes. Online education is a resource that should be used for individuals, regardless of their age, to provide novel academic opportunities.

In order to ensure that more individuals do not join terrorist organizations or turn to radicalism, education should instill quality skills, such as acceptance and tolerance. If, from a young age and a lower level of education, educators are able to provide quality academic experiences, even through online systems, that instill the notion that it is every individuals responsibility to contribute to the fight against terrorism, then it may be possible to build a future that relies on peaceful resolutions and witnesses lower percentage of the population turning to terrorism.

It is important to also take into consideration that a swift, immediate change in public perception and cultural normality cannot be expected. The issue should not revolve around the time it will take in order for a successful, positive, paradigm shift, but rather should revolve around the tools and resources needed to achieve the positive, ultimate goal. The goal of preventing individuals from turning to terrorism, in addition to eliminating current issues with terrorism relates to an ideological or internal issue; therefore, it should be noted that peace education can be used as a vital tool to highlight novel perspectives, new means of achieving goals, and the proper ways to fit into society to achieve goals without having to turn to radicalism or terrorism.

Some individuals may not support online education as a primary tool to promote peace education, yet subjective opinion should not override objective analyses; thus, as aforementioned, practitioners must continue to conduct research into the topic in order to highlight the pros and cons of moving forward with online education as it pertains to more educational opportunities to a wider proportion of the population. The advent of advanced technology may be used for social purposes, but individuals across the globe should take a step further to use the novel developments of the twenty-first century for more wholesome, prosperous purposes, such as educating the new generation.

Currently, the majority of discussions related to cyber systems focus on espionage and/or surveillance. While these are major issues that deserve attention, the debates and discussions of cyber systems should now also place a spotlight on the educational opportunities that can be offered through these systems. Rather than focusing solely on the negativity related to the cyber arena, the public should be informed of the actual ways in which the cyber arena can be used to establish positive changes at a global level. It is the responsibility of researchers, educators, and even news officials to make the public more aware of how they can contribute to the security of their country, without having to be directly working for law enforcement agencies or organizations. The security arena should not be viewed as that which is restricted to those with backgrounds or employment at law enforcement or intelligence agencies. Although the intelligence and security fields are generally covert in nature and require security clearances in order to take part in detailed operations, the public should be aware that they could equally contribute to the prevention of terrorism by placing a focus on peace education, especially though online courses.

REFERENCES

Bingham, J. (2013). Margaret Thatcher: Seconds from Death at Hands of an IRA Bomber. *The Telegraph*. Retrieved from http://www.telegraph.co.uk/news/politics/margaret-thatcher/9979915/Margaret-Thatcher-Seconds-from-death-at-the-hands-of-an-IRA-bomber.html

Botelho, G. (2015). Terror Attacks on 3 Continents; ISIS Claims Responsibility in Tunisia, Kuwait. *CNN*. Retrieved from http://www.cnn.com/2015/06/26/africa/tunisia-terror-attack/

Fountain, S. (1999). *Peace Education in UNICEF.* Retrieved from http://www.unicef.org/education/files/PeaceEducation.pdf

Hezbollah Video Game - War with Israel. (2007). *CNN*. Retrieved from http://www.cnn.com/2007/WORLD/meast/08/16/hezbollah.game.reut/

Reforms and Initiatives: We Can End Terrorism Through Quality Education. (2015). *The Tribune*. Retrieved from http://tribune.com.pk/story/818470/reforms-and-initiatives-we-can-end-terrorism-through-quality-education/

UNESCO.org. (1999). Declaration and Program of Action on a Culture of Peace. Retrieved from http://www3.unesco.org/iycp/kits/uk_res_243.pdf

University for Peace Accreditation. (2015). Retrieved from https://www.upeace.org/about-upeace/accreditation

What are Human Rights? (2015). Retrieved from http://www.ohchr.org/EN/Issues/Pages/WhatareHumanRights.aspx

Yanagizawa-Drott, D. (2011). *Propaganda vs. Education: A Case Study of Hate Radio in Rwanda.* Retrieved from http://www.hks.harvard.edu/fs/dyanagi/Research/Propaganda_vs_Education.pdf

KEY TERMS AND DEFINITIONS

Extremism: The holding of extreme beliefs that are especially political or religious in nature.

Online Education: Any educational activities or academic pursuits that are carried out through online systems, rather than in a brick and mortar setting.

Peace Education: The process of promoting the knowledge, skills, attitudes and values needed to bring about behavior changes that will enable children, youth and adults to prevent conflict and violence, both overt and structural; to resolve conflict peacefully; and to create the conditions conducive to peace, whether at an intrapersonal, interpersonal, intergroup, national or international level (Fountain, p.1).

Propaganda: Biased information used to further one's own agenda, especially by misleading or mischaracterizing facts.

Radicalization: The process wherein individuals are taught extreme beliefs pertaining to specific agendas (political, religious, racial, economic, etc.).

Terrorism: Violent acts, or the threat of violent acts, that are used to further political, economic, religious, racial, or other similar agenda.

Traditional Education: Education that takes place in on-ground, brick and mortar settings and primarily focuses on teacher-centered learning, rather than student-centered learning.

Chapter 13
The Role of State Actors in Cybersecurity:
Can State Actors Find Their Role in Cyberspace?

Seunghwan Yeo
Virtual Research Associates, Inc., USA

Amanda Sue Birch
The Fletcher School, Tufts University, USA

Hans Ingvar Jörgen Bengtsson
The Fletcher School, Tufts University, USA

ABSTRACT

The growing impact of cyber activities across political, social, economic, and military domains makes cyberspace an essential dimension of human security. The role of states in cybersecurity requires a different approach from conventional security models because the classic concept of statehood comprising territory, population, and nationality is absent in cyberspace. Additionally, security issues in cyberspace are not always between or among states and they frequently lack clear attribution and motivation. This new paradigm of individual and knowledge-centered cyberpower means state actors no longer fully monopolize violence, per Max Weber's definition of a state. Furthermore, unlike the interstate dynamic between nuclear powers, cyber warfare is offense-dominant due to the absence of efficient deterrence. The immediate security concern should be addressing the protection of cybercitizens across borders. Therefore, state actors must cooperate to establish a multilateral uninterrupted network in order to safeguard the cyber commons via mutually assured collective cybersecurity.

DOI: 10.4018/978-1-4666-9661-7.ch013

INTRODUCTION

Cybersecurity consists of measures to protect the operations of a computer system or the integrity of its data from hostile action. (Kello, 2013, p. 18)

Can state actors fulfill traditional security roles in cyberspace? This paper explores national and international cybersecurity by examining the feasibility of securing the power of a state actor in cyberspace. The analysis includes examining differences between classical security and cybersecurity and explores why nation states' attempts to command and control the digital commons so far have not been successful.

The role of government in the cyber realm is important but still elusive. Conventional military strategies and tactics do not adapt well to the constantly evolving cyber domain. Furthermore, cyber anxiety and cyber threats entice governments to spend more to improve cybersecurity. Worldwide spending on cybersecurity for both the public and private sectors is projected to reach nearly $80 billion dollars in 2015 (Ranger, 2015; Gatner Inc., 2015). But the quest for security is at odds with the underlying purposes of cyber technology. The purpose of most cyber innovations is to improve convenience and productivity, but preserving this convenience via overreaching cybersecurity measures may impose inconveniences and decrease productivity. Finding the right balance point is both elusive and essential.

The objective of this paper is to further explore the role of state actors in cyberspace in three main sections. The first section defines actors in cyberspace. The second section describes the rise of a new security paradigm, explores the resulting cybersecurity framework, and identifies the nature of cyberpower. The third section addresses why state actors find it difficult to take the role of peacekeepers in cyberspace. Finally, case studies illustrate historical state intervention in cybersecurity to explain why the classic state role is not effective in cyberspace.

BACKGROUND

Two terms that will be used throughout this paper merit mention up front. The term 'actor' in this paper only refers to cyber actors in a technical security sense. This definition excludes individuals with broad social media impacts on platforms such as Twitter and YouTube who do not have technical computer programming skills. The second term to mention up front is 'cyberspace.' This paper uses Singer's definition: "the realm of computer networks and users behind them." (Singer & Friedman, 2014, p.13). This includes all networked systems that support improved human activities ranging from closed military networks to internal networks and to the World Wide Web (Kello, 2013, p.17).

Networks are made up of people connected beyond spatiotemporal restrictions. The number of Internet users was nearly three billion worldwide by the end of 2014 according to The International Telecommunications Union (ITU) (ITU, 2014). In the 1970s, only large corporations, governments, and organizations could have networked computers and only a few authorized operators could even touch those computers. This lasted until the personal computer (PC) evolution in the 1980s. Nowadays, palm-sized smartphones have more computing power than the mainframes in the late 1980s. No one at the time could have predicted that computers would be as prevalent as they are today.

Most people can access the Internet easily but few users understand what the threats are, what to defend, and how to defend. Only security providers exclusively control both collective and personal cyber defense. As the evolution of smart devices continues, the architecture becomes more complex and users therefore tend to rely on cyber specialists. In fact, Microsoft Windows users in the late 1990s and early 2000s had higher administration privileges on their machines than smart device users have today. Operating system manufacturers like Apple and Google no longer allow device owners to be super-users with powerful rights or permissions known as root, administrator, admin, or supervisor. To meet users' desires for convenience, users decide voluntarily to become consumers of the predefined user interface by giving up rights to access the system core. Users legitimately gain device ownership by purchase, but the owners no longer have administrative access to their devices and are therefore consumers or mere purchasers of a service. Only system creators can access the root of the system without consumer disadvantages such as voiding the warranty. Likewise, global software companies and device manufacturers authoritatively control connections to cyberspace. Almost all users are consumers in cyberspace but very few are actors.

Actors: Who Are the Actors Managing Cybersecurity?

Private companies and skilled individuals, rather than states and their citizens, are the primary actors in cyberspace. There is not much that ordinary users can do about cybersecurity. Complicated passwords do not guarantee higher security because the public has no right to access the property and technical decisions of private companies. The strongest actors in terms of cyberpower may not be state actors but private companies such as Google, Apple, and Microsoft. A highly skilled individual may also become an actor in cyberspace if he or she knows system vulnerabilities and has administrative access to a critical system, thus having power to inflict catastrophic damages to the system.

There is no state monopoly on violence in cyberspace and nation states may not be able to stage cyber wars. Governments can hire hackers for offensive cyber warfare, but superiority in numbers (more engineers and more computers) does not guarantee a series of victories in cyber conflicts. There is no reliable standard to measure cyberpower. Nonetheless, being a superior actor in cyberspace requires either large amounts of collected user data or the software engineering know-how to design, build, and maintain cyber systems. Therefore cyber superiority can rest with any actor, even individuals, based on data acquisition capabilities and technological leadership.

Actorhood in Cyberspace

The Montevideo Convention on the Rights and Duties of States codified the term 'statehood' as the possession of a permanent population, a defined territory, a government, and a capacity to enter into relations with other states ("Montevideo Convention on the Rights and Duties of States," 1933). But fulfillment of the statehood criteria does not necessarily make a state an actor in cyberspace.

For an actor in cyberspace, the following qualifications of actorhood should be met (see Figure 1):

- **Structural Elements:** These include the pieces of cyber systems that provide a robust service. One structural element is human resources such as developers and administrators governing the service. Another element is skills to identify vulnerabilities. On one hand, these skills help establish a robust systemic defense. On the other hand, these skills relate to the capability of detecting vulnerabilities within potentially threatening systems, also leading to better offensive cyberpower. Access to equipment and infrastructure are, of course, necessary structural elements required for actorhood.

Figure 1. Cyclical Growth of an Actor in Cyberspace

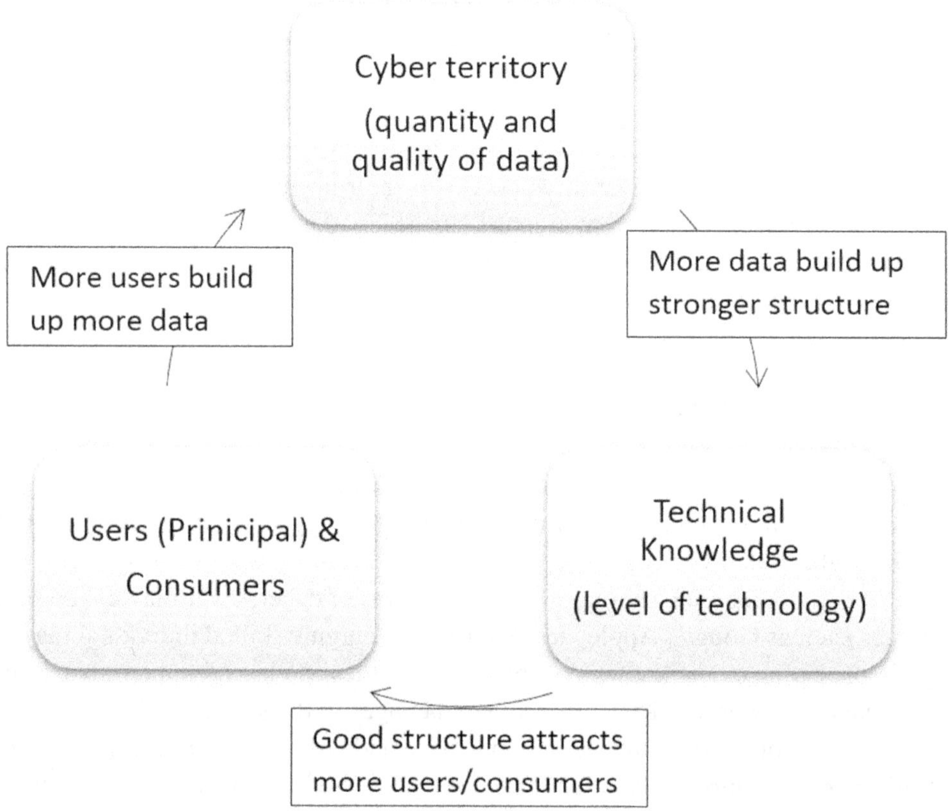

- **Population Elements:** The population includes all system users. More users mean that more information (and therefore power) is available to the actor.
- **Territorial Elements:** This includes ownership and access rights to user information, user-contributed content, and all types of core data, both collected and embedded. The level of access to user data defines the size of an actor's cyber territory.

Although the elements of actorhood described above cover bona fide actors in cyberspace, the definitions do not address all types of actors.

Normal and Flawed Actors

There are two types of actors in cyberspace: normal and flawed. Normal actors satisfy the three sequential elements of cyberpower defined above. For example, Google has a strong structural element in talented employees. It has the population element by its great number of users. This population's active participation contributes to Google's expanding territory of access rights, user information, and content. States are automatically categorized as normal or potential normal actors because governments can legitimately collect a data from their citizens and build systems facilitating their governance. But not all actors are normal.

Flawed actors often have great power to disrupt and harm. These actors conduct cyber activities without satisfying the pattern of cyclical growth. They access and exploit normal actors' data through understanding and using cyber weaknesses. For a normal actor it is more rational and beneficial to maintain a cycle of growth and get along well with other normal actors than it is to steal data, destroy systems, and hamper normal actors' cyber operations.

The activities of flawed actors can be characterized as goal-driven one offs such as cyberespionage and hacking. Flawed actors may have significant cyberpower with advanced structural technology to break into a target system, realizing physical outcomes as a result of their activities. These activities are unidirectional since they do not involve users relinquishing data (see Figure 2).

In Figure 2, flawed actors access the target system that contains the desired data. Once the preferred outcome is realized, the actor will terminate the process. This is the usual hacking pattern that is the focus of current cybersecurity research.

If a company holds private and critical user data such as email content, business communications, and proprietary knowledge saved on their servers, the company—the owner of the data—has no reason to use hacking techniques to obtain data since they already own the data through legitimate acquisition, absorption, and proper application of data (Lindsay, 2015, p.24). For instance Google monitors and aggregates data from its mail servers with 500 million active users, which makes the company a powerful actor in cyberspace.

Powerful non-state actors limit the power of states in cyberspace. States, however, may be able to access the privately collected data for the public good. It may therefore be assumed that the US government holds broad territory in cyberspace thanks to its advanced IT industry. For instance, Google voluntarily assists US law enforcement and proactively identifies child abuse suspects through message scanning technology (BBC, 2014). In China, in contrast to the United States and other democracies, authorities have access to all data without having to prove national security or public interest requirements. Internet companies in China are forced to cooperate with the Chinese government and their censorship by sign-

Figure 2. One-Off Action of Flawed Actor

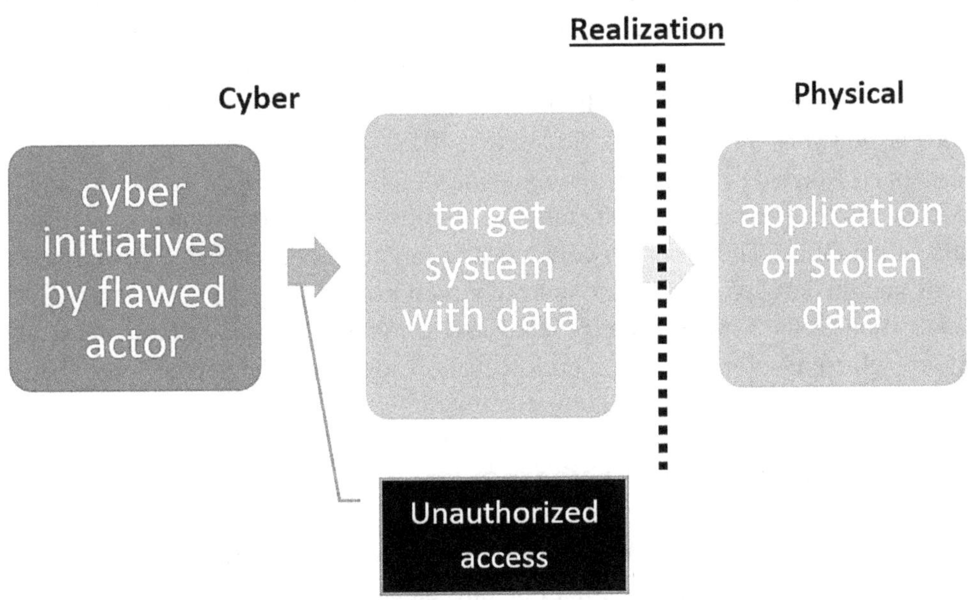

ing the Public Pledge of Self-Regulation and Professional Ethics for China Internet Industry, initiated by the Internet Society of China (ISC) (Internet Society of China, 2002). Cyber capability of illiberal authoritarian states with total domestic control can therefore be argued to include the total power of its private sector capabilities.

Data collected through territorial power by private normal actors may thus be credited to the cyber-power of the state. However the voluntary cooperation of the private sector may be a sensitive issue in democratic states (Der Spiegel, 2014). Setting aside states' legal controls over private actors, the security paradigm in cyberspace is driven by individuals and private organizations that satisfy both normal and flawed dimensions of actorhood. The next chapter discusses this security paradigm in cyberspace.

The Security Paradigm in Cyberspace

Cyberspace is still a new frontier. The birth of cyberspace had its origins in ARPANET—a US government project initiated in the 1960s. ARPANET was the first packet switching network to implement transmission control and Internet protocol (TCP/IP). In spite of its state sponsored origin, cyberspace in effect precludes state control in its context and implementation. Since cyber activities take place on the network and not in physical locations, traditional state jurisdiction is not applicable.

The primary goal of cyber technology is to connect people and devices beyond physical time and space. In other words, the term 'cyber' means an interconnection of two or more systems designed to cooperate and to create synergy beyond any physical restrictions.

Computer systems, the basic elements of cyberspace, must therefore be connected to be of value, but any connected system becomes immediately vulnerable to an attack (Kello, 2013, p.28). As more computers connect to each other, the combinations—and therefore the network vulnerabilities—grow exponentially (see Figure 3).

Unlike a hierarchy or a hub-and-spoke network, cyberspace has the characteristics of a neural network. If only two computers exist in the world, there will be a single network connecting the two. In cybersecurity, the most certain method to foil any type of unauthorized access is to cut the cable between the intruder and target computers. If three computers are connected, one may have to cut three cables. Four computers, six cables. Therefore network vulnerability will grow exponentially along with the network growth. About fifteen billion devices are estimated to be connected to the Internet in 2015, and the number of connections will be 105 billion, calculated from the combination of 15 billion devices (n=15 billion) taken two at a time (k =2) (Soderbery, 2013).

Even air-gapped isolated systems have a maintenance port that is open to the outside. Stuxnet, an advanced persistent attack that targeted the closed control system of Iran's nuclear program, is one example of this vulnerability. The cyber network has its primordial dilemma of connectivity; the number of connections and the level of security are inversely proportional.

Cyber innovation seeks to maximize efficiency and to minimize this inevitable vulnerability. A key question for strengthening cybersecurity, therefore, is how to narrow the gap between these conflicting concepts.

Definition and Measurement of Cyberpower

Joseph Nye defines cyberpower as "the ability to produce preferred outcomes within cyberspace or to use cyber instruments to produce benefits in other domains outside cyberspace. (Nye, 2010, p.4)" The term

Figure 3. Vulnerability Growth

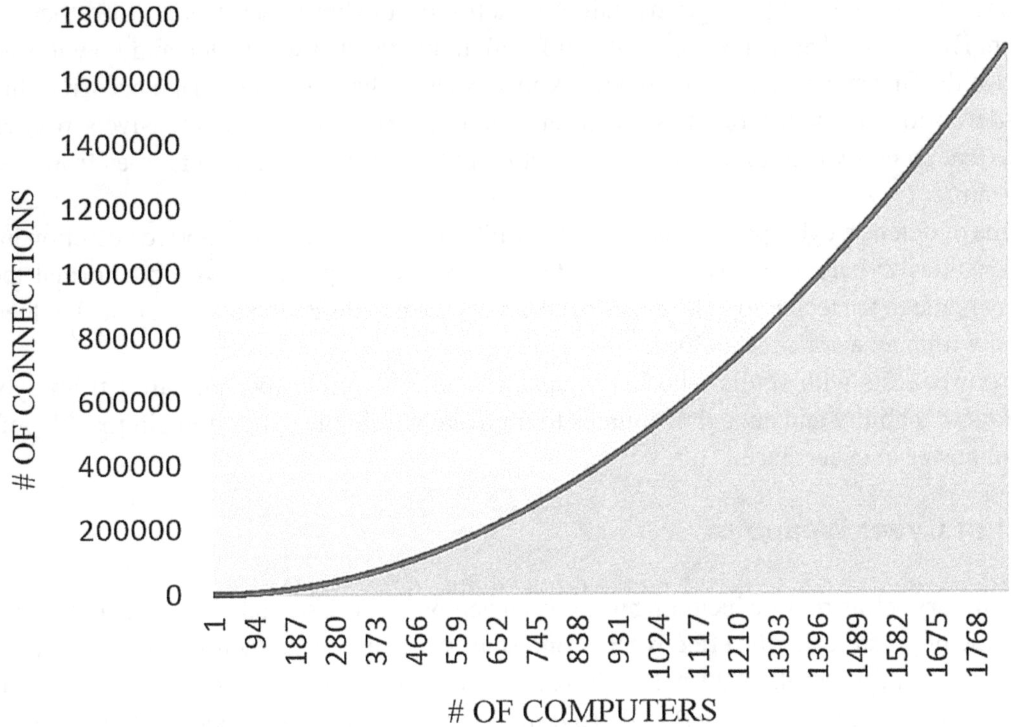

'preferred outcomes' could mean several things. It could represent the desired inoperability of the target infrastructure as in the Stuxnet case. It may also mean exploitation of confidential information (cyberespionage). Or it could be disrupted communication including sabotage activities through distributed denial of service (DDoS). However, the number of DDoS tools, spyware, or computer viruses do not equate to outcomes. Nor can outcomes be measured by the number of hired hackers and engineers on standby. In fact, there is no proven equation that presents a positive correlation between the resource input and the magnitude of outcomes. If a lone self-motivated hacker is able to find a critical vulnerability in the target system, he or she can inflict irreversible damage to the target with one calculated strike trigger.

The correlation between inputs and outcomes cannot yet be measured. Conceptually, however, cyberpower can be measured by:

Cyberpower = Territorial element (amount and quality of data) + Technical knowledge.

With this measurement equation, the next question becomes: who has power? It is a common misperception that "cyberpower as a strategic tool has diffused widely among all actors (Sheldon, 2011, p.95)." In fact, the actor spectrum in cyberspace has widened compared to the physical realm of international security where only states are actors; there are many opportunities to become a powerful actor in cyberspace. These opportunities are not limited to state actors or large organizations; they extend also to individuals with high technical skills. However, non-technical individuals in cyberspace enjoy less power than they do in the physical realm. Only a few people and a few organizations can see what happens behind the user interface.

Protecting cyber property is much less intuitive than guarding physical assets; most intrusions happen beyond human sensory perceptions. Often a victim of a cyber-attack has no idea that something was stolen. Even if the theft is perceived, it is difficult to know what was stolen and how it was done. If not foiled at the first stage, victims often never know exactly what kind of damage occurred. In addition to Nye's definition, the definition of cyberpower should therefore include a defensive aspect clarifying to what extent an entity can foil the adversary's attempt to derive preferred outcomes from the entity's cyber system.

In terms of defense, cyberpower has a broad definition that includes preemptive detection in order to frustrate enemies' cyber intrusions. One absolute measure of cyberpower across both normal and flawed actors may relate to the technology level and specifically the capability to identify critical vulnerabilities embedded within an actor's technology.

Cyberpower rests with actors who have capability to draw preferred outcomes from cyberspace. Whoever has capability and enough resources to innovate within the cyber domain may therefore hold influential power in cyberspace.

Control of Cyber Weapons

Physical military infrastructure including weapons inventory is an essential element to calculate a state's power. In the physical realm the effectiveness of a state's coercive arms therefore becomes the ultimate measure of power (Tellis et al., 2000, p.26). However the definition of 'coercive arms' still remains elusive in cybersecurity. A denial of service (DoS) program was used in the 2007 cyberattacks targeting Estonia. However the DoS tools used in the cyberattacks were originally designed to test the stress resilience of a network beyond the limits of normal operation and not to take out a network (Roebuck, 2012). Cyber technology is a double-edged sword. It could become an industrial tool or a weapon depending on who owns it and the way it is used.

In terms of technology, normal and flawed actors are not much different. The current prevailing technology is based on user manipulation with full automation without notifying the service user of the trade-offs between service and privacy. The difference is that flawed actors are not innovative enough to attract users while legitimate industrial actors create value from the full cycle of constructive actorhood.

The trajectory of industrial development tends to be more intrusive as people's lives become more reliant on networks. For example, network beaconing (collecting information then transmitting it to a designated server) is a common technology mobile industries employ to collect and to analyze user activities for marketing purposes. Industrial technology for beaconing and cyberespionage tools are interchangeable. The cyber industry has been growing based on this value creation from exploiting, archiving, and analyzing personal data in exchange for free services to the public. Beaconing is an accepted application of a dual-use technology that could easily be applied as cyberespionage in another context.

Likewise, there is no such thing as purely malicious code designed for warfare. If both industrial and malicious actors use the same common tools and solutions, one cannot label a certain technology as a weapon. Code is a symbolic arrangement of instructions designed to perform a specific task. Code is merely a tool. This makes it difficult for states to control power in cyberspace.

Both normal and flawed actors are thus beyond governments' control because their technical intrusiveness outpaces the drafting of governmental and regulatory authority controls, and will likely continue to be well ahead of public awareness of the value of cyber and digital privacy. The velocity of development is too fast to control; once an activity proliferates and becomes a standard in cyberspace, it is often too late for states to react.

State Actors in Cyberspace: Companies that are Stronger than States

It is challenging for governments to control the world of bits and electrons. If an actor is able to develop an innovative and disruptive technology, the cyberpower centroid could shift in a relatively short period of time. A data encryption program was included in the United States Munitions List that had strict export regulations until 1993 when the United States started to lift export controls on cryptographic software (The PGPI Project, n.d.). In February 1993, the regulations on exporting cryptography had been largely nullified by Phil Zimmermann when he found a way to export his encryption and decryption program called Pretty Good Privacy (PGP) outside the United States. Zimmermann exported printed materials to Europe that contained every line of his computer program, since the export regulations only covered software in electronic form (Zimmermann, n.d.). The PGP encryption program, almost two decades old, is still believed to be indecipherable by most national intelligence agencies and leading IT companies (Brandom, 2014). Zimmermann's encryption program circumvents government controls, but individuals are unlikely to establish cyberspace superiority.

The rule of cyber actorhood is gravitational where the tipping point effect happens dramatically; a big player enjoys a bigger gravitational pull. This gravity affects the entire realm of cyberspace. A successful actor establishes cyberspace superiority in a short period of time. An innovative technology quickly drives out obsolete technologies. The same is true with cyberpower. Rather than diffusion, a rapid power concentration transition is happening among leading actors in cyberspace. Google's desktop search market share was 67.6% in 2014 (87% for mobile search). The top five leading companies occupy almost 99% of the search market and there are even fewer players in mobile: Google, Apple, and Microsoft.

The Internet's security landscape is changing fast. Horizontal power shifts happen in the private sector through constant innovation. With these rapid changes, many questions arise. Is governance in cyberspace by nation states necessary? What is the realistic role or impact of state actors with coercive capabilities in cyberspace? What is the threshold for successful cybersecurity led by state actors?

The established cyber structure does not assume the presence of governance. State actors reside outside of the cyber structure. Cyberspace is supranational but multiple state actors attempt to control cyberspace with conventional domestic frameworks and regulations (see Figure 4).

State actors' attempts to control cyberspace will likely fail because state jurisdiction borders are not applicable. Cyber governance by state actors should instead cover global public safety in cyberspace since most users lack actorhood and therefore are largely indefensible due to the technical complexity of the cyber domain.

States must focus on safe and uninterrupted cyber activities because corporate accountability in this area is often curtailed by the quest to maximize shareholder value. The public heavily relies on good intentions by global cyber powers. People rely on Google's slogan—don't be evil—and hope that Google does not act against its users (Bierend, 2012). Google—a private enterprise—seeks to maximize its profit and to minimize its costs. Its primary concern is not cyber safety per se. States, therefore, have an important role to play as cyberspace watchdogs. In the physical realm, civil society, the private sector, and media

Figure 4. State Actors and the Structure of Cyberspace

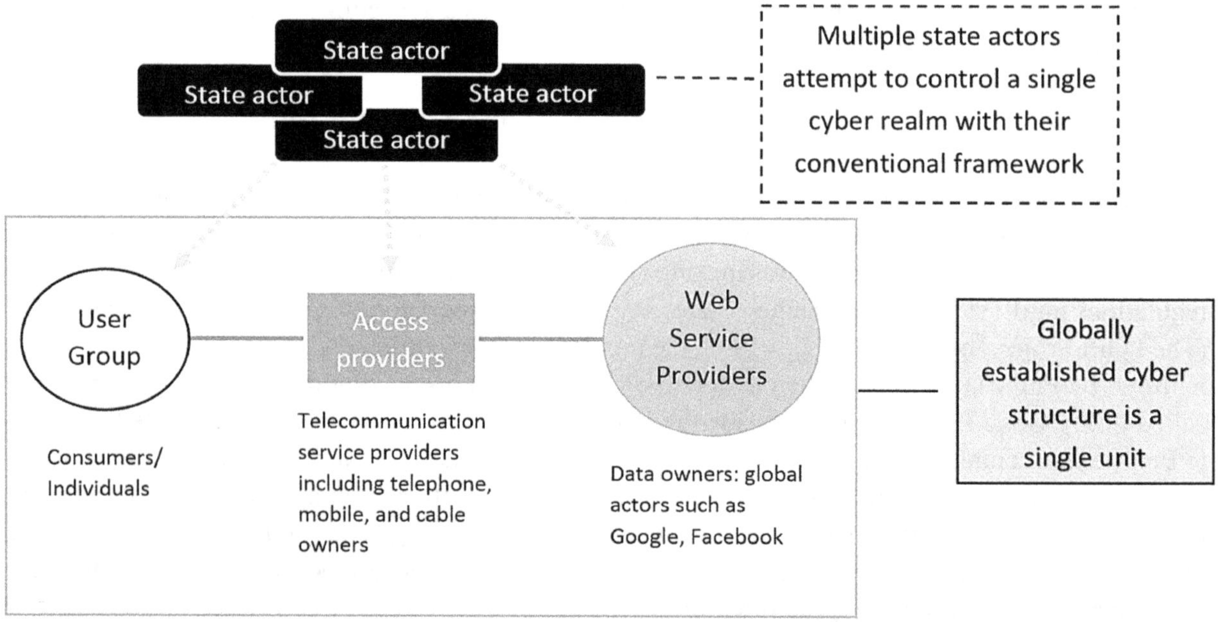

scrutinize the activities of democratic governments. In cyberspace, governments serve a public safety role for cybercitizens; however, these citizens differ from today's legal definitions of citizens. There is no nationality-based citizenship in cyberspace. Cybercitizens are, however, real elements of cyberspace.

Individuals in Cyberspace

Individuals generally have limited power in cyberspace with the exception of individuals who have ample knowledge about computer networks. There are a limited number of educated and trained individuals who understand vulnerabilities at both the individual and organizational level. Individual level players can be categorized as follows:

- **Consumers (Users):** most individuals are passive consumers in cyberspace. This group has no significant cyberpower.
- **Power Users:** individuals from the private sector (for instance Google and Apple engineers), from the public sector (for instance cyber professionals in the US military), or a combination of the two (Government contractors). Power users have technical skills, knowledge of programming, security capability, and database access skills. Due to high demand in the market, power users can move between and among these sectors. In terms of cybersecurity, power users are those who can find, exploit, or repair vulnerabilities. Power users fall into two subsets:
    - System developers or architects: system creators who design cybersecurity without supervision using proprietary techniques such as the creation of a backdoor.
    - System administrators: a person with administrative privileges for a system. For a large-scale or critical system, system administrators have unlimited access to the system and override management oversight.

From the individual user's perspective, cyberspace is the land of opportunity where innovative users can become power users. However, this does not mean that everyone can become a cyberspace actor. Most of the users in cyberspace are not actors but passive consumers. There are nevertheless a few individual actors who can inflict preferred outcomes. The US Director of National Intelligence, James Clapper, testified that there has never been an attack of the magnitude that would warrant an Armageddon label, but the frequency, scale, sophistication, and severity of small threats by flawed actors continue to increase (Harris, 2015). Threats are nonetheless real, so understanding the types of offensive cyberspace operators merits further attention.

Types of Actors in Offensive Cyberspace

Threats to cybersecurity come from flawed actors who benefit from using the offense-superior aspect of cyberspace (Kello, 2013, p.32). An offensive operation may originate from a state actor, an agent, or an individual. Offensive cyber operations fall into four categories (see Figure 5):

- **Type 1:** A state actor attacks another state. Rogue regimes use their offensive cyber capabilities to attack government entities and the critical infrastructure of another state. This might take the form of Advanced Persistent Threats (APTs) by intelligence agencies. An example is an attack designed to disable the target state's nuclear program or traditional signal intelligence (SIGINT).
- **Type 2:** State-sponsored cyberespionage targeting foreign companies. This type includes state-sponsored industrial espionage and exploitation of private sector information.
- **Type 3:** Self-inspired cyberterrorism against a target government. A civilian acts against a nation state. This type includes non-official nationalist groups and politically motivated civilians.
- **Type 4:** The great majority of cyberattacks can be characterized as type 4 including theft of personal data for financial purposes, industrial espionage for trade secrets, obtaining pecuniary advantages from intellectual property, identity theft, credit card access, or bank account breaches (Yadron & Glazer, 2014).

Figure 5. Types of Cyberspace Threats

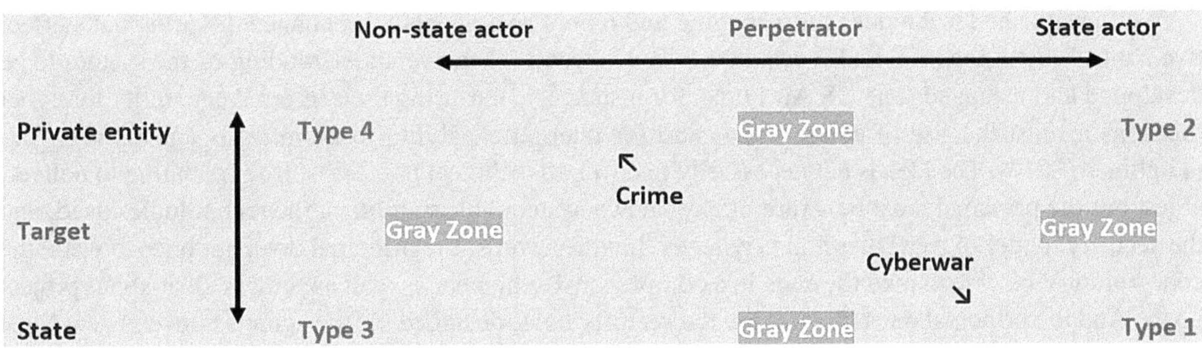

Principal-Agent Problem in Cyber Projects

The principal-agent problem is the single most important issue in cybersecurity management and centers on the absence of loyalty and quality control in the relationship. Regardless of the recent development of counter-hacking techniques, computer encryption, and entry management for cybersecurity, vulnerabilities still persist from inevitable principal-agent issues (Nye, 2010, p.11). People tend to rely on specialists or special services to perform cyber activities from the use of public email to the development of cyber projects.

Cyber outsourcing involves more serious principal-agent issues than physical projects conducted by agents. The problems in cyber outsourcing have more inherent risks than other agent-based activities because agents are often more knowledgeable than the principal about the technical details and, in some cases, the entire project. Cyber agents should seek to realize the principal's will, but in many cases the principal does not fully understand the requirements. As Steve Jobs noted in an interview: "A lot of times, people don't know what they want until you show it to them. (Reinhardt, 1998)" This is different from doctor-patient relationships or technician-customer relationships that normally involve tangible problem solving processes. Nearly all significant cyber activities are conducted by agents without an official license and without being under oaths of office and enlistment (U.S. Army, n.d.).[1]

There are nonetheless many reasons to use agents in cyber activities, namely 1) organizational necessity, 2) expertise, 3) time, 4) resources and networks, 5) distance from political influence, and finally 6) tactical advantage. On the other hand, disadvantages of using agents may include: 1) high costs and long implementation time, 2) added complexity which makes it difficult for the principal to maintain control, and most importantly 3) undesired actions. Outsourcing cybersecurity tasks to third-party vendors is, however, mostly inevitable for technological reasons.

The principal-agent problem is mainly because of the immaterial characteristics of digital projects, which makes direct supervision difficult. Agents often therefore serve their own interests above the best interests of the principal. The Edward Snowden case is a classic example of this problem. Snowden, an outsourced system administrator working for the NSA, leaked classified information from the state agency and severely damaged the principal's interests. Snowden prioritized his own interests over the rules established by the principal.

This phenomenon is largely made possible through the power asymmetry between the principal and the agent. The agent often has access to the system with more privileges than the principal. In order to avoid this problem, principals must carefully select agents and create effective management, monitoring, and incentives to avoid any breach of faith and contract.

Well-established techniques for managing and monitoring agents can enhance the principal's effective control. First, the principal is required to have a comprehensive understanding of the system to be developed and managed. The US Air Force, for instance, is nurturing their internal capability for cyber missions against the rise of cyber threats and for internal capability to monitor its agent's activities (Tilghman, 2014). The idea is not necessarily to cover all technical processes, from planning to deliverables, but the principal must be aware of any known system vulnerabilities, the technologies used, and the security model of user roles and privileges. In other words, the principal does not have to write the code but must be able to read the code in a comprehensive manner as well as remain clear about project goals. And the principal must be aware of the security holes designed for the agent's convenience. Most software engineers require a service port to test and to troubleshoot software glitches.

Cyberattack or Mistake: What Happened to the Agriculture Bank of South Korea?

In April 2011, there was a complete system shutdown at the biggest bank in South Korea. Unlike the famous case of the denial of service attacks on banks in Estonia in 2007, the Agricultural Bank of Korea case in 2011 had more serious impacts. The entire system including the customer database was completely purged by a handful of characters in this simple UNIX command: *rm –rf /.* In human language these symbols mean *force the recursive removal of the entire system* (Indiana University, n.d.). Until now, no one has identified who did it and for what purpose. Since the Agricultural Bank is under the Korean government's control, the government was pressured to find someone to blame and accused North Korea. However no hard evidence has been publically disclosed so far.

The Agricultural Bank of Korea's gray box that held the most important data was not a usual Windows system but a robust UNIX-based system. The best guess for the plot behind this incident is a staged attack that started from an infected Windows laptop computer used by a management engineer to configure the mainframe. Whether or not this is due to the engineer's negligence or malicious intent, an agent—a maintenance contractor for the principal—perpetrated it.

There is a persistent principal-agent contractual dilemma because cyber projects require high-tech computer engineering skills that demand significant time to master (Ritchie, 2003). The technology decisions are delegated to the development team including the architect, developer, and project manager, but decisions rarely involve the principal. The principal only sees the user interface functions of deliverables from the end-user's point of view, presumably because of insufficient knowledge and ineffective oversight, which generate a potential conflict of interests between the principal and agent. Principals that have the technological expertise to secure systemic robustness are therefore key elements of cybersecurity.

Cyber Warfare: Attribution and Deterrence Problems

States that aim to enlarge and project national power in cyberspace must establish cyberspace superiority in both offensive and defensive operations (Geers, 2013). Admiral Michael Rogers noted that it is time to consider boosting the military's cyber offense capability because a purely defensive, reactive strategy will have long response times and be resource intensive (Nakashima, 2015). The question is: can cyber offense measures locate and identify a target, strike it accurately in a timely fashion, and determine whether desired effects have been achieved? Do cyber weapons have capacity to strike a specific cyber target and to make cyber warfare an effective defensive countermeasure?

Cyber defense is centered on building a robust architecture against malicious attempts. The coercive effect of offense capabilities may also generate a good defense. With regard to cyberspace, however, there cannot be an immediate counterattack or response-on-demand from the defending side. Effective cyber deterrence therefore comes from how efficiently the system frustrates the attacker at the architectural level. Once built, the system architecture must defend itself unattended.

Effective responses to potential and imminent threats are challenging. In military operations, there is a concept called a kill chain of F2T2EA which includes six steps of 1) find, 2) fix, 3) track, 4) target, 5) engage, and 6) assess (US Air Force, 2014). The latest kill chain technology is fairly advanced and even addresses constantly moving time sensitive targets (TST) supported by real-time surveillance systems (US Air Force, 2014). Technology has dramatically reduced the time of the entire kill chain steps of detection, analysis, and strike to a matter of an hour. However, this great advance may not be applicable for cyber defense.

How is it possible to find and fix the target to begin the kill-chain against cyber threats? What is possible today is finding and fixing (politically) the geopolitical target by collecting circumstantial evidence over the course of months or even years of investigation. The last piece of the kill-chain, assessment, also seems to be problematic in cyber warfare. It is hard to assess if the defender's response disabled or destroyed the proper target with any degree of confidence. Some speculate, for instance, that the US may have been behind a shutdown of key North Korean websites in December 2014 (Swenson-Wright, 2014). At the current stage of technology, a shutdown of an enemy's websites by a denial of service (DoS) attack might have been the most timely feasible and assessable response method even for a top-tech state actor like the United States. An immediate response using a near real-time kill chain aimed at the proper target with some degree of accuracy would have an ideal deterrence effect against any type of offense, but the realization of this capability seems remote in cyber conflicts.

Attribution Problem: Identifying Perpetrators

A cyber-attack must first be attributed before any countermeasures can be applied. But digital bits do not leave fingerprints. All activities take place beyond geographical constraints and do not require the physical presence of the actor on the scene, therefore, the attribution of cyberattacks is extremely difficult and, in many cases, impossible (Kostadinov, 2013). Arquilla points out that "the biggest challenge to deterring, defending against, or retaliating for cyberattacks is the problem of correctly identifying the perpetrator (as cited in Gilbert, 2013)." At the current stage of technology, it is difficult to identify comprehensively who did what to whom, particularly for unattended M2M (machine to machine) threats not involving any human intervention.[2] The future of cyber conflicts will therefore likely have both offensive and defensive characteristics relying on architecture that is pre-programmed both for offense and for defense.

The US Government Accountability Office estimated that only five percent of known cybercriminals were arrested or convicted in 2006, and the arrest rate has not increased since (Perez & Prokupecz, 2013). Cybercrime is stealthy by nature. Even when government and private sector security professionals make significant advances in detecting and attributing cyber intrusions, damages tend to remain unknown for a long period because it simply takes time to discover the causal connection between a malicious cyber attempt and actual damage (Lewis & Baker, 2013, p.4). In cybercrime, the full-disclosure of who did what and how remains an enigma.

- Who: this is a question about the attribution of responsibility for a cyber-attack and its associated human actors. This is particularly difficult to identify if the perpetrator deliberately leaves no trace. Spoofing an IP address using a virtual private network (VPN) is a classic method that requires minimal IT knowledge. There are also many vulnerable servers in both the private and public sectors housing critical information. Some government servers in emerging economies run without basic mechanical protection and security protocols. Furthermore, these nations often depend on offshore technology outsourcing. Their computers are not only susceptible to cyberattacks but also likely to be used as staging devices for hacking attempts.
- What: many hacking activities, particularly in the case of information exploitation, happen without being noticed. Damage inventories require significant time to compile and assess. It is often

difficult to even know what the hackers took. Unlike the physical realm, digital content enables near-perfect duplication during the exploitation process (Rayburn, 2007, p.40). Therefore early damage estimates must assume that the database was entirely breached if there is a single trace of an intrusion log. Thorough damage assessment requires high-level forensic reverse hacking to potentially identify the perpetrator.

- How: which architecture was targeted? Was it the target data, a program, or the infrastructure itself? The answers to these questions assist with vulnerability assessments after hacking attempts.

Reverse-hacking techniques are still in the embryonic stage of development. For advanced persistent threats (APTs), however, it is possible to identify a likely culprit from circumstantial geopolitical dynamics. Moreover, persistent offensive attempts increase the probability of leaving inadvertent traces. For example, the FBI revealed evidence of undisguised IP addresses suggesting that North Korea was responsible for the Sony Pictures Entertainment hack in December 2014 (Laughl, 2015). This may have been a careless operational mistake by North Korea's cyber offense unit.

APTs use expensive customized malware targeting critical strategic infrastructure using a programmable logic controller (PLC) that individuals cannot easily obtain (Greenberg, 2012). State actors likely sponsor these actions, targeting a specific entity over a long period of time with limited prospects for immediate return. However all evidence remains circumstantial unless the attacker makes a mistake during a hacking attempt.

Difficulties in Establishing Pure Cyber Deterrence

It is difficult to measure a state actor's cyberpower in conventional terms of state power frameworks. The current security framework is relative and is based on a mutual understanding of what damage other nations may inflict with their national instruments of power. During the Cold War, the Mutual Assured Destruction (MAD) policy emerged because the two superpowers had a second-strike capability through the development of new nuclear warhead delivery systems. The United States and the Soviet Union realized that a nuclear war would produce a catastrophic result for both sides and would therefore be undesirable. In contrast, there is no controlled coercive power that can be entirely managed by state actors in cyberspace.

When there is tension in the Middle East or East Asia, the United States Navy can dispatch carrier strike groups to the region to coerce the adversary not to harm US interests. Unlike land, sea, and airpower, cyberpower is largely a complementary instrument (Sheldon, 2011, p.99). A conventional coercive strategy is difficult to apply in the realm of cybersecurity alone. In the conventional security framework, the physical possession of weapons brings coercive power to the state; however, states with offensive cyber weapons do not declare what their cyber weapons can do in detail against adversaries because most cyberattacks target systemic vulnerabilities.

"We have your password" will make the targets change their passwords. "We have a tool to destroy your system" will make adversaries patch or switch their systems. Thus offensive cyber weapons share characteristics with a Trojan horse; they are only successful if the real effect remains unknown. Of course, if one state has overwhelming cyber capabilities, then other rival states will hesitate to launch an attack against that state. Perhaps peace is more plausible in cyberspace if associated with other types of physical power; however it is difficult to coerce purely within cyberspace.

The denial mechanism linking coercive threats to adversaries' decisions works when adversaries recognize that they cannot achieve gains and will continue to pay unacceptable costs if they do not concede (Byman & Waxman, 2002, p.78). Basic deterrence theory assumes the presence of transparent capabilities for an adversary to be aware that the deterring actor possesses the capacity to act as promised; an adversary must realize that the deterring actor will respond to a threat (Wrenn, 2012, p.25). However due to the clandestine nature of cyber weapons, the deterring actor may find it difficult to make the capability transparent, therefore deterrence in the cyber domain alone is impotent.

Another reason that coercion does not work well in the cyber domain is the presence of technical alternatives. There will be always an easy alternative solution in cyber defense against any specific offensive measures if the threat is based on a known technology (how) and target (where). Going back to the Snowden case, his disclosure of what the NSA is doing and can do largely changed the paradigm of communications security. As soon as terrorist groups learned that the NSA had surveillance on Western-based email systems, they preferred Chinese communication services instead. Chinese service providers will not voluntarily share critical user information with the US government. There will always be innovative alternatives nullifying surveillance or offensive threats from strong state actors if threat capabilities are disclosed to the defenders. In addition, clandestine organizations can adopt alternate-domain solutions as Osama Bin Laden did for his post 9/11 operations.

It is difficult to use coercion purely to enhance cybersecurity within the cyber domain because the nature of cyberattacks excludes the possible presentation of cyber weapons. The mere implication of a possible backdoor presence exclusively for NSA on Microsoft Windows made the entire Chinese government replace their systems with a customized Linux solution (Reuters Shanghai, 2014). A circumstantial rumor that Chinese-made smartphones may have a beaconing backdoor to the Chinese government made the Indian military curb use of Chinese-made smartphones (BBC, 2014). Also the Chinese IT giant Huawei is banned from bidding on the US government contracts because of its alleged espionage attempts. However cross-domain deterrence remains an option if one can clearly resolve the attribution issue of who did what (Holl & Spetalnick, 2014). For example, a defensive team can promise to respond kinetically or to impose economic sanctions against anyone who perpetrates a cyber-attack.

Lastly and most importantly, individual flawed actors are largely immune to cyber deterrence. Potential threats from individual flawed actors should not be ignored because an individual, even a child, may threaten critical infrastructure without being constrained by spatiotemporal limits.

These five aforementioned aspects of cybersecurity are all interrelated: 1) weak presence of the nation state, 2) horizontal power transition to non-classical security actors, 3) the variety of actors, 4) difficulties in establishing deterrence purely in the cyber domain, and 5) the attribution problem. There are few power differences between state actors and individuals in cyberspace alone even when states have access to the nation's domestic cyber resources as well as other instruments of national power. By definition, individuals, organizations, and state actors all hold equal potential power in cyberspace. This power asymmetry invites a wide range of actors to the cyber domain and makes the attribution of cyberspace activities challenging. Furthermore, cyber deterrence by offensive supremacy is unlikely because of the lack of instrumental coercion.

These aspects of cybersecurity return this work to the central question of the role of state actors in cyberspace. A fundamental role of the state is security, but how does this apply in the cyber domain? The following case studies examine the challenges of misinterpretations of the role of state actors in cyberspace.

CASE STUDIES

Assured Access to Shared Spaces as the Strategic Objective

Anarchy is a society without governance; cyberspace is anarchic by its nature. The pioneers of cyberspace believed that cyberspace is where all can realize an absolute freedom from governance (Bey, 2015). Today's reality shatters this vision. Cyberspace has become a place where the few can intimidate and thwart the majority. There is no doubt that cyberspace requires urgent leadership to secure cyber freedoms for all. The US confirms this vision and role in the 2015 National Security Strategy: "as the birthplace of the Internet, the United States has a special responsibility to lead a networked world (The White House, 2015, p.12)." The United States has the most advanced cyber technologies in the world, but this fact alone does not necessarily make the United States the strongest actor in cyberspace.

No matter how advanced a state's cyber industry is, it makes little sense to speak of state actor cyberspace superiority in the same way as the physical commons of sea, air, and space (Posen, 2003, p.5). Cyberspace is a virtual digital common that traverses geographic mediums (Kello, 2013, p.22). In 2003, when Barry Posen discussed the US command of the commons, he did not mention cyberspace. The role of cyberspace calls for a new term in Posen's taxonomy: the unregulated commons.

The 2015 US National Security Strategy also calls for assuring access to shared spaces—cyber, space, air, and sea (The White House, 2015, p.12).[3] In particular, the digital shared spaces are crucial for US-led security because future challenges against US power will inevitably include cyber threats (The White House, 2015). The US Department of Defense is seeking cyber superiority with increased funding and budget allocations to secure both offensive and defensive cyber capabilities, yet few argue that the US has satisfied the pressing need for cybersecurity and network resilience in the global cyber commons (US Department of Defense [US DoD], 2013).[4]

Within the fundamentally anarchic environment of cyberspace, states still attempt to maximize their strength and extend their power and control (Krause, 2013, p.273). The use of nationalism and fear mongering among the population can help the state to mobilize its domestic support, to allow it to curtail domestic freedoms, and to outbid other nations in the power competition. In this competitive situation, the primary public goal of freedom of perpetual access at tolerable risk levels becomes subordinated to state institutional goals. The figure below illustrates the conflict of the strategic objectives of the public and the institutional objectives of states in a two-level outcomes matrix (Krause, 2013, p.278). The point is that the anarchic structure and borderless nature of cyberspace drive the state to pursue the state objective—command of the cyber commons—over public objectives (see Figure 6).

The four outcomes shown previously are described as follows.

- Total failure is a foreign-imposed curtailment of cyber freedom.
- Selfless success is the realization of uninterrupted cyberspace access without state-actor cyberspace superiority.
- Selfish success includes a dominant state actor in cyberspace. The state's institutional objective is realized but other states' access to cyberspace is curtailed.
- Total success is maximized freedom of access (no state control) with the protection of individuals from all types of cyber threats. Unfortunately this ideal win-win situation is unlikely because of a paradox—one actor's freedom collides with the unfettered freedom of another actor's choices.

Figure 6. Objectives of Public and State

Institutional objectives of states	Strategic objectives for public: Failure	Strategic objectives for public: Success
Failure	Total Failure	Selfless success
Success	Selfish success	Win-Win: Total success

Cyber superiority is best achieved through freedom of access and resilient networks. However, some state actors see cyberspace as an arena where interests collide. Therefore they seek cyberspace superiority to maximize national interests. This can be a classic case of the prisoner's dilemma. Despite the fact that mutual cooperation between states is the best option to deter or to derail motivated offenders—state-sponsored or individual—rational players might not cooperate to achieve broader public goods, thus creating a cybersecurity dilemma (Kostyuk, 2013). As Will Hutton points out, "the fight for security, prosperity and justice can no longer be won on any one nation's ground (Svendsen, 2010, p.395)." This is particularly true for cyberspace where borders were non-existent from the beginning. The official policy of the US on cybersecurity is: "Collective action is needed to assure access to the shared spaces—cyber, space, air, and oceans—where the dangerous behaviors of some threaten us all (The White House, 2015, p.7)." International cooperation initiatives are however relatively few with only thirteen bilateral agreements and six million dollars of international co-funding between 2004 and 2013 (Maughan, 2013, p.15).

As addressed previously, cyberattacks can only be deterred by a system that makes malicious attempts costly. The best results are most likely achieved through shared collective action among all actors.

The universal norms for cybersecurity require coordination across government agencies and non-state actors within agreed legal frameworks. Cyberspace is a new arena for international cooperation. Cooperative strategies assure free and perpetual network access with acceptable risks for the benefit of all.

Failure of State Control over Cyberspace: South Korea

States will continue to claim their sovereignty by attempting to draw borders in cyberspace. Some states also seek to curb cyber technology with goals of controlling cyberspace to enhance prosperity (Fitzpatrick, 2008). Even if technical restrictions can be made, if there is a need to protect the population's welfare, governments cannot prevent code from being freely created and disseminated (PBS Frontline, 2014). It may therefore be argued that South Korea's restrictions on the freedom of technology development do more harm than good.

South Korea has long been proud of its nationwide high-speed network and its e-government system. Since 2010, the country has retained the top spot in e-government innovation according to the United Nations (United Nations, 2014). Nonetheless, South Korea has never exported its technology to other governments because of its incompatibility with global standards. South Korea is an example of how state policies can crowd out innovation in the IT industry.

Governments can take steps to subsidize network infrastructure, computer education, and protection of intellectual property that will encourage or discourage the development of capabilities within their borders and systems (Korean Internet and Security Agency [KISA], 1999). The South Korean government did play a great role in putting critical cyber infrastructure in place. But allowing the state to lead development in cyberspace ultimately did not contribute to South Korea's state goals. South Korea tried to emulate state industrial development policies that led to rapid economic growth in the 1970s and 1980s, but these hierarchical models proved to be ineffective within the networked nature of cyberspace.

Since the late 1990s and until recently, South Korea has had the fastest average Internet speed in the world (Sutter, 2010). The nation-wide high-speed network was established by the state-led development plan for domestic IT industries including public services and e-banking. E-banking requires the best class encryption protocols but there was no available cryptography for sale sufficient for e-banking in the 1990s. South Korea decided to develop its own technology with a long-term perspective in mind. As a result, the domestically produced SEED cryptology became the Korean national industrial standard for online banking and personal identification in 1999[5]. In addition, the government passed a law in the late 1990s sponsoring the state-developed technology to facilitate e-commerce security (Seltzer, 2013). The technology was a fairly complex 128-bit, symmetric key encryption protocol, similar to the US Advanced Encryption Standard (AES) (KISA, 1999).

No other countries were pursing e-government and e-banking at the time due to the restricted export of cryptography from the US. The longest key size allowed for exporting outside the US was 40-bit encryption, which is rudimentary and takes only three to four hours to break even when using mid-1990s computing power. Even in the United States, less than 0.4% of households were using web-based online banking at the end of 20th century (Online Banking Database, n.d.). Fortunately or maybe unfortunately, the South Korean government was successful in developing their own cryptology that met the requirements for online banking and secure services. Initially, South Korea outpaced even the US in encryption innovation.

Domestic security standards originated from good intentions but ultimately produced undesirable outcomes. The government's plan was ambitious and looked successful for several years. The SEED cryptography inaugurated well-encrypted protection on sensitive e-banking and e-government services, but the unique technology hampered continuous development alongside global standards. Furthermore, the unique standard discouraged merit-based free competition. It nurtured government-friendly firms who understood and implemented the government's policy faithfully. This discouraged domestic innovative technologies and lowered global competitiveness.

The cybersecurity market then became the battlefield for lobbyists in South Korea. Cyber technology began to suffer high costs, low competitiveness, and unacceptable vulnerabilities. The entire national cyber system became monophyletic, remained isolated from the global standard, and continued to lose attractiveness. Eventually South Korea started to suffer from a less secure and less efficient cyber environment when compared to international state-of-the-art technology.

The obsolete technology became a permanent structure. Security providers could maximize their profits while benefitting from government protection. The biggest problem was that the government-sponsored exclusive technology became obsolete earlier than the policy makers anticipated. The fixed technology resisted continuous upgrades and created oligopolies—a perfect storm for the Korean cyber industry. Regardless of the first-mover advantage that Korea had in the early 2000s, the government's insights and plans later turned out to be the biggest challenge for the future of technological innovation in cyberspace.

The proprietary technology started a vicious cycle that could not be easily modified to adapt to state-of-the-art technical solutions. The South Korean cyber experiment, driven by the government, failed simply because the decision makers did not understand that "regulations can inhibit new technologies," even more so when it comes to the fast-changing norms in cyberspace (Dvorak, 2013).

RECOMMENDATIONS

Develop a Hierarchy of Policies

An effective role for states would be to establish a four-level hierarchy of policies. The first hierarchy of policies should emphasize the responsibilities of individual users who wish to maintain their freedoms and rights in cyberspace. All rights carry responsibilities; those who seek freedom in the cyber domain must not simply be passive consumers in the community. As in the physical domain, people have little sympathy for a victim of theft who refuses to take on the basic responsibility of installing and using a lock (even if people would prefer to live in a utopia where no crimes occur).

The second hierarchy of policies should be at the domestic collective action level. All within a society share security responsibilities beyond installing their own locks. Neighbors, businesses, and law enforcement agencies all share community security responsibilities. Each should find their role and find mechanisms to hold one another mutually accountable. The third hierarchy of policies should address international cooperation. In the cyber domain, the global community is ever-shrinking. International collective action will be required to secure liberty for all. The final hierarchy of policies should address the use of force in case individual responsibilities, domestic collective action responsibilities, and international collective action responsibilities all fail. This hierarchy will ensure that balanced policies of liberty and security in cyberspace will prevail over organizational objectives of government institutions.

At the macro level, governments must create an effective hierarchy of policies. At the other end of the spectrum, at the micro level, those involved with coding in both the government and private sectors must also play an important role in cybersecurity: parsimonious coding.

Mitigate Risks with Parsimonious Coding

Constructing robust cyber infrastructure through sustainable information technology takes copious time and effort by trained and experienced engineers. On the other hand, destruction in the cyber realm is relatively easy. A single programming command takes a millisecond to launch but can wipe out years of effort and the digital commons for billions of people.

The most secure system is the one that the user knows how to secure. Programmers and those who employ them must aim for resilient coding that includes shorter program lines with maximum readability. Parsimonious architectures do not raise security alone, but they provide a resilient structure to see and to address vulnerabilities. They allow quick reactions that can minimize damage at an early stage.

Secondly a high project price tag does not necessarily guarantee the best performance. A better measure of quality is as few program code lines as possible to perform the same expected function. A simple code structure helps human actors reduce risks even if no program is bug-free. This is true for even simple programs like printing "Hello, world!" (Kernighan & Ritchie, 1988, p.6)

```
main() { puts("Hello, world!"); return 0;}
```

This single line of code looks perfectly bug-free, but it still contains unmanageable risks because of the underlying compiler and operating system. Bugs, glitches, and flaws are persistent in cyberspace. There is no such thing as a bug-free program. Programs become exponentially complex when protective "if-then-else" conditional statements increase. Programmers should opt to mitigate risks with quick responses rather than try to eliminate every bug.

Cyber incidents happen at the intersection of three vulnerabilities: human error, systemic problems including operating procedure flaws, and lastly an unknown area of pure risk (Perrow, 1999).

Cyber incident = human error + systemic problem+ unknown area (pure risk)

In the equation above, 'unknown area' is where no one can take responsibility and little can be done, similar to an unpredictable natural disaster. Human errors and systemic problems, on the other hand, are manageable risks, though they cannot be completely eliminated. Effective cybersecurity focuses on managing these risks through the combination of quick detection and early damage control (Dyck et al. 2005, p.1229). Simplicity, therefore, must be weighted more than all other source selection factors; parsimonious code assists in mitigating manageable risks.

Cybersecurity and convenience correlate negatively. A security-only policy results in less convenience, and more convenience comes with less security. If a computer program is too complex for users to understand, they lose both crucial elements of cyber technology: security and convenience. If a private company commits a disastrous mistake, the market will drive the company out of business, but when a state actor introduces erratic regulations and rules, the entire state may have to pay for the mistake.

The Role of State Actors

Cyberspace demands two new roles for state actors: 1) leadership in freedom of perpetual public cyberspace access at tolerable risk levels and 2) international cross-domain cooperation to develop new security norms. The disparity in cybersecurity capability exists across physical regions. For leading states, advanced security measures protect cyber infrastructure, but many developing states remain vulnerable and reliant on open source solutions developed by a few unpaid volunteers. Many individuals, businesses, and even government agencies benefit from the open source security tools thanks to idealistic cyber volunteers investing their time and effort to secure cyberspace liberties. But there are limits to reducing systemic vulnerabilities and risk factors through volunteerism (Chiusano, 2014). The rapid increase of public reliance on cyber technology invites more flawed actors who constantly try to exploit benefits from vulnerabilities. This problem will eventually call for state actors to take action. Freedom to access the cyber domain merits the attention of state actors.

Self-interested actors create strong inertia that entices the public to cede privacy rights in exchange for convenience and social norms. In the past, people entered their IDs and passwords every time they accessed Internet services. Today, most services allow constant signed-in status to enable monitoring activities across cyberspace, mainly for marketing purposes, represented for instance by the statement "Google knows you better than you know yourself (Carmichael, 2014)." Empowered by data tools that collect patterns and behaviors, major service providers beacon all users' movements to their central database. Thanks to the mass propagation of smart devices, individual access to cyberspace is no longer anonymous. All Internet users are associated with a unique identity that leads to the user's physical self.

No one has yet answered these questions: 1) are customers paying the right price for Internet services in return for giving up their privacy, 2) is the Internet a safe space, and 3) what can be gained or lost from Internet access? State actors must set the conditions to allow society to answer these questions and formulate policies at the four levels discussed above, with the preference and priority being for the individual and community levels. First, state actors must prioritize empowering individuals to exercise not only their rights, but also their responsibilities in the cyber domain. Second, state actors must enable domestic collective action and development of societal norms that ensure freedoms and fair trades between neighbors, businesses, and government institutions. Third, state actors must engage other states on behalf of their citizens for international cyber defense cooperation to ensure prosperity and security for everyone.

Furthermore, the media must step forward to perform their fourth-estate watchdog role, highlighting threats to citizens that may come not only from intrusive foreign or domestic governments, but also from intrusive private firms. Governments and the private sector must cooperate for cyberspace liberty and security. Furthermore, it is not viable for a single government to undertake initiatives in isolation.

State actors, above all, must focus on mutually assured cybersecurity to guarantee liberty and prosperity for all in cyberspace.

FUTURE RESEARCH DIRECTIONS

Cyberterrorism

Cyberterrorism is the intentional use of threatening and disruptive actions against computers, networks, and the Internet performed by politically motivated individuals or groups (Matusitz, 2005, p.137). Cyberterrorism has thus far been rare, but it could grow in the future as a means of social engineering or inciting political unrest. The easiest way to breed social unrest without physical presence on the ground is cyberterrorism. Cyberterrorism is cheap and leaves few traces. Nye explains "cyberattacks are not the most attractive route for terrorists today, but as groups develop their capacity to wreak great damage against infrastructure over the coming years, the temptation will grow (Nye, 2010, p.17)." Even though cyberterrorism cases are scarce, one cannot rule out the possibility of destructive cyberterrorism in the future that can inflict physical causalities and damage beyond the stolen data and software destruction.

Proper Cyber Investment Policy for State Actors

Where should states make their biggest cyber investments? Establishing reliable security measures against global threats of criminals, terrorists, and rogue state governments who do not work for the public interest have been discussed in this paper, but detailed policies and implementation logistics require more research and cases studies.

Global Cyberspace Standards

The IT industry, particularly the software business, is transnational by nature. Domestic authorities cannot regulate private operations in cyberspace without cooperation with other state actors. The cyberspace market has multiple ways to bypass trade blocs, protectionism, and national taxation. Global cooperation is necessary not only for state cybersecurity; it is also relevant for cyber-related trade, taxes, and economic prosperity.

Global Cooperation Unit for Cybersecurity

The International Telecommunication Union (ITU) or other global organizations should explore establishing a permanent body for cybersecurity. Ideally this body must allow access for all without impeding strong leadership candidates to assure access to the cyber commons.

CONCLUSION

Cyberspace does not square easily with the Westphalian concept of state. State control and legislation is to a large extent ineffectual. States are therefore often unable to fulfill their traditional role of providing security when it comes to the cyber domain. Cyber deterrence is often to no avail in the offense-dominant cyber realm. The most powerful actors in cyberspace are not states and are not necessarily concerned with cybersecurity, an area where states have a crucial role to play. Individual responsibility, community cooperation, and international cooperation among states are therefore all necessary parts of a multi-faceted approach that is essential when responding to pressing global cybersecurity needs.

REFERENCES

Bey, H. (n. d.). *The Information War*. Hermetic Library. Retrieved from http://hermetic.com/bey/infowar.html

Bierend, D. (2012, June 12). Google Is Evil. *Wired*. Retrieved from http://www.wired.com/2012/06/opinion-google-is-evil/

Brandom, R. (2014, December 28). New documents reveal which encryption tools the NSA couldn't crack. *The Verge*. Retrieved from http://www.theverge.com/2014/12/28/7458159/encryption-standards-the-nsa-cant-crack-pgp-tor-otr-snowden

Byman, D., & Waxman, M. (2002). *The Dynamics of Coercion: American Foreign Policy and the Limits of Military Might* (p. 78). New York: Cambridge University Press.

Carmichael, J. (2014, August 19). Google Knows You Better Than You Know Yourself. *The Atlantic*. Retrieved from http://www.theatlantic.com/technology/archive/2014/08/google-knows-you-better-than-you-know-yourself/378608/

China targets own operating system to take on likes of Microsoft, Google. (2014, August 24). *Reuters*. Retrieved from http://www.reuters.com/article/2014/08/24/china-technology-idUSL3N0QU07420140824

Chiusano, P. (2014, December 8). *The failed economics of our software commons, and what you can about it right now.* Retrieved from http://pchiusano.github.io/2014-12-08/failed-software-economics

Defense Budget Priorities and Choices—Fiscal Year 2014. (April 2013). The United States Department of Defense.

Dvorak, K. (2013, June 18). Old regulations inhibit new technologies. *The Hill*. Retrieved from http://thehill.com/opinion/op-ed/306377-old-regulations-inhibit-new-technologies

Dyck, C., Frese, M., Baer, M., & Sonnentag, S. (2005). Organizational error management culture and its impact on performance: A two-study replication. *The Journal of Applied Psychology*, *90*(6), 1228–1240. doi:10.1037/0021-9010.90.6.1228 PMID:16316276

Fitzpatrick, M. (2008, October 7). South Korea wants to gag the noisy Internet rabble. *The Guardian*. Retrieved from http://www.theguardian.com/technology/2008/oct/09/news.Internet

Gartner. (2014, August 22). *Gartner Says Worldwide Information Security Spending Will Grow Almost 8 Percent in 2014 as Organizations Become More Threat-Aware*. Retrieved from http://www.gartner.com/newsroom/id/2828722

Geers, K. (2013, October 17). サイバー世界大戦:国家レベルの高度なサイバー攻撃 の背景を理解する (*World War C: Understanding Nation-State Motives Behind Today's Cyber Attacks*). Retrieved from https://www.fireeye.com/resources/pdfs/fireeye-wwc-report.pdf

Gilbert, D. (September 30, 2013). World War C: How Understanding Geopolitics Can Help Protect Against Cyber Attacks, *International Business Times*. Retrieved from http://www.ibtimes.co.uk/world-war-c-cyber-attacks-motives-nation-510234

Google reveals child porn user. (2014, August 4). *BBC News*. Retrieved from http://www.bbc.com/news/technology-28639628

Greenberg, A. (2012, March 21). Meet The Hackers Who Sell Spies The Tools To Crack Your PC (And Get Paid Six-Figure Fees). *Forbes*. Retrieved from http://www.forbes.com/sites/andygreenberg/2012/03/21/meet-the-hackers-who-sell-spies-the-tools-to-crack-your-pc-and-get-paid-six-figure-fees/

Harris, S. (2015, February 26). Top Spy: Small Hacks Are Bigger Threat Than "Cyber Armageddon." *The Daily Beast*. Retrieved from http://www.thedailybeast.com/articles/2015/02/26/top-spy-small-hacks-are-bigger-threat-than-cyber-armageddon.html

Holl, S., & Spetalnick, M. (2014, December 19). Obama vows U.S. response to North Korea over Sony cyber attack. *Reuters*. Retrieved from http://www.reuters.com/article/2014/12/19/us-sony-cybersecurity-usa-idUSKBN0JX1MH20141219

Indiana University Knowledgebase. (n. d.). *Introduction to Unix commands*. Retrieved from https://kb.iu.edu/d/afsk

Inside the NSA's War on Internet Security. (2014, December 28). *Der Spiegel Online*. Retrieved from http://www.spiegel.de/international/germany/inside-the-nsa-s-war-on-Internet-security-a-1010361.html

International Telecommunication Union (ITU). (2014). *Measuring the Information Society Report*. Geneva, Switzerland: International Telecommunication Union.

Internet Society of China. (2002, March). *Public Pledge of Self-Regulation and Professional Ethics for China Internet Industry*.

Justice, J. (n. d.). *Frontline Facts & Stats. PBS*. Retrieved from http://www.pbs.org/wgbh/pages/frontline/shows/juvenile/stats/states.html

Kello, L. (2013). The meaning of the cyber revolution: Perils to theory and statecraft. *International Security, 38*(2), 7–40. doi:10.1162/ISEC_a_00138

Kepes, B. (2013, December 4). Google Users—You're The Product, Not The Customer. *Forbes*. Retrieved from http://www.forbes.com/sites/benkepes/2013/12/04/google-users-youre-the-product-not-the-customer/

Kernighan, B. W., & Ritchie, D. M. (1988). *The C Programming Language* (2nd ed., p. 6). Englewood Cliffs, N.J: Prentice Hall.

Kostadinov, D. (2013, February 1). The Attribution Problem in CyberAttacks, *InfoSec Institute,* Retrieved from http://resources.infosecinstitute.com/attribution-problem-in-cyber-attacks/

Kostyuk, N. (2013). The Digital Prisoner's Dilemma: Challenges and Opportunities for Cooperation., World Cyberspace Cooperation Summit IV (WCC4), 2013, Worldwide Cybersecurity Initiative. New York, NY, USA: East West Institute. Retrieved from http://cybersummit.info/sites/cybersummit.info/files/The%20Digital%20Prisoner%27s%20Dilemma-Challenges%20and%20Opportunities%20for%20Cooperation_Nadiya%20Kostyuk%20.pdf

Krause, P. (2013). The Political Effectiveness of Non-State Violence: A Two-Level Framework to Transform a Deceptive Debate. *Security Studies. 22*(2), 259, 273.

Laughl, O. (2015, January 7). FBI director stands by claim that North Korea was source of Sony cyberattack. *The Guardian.* from http://www.theguardian.com/world/2015/jan/07/fbi-director-north-korea-source-sony-cyber-attack-james-comey

Liaropoulos, A., & Tsihrintzis, G. (2014). *Proceedings of the 13th European Conference on Cyber warefare and Security*: ECCWS 2014 (p. 138). Academic Conferences Limited.

Lindsay, J. R. (2014). 2015). The impact of china on cybersecurity: Fiction and friction. *International Security, 39*(3), 7–47. doi:10.1162/ISEC_a_00189

Machine-to-machine (M2M) is a term that digital devices of the same type communicate with one another, take measurements, and make decisions without human intervention.

Matusitz, J. (2005). Cyberterrorism: How can American foreign policy be strengthened in the information age? *American Foreign Policy Interests, 27*(2), 137–147. doi:10.1080/10803920590935376

Maughan, D. (2013, August). Homeland Security Advanced Research Projects Agency: *The Bigger Picture: S&T's Role in Cyber Security* (Slide 15). Homeland Security, Science and Technology division. Retrieved from http://www.dhs.gov/sites/default/files/publications/csd-ttp-finance-two.pdf

McHugh, J. (n. d.). Google vs. Evil, *Wired 11.01*, Retrieved from http://archive.wired.com/wired/archive/11.01/google_pr.html

Montevideo Convention on the Rights and Duties of States. (1933, December 26). International Conference of American States in Montevideo, Uruguay.

Nakashima, E. (2015, March 19). Cyber chief: Efforts to deter attacks against the U.S. are not working. *The Washington Post.* Retrieved from http://www.washingtonpost.com/world/national-security/head-of-cyber-command-us-may-need-to-boost-offensive-cyber-powers/2015/03/19/1ad79a34-ce4e-11e4-a2a7-9517a3a70506_story.html

National Security Strategy of the United States. (2015, February). The White House. Retrieved from http://www.whitehouse.gov/sites/default/files/docs/2015_national_security_strategy_2.pdf

Negroponte, N. (1996). *Being Digital* (1st ed., p. 4). New York: Vintage.

Nye, J. S. (2010). *Cyber power. Belfer Center for Science and International Affairs.* Cambridge: Harvard Kennedy School.

Oaths of Enlistment and Oaths of Office—U.S. Army Center of Military History. Retrieved from http://www.history.army.mil/html/faq/oaths.html

Online banking report Database. (n. d.). Retrieved from http://www.onlinebankingreport.com/

Perez, E., & Prokupecz, S. (2014, May 19). Inside FBI's massive cybercrime bust. *CNN Money,* Retrieved from http://money.cnn.com/2014/05/19/technology/security/cyber-crime-bust-blackshades/index.html

Perrow, C. (1999). *Normal Accidents: Living with High-Risk Technologies (Updated edition with a New afterword and a new postscript by the author edition)*. Princeton, N.J: Princeton University Press.

Phil Zimmermann's Home Page. (n. d.). Retrieved from http://www.mit.edu/~prz/EN/background/index.html

Posen, B. R. (2003). Command of the commons: The military foundation of U.S. hegemony. *International Security*, *28*(1), 5–46. doi:10.1162/016228803322427965

Ranger, S. (n. d.). Inside the secret digital arms race: Facing the threat of a global cyberwar. *Tech Republic*, Retrieved from http://www.techrepublic.com/article/inside-the-secret-digital-arms-race/

Rayburn, D. (2007). Streaming and Digital Media: Understanding the Business and Technology (1 ed., p. 40). Amsterdam; Burlington, MA: Focal Press.

Reinhardt, A. (1998, May 12) Steve Jobs on Apple's resurgence. *Business Week*. Retrieved from http://allaboutstevejobs.com/sayings/stevejobsinterviews/bw98.php

Ritchie, D. M. (2003). *The Development of the C Language*. Retrieved from http://cm.bell-labs.com/who/dmr/chist.html

Roebuck, K. (2012). Application Testing as a Service (TaaS): High-impact Technology—What You Need to Know: Definitions, Adoptions, Impact, Benefits, Maturity, Vendors (p. 266). Emereo Publishing.

Schmitt, M.N. (2005). Precision attack and international humanitarian law. *International Review of the Red Cross, 859*, 445-466, 445.

Securing Cyber Space—President Obama Announces New Cybersecurity Legislative Proposal and Other Cybersecurity Efforts. (2015, January 13). The White House. Retrieved from https://www.whitehouse.gov/node/316726

SEED 128 Algorithm Specification. (1999). Korea Internet and Security Agency http://seed.kisa.or.kr/html/egovframework/iwt/ds/ko/ref/%5B2%5D_SEED+128_Specification_english_M.pdf

Seltzer, L. (2013, November 5). South Koreans use Internet Explorer: It's the law. *ZDNet*. Retrieved from http://www.zdnet.com/article/south-koreans-use-Internet-explorer-its-the-law/

Sheldon, J. B. (2011). Deciphering cyberpower strategic purpose in peace and war. *Strategic Studies Quarterly*, *5*(2), 95.

Singer, P. W., & Friedman, A. (2014). *Cybersecurity and Cyberwar: What Everyone Needs to Know* (p. 13). Oxford, New York: Oxford University Press.

Soderbery, R. (2013, January 7). How Many Things Are Currently Connected To The "Internet of Things" (IoT)? *Forbes*. Retrieved from http://www.forbes.com/sites/quora/2013/01/07/how-many-things-are-currently-connected-to-the-Internet-of-things-iot/

Sutter, J. D. (2010, March 31). Why Internet connections are fastest in South Korea. *CNN*. Retrieved from http://www.cnn.com

Svendsen, A. (2010). Strategy and disproportionality in contemporary conflicts. *The Journal of Strategic Studies*, *33*(3), 367–399. doi:10.1080/01402390903189576

Telegraph Video. (2014, December 23). Analyst: US possibly behind North Korea's Internet shutdown. *The Telegraph*, Retrieved from http://www.telegraph.co.uk/news/worldnews/asia/northkorea/11310314/Analyst-US-behind-North-Koreas-Internet-shutdown.html

Tellis, A. J., Bially, J., Layne, C., MacPherson, M., & Sollinger, J. M. (2000). *Measuring National Power in the Postindustrial Age: Analyst's Handbook*. Santa Monica, Calif: RAND Corporation, 28. *The PGPi scanning project*. Retrieved from http://www.pgpi.org/pgpi/project/scanning/

The US Air Force. (2014, January). Dynamic Targeting and The Tasking Process, *Annex 3-60 Targeting*. LeMay Center for Doctrine Development and Education. Retrieved from https://doctrine.af.mil/download.jsp?filename=3-60-D17-Target-Dynamic-Task.pdf

Tilghman, A. (2014, September 22). Active, reserve components spar over "sexy" cyber mission. *Air Force Times*. Retrieved from http://archive.airforcetimes.com/article/20140922/NEWS04/309220034/Active-reserve-components-spar-over-sexy-cyber-mission

United Nations E-government Survey 2014. (n. d.). The United Nations. Retrieved from http://unpan3.un.org/egovkb/Portals/egovkb/Documents/un/2014-Survey/E-Gov_Complete_Survey-2014.pdf

US spy chief James Clapper highlights cyber threats. (2015, February 27). *BBC News*. Retrieved from http://www.bbc.com/news/world-us-canada-31654050

Walker, J. (2015, February 13). Battle For Search Market Share Heats Up Again. *Media Post*. Retrieved from http://www.mediapost.com/publications/article/243791/battle-for-search-market-share-heats-up-again.html

Weber, M. (2004). The Vocation Lectures. (R. Livingstone, Trans., D. Owen and T. B. Strong, Eds.) (p. 33). Indianapolis: Hackett Publishing Company, Inc.

Wrenn, C. F. (2012). Strategic cyber deterrence, (p. 25). Fletcher School of Law and Diplomacy.

Xiaomi to open India data centre to allay privacy fears. (2014, October 27). *BBC News*. Retrieved from http://www.bbc.com/news/technology-29786324

Yadron, D., & Glazer, E. (2014, October 31). J.P. Morgan Found Hackers Through Breach of Road-Race Website. *Wall Street Journal*. Retrieved from http://www.wsj.com/articles/j-p-morgan-found-hackers-after-finding-breach-of-race-website-1414766443

Yueh, L. (2014, October 16). Huawei boss says US ban "not very important." *BBC News*. Retrieved from http://www.bbc.com/news/business-29620442

KEY TERMS AND DEFINITIONS

Advanced Persistent Threat (APT): A set of continuous computer hacking processes with a high degree of covertness, often orchestrated by human actors targeting organizations or states for economic benefits and/or political motives. Unlike other hacking attempts, APT is being conducted over a longer period of time targeting a specific entity.

Code Readability: A logical easiness to follow the code.

Code: A programming language designed to communicate instructions between human and a computer. The code is used to create computer programs to control the behavior of a machine or to express algorithms.

Cyber Actorhood: Three sequential elements of 1) cyber structure 2) users 3) data acquisition and its proper application.

Distributed Denial of Service (DDoS): A mechanical attempt to make a machine or network resource unavailable by overloading the system thereby causing denial of service to its intended users.

Hacker: Someone who seeks and exploits weaknesses in a computer system or computer network.

Internet-of-Things: The ability to transfer data among machines over a network without requiring human-to-human or human-to-machine interaction.

IP: Internet Protocol (IP) is the principal set of communications protocol of digital message formats and rules for exchanging messages between computers across a single network or a series of interconnected networks (Internet), using the Internet Protocol Suite.

PLC: A programmable logic controller (PLC) is a digital computer used for automation of typically industrial electromechanical processes, such as control of machinery on factory assembly lines, amusement rides, or light fixtures.

SEED: Korean Certificate based Digital Signature Algorithm. Not an acronym but a proper noun.

Software Bug: An error, flaw, failure, or fault in a computer program or system that causes it to produce an incorrect or unexpected result, or to behave in unintended ways.

Stuxnet: A computer worm that was designed to attack industrial programmable logic controllers (PLCs) of the Iranian nuclear program.

Virtual Private Network (VPN): An extended private network across a public network. It enables a networked device to send and receive data across the Internet as if it were directly connected to the private network.

Vulnerability: A cyber-security term that refers to a flaw in a system that can leave it susceptible to attack. Cutting down vulnerabilities provides fewer options for malicious users to gain access to secure information.

Zero Day Vulnerability: A security flaw in a computer program remaining unknown to the creator. This vulnerability can be exploited by hackers before the creator becomes aware and rushes to fix the flaw. This attempt by hackers is called a zero day attack.

ENDNOTES

1 US Army "Oaths of Enlistment and Oaths of Office"

2 Machine-to-machine (M2M) is a term that digital devices of the same type communicate with one another, take measurements, and make decisions without human intervention.

3 National Security Strategy of the United States (February 2015). *The White House*

4 Defense Budget Priorities and Choices—Fiscal Year 2014 (April 2013). *The United States Department of Defense.*

5 SEED is a proper noun, not an acronym. It denotes "Korean Certificate based Digital Signature Algorithm."

Chapter 14
Intelligence Studies, Theory, and Intergroup Conflict and Resolution:
Theory and Beyond

Elena Mastors
University of Phoenix, USA

Joseph H. Campos
University of Hawaii, USA

ABSTRACT

The study of intelligence traditionally relies on descriptive and case study approaches. However, the study of intelligence should shift from this reliance on case study approaches to one grounded in multidisciplinary theory. In particular, social psychological approaches should be fully integrated into an intelligence studies curriculum. These theories inform our understanding of intergroup processes, specifically intergroup conflict, so that we can begin to develop appropriate conflict resolution strategies.

DOI: 10.4018/978-1-4666-9661-7.ch014

INTRODUCTION

Intelligence Studies programs tend to emphasize descriptive approaches to the understanding of intelligence. This includes describing the evolution and function of intelligence bodies; aspects of intelligence roles, including how to effectively carry out these roles; processes; structured analysis techniques; and other pertinent information. The study of intelligence also focuses on case studies to illustrate various aspects of intelligence. Several authors provide good insight into the history of intelligence through the use of case studies (see Aldrich, 2002; Cockburn & Cockburn, 1991; Jakub, 1998). There is no doubt that having a solid foundation of the aforementioned descriptive aspects is important, and that the dependence on case studies using declassified documentation exposes students of intelligence studies to the various important aspects of intelligence. However, having this solid foundation in intelligence is no longer enough. Despite the benefits of using case studies, we must recognize that it runs the risk of creating well-versed historians of intelligence. Thus, overreliance on case study approach may result in intelligence analysts who become clouded in historical imperatives and are not able to extrapolate the historical lessons to current situations and events. Foundation in multidisciplinary theory is crucial to move the study of intelligence from a descriptive case study-based discipline to one grounded in theory that can analyze, interpret, explain, and even predict issues, events, and situations. Social psychological theories in particular help inform our understanding of both the reasons for conflict and appropriate avenues of conflict resolution.

BACKGROUND

The Intelligence Reform and Terrorism Prevention Act of 2004 took great pains to enhance the concept of national intelligence. Traditional notions of intelligence, with an emphasis on a distinction between international and domestic concerns, are organized around specific sources and limited methods. The Act, instead, emphasized timeliness and accuracy, demanding that intelligence be organized around issues or problems, not solely sources:

Paragraph (5) of section 3 of the National Security Act of1947 (50 U.S.C. 401a) is amended to read as follows:

"(5) The terms 'national intelligence' and 'intelligence related to national security' refer to all intelligence, regardless of the source from which derived and including information gathered within or outside the United States, that—

"(A) pertains, as determined consistent with any guidance issued by the President, to more than one United

States Government agency; and

"(B) that involves—

"(i) threats to the United States, its people, property, or interests;

"(ii) the development, proliferation, or use of weapons of mass destruction; or

"(iii) any other matter bearing on United States national or homeland security.". (Intelligence Prevention and Reform Act, 2004).

Intelligence analysts must be able to assess a variety of situations through diverse perspectives, rather than just rely on source-based information. This in turn requires that intelligence analysts have the skills and knowledge to analyze, interpret, and explain issues, events, and situations based on a variety of variables. Unfortunately, based in large part on the focus on case studies and source intelligence, intelligence studies, unlike other disciplines, does not have a body of theoretical work on which to base this new and definitely necessary emphasis. However, there are a variety of theories from multiple disciplines from which intelligence studies can borrow that may immensely benefit the intelligence studies field. It is important to note that theories are not topic-or content-specific, but are abstract and provide a foundation through which analysts can interpret a variety of situations. Each theory has a specific vocabulary and utilizes different techniques when approaching situations. Thus, analysts need to be exposed to a variety of theories given the multidisciplinary nature of intelligence. As the field of intelligence studies grows and more emphasis is placed on being able to analyze, interpret, explain, and predict complex issues, events, and situations, using borrowed theories from other fields may possibly even transform thinking and foster growth in intelligence-based theories in their own right. The reliance on problem- and issue-based analysis will develop new theories, and strengthen the field of intelligence studies.

A good place to start is in the realm of the social sciences. In general, these theories are used to examine a variety of phenomena about the world around us. Social science disciplines such as anthropology, psychology, political science, international relations, and economics offer some enlightening theories pertinent to the field of intelligence studies. Conflicts within and among countries are of important concern to intelligence studies. In particular, the discipline of psychology offers relevant theoretical insights into the study of this important topic.

MAIN FOCUS OF THE CHAPTER

There is no doubt that conflict amongst groups in the global community, and the detrimental manifestations of these conflicts, are pressing national security concerns for governments throughout the world. There are many types of conflict that exist. The particular types of conflict we refer to in thischapter are those that occur within countries and among them. Conflict can involve states, various ethnic and national groups, and human, state, and international security. Social psychology-based theories are concerned with explaining the functioning groups and relationships between them. As such, there is an important role for social psychology in explaining intergroup conflict and conflict resolution. In other words, the body of literature provides explanations for questions regarding intergroup behavior and intergroup conflict so that we can begin to develop appropriate conflict resolution strategies. Clearly, social psychology should be fully integrated into the curriculum of intelligence- and national security-based programs. Through the integration of social psychology intelligence- and national security-based programs we will be able to foster an environment that encourages the understanding of the factors that lead individuals to behave in specific ways and the conditions under which behavior and action occur.

ISSUES, CONTROVERSIES, PROBLEMS

In pioneering work on intergroup relations, social psychologist Henri Tajfel (1970) and colleagues (see, for example, Tajfel, Billig, Bundy, &Flament,1971) published findings on a series of experiments conducted about intergroup relations. The findings of these experiments, and further postulations about intergroup behavior, eventually became known as social identity theory (SIT). Tajfel and colleagues argue that we classify ourselves and others into groups, and that identity is derived through group affiliation (Brown, 2000).

In the world of group membership, groups we belong to are in-groups, and those we do not belong to are considered out-groups. Groups compare themselves to other groups, and strive to have positive distinctiveness through intergroup comparison. As Brown (2000) elaborates, "the outcome of these intergroup comparisons is critical for us because indirectly it contributes to our own self-esteem. If our own group can be perceived as clearly superior on some dimension of value (like skill or sociability) then we, too, can bask in that reflected glory" (p. 312).

Tajfel and others based their theoretical postulations on experiments that were based on the "minimal group paradigm" in which individuals were randomly assigned to two groups. For example, in one experiment, individuals were distributed into groups because of their under- or overestimation of dots shown on a screen. The arbitrary distribution into groups was necessary for several reasons. According to Cottam, Mastors, Preston, and Dietz-Uhler (2010),

First, it ensured that there was no personal reason for one group to discriminate against the other group. An individual presumably had nothing to gain personally by discriminating against the other group. Second, the procedure ensured that there was no existing hostility between the groups. Prior to categorization, individuals never thought of themselves as being a member of the group that tends to underestimate, or that other individuals are members of a group that overestimate, for example. Further, there was no chance for the groups to interact with one another, thus eliminating any possibility that group members would come to like the in-group or dislike the out-group. Third, such a procedure ensured that individuals had no conflicts of interest. There was nothing inherently valuable about being a member of a group that under- or overestimates. (p. 47)

Individuals were then asked to assign money to group members. They assigned more money to their own group than to the other groups. According to Tajfel and Turner (1986), the discovery regarding in-group favoritism and out-group discrimination based on "minimal in-group affiliation, anonymity of group membership, absence of conflict of interest, and absence of previous hostility between the groups," resulted in further conclusions about intergroup relations (p. 8). For example, Tajfel and Turner (1986) contend that once group comparison takes place, there are certain strategies available to deal with a negative or threatened outcome of group comparison (status). The first is individual mobility whereby an individual can leave the perceived low status group in favor of the higher status group, thus disassociating from the in-group. Another strategy is social creativity whereby elements of the comparative situation are altered or redefined. This involves:

a) Comparing the in-group to the out-group on some new dimension… b) Changing the values assigned to the attributes of the group, so that the comparisons which were previously negative are now perceived as positive… c) Changing the out-group (or selecting the out-group) with which the in-group is com-

pared–in particular, ceasing or avoiding to use the high-status out-group as a comparative frame of reference. (Tajfel & Turner, 1986,p. 20)

The last strategy is social competition whereby groups directly compete to achieve positive distinctiveness or identity. As the authors elaborate, "the group members may seek positive distinctiveness through direct competition with the out-group. They may try to reverse the relative positions of the in-group and the out-group on salient dimensions" (p. 20).

The relationship between interpersonal and intergroup should be seen as a continuum. As Turner and Reynolds (2004) elaborate:

Tajfel developed the idea of the "interpersonal-intergroup continuum" (the extent to which one acted as an individual in terms of interpersonal relationships or as a group member in terms of intergroup relationships) to explain when social identity processes were likely to come into operation and how social interaction differed qualitatively between these extremes....He argued that as behavior became more intergroup, attitudes to the out-group within the in-group tended to become more consensual and that out-group members tended to be seen as homogenous and undifferentiated members of their social category. (p. 261)

Thus, there was the interpersonal (acting in terms of self, but not personal identity) and intergroup "acting in terms of group" (Turner& Reynolds, 2004, p. 261).

Later, to address the distinction between personal and social identity, Turner and colleagues proposed self-categorization theory (see for example, Turner, et al., 1987). "Defining self as an individual person to self in terms of social identity, group behavior becomes possible and emerges" (Turner & Reynolds, 2004, p. 261). Salience [relevant] is also important. Not all groups are salient at one time. Those that are salient are influential. A number of studies show that salience is affected by different factors such as "the other people present and the groups to which they are members, how positively they are viewed, and the mood of the individuals and others present share" (see Coutant, Worchel, & Hanza, 2011, p. 41).

However, ethnocentrism is not universal, and in-group bias (positively valued in-group distinctiveness) does not automatically equate with social conflict and prejudice (Coutant et al., 2011; Turner & Reynolds, 2004). Further, it is important to note that in social identity theory, in-group bias is not the same thing as prejudice (Turner & Reynolds, 2004). For example, it is possible to have a situation where there is in-group favoritism, but not out-group discrimination and conflict; it is also possible to have in-group favoritism and fairness or out-group favoritism on negative dimensions. In-group favoritism in the negative dimension happens when the positive distinctiveness of the in-group is threatened (defined as low status) (Turner & Reynolds, 2004). Out-group favoritism is possible, for example, because low status in-groups are satisfied with that relationship, and with being inferior on that dimension (Turner & Reynolds, 2004). In other research, Brewer (2011) argues that perception of threat is important in justifying conflict and highly negative views of the out-group. Thus, "to justify out-group hate and intergroup conflict, the very existence of the out-group, or its goals and values, must be seen as a threat to the maintenance of the in-group and to one's own social identity" (Brewer, 2011,p. 132).

Social psychologists also introduced work on stereotypes, which are important to categorization and intergroup comparison. Stereotypes are beliefs about the traits or characteristics shared by members of groups (Baron & Byrne, 1997). According to the social cognition literature, stereotypes are not entirely accurate representations, and can overestimate or underestimate differences between individuals, distort reality, and serve to denigrate the out-group (Pennington, 2000). Other social psychologists (see Turner & Reynolds, 2004) do not see stereotypes as erroneous. While stereotypes may not always be valid, they should be seen as being "products of group interaction and anchored in group membership" (Turner & Reynolds, 2004,p. 271). Validity of stereotypes is not just psychological, but social and political.

Other research (Corenblum & Stephan, 2001; Stephan & Stephan, 2000) examined types of threat. For instance, integrated threat theory looks at four types of threat: realistic, symbolic, intergroup, and anxiety and negative stereotypes (see Stephan, Renfro & Davis, 2008). Later, refinements to the theory postulated that there are symbolic threats pertaining to values, beliefs, worldview, and collective identity, as well as realistic threats, relevant to, economic and political welfare, the former being just as important as the latter (Brewer, 2011; Coutant et al., 2011;Stephan, Renfro,& Davis, 2008). Antecedents that can threaten out-groups include relations between groups, individual difference variables, cultural dimensions, and situational factors (Stephan et al., 2008). Worchel and Coutant (2008) argue that fears related to group security and existence lead to protracted conflict (Coutant et al., 2011). Some investigated the strength of identification (Bransombe, Ellemers, Spears, &Doosje, 1999), which "determines how much a threat to the in-group matters to individuals and how likely they are to mobilize in defense of in-group interests" (Brewer, 2011, p.133). Still other research shows that strength of identification is also related to the degree of emotional response, and in the initial perception of threat (see Brewer, 2011).

Other research looks at intragroup cohesion factors such as leadership, conformity, deindividuation, and so forth to explain collective action. Here the literature is robust, and we highlight some key aspects here. From a social psychological perspective, leaders are still important to groups. From this perspective, there are prototypical members in groups, and those that conform to prototypicality appear to have influence. This influence becomes a reality because of depersonalized social attraction (Hogg, 2001). Further, conformity in groups is important, and individuals change their behavior to be consistent with the group (Sherif, 1936). Thus, all groups have norms—"a scale values which defines a range of acceptable (and unacceptable) attitudes and behaviors" (Brown, 2000). Finally, Zimbardo (2007) suggests that deindividuation occurs when personal accountability and responsibility shift from the individual to the group.

The crowd psychology literature (Coutant et al., 2011, see also Reicher, 2011 for a review) is another avenue of research where the focus is not on the individual to explain collective action. In a sub-set of this work, Reicher's (1996, 2001) conclusions about crowds rest on a social identity model. In crowd behavior, group identity is highly salient and dictates conduct. Collective memories also play an important role in intergroup conflict. Paez and Hou-fu Liu (2011) discuss that "CM [collective memories] is a widely shared knowledge of past social events that may not have been personally experienced but are collectively constructed through communicative social functions.... These social representations, or shared knowledge about the past, are elaborated, transmitted and conserved in a society through both interpersonal and institutional communications" (p. 105).

SOLUTIONS AND RECOMMENDATIONS

Once conflicts erupt, resolving them, or conflict resolution, is often difficult. But before delving into the literature, clarification of the term conflict resolution is necessary. Terms regarding conflict resolution are used differently throughout the literature. Fisher (2006) defines conflict resolution as when the relationship and situation is transformative and sustainable in the long run (Reykowski & Cislak, 2011).

However, Reykowski & Cislak (2011) maintain that in reality, a more limited model can be acceptable because conflict can never entirely be "resolved." They state that in this limited perspective, "conflict is resolved, if all or most of its major causes are eliminated or reduced, and the parties have learned how to live and work together avoiding violent encounters and hostile actions" (2011, p.241). It is not only the outcome, but the process.

Rouhana (2011) characterizes conflict settlement as "a formal termination of open violent conflict based on mutual interests" (p. 294). Alternatively, "conflict resolution activities seek to address the underlying causes of conflict and accordingly reach an agreement designed to address the basic human needs of both sides, regardless of the power relations with them" (p. 294). For Rouhana, transformative change to the relationship occurs in what the author coins "reconciliation." As will be discussed below, conflict drivers and attempts to resolve or reconcile them involve complex elements in which psychological processes are important. We will use the broader reference of conflict resolution to denote the end of hostilities, and the beginning of strategies aimed at transformation.

The social psychological literature addresses different aspects of conflict resolution. Reykowski and Cislak (2011) maintain that the origin of the conflict is important when ascertaining an approach to conflict resolution. Thus, those conflicts over divergent perspectives such as beliefs, opinions, narratives, and so forth can be debated. Those over divergent interest, such as resources are handled by bargaining, trade-offs, concessions, or compromises. The latter can be effective if not perceived in zero-sum terms. On the other hand, reaching understanding in conflicts over basic needs, sacred values (freedom, justice, legitimacy, and so forth), or values of the self (identity, prestige, dignity, positive self-image), "requires from the protagonists mutual recognitions of their needs and values…they have to make the necessary accommodations within the same relational dimension" (p. 242). Mutual forgiveness and reconciliation are important components. But many conflicts are complicated, and involve many of the issues described above, making them intractable. The authors argue that in these cases, the intention of the parties, whether competitive or cooperative, is important. That being said, cooperative intentions drive agreement, solution seeking, reduction in tensions, or elimination of the cause of the conflict, whereas competitive intensions drive more destructive behavior. In some cases of conflict, both intentions are evident. Reykowski and Cislak contend that what is chosen depends on the "cognitive construal" of the situation. Thus, divergent perspectives likely lead to cooperative problem solving. Others defined in threatening or harmful terms can evoke fear, anger, and hostility, leading to aggression. However, they note that solutions are possible if the other is not seen as a "mortal enemy."

Clearly, as Reykowski and Cislak demonstrate, emotions are important to any discussion of conflict resolution (Cottam et al., 2010; Halperin, Sharvit, & Gross, 2011; Moaz, 2004; Rouhana, 2011). In their work, for example, Halperin, Sharvit, and Gross (2011) examine the role of emotions and their relevance to conflict situations and conflict resolution. According to them, collective emotions such as anger, fear, and hatred can play a role in conflict outbreak and escalation. While these emotions escalate conflict, they suggest focusing on strategies to avoid escalation such as highlighting high risks involved with military action by emphasizing one's own weakness and the strength of the other side. Further, they suggest a balanced message of responsibility of both sides, which can lead to a reduction of anger and perceptions of unfairness and injustice. To reduce long-term hatred and situational hopelessness, they also advocate focusing on humaneness and heterogeneity of the out-group, and the "ability of individuals and groups to change their characteristics, moral-values, positions and behavior" (p. 93). In addition, to ascertain the motives and goals of the other, strategies of perspective taking can be used. As the authors conclude, "we propose that such long-term processes, disseminated through education channels, cultural products and other societal mechanisms, will alter the behavioral manifestations of reactive negative emotions, which are themselves natural and legitimate responses to offensive acts or provocations" (p. 93). Fear and hope and shame play a role in de-escalation of conflict. The authors suggest up-regulating guilt, but not shame, and in the long-term focusing on hope about the future. Finally, during the reconciliation phase, relevant emotions are forgiveness and empathy to toward the out-group.

Other literature focuses on identity transformation; that is, a shared identity. This would require groups in conflict to favor a third identity. While an appealing notion, given the strength of group identity that led to conflict in the first place, it is difficult to achieve in practice. One such solution is that while a superordinate identity is put in place, other identities could be maintained (Kelman, 2004). However, other research proposes that even this is difficult to accomplish or sustain (Brewer, 2011). Another possible avenue is the work on crosscutting memberships (Maalouf, 2000). As Brewer (2011) explains, cross-cutting memberships,

...involve only partial overlap between memberships in two different in-groups; one in-group is not full subsumed with the other. Instead, from the standpoint of a particular person, other individuals may be fellow in-group members on one dimension of category differentiation but out-group members on another. (p. 137)

Other strategies proposed to ameliorate identity conflict include shared sovereignty, where some element of self-rule—regional autonomy, statewide federation or confederation—is provided to groups (Rabie, 1994). Yet, as Cottam and colleagues (2010) illustrate, "people must be confident that the integrity, indeed the very continuity, of their primary identity groups will be secure, for these groups to be resolvable" (Cottam et al., 2010, p. 326). They further maintain that the best strategy depends on the nature of group interaction, and on settlement patterns. But in reality, both promoting equality and changing stereotypes require that one not only think, but also act differently. Here again, perspective taking could serve to diminish stereotyping. On the other hand, utilitarian integration strategies, which serve to provide equal access, are available when the groups in conflict are intermingled or when minority groups are not sufficiently powerful. Because of social distance, reform change can come slowly. Extent of institutional discrimination and memories of the past are also factors.

Related to this notion of memories and their relevance to conflict resolution, Paez & Hou-fu Liu (2011) argue that it is important to accept past events to move "toward the negotiation of a shared representation of the past." (p. 117). Truth and reconciliation commissions are one such example of this. According to Cottam and co-authors (2010), truth and reconciliation commissions "are designed to reveal the truths of political violence, to let the revelation of truth allow the victims or their survivors to grieve, and to achieve some measure of reconciliation and forgiveness" and "gather evidence, determine accountability and often recommend policies for the treatment of victims and perpetrators" (p. 321).

Another approach to conflict resolution stems from the intergroup contact hypothesis (Allport, 1954; Pettigrew, 1998). This hypothesis maintains that increasing intergroup contact can serve to demonstrate the complexity of group members, and break down stereotypes. However, later, some caveats were noted such as that this only works under conditions of protracted contact, with groups of equal status, and in supportive environments. Further, it is possible that a member of the group may be seen as different from stereotypical members. Therefore, the perception of the group does not change (Cottam et al., 2010). Important work on the contact hypothesis continues to be done (see Wagner, Tropp, Finchilescu, & Tredoux, 2008 for other research).

FUTURE RESEARCH DIRECTIONS

Social psychologists provide a strong foundation on the nature and reason for intergroup conflict. For this reason, intelligence analysts should be well versed in this theoretical body of knowledge. Further, this body of knowledge on intergroup conflict demonstrates ameliorating conflict can be very difficult to achieve in practice. The very nature of conflicts is often complex and can involve multiple factors, including strong emotions. Thus, this should realistically factor into analysts' conclusions and policy recommendations. While social psychology provides ample insight into the nature and reason for conflict, further social psychological research should focus on integrating current findings from the different theoretical schools, finding proven pathways, and continuing to focus on viable strategies for ending and resolving conflict.

CONCLUSION

Moving from a case study-based approach to a focus issues, events, and situations is important to advance the discipline of intelligence studies. Grounding in multidisciplinary theory is crucial to the discipline. This chapter demonstrated how knowledge of social psychological theory within the discipline of psychology informs our understanding of intergroup conflict and conflict resolution. This is just one example. Creating or refining intelligence studies programs should not only integrate social psychology but also other theories within psychology and other pertinent social science disciplines. This will transform thinking, and possibly lead to the creation of new theory.

REFERENCES

Aldrich, R. J. (2002). *The hidden hand: Britain, America, and cold war secret intelligence*. New York: Overlook Press.

Allport, G. W. (1954). *The nature of prejudice*. Garden City: Doubleday.

Bransombe, N. R., Ellemers, N., Spears, R., & Doosje, B. (1999). The context and content of social identity threat. In N. Ellemers, R. Spears, & B. Doosje (Eds.), *Social identity: Context, commitment, content* (pp. 35–58). Oxford: Blackwell.

Brewer, M. B. (2011). Identity and conflict. In D. Bar-Tal (Ed.), *Intergroup conflicts and their resolution: A social psychological perspective* (pp. 125–143). New York: Psychology Press.

Brown, R. (2000). *Group processes*. Malden, MA: Blackwell.

Cockburn, A., & Cockburn, L. (1991). *Dangerous liaisons: The inside story of the U.S.-Israeli covert relationship*. New York: HarperCollins.

Corenblum, B., & Stephan, W. G. (2001). White fears and native apprehensions: An integrated threat theory approach to intergroup attitudes. *Canadian Journal of Behavioural Science, 33*(4), 251–268. doi:10.1037/h0087147

Cottam, M. L., Mastors, E., Preston, T., & Dietz-Uhler, B. (2010). *Introduction to political psychology*. New York: Psychology Press.

Coutant, D. K., Worchel, S., & Hanza, M. (2011). Pigs, slingshots, and other foundations of intergroup conflict. In D. Bar-Tal (Ed.), *Intergroup conflicts and their resolution: A social psychological perspective* (pp. 39–59). New York: Psychology Press.

Fischer, R. J. (2006). Intergroup conflict. In M. Deutsch, P. T. Coleman, & E. E. Marcus (Eds.), *The handbook of conflict resolution* (pp. 176–196). San Francisco: Jossey-Bass.

Gallagher, A. M. (1989). Social identity and the Northern Ireland conflict. *Human Relations, 42*(10), 917–935. doi:10.1177/001872678904201004

Halpern, E., Sharvit, K., & Gross, J. J. (2011). Emotion and emotion regulation in intergroup conflict. In D. Bar-Tal (Ed.), *Intergroup conflicts and their resolution: A social psychological perspective* (pp. 83–102). New York: Psychology Press.

Hogg, M. A. (2001). A social identity theory of leadership. *Personality and Social Psychology Review, 5*(3), 184–200. doi:10.1207/S15327957PSPR0503_1

Hogg, M. A. (2001). Social categorization, depersonalization, and group behavior. In M. A. Hogg & S. Tindale (Eds.), *Group processes* (pp. 56–85). Malden, MA: Blackwell.

Jakub, J. (1998). *Spies and saboteurs: Anglo-American collaboration and rivalry in human intelligence collection and special operations, 1940-1945*. London: Macmillan.

Kelman, H. C. (2004). Reconciliation as identity change: A social psychological perspective. In Y. Bar-Siman-Tov (Ed.), *From conflict resolution to reconciliation* (pp. 11–124). Oxford: Oxford University Press. doi:10.1093/acprof:oso/9780195166439.003.0006

Maalouf, A. (2000). *In the name of identity*. New York: Penguin Books.

Moaz, I. (2004). Social-cognitive mechanisms in reconciliation. In Y. Bar-Siman-Tov (Ed.), *From conflict resolution to reconciliation* (pp. 197–224). Oxford: Oxford University Press. doi:10.1093/acprof:oso/9780195166439.003.0011

Paez, D.R., & Hou-fu Liu, J. (2011). Collective memory in conflicts. In D. Bar-Tal (Ed.), *Intergroup conflicts and their resolution: A social psychological perspective* (pp. 105-124). New York: Psychology Press.

Pennington, D. C. (2000). *Social cognition*. London: Routledge.

Pettigrew, T. F. (1998). Intergroup contact theory. *Annual Review of Psychology*, *49*(1), 65–85. doi:10.1146/annurev.psych.49.1.65 PMID:15012467

Rabie, M. (1994). *Conflict resolution and ethnicity*. Westport, CT: Praeger.

Reicher, S. D. (1996). 'The battle of Westminster': Developing the social identity model of crowd behavior in order to explain the initiation and development of collective conflict. *European Journal of Social Psychology*, *26*(1), 115–134. doi:10.1002/(SICI)1099-0992(199601)26:1<115::AID-EJSP740>3.0.CO;2-Z

Reicher, S. D. (2001). The psychology of crowd dynamics. In M. A. Hogg & S. Tindale (Eds.), *Group processes* (pp. 182–208). Malden, MA: Blackwell.

Reykowski, J., & Cislak, A. (2011). Socio-psychological approaches to conflict resolution. In D. Bar-Tal (Ed.), *Intergroup conflicts and their resolution: A social psychological perspective* (pp. 241–266). New York: Psychology Press.

Rouhana, N. N. (2011). Key issues in reconciliation: Challenging traditional assumptions on conflict resolution and power dynamics. In D. Bar-Tal (Ed.), *Intergroup conflicts and their resolution: A social psychological perspective* (pp. 291–311). New York: Psychology Press.

Rubin, M., & Hewstone, M. (1998). Social identity theory's self-esteem hypothesis: A review and some suggestions for clarification. *Personality and Social Psychology Review*, *2*(1), 40–62. doi:10.1207/s15327957pspr0201_3 PMID:15647150

Sherif, M. (1936). *The psychology of social norms*. New York: Harper & Row.

Stephan, W. G., Renfro, L., & Davis, M. D. (2008). The role of threat in intergroup relations. In U. Wagner, L. R. Tropp, G. Finchilescu, & C. Tredoux (Eds.), *Improving intergroup relations: Building on the legacy of Thomas F. Pettigrew* (pp. 55–72). Malden, MA: Blackwell. doi:10.1002/9781444303117.ch5

Stephan, W. G., & Stephan, C. W. (2000). An integrated threat theory of prejudice. In S. Oskamp (Ed.), *Reducing prejudice and discrimination* (pp. 23–45). Mahwah, NJ: Erlbaum.

Tajfel, H. (1970). Experiments in intergroup discrimination. *Scientific American*, *223*(5), 96–102. doi:10.1038/scientificamerican1170-96 PMID:5482577

Tajfel, H., Billig, M., Bundy, R. P., & Flament, C. (1971). Social categorization and intergroup behavior. *European Journal of Social Psychology, 1*(2), 149–178. doi:10.1002/ejsp.2420010202

Tajfel, H., & Turner, J. C. (1986). The social identity theory of intergroup behavior. In S. Worchel & W. G. Austin (Eds.), *Psychology of intergroup relations* (2nd ed., pp. 7–24). Chicago: Nelson-Hall.

Turner, J. C., Hogg, M. A., Oakes, P. J., Richer, S. D., & Wetherell, M. S. (1987). *Rediscovering the social group*. Oxford: Basil Blackwell.

Turner, J. C., & Reynolds, K. J. (2004). The social identity perspective in intergroup relations: Theories, themes, and controversies. In M. B. Brewer & M. Hewstone (Eds.), *Self and social identity* (pp. 259–277). Malden, MA: Blackwell.

US Government. (2004, December 17). Intelligence Reform and Prevention of Terrorism Act 2004, Pub. L. No. 108–458. Retrieved from http://www.gpo.gov/fdsys/pkg/PLAW-108publ458/pdf/PLAW-108publ458.pdf.

Wagner, U., Tropp, L. R., Finchilescu, G., & Tredoux, C. (2008). *Improving intergroup relations: Building on the legacy of Thomas F. Pettigrew*. Malden, MA: Blackwell. doi:10.1002/9781444303117

Zimbardo, P. (2007). *The Lucifer effect*. New York: Random House.

KEY TERMS AND DEFINITIONS

Collective Memories: Widely shared knowledge of past social events.

Contact Hypothesis: Increasing intergroup contact to break down stereotypes.

Crowd Psychology: A branch of social psychology concerned with the study of crowd behavior.

Deindividuation: When personal responsibility shifts from the individual to the group.

Individual Mobility: When an individual leaves a perceived low status group for another high status group.

Realistic Threats: Threats to material, economic, and political welfare of a group.

Social Competition: When groups directly compete to achieve positive distinctiveness or identity.

Social Creativity: Altering or redefining the comparative situation.

Social Psychology: A branch of the field of psychology that is concerned with individuals in the social context.

Stereotypes: Beliefs about the traits or characteristics shared by members of groups.

Symbolic Threats: Threats to a group that pertain to values, beliefs, worldview and collective identity.

Chapter 15

Detecting Individual-Level Deception in the Digital Age: The DETECT Model ©

Eugenie de Silva
University of Leicester, UK & Virginia Research Institute, USA

ABSTRACT

This chapter presents a discussion of a new model titled, "DETECT (Determining and Evaluating Truthfulness through Explicit Cue Testing) which relies upon the assessment of verbal and non-verbal cues. The author presents the argument that the digital age has posed novel challenges to law enforcement and intelligence personnel; hence, the author further explains the ways in which the DETECT model (©, Eugenie de Silva, 2014) can be used to determine deceptive activities at the individual-level even in a technologically advanced society. The chapter touches upon Denial and Deception (D&D), and how the detection of deception must be carried out in the twenty-first century, especially through rigorous monitoring within the established legal framework.

DOI: 10.4018/978-1-4666-9661-7.ch015

INTRODUCTION

It seems counterintuitive that deception could be detected, since the very act is executed to mislead others. Yet, this chapter expands upon the notion of utilizing verbal (e.g. spoken) and non-verbal (e.g. body movements) cues to detect deception to precisely explicate the extent to which deception can be detected in the twenty-first century.

Denial and Deception (D&D) is an all-inclusive term that commonly refers to activities that involve distorting information, manipulating facts to establish a false story, or even withholding data from an adversary. Whilst denial and deception can be utilized as two individual terms, they are undoubtedly interlinked and can be used to strengthen operations aimed at feeding false information to adversaries. In 2000, Roy Godson and James Wirtz explicitly reinstated this information by denoting that denial and deception are intertwined terms that work uniquely as a blend to essentially pull wool over the eyes of opponents or enemies (2000, 5). The denial of information results in a misinformed perception of an event, whereas deception can result in a completely distorted view of a scenario or the distortion to various degrees of specific aspects of cases. Accordingly, when used in combination, an individual can relay a completely false story to a targeted opponent to whom it would seem completely feasible and truthful. The use of realistic characteristics is what makes D&D such a dominating tool.

With regard to the disciplines of law enforcement and intelligence, deception must be identified at its earliest stages in order to avert any possible dangers aimed at damaging the national security of the U.S. This being the case, it is imperative to recognize that a successful deceptive story will commonly take advantage of the opponent's weaknesses and/or known perceptions of the world. Through the recognition of these weaknesses, an opponent may specifically tailor a deception activity to ensure that the false story is believable to his/her adversary. As a result, if one seeks to identify deception, then one should not be oblivious to the actual facts that may have been hidden or altered, based on the given set of data. Further, as history has shown, it is necessary to take into consideration all activities as they relate to other on-going operations.

Indubitably, officials who have daily interactions with individuals will encounter acts of trickery and guile. For an officer specialized in the recognition of deception, there is assuredly a higher probability of having the ability to detect duplicity at a faster rate than in cases of untrained individuals. Thus, there is a necessity to establish a model that would aid in the prediction and/or identification of deception solely by observing, and then analyzing an individual's actions or inactions, in addition to their spoken words. For the purpose of distinguishing the truth from lies without requiring an in-depth background in the field, any proposed model must not necessitate any outside or previous knowledge. Thus, the DETECT model in this chapter simply requires that individuals study the requirements of the model itself, which lessens the responsibility of having to learn an entirely new subject in order to know how to detect deception.

One scenario that explicates the necessity of a more personal approach to solving problems is the 2001 U.S. terrorist attacks. During this period, intelligence analysts in the U.S. had devoted much time to conduct research and finalize reports to determine when and where an imminent attack would take place. For those working in the Central Intelligence Agency (CIA), the identification of several suspects had already been successful. The list of these individuals had been sent to the Federal Bureau of Intelligence (FBI), yet it had not been transferred to local state troopers, and the information that had been sent were not the complete lists (de Silva, 2003, 113). As a result, although the suspected terrorist was stopped for traffic violations, he was not detained due to the troopers' lack of knowledge on the topic (de Silva, 2003, 113). This should be deemed a noteworthy instance of a failure to share information among intelligence officers and law enforcement personnel, in addition to the ways in which even advanced technology did not offer support; however, this also represents a perfect scenario in which the utilization of verbal and non-verbal cues could have been effective. Whilst the troopers were not made aware of the suspected individuals, had they been provided information about the ways to detect deception, there could have been a higher probability that they would have at least asked the individuals more pressing questions to determine the truthfulness of their statements which would have possibly led to further inquiry, recognition, and then detainment of the terrorists prior to the attacks. Although it is not certain whether the application of the DETECT model would have resulted in the definitive detainment of the terrorists prior to the attack, it is certain that offering greater opportunities to investigate and determine deception can always improve the probabilities of accurate and effective detection and handling of situations.

Unfortunately, there is no factually significant way in which to determine the most probable success rate of the troopers' utilizing verbal and non-verbal cues to either make an arrest or gather more information on the suspects. Nevertheless, based on the success of the DETECT model in prior research and in practical situations (especially the testing on "rehabilitated" terrorists), it has been herein assumed that the model would have, at the very least, provided the law enforcement officers with a more concrete basis to prevent the terrorist attacks.

Along these lines, this chapter has focused on the applicability of the DETECT model to evaluate truthfulness in the twenty-first century by taking into consideration the technologically-dependent and advanced culture of present society. The author of this chapter has sought to provide readers with a basic understanding of D&D, how it can be detected at an individual-level, and the ways in which technology may make the detection of deception an easier process, whilst simultaneously highlighting greater challenges than were previously present.

BACKGROUND

It has been reported that for average individuals and even specialists, detecting deception can be a strenuous challenge (Da Silva & Leach, 2013, 116). For instance, it has even been established that for average individuals without a background in the field the "accuracy rate [of detecting deception for laypersons] [...] was 54%: 61% of truths and 47% of lies [that] were correctly identified" (Da Silva & Leach, 2013, 115). In the research, it was established that the detection of deception for specialists was only marginally higher than those without a background in the discipline. Accordingly, although it can be a struggle to recognize deception, there have been researchers who have taken the initiatives to establish and verify a list of verbal and non-verbal cues that have been explicitly linked to deceptive practices. These lists, as illustrated later in this chapter, were utilized as the exhaustive lists of cues for personnel who are interested in detecting deception in the DETECT model.

Biometrics has also been a major point of focus for other researchers in the field. According to the U.S. Federal Government's biometrics website, the term biometrics can be used to refer to either a process or a characteristic. A biometric, as a process, is defined as, "an automated method of recognizing an individual based on measurable biological (anatomical and physiological) and behavioral characteristics" ("Biometrics," 2006). On the other hand, a biometric, as a characteristic, is a measurable biological characteristic that may be utilized for "automated recognition" ("Biometrics," 2006). Accordingly, whereas there has been research elsewhere that specifically focuses on the study of biometrics through advanced technology, such as live-scan facial recognition systems, voice recognition, and retina recognition, the

DETECT model primarily focused on the detection of deception without a reliance on such resources. These technologies can certainly be practical for officers who wish to conduct concrete analyses of individuals, yet these resources do not aid in the timely identification of deception on a daily basis for personnel without access to these systems. This leads to an important point pertaining to the usefulness of DETECT in a technologically-advanced society. Take for instance a police officer who must monitor a major highway and stop individuals who are driving over the limit, driving with faulty brake lights, failing to follow legal regulations, etc. This officer must, within a few minutes, determine whether the individual at-hand is trying to establish a deceitful story or is actually telling the truth. In such instances, it may be impractical to expect the law enforcement officer to utilize advanced technologies. The process of detecting deception should be made easier, not complicated for those who have dedicated their lives to ensure the safety of the nation. The use of social media may be useful for intelligence officers who require an understanding of the social, political, or even economic dynamics of a certain region or seek background information of a specific individual; however, law enforcement officers who work at a fast-pace in dangerous situations do not have the freedom or opportunities to take advantage of such social advancements in order to carry out their responsibilities. Thus, having an understanding of specific cues that can be used to ascertain the truthfulness of an individual's statements can make easier the responsibilities that are allocated to law enforcement personnel.

Since the 9/11 attacks of 2001, there has been a progressive shift in threats aimed at the U.S. Whereas al-Qaida and other religiously/politically motivated terrorists groups may have been at the forefront of intelligence and law enforcement analyses in 2001, one of the most prominent threats in 2013 were cyber-attacks. In fact, in 2015, the Worldwide Threat Assessment from the Office of the Director of National Intelligence (ODNI) did not even highlight Iran or Hezbollah as terrorist threats (Clapper, 2015). Therefore, it is undeniable that the threats that were previously present, no longer pose as harsh threats in the current time. In fact, a simple glance at the threat assessment proves that many of the current threats relate to cyber security, economic espionage, and other insider threats aimed at damaging the U.S. critical infrastructure. However, amidst these threats are two specific forms of terrorism that could render the U.S. virtually victim to countless domestic attacks; Homegrown Violent Extremism (HVE) and lone-wolf terrorism. For those who are radicalized within the nation, their goals are made easier by the civil rights, protections, and constitutional guarantees that are granted to those in the U.S. Accordingly, these individuals do not have to be concerned about issues that would have otherwise been raised, such as gaining security clearances and passing through border control, had they been based in another country and wanted to enter the U.S. to initiate an attack.

According to reports, HVE has essentially become the "'new face' of terrorism" (*Homegrown Violent Extremism,* n.d.). Threats of radicalization, extremism, and/or lone-wolf terrorism rise amidst political, social, and economic turmoil. When individuals feel as though they are not accepted, they commonly seek acceptance and find it in terrorist, radical, or extremist groups. The propaganda and deception used by such groups to recruit individuals, especially through the use of advanced technology and social media make it quite simple to convince individuals that their own objectives and goals can be achieved by joining the group. Disgruntled citizens who yearn to find ways to feel as though their ideologies are respected are at risk of falling victim to the D&D of the aforementioned groups. These individuals align their activities with the groups (which further criminal activities) in the process of trying to improve their own situations.

U.S. law enforcement personnel at the local, state, and federal levels are explicitly accountable for protecting the nation from these individuals who have been radicalized. Of course, the utilization of the intelligence cycle to gather, analyze, and then disseminate reports can be a useful tool; yet, it does not always foster the necessary protection to predict, and then prevent such attacks. In addition, placing high reliance on technology is a less personal/human means of handling intelligence issues, which may not always allow the government to attain their intelligence goals. In 2015, these issues are particularly pressing, due to the ways in which social media has provided terrorist organizations with the opportunity to recruit and radicalize individuals to carry out actions from within the U.S.; in fact, Islamic State of Iraq and Syria (ISIS) is one terrorist group that has significantly taken advantage of these resources to further its agenda.

For years, the topic of detecting deception has been investigated by researchers who have developed academic reports on the ways in which interviewing strategies can be improved to increase the likelihood of distinguishing the truth from the lies. Whereas other topics have been diligently researched for years, the detection of deception through verbal and non-verbal cues has not been at the forefront of recent discussions in the fields of political science and law enforcement. As was previously mentioned, the recognition of deceit is a necessary and useful tactic for law enforcement personnel who must work with individuals on a daily basis.

Verbal and non-verbal cues have been analyzed in the field as early as 1987, yet a common weakness of the research has been the lack of rigorous testing of the effectiveness of the utilization of the cues as a means of recognizing deception. In addition, there has been a failure to identify the applicability and usefulness of both cues in law enforcement and intelligence environments. Accordingly, in 2013, the author of this chapter conducted a rigorous research project wherein individuals were interviewed and tested to detect their truthfulness based on the author's novel model "DETECT." This model was based on several verbal and non-verbal cues that had been carefully identified through an extensive review of existing literature. There are many verbal and non-verbal cues that can be used to detect deception as has been highlighted through research over the years. Moreover, since there are cues that are specific to individuals of certain genders, each of the cues have been listed below with either M to indicate that it is predominately noticed in males, F to indicate that it is commonly recognized in females, or M/F to highlight that it is commonly noticed in both males and females. The cues that are listed below form the basis of the DETECT model:

Verbal Cues:

1. Speech Stumbles (M/F) = Use of filler words (e.g. "umm" or "uhh") sign of deception.
2. Including long pauses before answering (M/F) = High probability of deception
3. Evading answering the question (M/F) = High probability of deception
4. Beginning answers with the word "well" (M/F) = Major sign of deception
5. Utilizing negative statements (M/F) – Use of words, such as "no," "do not," or "cannot" are signs of deception.
6. Using higher tone and pitch of voice (M/F) – Associated with deception

Nonverbal Cues:

1. Maintaining steady eye contact (M/F) = Habitual liars believe looking away will lead the interviewer to suspect they are lying.

2. Rubbing nose (M/F) = Stress causes an increase of blood to the extremities which causes tingling in the nose; hence, individuals rub their nose when they feel discomfort.
3. Crossing/Folding arms (M/F) = A barrier in communication.
4. Touching/Placing hand on suprasternal notch or the base of throat (F) = Researcher Joe Navarro recognized women do this when they are stressed (2012).
5. Using item to cover themselves (e.g. jacket, cup, paper) (M/F) = Barrier in communication
6. Holding hands together or clasping hands (M/F) = Barrier in communication
7. Positioning feet at the closest exit (M/F) = Represents where an individual actually wants to be at the time.
8. Using hand gestures that do not explicitly match what is being stated (M/F) = Liars must juggle conflicting information to present a believable story; hence, hand gestures are not in synch with their statements.
9. Not using hand gestures (M/F) = Focus is on establishing a truthful story, so the individual forgets to use hand gestures as they would in general situations.
10. Fanning themselves with their hands or other items (M/F) = Stress causes individuals to feel hot, which forces them to fan themselves to cool down.
11. Pupil dilation increasing (M/F) = Sign of deception
12. More blinking (M/F) – Researcher note this as a sign of deception
13. Moving fingers – Identified later in research as being a common movement
14. Crossing legs – Sign of barrier in communication

In an effort to establish a general outline of basic qualifiers of deception, John L. Waltman and Golen published "Detecting Deception during Interviews" in 1993, which pertained to the identification of deception during interviews when auditing. Waltman and Golen were both faculty members at Eastern Michigan University ("EMU Faculty Publications," 2001). The combination of their expertise and backgrounds in the field substantially aided in the establishment of a body of work focused on leakage and the common non-verbal behavioral patterns or body movements of liars. Moving forward, the work provided assessments that determined that many advanced liars have learned to control their faces; hence, the author discussed the importance of assessing situations through the analysis of other areas of an individual's body (Waltman & Golen, 1993, 61.) Furthermore, the authors also brought their work to an end by identifying that the behavioral norms of individuals vary from person-to-person (Waltman & Golen, 1993, 63.) Based on this information, the importance of identifying the norm of an individual prior to judging their actions and assessing for deception was confirmed.

The data offered by these authors acted as the guiding factors in the development of "DETECT." Although the articles may not have been written in relation to the technological advances of the twenty-first century, they establish the underlying basis that is necessary to understand deception activities. Along these lines, it was also necessary to take into consideration that by being objective and not generalizing each individual, one can improve the chances of successful detection of deception. Complete reliance on current technology would thus require one to generalize most individuals; this would further exacerbate issues in detecting deception.

In 2000, Barton Whaley and Jeffrey Busby developed "Detecting Deception: Practice, Practitioners, and Theory," which provided readers with an introduction to deception, a description of the practitioners of deception, and how deception can be detected. Whaley and Busby's work significantly contributed to the field by making known that although experts are the individuals who commonly have more success in detecting deception due to the organized manner in which they approach situations, non-experts could also be deemed detectives since every individual applies skills of detection to identify deception on a daily basis (2000, 73).

Along these lines, the author of this chapter reflected upon the notion of how technological advancement plays a role in the extent to which members of the public feel that they are apt and adequately prepared to counter deceptive ploys, and detect any propaganda if it were being aimed at them. These beliefs are typically what make deception campaigns successful, since unrealistic beliefs that one can easily detect deception, and ill-informed views of deception and propaganda allow one to be more easily swayed.

As more research was conducted, it was found that in 2007, Kevin Colwell published an article known as "Assessment Criteria Indicative of Deception (ACID): an integrated system of investigative interviewing and detecting deception." Colwell's background as a professor of psychology specialized in detecting deception clearly aided in the development of a foundation for the work ("Kevin Colwell," 2014). Consequent to providing a brief overview of the extent to which content analyses have been conducted to determine patterns in deceptive statements during interviews, Colwell further explicated that interviewing strategies that can increase the cognitive load of the individuals being interviewed can improve the effort to detect deception (2007, 168).

This also leads back to the issue of the public view of D&D. What is portrayed in the media (e.g. news, television, movies, dramas, etc.) is certainly not always the most credible or accurate information. However, if one takes into consideration the extent to which most individuals rely on the media for their information, without conducting outside, academic research, then it becomes possible to realize the ways in which the public makes D&D campaigns easier. With the knowledge that experts and practitioners hold with regard to D&D campaigns, and the lack of understanding by a majority of the public, influencing views to attain tactical and strategic success can be a simple process. For instance, it is understood that by increasing the cognitive load of individuals, the detection of deception is made easier, since the individual must make an effort to manage more cognitive processes; thus, whilst an individual is forced to increase their cognitive load, the lack of knowledge on how their ideologies could be manipulated sets the path for the interrogator/researcher/practitioner to easily detect the common signs of deception. The increase in cognitive load ensures that an individual is unable to maintain deceptive stories in ways that would have otherwise been possible. In the cyber arena, this increase in cognitive load is difficult to carry out; yet, it can be possible through extensive online discussions that require the subject at-hand to become emotionally or psychologically involved in the discussion(s). Detecting individual-level deception is made easier on a face-to-face basis, especially through the application of the DETECT model, which allows practitioners to assess based on verbal and physical cues; however, it is also certainly possible to detect deception through cyber systems by gaining essential background information, and tactically questioning an individual to gather information.

Moving forward, in 2012, an FBI article written by Joe Navarro was published. It was titled, "Detecting Deception." Navarro briefly touched upon the necessity of law enforcement officials to have an adequate understanding of human behavior, since it would provide more opportunities to gather data and conduct assessments (2012). Subsequently, he pondered on several non-verbal characteristics that were known to be associated with deception (Navarro, 2012). However, Navarro also spoke about the importance of having an adequate setting to conduct an interview of an individual to determine deception (2012). This is a point that was taken into consideration through the research to establish the DETECT model; the model was designed to have the flexibility to be tailored according to the needs of individual officers. Technology can be used to detect deception as has been proven through other research;

however, without generalizing all individuals or understanding human behavior, technology itself cannot be the sole or primary identifier of deception. The individuals who program the technology may understand human behavior, yet if the technology is not appropriately programmed or fine-tuned, then the technology simply becomes an assistive maneuver, rather than a primary technique in the detection of deception. This is the reason why this chapter promotes the use of the DETECT model to make the initial determinations of deception at an individual-level. Technology can be used in combination with the model, yet it is not required.

Furthermore, Walter Weintraub's 2005 work "Verbal Behavior and Personality Assessment" explicated that if verbal trait analyses are to be conducted, the speech samples must be collected from speech under conditions that are only moderately stressful (2005, 140). He also explained that if the verbal samples were collected from scenarios in which the stress levels were too high or too low, any analyses of the data would not be rendered useful or applicable (Weintraub, 2005, 140). Further, Weintraub did include information about grammatical commonalities and the utilization of verbal patterns to recognize personality norms for individuals. Weintraub explicitly focused on the grammatical ways in which sentences are structured; yet, the DETECT model relies on previously identified specific verbal cues on which to focus. Thus, the main point that has been derived from Weintraub's work was the necessity of focusing on spontaneous material that was presented by the individuals being interviewed.

Later in 2011, Maria Hartwig, Par A. Granhag, Leif Stromwall, Ann G. Wolf, Aldert Vrij, and Emma Roos Hjelmsater published an article titled "Detecting deception in suspects: verbal cues as a function of interview strategy" which was dedicated to the utilization of verbal cues as a way of detecting deception. By conducting observations of ninety-six undergraduates, Hartwig, et. al. were able to highlight the veracity of the extent to which verbal cues could be used to recognize deceptive practices (2011, 654). The study concluded by also stating that many innocent suspects believed that "telling the truth is sufficient for exoneration" whereas officials mainly require corroborating evidence to determine an individual's innocence (Hartwig, et. al., 2011, 645). Furthermore, it was also made clear that the accuracy rate was not as high as predicted when the basis was the verbal cues; accordingly, the authors hinted to the possibility that the examination of non-verbal cues may have provided greater insight. This acted as further impetus in the development of the DETECT model.

On another note, the work of Lara Warmelink, Aldert, Vrij, Samantha Mann, and Par Anders Granhag from 2013 titled "Spatial and Temporal Details in Intentions: A Cue to Detecting Deception" was able to emphasize that individuals have a tendency to provide a wealth of detail in describing their intentions, whereas details were minimized when one was not discussing their intentions (Warmelink, Vrij, Mann, Granhag, 2013, 105). For the purposes of Warmelink, et. al.'s work, it was hypothesized, and then verified that the individuals tested in their research offered significantly more detail in their answers to questions when being truthful about their intentions, whilst less details were provided when the individuals were lying (Warmelink, et. al., 105).

With the aforementioned research taken into consideration, in 2011, David Matsumoto, Hyi Sung Hwang, Lisa Skinner, and Mark Frank published an article in the Federal Bureau of Investigation (FBI) bulletin entitled, "Evaluating Truthfulness and Detecting Deception." The article relayed the ideas that law enforcement should recognize that there is not one standard, nor perfect technique or model to detect deception; however, the authors did mention that through systematic awareness of non-verbal cues, individuals could more easily recognize deception (Matsumoto, Hwang, Skinner, and Frank, 2011). For example, the authors made clear that many law enforcement officers commonly focus on what an individual is saying, rather than also being aware of how the individual is saying the information (Matsumoto, et. al., 2011). However, the work relayed the notion that the officers should not just focus on non-verbal characteristics, but should also try to multitask and take into consideration both cues, while assessing how they are working in coordination with one another (Matsumoto, et. al., 2011). Accordingly, the work was useful to highlight the actual importance of the DETECT model; the model is not to be applied as a perfect model that will provide continuous, accurate results. Rather, the model provides practitioners with greater opportunities to detect deception, which further makes the probability of successfully detecting deception much higher.

MAIN FOCUS OF THE CHAPTER

DETECT Model: Application

The application of the DETECT model was simplified during inception in order to ensure that law enforcement and intelligence officers would not be required to undergo intense training. To successfully apply the model, the practitioner (the individual applying the model) must be aware of the verbal and non-verbal cues. Since most practitioners will not be able to mentally remember each of the cues, the tables below may be used to provide the practitioners with easier ways in which to note any identified cues. Due to the fact that there are more non-verbal cues than verbal cues, the non-verbal cue table may be broken into three separate components, and then totaled in the final "Cue Evaluation" table (see Figures 1-5).

As can be determined from the above tables, the application of the model is quite simple. Once the practitioners become comfortable with the system, the time it takes to enter the information into the

Figure 1. Verbal Cue Checklist Outline

Date	Time	Name	Cue 1: Speech Stumble	Cue 2: Long Pauses Prior to Answering	Cue 3: Answers Begin w/ "Well."	Cue 4: Negative Statements	Cue 5: Higher Tone and Pitch of Voice	Cue 6: Evading Answering	Total Cues Out of 6

Figure 2. Non-Verbal Cue Checklist Outline – Part 1

Date	Time	Name	Cue 1: Steady Eye Contact	Cue 2: Rubbing Nose	Cue 3: Crossing Arms	Cue 4: Touching Suprasternal Notch/Base of Throat	Cue 5: Using Item to Cover Themselves	Cue 6: Holding Hands Together / Clasping Hands	Total Cues Out of 6:

Figure 3. Non-Verbal Cue Checklist Outline – Part 2

Date	Time	Name	Cue 1: Positioning Feet at Closest Exit	Cue 2: Hand Gestures Do Not Match Statements	Cue 3: Not Using Hand Gestures	Cue 4: Fanning Themselves w/ Hands or Other Items	Cue 5: Pupil Dilation Increasing	Cue 6: More Blinking	Total Cues Out of 6:

Figure 4. Non-Verbal Cue Checklist Outline – Part 3

Date	Time	Name	Cue 1: Crossing Legs	Cue 2: Moving Fingers	Total Cues Out of 2:

Figure 5. Final Cue Evaluation

Date	Time	Name	1. Number of Verbal Cues	2. Number of Non-Verbal Cues	3. 3 or More Verbal Cues Detected? YES/NO	4. 7 or More Non-Verbal Cues Detected? YES/NO	If You Entered "YES" in Boxes 3 or 4, Enter Check Mark in This Box. 50% or More Signs of Either Cues Equals High Probability of Deception. Seek Further Investigation.

tables will lessen. The DETECT model was developed through non-parametric, statistical analyses that further relied on the McNemar Test. Furthermore, the evaluation of participants in the initial Institutional Review Board (IRB) approved investigations for the development of the model resulted in the determination that if an individual displayed fifty-percent or more of either of the cues (e.g. 3 out of 6 verbal cues or 7 out of 14 non-verbal cues), then that individual was more likely to be deceiving the practitioner.

Issues, Controversies, and Problems

The U.S., in 2015, is faced with the challenges that arise due to the evolving times, such as increased cyber threats, homegrown violent extremism, insider threats in intelligence agencies, etc. Therefore, those who are involved in security sectors are presented with the challenges of identifying appropriate strategies to counter the threats, while also maintaining the standards of the institution according to the relevant legal regulations. The extensive reliance on cyber infrastructure further exacerbates the threats by allowing criminals to carry out activities that would not have been possible without advanced technology. Although this poses a wide array of challenges to intelligence and law enforcement personnel, it particularly makes the detection of deception less feasible. The DETECT model focuses on face-to-face interaction that provides individuals with opportunities to assess verbal and non-verbal cues; the application of this model in the cyber arena would ultimately rely on written words, which would ultimately require an expansion of the model to train practitioners with regard to understanding how grammar, punctuation, and other written characteristics can be used to first gain an understanding of an individual's personality, and then begin to detect deception.

Deception strategies vary depending on the area of the world in which they are executed. To date, investigations and analyses into the subject have resulted in the determination that "[t]errorist sympathizers will probably conduct low-level cyber-attacks on behalf of terrorist groups and attract attention of the media, which might exaggerate the capabilities and threat posed by these actors" (Clapper, 2015, p.2). As aforementioned, HVE and lone-wolf terrorism are growing threats. In fact, HVE related to ISIS and the fight to carry out the objectives of ISIS by traveling to Syria and/or conducting illegal activities in the U.S. have clearly been major threats to U.S. homeland security (Clapper, 2015, p.5). Although the monitoring of social media will be vital in the determination of whether individuals are being radicalized, it will be important to find ways for law enforcement at all levels to be integrated in a manner that will be conducive to the maintenance of national security. Therefore, social media not only poses issues pertaining the radicalization in individuals, but it also creates a barrier when law enforcement or intelligence personnel want to investigate the verbal and non-verbal cues.

Another issue with which practitioners of detecting deception are faced is the cooperation between the public and law enforcement. The Edward Snowden case resulted in much uproar amongst U.S. citizens, and individuals across the globe; although law enforcement and intelligence personnel could have used the situation as a basis of reform to regain the public's trust, more issues arose after this time. In particular, in recent months, law enforcement have been involved in the shooting and killing of many unarmed citizens. These killings have led to protests pertaining to tactics employed by law enforcement and the motives behind the shootings. Therefore, individuals may hide their true intentions or purposefully react in irregular ways when questioned by law enforcement personnel. This could lead to incorrect determinations based on the assessment of verbal or non-verbal cues.

Solutions and Recommendations

Overall, the application of the DETECT model allows practitioners to detect deception at early stages without having to gather much background data in order to make an initial determination. With regard to the issue of terrorist activities and terrorist sympathizers, the management of these threats may include the application of the DETECT model. Law enforcement personnel at all levels (e.g. local, state, and federal), whilst carrying out their allocated responsibilities, should maintain awareness of common signs of deception. Thus, law enforcement should go beyond what is required of them in order to ensure that they do not allow an individual with malicious intentions to slip through their grip without notice. This also relates back to the mistakes made prior to 9/11 by the law enforcement officer who did not appropriately investigate the terrorist who had been stopped while driving.

Along these lines, through social media, it can be difficult for law enforcement to determine whether or not an individual is being deceitful through verbal/non-verbal cues. The ways in which individuals type may not be the ways in which the individuals verbally speak. Therefore, it will always be more useful to take advantage of the advancements in social media through voice and video chat. Take for instance the popular social networking site Facebook, which allows users to use their webcams and microphones to speak, rather than solely relying on the messenger feature within the site. In cases wherein there are reasonable suspicions of criminal activity, law enforcement/intelligence personnel may befriend an individual through a fake profile, and then initiate contact with the individual in question. The process may take time, since the officer must gain the trust of the individual in question; however, once a appropriate time has passed, the use of Facebook's webcam and microphone chat features will be useful for the officer to hear how the individual speaks, and the ways in which they carry themselves during a conversation. Once the officer has an understanding of the individual's behavior, questions could be asked through the features or the individual could be called in for questioning wherein the DETECT model could be further applied. In addition, other resources, such as Skype, ooVoo, WhatsApp, KiK, etc., could similarly be used to apply the DETECT model without requiring physical interviews with an individual; although, the latter will always be more useful in detecting deception based on verbal and non-verbal cues.

With regard to the issue of public frustration and distrust of law enforcement and intelligence personnel, the main solution will be public outreach and education. If law enforcement and intelligence personnel place a priority on establishing a more open relationship with the public, it may be possible to regain trust. This will not be a fast solution, yet it will promote a cooperative relationship conducive to the detection of deception whenever necessary. Furthermore, if individuals act irrationally or in irregular ways when confronted by law enforcement personnel, then it will, as aforementioned, be difficult to clearly assess verbal or non-verbal cues. However, it will be more useful to incorrectly assume that an individual is being deceitful an initiate further investigations, rather than incorrectly assume that an individual is being truthful and allow the individual to freely leave. Law enforcement personnel, however, should realize that assuming an individual is being deceitful based on the DETECT model does not mean that the individual is guilty of a crime, and also does not provide the law enforcement with the right to freely use excessive force. The results of the DETECT model simply provide law enforcement with a basis to initiate further investigations.

The following are also strategies that should be taken into consideration in order to more appropriately detect deception, and improve the way in which security officials conduct activities:

1. **When Conducting In-Depth Interviews, Follow the Common Practices and Tactics Enlisted in Cognitive Interviews (CI):** When officials interview eyewitnesses and victims of crimes, CIs are commonly utilized to ensure that the individuals being interviewed have improved opportunities to explain themselves and provide more complete and real explanations of information. In the case of detecting deception, the common practices of this form of interviewing should be used. Firstly, officers should instruct the individuals to "think-aloud" during the interview. During this form of interviewing, law enforcement and intelligence personnel should "read each question to the subject, and then record and/or otherwise note the processes that subject uses in arriving at an answer to the question" (Willis, 1999, 1). Accordingly, the interviewer should also ask the interviewee what they are thinking whenever they take long pauses (Willis, 1999, 1). Another strategy of CI that could be applied is known as verbal probing; here, the officer "asks the survey question [does not have to be a survey question in the case of detecting deception], and the subject answers, the interviewer then asks for other, specific information relevant to the question, or to the specific answer given" (Willis, 1999, 5). It is important to recognize that for the purposes of detecting deception, the specific details of the CI method are not entirely applicable. However, the two above-mentioned

techniques will particularly allow the personnel interviewing subjects more time to identify whether the subjects are showing any of the noted verbal or non-verbal cues. **NOTE:** This may not apply to daily discussions of law enforcement/intelligence personnel who must conduct brief interviews with individuals.

2. **When Analyzing Individual Responses, Do Not Over-Analyze and/or Allow Personal Beliefs or Biases to Skew Judgment:** It is important to quickly identify the cues without spending too much time on whether or not there is a possibility that the individual is lying or telling the truth and in-turn more closely trying to purposefully identify specific cues to fulfill a biased agenda. This also expands to scenarios in which officers must interrogate several individuals with regard to the same case. Consequent to interviewing several individuals, it is apparent that there will be components of the stories that corroborate and complement one another. Nevertheless, in order for the model to work effectively, it will be important that the individuals are analyzed objectively. It may be possible for the interviewers to identify common patterns, yet the model should not be used to fulfill biased opinions with regard to patterns in individuals' stories. Therefore, the model should be applied without biases; otherwise, it will merely become a tool that can be used to substantiate and validate subjective claims.
3. **Taking Notes is Not Mandatory, But Can Be Conducive to Appropriate Detection of Deception:** There are fourteen non-verbal cues, whereas there are only six verbal cues; therefore, it may be possible to remember the six cues and mentally observe the individuals being interviewed. However, to remember each of the fourteen cues would require at least general training, yet even in these cases it may be difficult for officials to take into consideration the cues whilst also ensuring that they are asking the most appropriate questions and gaining all information that is necessary under the specific circumstances. Therefore, the use of a worksheet that would list out the cues would provide the officials with an opportunity to speak to the individuals, and then check any cues that are noticed without having to remember the cues at the time. This is the reason why the verbal and non-verbal cue tables were incorporated in this chapter.

FUTURE RESEARCH DIRECTIONS

Officials who plan to utilize the model should take the three aforementioned suggestions into consideration. Accordingly, if this model is to be used in professional settings it may be more appropriate to establish a training course that would prepare officials to use the model on a timely basis. As is the case with any novel implementation, individuals may have difficulties in becoming comfortable with the new techniques; thus, it is of the utmost importance that the individuals are able to effectively use the model prior to applying it in the field. A training course to direct the officers on how to use the model would not require months, or many weeks. Rather the training could be broken down into four major components and taught throughout a six-week process. Each of the weeks would require devotion to the learning of the model, yet it would not overwhelm the officers by taking too much time out of their daily lives.

- **1st Week:** Officers are provided with worksheets and readings that allow them to immerse themselves in the understanding of what is deception, common deceptive practices, and how the model itself works. This week will be the introductory phase that would establish a basis for officers to understand what is expected in detecting deception. This week would be representative of a "flipped classroom" whereby students are provided materials to read and/or watch, and then attend the classes to discuss what has been learnt. The officers should feel comfortable to openly discuss the material, explain any challenges in understanding the materials, and actively engage in discussions with fellow officers to ensure that every individual in the course has progressed at the same pace.

- **2nd Week:** This week should be devoted to allowing the officers to watch videos of individuals who are telling the truth and/or lying. When the analyses for this research were conducted, the entire process was new, since no training had been undergone prior to the beginning of the project. Whilst the results have proven that the model can be used by those without training, the six-week course would be useful for those officers who wish to further learn about the processes that are involved in detecting deception. Accordingly, this week would be the prime time for officers to become accustomed to watching brief interviews with individuals and identify the non-verbal and verbal cues. The instructors in this course, especially during this week, should allow the officers to learn their most comfortable strategies to identify the cues and note them down. For instance, when the research was conducted for this work, the verbal and non-verbal cues were listed on two separate excel sheets. As the cues were recognized, a check mark was entered into the graph, which ultimately allowed for further analyses.
- **3rd Week:** By the end of week 2, the officers should be well aware of the discipline of detecting deception and should feel more comfortable in watching interviews and recognizing the cues. Therefore, this week should be devoted to allowing the officers to conduct interviews amongst themselves within the regulations of their divisions, while also noting the cues exemplified by the interviewees. They should also be made aware, if not already, of the CI method. The officers should recognize the extent to which the model can be applied and how they can personalize their own interviewing styles to incorporate the use of the model. This week should allow the officers to experiment with the model.
- **4th Week:** Based on the results of the previous research to develop the DETECT model, there was a lack of cultural variety in the selected participants. Since each of the participants were born and raised in and around the same areas in Eastern Tennessee (e.g. Tazewell, TN, Claiborne, TN, & Harrogate, TN), there was a lack of context to establish the possible differences that may have arisen had there been a broader range of individuals with a wider variety of backgrounds. Thus, for those who have chosen to take the course, this training week would be extremely useful to allow the officials to interview individuals and determine the different ways in which certain individuals answer questions based on their background. Overall, this week would be a continuation of the practices for week 3.
- **5th Week:** This week should be a review week for the officers to once again gather around and take part in lively discussions. Furthermore, these discussions would allow the officers to discuss patterns or strategies that they have developed over the course of the past weeks. The instructors should facilitate detailed discussions to determine whether or not the individuals seem to have a strong understanding of what has been taught and what is required in the use of the model. The instructor should ask general questions and ask all the participants to discuss their answers with one another. The individuals should also be asked to complete minimum one-page essays wherein they must prove their knowledge of the model and the background of detecting deception.

- **6th Week:** The fifth week is essentially the week of the course in which the instructor determines whether or not the participants have an adequate understanding of the model and the discipline. This week the instructor must return the graded papers with either a P for pass or an F for fail. The participants will be allowed to engage in group detection of deception activities in which they will be once again allowed to practice their skills. However, in this case, the officers will be working in groups, rather than on their own. This week will ultimately act as a cumulative review of all information that has been taught over the course of the six weeks.

CONCLUSION

In its entirety, the DETECT model is an effective resource for law enforcement and intelligence personnel to detect individual-level deception without reliance on advanced technology. The model is flexible and can be applied in a wide range of situations without requiring the practitioner to physically be in the presence of an individual. This is particularly useful in a society wherein a majority of activities revolve around technology and social media. Thus, the DETECT model can be applied on a face-to-face basis (which the author suggests is the most effective strategy), yet can also be executed through social media and online networking sites.

Furthermore, due to the issues pertaining to the trust amongst the public and law enforcement and intelligence personnel, there will be greater hurdles in appropriately applying the DETECT model. If the public purposefully act in irregular manners, due to their angst over the ways in which law enforcement and intelligence matters have been handled in recent times, then the DETECT model may result in incorrect results. However, prior research on the DETECT model only proved one case wherein an incorrect determination was made; in that case, the individual was being truthful, yet the model assessed that the individual was being deceitful. Therefore, it is herein argued that the DETECT model will still be useful in cases of odd behavior by individuals, since it will be safer to incorrectly assume that an individual is being deceitful and investigate further, rather incorrectly assume that an individual is being truthful and allow him/her to flee without further questioning.

Deception is not that which laymen can easily detect with high accuracy without training in the discipline. Accordingly, the DETECT model itself was designed for law enforcement officials, such as police officers, and intelligence personnel who must conduct individual-level interviews to determine deception. Further investigation could lead to the determination that this model would be particularly useful for the Transportation Security Administration (TSA), since these professionals encounter countless individuals on a daily basis, and they must, at times, ask questions that only require one-word answers. Through the use of DETECT, the officers would most probably have higher probability rates of detecting deception and further securing U.S. borders at the domestic and international levels. The future of detecting deception will rely on the research that is conducted today, in the twenty-first century. There will be no major improvements that can aid in the safeguarding of intelligence systems and the upholding of the national security of the country if there is no impetus to focus on this research topic and place a priority on improving the ways in which government officials can determine if an individual is being deceptive. If a government official cannot detect deception, then the risk of falling victim to D&D, and then compromising the security of the country is raised. As more of these officials fail to recognize deceit, the overall safety standards of the country will begin to waver. Therefore, the research work that has been presented here adds to the existing body of knowledge by providing a novel avenue whereby law enforcement officers and intelligence officers may detect deception on a timely basis. Of course, there may be instances in which the model cannot be applied; yet, in a majority of the instances, the utilization of the model is plausible. Thus, the work has added a novel facet to be further explored and investigated by researchers in the field who have an avid, yet unbiased interest in the determination of the overall effectiveness of the model in a wide array of circumstances.

Finally, it is paramount to note that as technology advances, law enforcement and intelligence personnel may feel more enthusiastically about utilizing novel technological devises to detect deception, rather than relying upon models that require traditional methods of writing and examining data. However, the responsibility of law enforcement and intelligence officers is to aid in the efforts to protect the nation domestically and internationally; therefore, the most useful model should be utilized, not the one that has gained the most publicity or acknowledgment from the media. The pure goal of detecting deception for government officials is to predict, and then prevent any deceptive practices that may cause harm to the country or those living within the nation. In its entirety, DETECT is a model that has been tested through non-parametric statistical analyses and has proven to be acceptable and extremely useful in the successful identification of deception in a majority of individual-level interviews. Accordingly, it is hoped that this branch of research will become more widely known and an emphasis will be placed on the testing of this model scenarios different to those tested in previous research. Accordingly, as this research has come to a conclusion, it is imperative to note that DETECT may have a perfect place within the fields of intelligence and law enforcement; thus, the development and completion of this research is a call to fellow researchers to take an initiative to test, examine, and report about this model and aid in the improvement of this model to provide officers with an effective means of detecting deception.

REFERENCES

Biometrics.gov. (n.d.). *Biometrics.* Retrieved from http://www.biometrics.gov/mediaroom/fastfacts.aspx

Clapper, J. R. (2015). *Worldwide Threat Assessment of the US Intelligence Community.* Retrieved from http://www.dni.gov/files/documents/Unclassified_2015_ATA_SFR_-_SASC_FINAL.pdf

Colwell, K., Hiscock-Anisman, C. K., Memon, A., Taylor, L., & Prewett, J. (2007). Assessment Criteria Indicative of Deception (ACID): An integrated system of investigative interviewing and detecting deception. *Journal of Investigative Psychology and Offender Profiling*, *4*(3), 167–180. doi:10.1002/jip.73

Da Silva, C. S., & Leach, A. M. (2013). Detecting Deception in Second-Language Speakers. *Legal and Criminological Psychology*, *18*(1), 115–127. doi:10.1111/j.2044-8333.2011.02030.x

de Silva, E. (2003). Intelligence and Policy in Combating Terrorism. In R. Gunaratna (Ed.), *Terrorism in the Asia-Pacific. Threat and Response* (pp. 108–133). Singapore: Eastern Universities Press.

Eastern Michigan University. (2001). *EMU Faculty Publications.* Retrieved http://www.emich.edu/library/notablecollection/facpub/publist.php?department=Management%20and%20Law&page=10

Godson, R., & Wirtz, J. J. (2000). Strategic Denial and Deception. *Trends in Organized Crime*, *6*(6), 5–16. doi:10.1007/s12117-000-1002-2

Google Scholar. (2014). *Kevin Colwell.* Retrieved from http://scholar.google.com/citations?user=HWwtbD8AAAAJ&hl=en

Hartwig, M., Granhag, P. A., Stromwall, L., Wolf, A. G., Vrij, A., & Roos Hjelmsater, E. (2011). Detecting Deception in Suspects: Verbal Cues as a Function of Interview Strategy. *Psychology, Crime & Law*, *17*(7), 643–656. doi:10.1080/10683160903446982

Matsumoto, D., Hwang, H. S., Skinner, L., and Frank, M. (2011). Evaluating Truthfulness and Detecting Deception. *FBI Law Enforcement Bulletin*, (80), 1-8.

Navarro, J. (2012). Detecting Deception. *FBI Law Enforcement Bulletin*, (81), 7-11.

Waltman, J. L. & Golen, S. P. (1993). Detecting Deception During Interviews. *Internal Auditor*, 50, 61-63.

Warmelink, L., Vrij, A., Mann, S., & Granhag, P. A. (2013). Spatial and Temporal Details in Intentions: A Cue to Detecting Deception. *Applied Cognitive Psychology*, *27*(1), 101–106. doi:10.1002/acp.2878

Weintraub, W. (2005). Verbal Behavior and Personality Assessment. In J. M. Post (Ed.), *Psychological Assessment of Political Leaders: With Profiles of Saddam Hussein and Bill Clinton* (pp. 215–271). Michigan: University of Michigan Press.

Whaley, B., & Busby, J. (2000). Detecting Deception: Practice, Practitioners, and Theory. *Trends in Organized Crime*, *6*(6), 73–104. doi:10.1007/s12117-000-1007-x

Willis, G. B. (1999). *Cognitive Interviewing: A "How To" Guide.* Retrieved from http://www.uiowa.edu/~c07b209/interview.pdf

KEY TERMS AND DEFINITIONS

Cybersecurity: The strategies and measures that are taken to ensure the protection of computer systems.

Deception: The effort to ensure that an individual believes a false story that will ultimately result in a reaction that serves the benefit of the practitioner.

Denial and Deception (D&D): The blend of denial and deception to achieve one's own objectives; this can be separated into A-Type deception (causing ambiguity) and M-Type deception (misleading an adversary).

Denial: Blocking information to ensure that an individual cannot access the truth about a situation; thus, resulting in the individual's inability to appropriately react.

DETECT Model (©, Eugenie de Silva, 2014): This model is based on verbal and non-verbal cues to aid in the timely detection of deception at the individual-level. It was first designed and tested for law enforcement and intelligence personnel by Eugenie de Silva in 2014.

Intelligence Community (IC) (U.S.): The syndication of seventeen organizations and agencies that work in the U.S. to gather information and disseminate intelligence to aid in the maintenance of national security.

Non-Verbal Cues: Physical movements or non-movements exemplified by an individual.

Verbal Cues: The words or noises actually spoken or made by an individual.

Compilation of References

Inside the NSA's War on Internet Security. (2014, December 28). *Der Spiegel Online*. Retrieved from http://www.spiegel.de/international/germany/inside-the-nsa-s-war-on-Internet-security-a-1010361.html

A Framework for Understanding Terrorist Use of the Internet. (2006). *ITAC, 2*, The Canadian Centre for Intelligence and Security Studies, The Norman Paterson School of International Affairs, Carleton University. Retrieved from http://www4.carleton.ca/cifp/app/serve.php/1121.pdf

Abbate, J. (2001). Government, Business, and the Making of the Internet. *Business History Review* (Special Issue), *75*(1), 147-176.

Aid, M. (2013, June). Inside the NSA's ultra-secret China hacking group. *Foreign Policy*. Retrieved from http://foreignpolicy.com/2013/06/10/inside-the-nsas-ultra-secret-china-hacking-group/

Aid, M. (2012). *The Secret Sentry*. London: Bloomsbury.

Aldrich, R. (2006). *GCHQ*. London: Heinemann.

Aldrich, R. J. (2002). *The hidden hand: Britain, America, and cold war secret intelligence*. New York: Overlook Press.

Alexander, M. G., Levin, S., & Henry, P. J. (2005). Image theory, social identity, and social dominance: Structural characteristics and individual motives underlying international images. *Political Psychology*, *26*(1), 27–45. doi:10.1111/j.1467-9221.2005.00408.x

Alford, W. P. (2004). *To steal a book is an elegant offense*. Stanford, CA: Stanford University Press.

Allport, G. W. (1954). *The nature of prejudice*. Garden City: Doubleday.

Anonymous (n. d.). We are the ninety nine per cent [YouTube Video]. Retrieved 21 April 2014 from http://www.youtube.com/watch?v=o74sMCU_kPQ

Anonymous. (n. d.). We are Anonymous [YouTube Video] Retrieved 20 April 2014 from http://www.youtube.com/watch?v=AcDnjFemPuc

Anspaha, K. (2008, September 25). The Integration of Islam in Europe: Preventing the radicalization of Muslim Diasporas and counterterrorism policy. *Paper presented at the ECPR 4TH Pan-European conference on EU Politics*. Retrieved from http://www.jhubc.it/ecpr-riga/virtualpaperroom/026.pdf

Arendt, H. (1954). *Between Past and Future*. London: Penguin.

Arendt, H. (2005). *The Promise of Politics New York: Random House Hannah Arendt, (1951) The Origins of Totalitarianism*. New York: Houghton Mifflin Harcourt.

Aristotle, . (1946). *The Politics Oxford*. Clarendon Press.

Arquilla, J., & Ronfeldt, D. (2001). Networks and Netwars: The Future of Terror, Crime, and Militancy. Santa Monica, C.A.: RAND Publications.

Ashour, O. (2010). Online De-Radicalization? Countering Violent Extremist Narratives: Message, Messenger and Media Strategy, *Perspectives on Terrorism, 4*(6). Retrieved from http://www.terrorismanalysts.com/pt/index.php/pot/article/view/128/html

Axelrod, R., & Iliev, R. (2014). Timing of cyber conflict. *Proceedings of the National Academy of Sciences of the United States of America, 111*(4), 1298–1303. doi:10.1073/pnas.1322638111 PMID:24474752

BakerHostetter. (2015, May 23). *Data Breach Charts*. Retrieved from http://www.bakerlaw.com/files/Uploads/Documents/Data%20Breach%20documents/Data_Breach_Charts.pdf/

Bamford, J. (1983). *The Puzzle Palace*. London: Penguin Books.

Barnett, A. (2000). Corporate Populism and Partyless Democracy. *New Left Review*, (May-June): 1–8.

Barron-Lopez, L. (2014, June). Cyber threats put energy sector on red alert. *The Hill*. Retrieved from http://thehill.com/policy/technology/209116-cyber-threats-put-energy-sector-on-red-alert

Bazilian, M., Rogner, H., Howells, M., Hermann, S., Arent, D., Gielen, D., & Yumkella, K. K. et al. (2011). Considering the energy, water and food nexus: Towards an integrated modeling approach. *Energy Policy, 39*(12), 7896–7906. doi:10.1016/j.enpol.2011.09.039

Beam, L. (1992, January). Leaderless Resistance. *The Seditionist, 12*, 1–5.

Berwick, A. (2013). 2083 A European Declaration of Independence. London: self-published

Bey, H. (n. d.). *The Information War*. Hermetic Library. Retrieved from http://hermetic.com/bey/infowar.html

Bierend, D. (2012, June 12). Google Is Evil. *Wired*. Retrieved from http://www.wired.com/2012/06/opinion-google-is-evil/

Biersteker, T. J., & Eckert, S. E. (2007). *Countering the Financing of Terrorism*. Oxford: Routledge Press.

Bingham, J. (2013). Margaret Thatcher: Seconds from Death at Hands of an IRA Bomber. *The Telegraph*. Retrieved from http://www.telegraph.co.uk/news/politics/margaret-thatcher/9979915/Margaret-Thatcher-Seconds-from-death-at-the-hands-of-an-IRA-bomber.html

Biometrics.gov. (n.d.). *Biometrics*. Retrieved from http://www.biometrics.gov/mediaroom/fastfacts.aspx

Bono, M. (2015, January 20). The need for a national data breach law. *The Hill*. Retrieved from http://thehill.com/blogs/pundits-blog/technology/229968-the-need-for-a-national-data-breach-notification-law/

Bosco, F. (2013). Terrorist Use of the Internet. In U. Gürbuz (Ed.), *Capacity Building in the Fight Against Terrorism* (pp. 39–46). Amsterdam: IOS Press.

Botelho, G. (2015). Terror Attacks on 3 Continents; ISIS Claims Responsibility in Tunisia, Kuwait. *CNN*. Retrieved from http://www.cnn.com/2015/06/26/africa/tunisia-terror-attack/

Brandom, R. (2014, December 28). New documents reveal which encryption tools the NSA couldn't crack. *The Verge*. Retrieved from http://www.theverge.com/2014/12/28/7458159/encryption-standards-the-nsa-cant-crack-pgp-tor-otr-snowden

Brandon, J. (2009). *Unlocking Al-Qaeda - Islamist Extremism in British Prisons*. London: Quilliam.

Bransombe, N. R., Ellemers, N., Spears, R., & Doosje, B. (1999). The context and content of social identity threat. In N. Ellemers, R. Spears, & B. Doosje (Eds.), *Social identity: Context, commitment, content* (pp. 35–58). Oxford: Blackwell.

Brenner, J. (2011). *America the vulnerable: Inside the new threat matrix of digital espionage, crime, and warfare.* New York: Penguin Press.

Brewer, M. B. (2011). Identity and conflict. In D. Bar-Tal (Ed.), *Intergroup conflicts and their resolution: A social psychological perspective* (pp. 125–143). New York: Psychology Press.

Brinkmann, B. H., Bower, M. R., Stengel, K. A., Worrell, G. A., & Stead, M. (2009). Large-scale electrophysiology: Acquisition, compression, encryption, and storage of big data. *Journal of Neuroscience Methods, 180*(1), 185–192. doi:10.1016/j.jneumeth.2009.03.022 PMID:19427545

Brown, R. (2000). *Group processes.* Malden, MA: Blackwell.

Bukay, D. (2006, Fall). The Religious Foundations of Suicide Bombings Islamist Ideology. *Middle East Quarterly, 13*(4), 27–36. Retrieved from http://www.meforum.org/1003/the-religious-foundations-of-suicide-bombings

Buzan, B. (1998). *Ole Wver & Jaap De Wilde. Security: a new framework for analysis* (p. 239). Lynne Rienner Publishers.

Byman, D., & Waxman, M. (2002). *The Dynamics of Coercion: American Foreign Policy and the Limits of Military Might* (p. 78). New York: Cambridge University Press.

Caeiro, A. (2003, March 19-23). The European Council for Fatwa and Research. Proceedings of the *Fourth Mediterranean Social and Political Research Meeting*, European University Institute, Florence.

Cai, T., Zhao, C., & Xu, Q. (2012). Energy network dispatch optimization under emergency of local energy shortage. *Energy, 42*(1), 132–145. doi:10.1016/j.energy.2012.04.001

Carmichael, J. (2014, August 19). Google Knows You Better Than You Know Yourself. *The Atlantic.* Retrieved from http://www.theatlantic.com/technology/archive/2014/08/google-knows-you-better-than-you-know-yourself/378608/

Carnegie Endowment for International Peace. (2013). *U.S.-China security perceptions survey: findings and implications.* Washington, D.C. Retrieved from http://cusef.org.hk/wp-content/uploads/2014/05/02_eng.pdf

Carr, C. (Ed.). (2000). *The book of war: Sun-Tzu the art of warfare & Karl Von Clausewitz on war.* New York: The Modern Library.

Carswell, D. (2013, October 22). The Front national is the most popular party in France. The Telegraph. Retrieved from http://blogs.telegraph.co.uk/news/douglascarswellmp/100242451/the-front-national-is-the-most-popular-party-in-france-are-you-happy-now-eurocrats/

Carter, J. A., Maher, S., & Neumann, P. R. (2014). #Greenbirds: Measuring Importance and Influence in Syrian Foreign Fighter Networks. *ICSR* report. King's College, London. Retrieved from http://icsr.info/wp-content/uploads/2014/04/ICSR-Report-Greenbirds-Measuring-Importance-and-Infleunce-in-Syrian-Foreign-Fighter-Networks.pdf

Cartin, J. M. (2014). Don't forget the humans: Toward a 21st century offensive cyber strategy. *Global Security Studies, 5*(2), 1–26.

Castells, M. (1996). The Information Age: Economy. Society and Culture: Vol. 1. *The Rise of the Network Society.* Oxford: Blackwell Publishing.

Castells, M. (1997). *The Power of Identity: The Information Age, Economy, Society, and Culture* (Vol. 2). Oxford: Blackwell Publishers.

CBS News. (2010). *Cyber War: Sabotaging the System.* Retrieved from http://www.cbsnews.com/news/cyber-war-sabotaging-the-system-10-06-2010/5/

Center for Strategic and International Studies. (2010). *U.S. Cybersecurity Policy and the Role of U.S. Cybercom: Cyber Security Policy Debate Series.* Retrieved from https://www.nsa.gov/public_info/_files/speeches_testimonies/100603_alexander_transcript.pdf

Chandrasekaran, R., & Corcoran, E. (1997, July 18). Human Errors Block E-Mail, Web Sites in Internet Failure: Garbled Address Files From Va. Firm Blamed. *The Washington Post,* A1.

Chen, D. (2013). China's state-owned enterprises: How much do we know? From CNOOC to its siblings. *The School of Public Policy*, 6(19), 1-27. Retrieved from http://www.policyschool.ucalgary.ca/sites/default/files/research/china-soes-final.pdf

Chen, D. Q., Chen, W. B., Soong, M., Soong, S. J., & Orthner, H. F. (2009). Turning Access (TM) into a web-enabled secure information system for clinical trials. *Clinical Trials*, *6*(4), 378–385. doi:10.1177/1740774509338228 PMID:19625330

Cheng, J. Y. S. (2012). Convincing the world of China's tradition to pursue universal harmony. *Journal of Chinese Political Science*, *17*(2), 165–185. doi:10.1007/s11366-012-9191-5

China targets own operating system to take on likes of Microsoft, Google. (2014, August 24). *Reuters*. Retrieved from http://www.reuters.com/article/2014/08/24/china-technology-idUSL3N0QU07420140824

Chiusano, P. (2014, December 8). *The failed economics of our software commons, and what you can about it right now.* Retrieved from http://pchiusano.github.io/2014-12-08/failed-software-economics

Chomsky, N. (2004). *Hegemony and Survival, America's Quest for Global Dominance London.* Penguin.

Cho, Y. C., & Pan, J. Y. (2014). Hybrid Network Defense Model Based on Fuzzy Evaluation. *TheScientificWorldJournal*, *2014*,1–12. doi:10.1155/2014/178937 PMID:24574870

Chun, S., Shulman, S., Sandoval, R., & Hovy, E. (2010). Government 2.0: Making Connections between Citizens, Data and Government. *Information Polity Journal*, *15*(1–2), 1–9.

Church of Jesus Christ Christian Aryan Nations Converse. (n. d.). Retrieved from https://www.aryan-nations.org

Clapper, J. R. (2015). *Worldwide Threat Assessment of the US Intelligence Community.* Retrieved from http://www.dni.gov/files/documents/Unclassified_2015_ATA_SFR_-_SASC_FINAL.pdf

Clark, D.D. & Landau, S. (2011). Untangling Attribution. *Harvard National Security Journal*, *2*(1), 30.

Clastres, C. (2011). Smart grids: Another step towards competition, energy security and climate change objectives. *Energy Policy*, *39*(9), 5399–5408. doi:10.1016/j.enpol.2011.05.024

Coates, S. (2014, January). Voters' trust in society is collapsing, says Ashdown. *The Times.*

Cockburn, A., & Cockburn, L. (1991). *Dangerous liaisons: The inside story of the U.S.-Israeli covert relationship.* New York: HarperCollins.

Cohen, N. (2007). *What's Left? How the Left lost it's way.* London: Harper.

Cohn, N. (1969). *The Pursuit of the Millennium.* London: Paladin.

Coll, S., & Glasser, S. B. (2005, August 7). Terrorists turn to the Web as base of operations, *The Washington Post*, A1.

Collins, K. (2014). *Guns, Gore and Girls: The Rise of Cyber Cartels.* Retrieved from http://www.wired.co.uk/news/archive/2014-11/05/cyber-cartels

Colwell, K., Hiscock-Anisman, C. K., Memon, A., Taylor, L., & Prewett, J. (2007). Assessment Criteria Indicative of Deception (ACID): An integrated system of investigative interviewing and detecting deception. *Journal of Investigative Psychology and Offender Profiling*, *4*(3), 167–180. doi:10.1002/jip.73

Committee on Energy and Commerce. (2015). Data security and breach notification act of 2015. Retrieved from http://energycommerce.house.gov/sites/republicans.energycommerce.house.gov/files/analysis/20150312DataSecuritySummary.pdf

Conway, M. (2006). Terrorism and the Internet: New Media - New Threat? *Parliamentary Affairs*, *59*(2), 283–298. doi:10.1093/pa/gsl009

Cooper, A. (2015, March 2). *Air Traffic Control System Vulnerable to Cyberattack.* Retrieved from http://www.cnn.com/2015/03/02/politics/cyberattack-faa-air-traffic-control-hacking/

Cooper, B. (1999). *Eric Voegelin and the Foundations of Modern Political Science* Columbia: University of Missouri Press Bernard Crick (1962, 2005). In *Defence of Politics*. London: Continuum.

Corenblum, B., & Stephan, W. G. (2001). White fears and native apprehensions: An integrated threat theory approach to intergroup attitudes. *Canadian Journal of Behavioural Science*, *33*(4), 251–268. doi:10.1037/h0087147

Cottam, M. (1994). *Images &intervention: U.S. policies in Latin America*. Pittsburgh, PA: University of Pittsburgh Press.

Cottam, M., Dietz-Uhler, B., Mastors, E. M., & Preston, T. (2004). *Introduction to political psychology*. Mahwah, New Jersey: Lawrence Erlbaum Associates.

Cottam, R. (1977). *Foreign policy motivation: A general theory and a case study*. Pittsburgh, PA: University of Pittsburgh Press.

Coutant, D. K., Worchel, S., & Hanza, M. (2011). Pigs, slingshots, and other foundations of intergroup conflict. In D. Bar-Tal (Ed.), *Intergroup conflicts and their resolution: A social psychological perspective* (pp. 39–59). New York: Psychology Press.

Da Silva, C. S., & Leach, A. M. (2013). Detecting Deception in Second-Language Speakers. *Legal and Criminological Psychology*, *18*(1), 115–127. doi:10.1111/j.2044-8333.2011.02030.x

Dahl, R. (1989). Democracy and its Critics. New Haven, C.T.: Yale University Press.

Danitz, T., & Stobel, W. P. (2001). Networking Dissent: Cyber Activists Use the Internet to Promote Democracy in Burma. In J. Arquilla & D. Ronfeldt (Eds.), Networks and Netwars: The Future of Terror, Crime, and Militancy (pp. 129-170). Santa Monica, C.A.: RAND Publications.

Davis, R. T. (Ed.), (2010). U.S. Foreign Policy and National Security: Chronology and Index for the 20th Century (Praeger Security International Series Illustrated ed.) (pp. xiii–xiv). ABC-CLIO.

de Armond, P. (2001). Netwar in the Emerald City: WTO Protest Strategy and Tactics. In J. Arquilla & D. Ronfeldt (Eds.), Networks and Netwars: The Future of Terror, Crime, and Militancy (pp. 201-238). Santa Monica, C.A.: RAND Publications.

de Silva, E. (2003). Intelligence and Policy in Combating Terrorism. In R. Gunaratna (Ed.), *Terrorism in the Asia-Pacific. Threat and Response* (pp. 108–133). Singapore: Eastern Universities Press.

Defense Budget Priorities and Choices—Fiscal Year 2014. (April 2013). The United States Department of Defense.

Deibert, R. J. (2002). The Politics of Internet Design: Securing the Foundations for Global Civil Society Networks. *Institute of Intergovernmental Relations Conference Paper*. Retrieved from http://www.iigr.ca/conferences/archive/pdfs1/deibert.pdf

Deibert, R. J. (2000). International Plug 'n Play?: Citizen Activism, the Internet and Global Public Policy. *International Studies Perspectives*, *1*(3), 255–272. doi:10.1111/1528-3577.00026

del Valle, A. (2010) I Rossi Neri, Verdi: la convergenza degli Estremi opposti. Islamismo, comunismo, neonazismo, Torino: Lindau

Denning, D. E. (2001). Activism, Hactivism and Cyberterrorism: The Internet as a Tool for Influencing Foreign Policy. In J. Arquilla & D. Ronfeldt (Eds.), Networks and Netwars: The Future of Crime, Terrorism and Militancy (pp. 171-199). Santa Monica, C.A.: RAND Publications.

Devanny, J., & Harris, J. (2014). The National Security Council: national security at the centre of government. Institute for Government & King's College London.

Diamond, J. (2005). Malthus in Africa: Rwanda's Genocide. In Collapse: How societies choose to fail or succeed.

Dice, M. (2014), *FBI Citizens Academy: Counterintelligence*. Retrieved from http://www.counton2.com/story/26181957/fbi-citizens-academy-counterintelligence

Dilanian, K. (2011, October 4). China cyber attacks threaten U.S. security, official says. *Los Angeles Times*. Retrieved from http://articles.latimes.com/2011/oct/04/news/la-pn-china-cyberattacks-20111004

Drogin, B., & Goetz, J. (2005). *How U.S. Fell Under the Spell of Curveball*. Retrieved from http://downloadswww.leadingtowar.com/PDFsources_claims_nomobile/2000_2001_Jan_Sept_comndrms.pdf

Dutton, W. H., Gillet, S. E., McKnight, L. W., & Peltu, M. (2003, August). Broadband Internet: The Power to Reconfigure Access. *Oxford Internet Institute Forum Discussion Paper No. 1*.

Dvorak, K. (2013, June 18). Old regulations inhibit new technologies. *The Hill*. Retrieved from http://thehill.com/opinion/op-ed/306377-old-regulations-inhibit-new-technologies

Dyck, C., Frese, M., Baer, M., & Sonnentag, S. (2005). Organizational error management culture and its impact on performance: A two-study replication. *The Journal of Applied Psychology*, *90*(6), 1228–1240. doi:10.1037/0021-9010.90.6.1228 PMID:16316276

Eastern Michigan University. (2001). *EMU Faculty Publications*. Retrieved http://www.emich.edu/library/notablecollection/facpub/publist.php?department=Management%20and%20Law&page=10

Egan, M. (2014, December 22). *Thank you Sony! Cybersecurity Stock Soar*. Retrieved from http://money.cnn.com/2014/12/22/investing/sony-cybersecurity-stocks/

Eickelman, D. F. (1998, Winter). Inside the Islamic Reformation. *The Wilson Quarterly*, *22*(1), 80–89.

Eickelman, D. F., & Piscatori, J. (Eds.), (1990). *Muslim Travellers: Piegrimage, Migration and the Religious Imagination*. Berkeley: University of California Press.

Esman, A. R. (2014, April 25). Experts Warn More European Muslim Youth Are Radicalizing. *IPT News*. Retrieved from http://www.investigativeproject.org/4362/experts-warn-more-european-muslim-youth-are#

Executive Office of the President. (2011). *A Policy Framework for the 21st Century Grid: Enabling Our Secure Energy Future*. Retrieved from http://www.whitehouse.gov/sites/default/files/microsites/ostp/nstc-smart-grid-june2011.pdf

Executive Office of the President. (2013). *Economic Benefits of Increasing Electric Grid Resilience to Weather Outages.* Retrieved from http://energy.gov/sites/prod/files/2013/08/f2/Grid%20Resiliency%20Report_FINAL.pdf

Fan, L. J., Wang, Y. Z., Jin, X. L., Li, J. Y., Cheng, X. Q., & Jin, S. Y. (2013). Comprehensive Quantitative Analysis on Privacy Leak Behavior. *Plos One, 8*(9). DOI:10.1371/journal.pone.0073410

Federal Bureau of Investigation. (2013). *Six Chinese Nationals Indicted for Conspiring to Steal Trade Secrets from U.S. Seed Companies.* Retrieved from http://www.fbi.gov/omaha/press-releases/2013/six-chinese-nationals-indicted-for-conspiring-to-steal-trade-secrets-from-u.s.-seed-companies

Federation of American Scientists. (2011). *Terms and Definitions of Interest for DoD Counterintelligence Professionals.* Retrieved from http://fas.org/irp/eprint/ci-glossary.pdf

Fenton, N. (2007). Contesting Global Capital, New Media, Solidarity and the Role of a Social Imaginary. In B. Cammaerts & N. Carpentier (Eds.), *Reclaiming the Media: Communication Rights and Democratic Media Roles* (pp. 225–242). Brussels: ECREA Series - Intellect.

Filipkowski, W. (2008). Cyber Laundering: An Analysis of Typology and Techniques. *International Journal of Criminal Justice Sciences*, 15-27.

Fink, N. C., & Hearne, E. B. (2008, October). Beyond Terrorism: Deradicalization and Disengagement from Violent Extremism. IPI Publications & International Peace Institute Report. Retrieved from http://www.ipinst.org/media/pdf/publications/beter.pdf

Finklea, K., & Theohary, C. A. (2013). *Cybercrime: Conceptual Issues for Congress and U.S. Law Enforcement.* Retrieved from http://fas.org/sgp/crs/misc/R42547.pdf

Fischer, R. J. (2006). Intergroup conflict. In M. Deutsch, P. T. Coleman, & E. E. Marcus (Eds.), *The handbook of conflict resolution* (pp. 176–196). San Francisco: Jossey-Bass.

Fishkin, J. S. (1995). *The Voice of the People*. New Haven, N.J.: Yale University Press.

Fitzpatrick, M. (2008, October 7). South Korea wants to gag the noisy Internet rabble. *The Guardian*. Retrieved from http://www.theguardian.com/technology/2008/oct/09/news.Internet

Flaccus, G. (2010). *Dongfan "Greg" Chung, Chinese Spy, Gets More Than 15 Years in Prison.* Retrieved from http://www.huffingtonpost.com/2010/02/08/dongfan-greg-chung-chines_n_454107.html

Fleisher, C. S., & Wright, S. (2009). Examining differences in competitive intelligence practice: China, Japan, and the West. *Thunderbird International Business Review*, *51*(3), 249–261. doi:10.1002/tie.20263

Fonte, J. (2002). Liberal Democracy versus Transnational Progressivism: The future of the ideological civil war within the West. *Orbis*, Summer, 1–14.

Fountain, S. (1999). *Peace Education in UNICEF.* Retrieved from http://www.unicef.org/education/files/PeaceEducation.pdf

Frangonikolopoulos, C. A. (2012). Global Civil Society and Deliberation in the Digital Age. *International Journal Electronic Governance*, *5*(1), 11–23. doi:10.1504/IJEG.2012.047440

Fry, J. (2006). Studying the Scholarly Web: How Disciplinary Culture Shapes Online Representations. *International Journal of Scientometrics, Informetrics and Bibliometrics, 10*(1).

Fry, J., & Talja, S. (2007). The Intellectual and Social Organization of Academic Fields and the Shaping of Digital Resources. *Journal of Information Science*, *33*(2), 115–133. doi:10.1177/0165551506068153

Fry, J., Virkar, S., & Schroeder, R. (2008). Search Engines and Expertise about Global Issues: Well-defined Landscape or Undomesticated Wilderness? In A. Spink & M. Zimmer (Eds.), *Web Search: Multidisciplinary Perspectives* (pp. 255–275). Berlin, Heidelberg: Springer Link-Verlag. doi:10.1007/978-3-540-75829-7_14

Gallagher, A. M. (1989). Social identity and the Northern Ireland conflict. *Human Relations*, *42*(10), 917–935. doi:10.1177/001872678904201004

Gartner. (2014, August 22). *Gartner Says Worldwide Information Security Spending Will Grow Almost 8 Percent in2014as Organizations Become More Threat-Aware*. Retrieved from http://www.gartner.com/newsroom/id/2828722

Geers, K. (2013, October 17). サイバー世界大戦:国家レベルの高度なサイバー攻撃 の背景を理解する (*World War C: Understanding Nation-State Motives Behind Today's Cyber Attacks*). Retrieved from https://www.fireeye.com/resources/pdfs/fireeye-wwc-report.pdf

Gelinas, R. R. (2010). Cyberdeterrence and the Problem of Attribution. Georgetown University, 1-26.

Gentile, E. M. R., & Mallett, R. (2000). The Sacralization of Politics: Definitions, Interpretations and Reflections on the Question of Secular Religion and Totalitarianism. *Totalitarian Movements and Political Religions*, *1*(1), 20–37. doi:10.1080/14690760008406923

George, A. (1979). The causal nexus between cognitive beliefs and decision-making behavior: The 'operational code. In L. S. Falkowski (Ed.), *Psychological Models in International Politics* (pp. 95–124). Boulder, CO: Westview Press.

German authorities arrest three people for alleged ties to Syrian radical group. (2014 March 31). *Deutsche Welle*. Retrieved from http://www.dw.de/german-authorities-arrest-three-people-for-alleged-ties-to-syrian-radical-group/a-17533472

German Right wing extremism. (n. d.). Retrieved from http://www.spiegel.de/international/topic/right_wing_extremism/

Gewirtz, D. (2011). Night dragon: Cyberwar meets corporate espionage. *Journal of Counterterrorism & Homeland Security International*, *17*(2), 6–8.

Gilbert, D. (September 30, 2013). World War C: How Understanding Geopolitics Can Help Protect Against Cyber Attacks, *International Business Times*. Retrieved from http://www.ibtimes.co.uk/world-war-c-cyber-attacks-motives-nation-510234

Gilligan, A. (2014, April 20). 'Trojan Horse' schools: the leaked inspectors report. *The Telegraph*. Retrieved from http://blogs.telegraph.co.uk/news/andrewgilligan/100268346/trojan-horse-schools-the-leaked-inspectors-report/

Glaser, B.S. (2014). US-China relations: Managing differences remains and urgent challenge. *Southeast Asian Affairs*, 76-82.

Godson, R., & Wirtz, J. J. (2000). Strategic Denial and Deception. *Trends in Organized Crime*, *6*(6), 5–16. doi:10.1007/s12117-000-1002-2

Goetinck, M. (2013, October 25). Syria: a magnet for European Radicalised Muslim Youngsters. *MEDEA Institute*. Retrieved from http://www.medea.be/2013/10/syria-a-magnet-for-european-radicalised-muslim-youngsters/

Golden, S. (2011). China's perception of risk and the concept of comprehensive national power. *The Copenhagen Journal of Asian Studies*, *29*(2), 79–109.

Google reveals child porn user. (2014, August 4). *BBC News*. Retrieved from http://www.bbc.com/news/technology-28639628

Google Scholar. (2014). *Kevin Colwell*. Retrieved from http://scholar.google.com/citations?user=HWwtbD8AAAAJ&hl=en

Government Digital Service. (2014). *Whistleblowing*. Retrieved from https://www.gov.uk/whistleblowing/overview

Greenberg, A. (2012, March 21). Meet The Hackers Who Sell Spies The Tools To Crack Your PC (And Get Paid Six-Figure Fees). *Forbes*. Retrieved from http://www.forbes.com/sites/andygreenberg/2012/03/21/meet-the-hackers-who-sell-spies-the-tools-to-crack-your-pc-and-get-paid-six-figure-fees/

Griffin, R. (1991). *The Nature of Fascism*. London: Pinter.

Guan, S. P., Zhang, Y., & Ji, Y. (2013). Privacy-Preserving Health Data Collection for Preschool Children. *Computational and Mathematical Methods in Medicine*. Doi:10.1155/2013/501607

Halpern, E., Sharvit, K., & Gross, J. J. (2011). Emotion and emotion regulation in intergroup conflict. In D. Bar-Tal (Ed.), *Intergroup conflicts and their resolution: A social psychological perspective* (pp. 83–102). New York: Psychology Press.

Harding, L. (2014). *The Snowden Files*. London: Faber and Faber.

Hardt, M., & Negri, A. (2001). *Empire*. Cambridge, Mass: Harvard University Press.

Harris, S. (2015, February 26). Top Spy: Small Hacks Are Bigger Threat Than "Cyber Armageddon." *The Daily Beast*. Retrieved from http://www.thedailybeast.com/articles/2015/02/26/top-spy-small-hacks-are-bigger-threat-than-cyber-armageddon.html

Hartwig, M., Granhag, P. A., Stromwall, L., Wolf, A. G., Vrij, A., & Roos Hjelmsater, E. (2011). Detecting Deception in Suspects: Verbal Cues as a Function of Interview Strategy. *Psychology, Crime & Law*, *17*(7), 643–656. doi:10.1080/10683160903446982

Harwood, P. G., & Lay, C. J. (2001, August-September). Surfing Alone: The Internet as a Facilitator of Social and Political Capital? *Paper prepared for the2001 Annual Meeting of American Political Science Association.*

Hathaway, M. (2014). Connected Choices: How the Internet is Changing Sovereign Decisions. *American Foreign Policy Interests*, *36*(5), 300–313. doi:10.1080/10803920.2014.969178

He, K. (2012). Undermining adversaries: Unipolarity, threat perception, and negative balancing strategies after the Cold War. *Security Studies*, *21*(2), 154–191. doi:10.1080/09636412.2012.679201

Herbig, K. (2008). *Changes in Espionage by Americans: 1947-2007*. Retrieved from http://fas.org/sgp/library/changes.pdf

Hermann, M. G. (2001). How decision units shape foreign policy: A theoretical framework. International Studies Association, 47-81.

Herrmann, R. K. (1985). *Perception and behavior in Soviet foreign policy*. Pittsburgh, PA: University of Pittsburgh Press.

Herrmann, R. K., & Keller, J. W. (2004). Beliefs, values, and strategic choice: U.S. leaders' decision to engage, contain, and use force in an era of globalization. *The Journal of Politics*, *66*(2), 557–580. doi:10.1111/j.1468-2508.2004.00164.x

Herrmann, R. K., Voss, J. F., Schooler, T., & Ciarrochi, J. (1997). Images in international relations: An experimental test of cognitive schemata. *International Studies Quarterly*, *41*(3), 403–433. doi:10.1111/0020-8833.00050

Hexter, J. H. (1973). *The Vision of Politics on the Eve of the Reformation*. New York: Basic Books.

Hezbollah Video Game - War with Israel. (2007). *CNN*. Retrieved from http://www.cnn.com/2007/WORLD/meast/08/16/hezbollah.game.reut/

Hillis, K., Petit, M., & Jarrett, K. (2013). *Google and the Culture of Search*. New York, N.Y.: Routledge Press.

Hindman, M., Tsioutsiouliklis, K., & Johnson, J. (2003). Googlearchy: How a Few Heavily-Linked Sites Dominate Politics on the Web. Proceedings of the *Annual Meeting of the Midwest Political Science Association*, Volume 4.

Hjortdal, M. (2011). China's use of cyber warfare: Espionage meets strategic deterrence. *Journal of Strategic Security*, *4*(2), 1–24. doi:10.5038/1944-0472.4.2.1

Hogg, M. A. (2001). A social identity theory of leadership. *Personality and Social Psychology Review*, *5*(3), 184–200. doi:10.1207/S15327957PSPR0503_1

Hogg, M. A. (2001). Social categorization, depersonalization, and group behavior. In M. A. Hogg & S. Tindale (Eds.), *Group processes* (pp. 56–85). Malden, MA: Blackwell.

Holl, S., & Spetalnick, M. (2014, December 19). Obama vows U.S. response to North Korea over Sony cyber attack. *Reuters*. Retrieved from http://www.reuters.com/article/2014/12/19/us-sony-cybersecurity-usa-idUSKBN0JX1MH20141219

Holsti, O. (1967). Cognitive dynamics and images of the enemy. In D. Finley, O. Holsti, & R. Fagen (Eds.), *Enemy in Politics* (pp. 25–96). Chicago: Rand McNally.

Hu, E. (2014, June 6). The 'cool war' with China is unseen, but comes with consequences. *National Public Radio*. Retrieved from http://www.npr.org/blogs/parallels/2014/06/06/318788569/the-cool-war-with-china-is-unseen-but-comes-with-consequences

Huysman, M., & Wulf, V. (2004). *Social Capital and Information Technology. Cambridge M.A.* M.I.T Press.

Indiana University Knowledgebase. (n. d.). *Introduction to Unix commands*. Retrieved from https://kb.iu.edu/d/afsk

Institute for Strategic Dialogue. (n. d.). The Role of Civil Society in counter-Radicalisation and De-Radicalisation, *PPN Working Paper*. Retrieved from http://www.strategicdialogue.org/allnewmats/idandsc2010/PPNPaper-CommunityEngagement.pdf

Interactive, C. B. S. (2015, February 6). *Car Hacked on 60 Minutes*. Retrieved from http://www.cbsnews.com/news/car-hacked-on-60-minutes/

International Telecommunication Union (ITU). (2014). *Measuring the Information Society Report*. Geneva, Switzerland: International Telecommunication Union.

Internet Society of China. (2002, March). *Public Pledge of Self-Regulation and Professional Ethics for China Internet Industry*.

ISC. (2013). *Intelligence and Security Committee*. Inquiry into Huawei.

ISC. (2014). Intelligence and Security Committee, Report on the Intelligence Relating to the Murder of Fusilier Lee Rigby.

Islam: Anti-terrorism fatwa launch in London. (2010, March 2). *SAJA FORUM*. Retrieved from http://www.sajaforum.org/2010/03/islam-antiterrorism-fatwa-to-be-issued-in-london.html

Jackson, J. (2013). NIST Denies Tampering with Encryption Standards. *PCWorld*, *10*(Sept), 13.

Jakub, J. (1998). *Spies and saboteurs: Anglo-American collaboration and rivalry in human intelligence collection and special operations, 1940-1945*. London: Macmillan.

Jansen, J. C., & Seebregts, A. J. (2010). Long-term energy services security: What is it and how can it be measured and valued? *Energy Policy*, *38*(4), 1654–1664. doi:10.1016/j.enpol.2009.02.047

Jervis, R. (1976). *Perception and misperception in international politics*. Princeton, NJ: Princeton University Press.

Johnson, B. (2014, March 2). The children taught at home about murder and bombings. *The Telegraph*. Retrieved from http://www.telegraph.co.uk/news/politics/10671841/The-children-taught-at-home-about-murder-and-bombings.html

Johnson, P. (1990). A Gale for all seasons'. *Spectator (London, England)*, *10*(November), 21–22.

Jones, D. M. (2005, Spring). Peace Through Conversation. *National Interest*, *79*, 1.

Jones, D. M., & Smith, M. L. R. (2014). *Sacred Violence Political Religion in a Secular Age*. London: Plagrave.

Jordan, T., & Taylor, P. A. (2004). *Hacktivism and Cyberwars: Rebels with a Cause?* London: Routledge Press.

Juris, J. S. (2005). The New Digital Media and Activist Networking within Anti–Corporate Globalization Movements. *The Annals of the American Academy of Political and Social Science*, *597*(1), 189–208. doi:10.1177/0002716204270338

Justice, J. (n. d.). *Frontline Facts & Stats. PBS*. Retrieved from http://www.pbs.org/wgbh/pages/frontline/shows/juvenile/stats/states.html

Kalathil, S., & Boas, T. C. (2010). *Open Networks, Closed Regimes: The Impact of the Internet on Authoritarian Rule*. Washington, D.C.: Carnegie Endowment for International Peace.

Kanwal, G. (2009). China's emerging cyber war doctrine. *Journal of Defense Studies*, *3*(3), 14–22.

Kaplowitz, N. (1984). Psychopolitical dimensions of international relations: The reciprocal effect of conflict strategies. *International Studies Quarterly*, *28*(4), 373–406. doi:10.2307/2600562

Katz, R. S., & Mair, P. (1995). Richard S Katz and Peter Mair, Changing Models of Party Organization and Party Democracy: The emergence of the cartel party. *Party Politics*, *1*(1), 5–31. doi:10.1177/1354068895001001001

Kello, L. (2013). The meaning of the cyber revolution: Perils to theory and statecraft. *International Security*, *38*(2), 7–40. doi:10.1162/ISEC_a_00138

Kelman, H. C. (2004). Reconciliation as identity change: A social psychological perspective. In Y. Bar-Siman-Tov (Ed.), *From conflict resolution to reconciliation* (pp. 11–124). Oxford: Oxford University Press. doi:10.1093/acprof:oso/9780195166439.003.0006

Kepes, B. (2013, December 4). Google Users—You're The Product, Not The Customer. *Forbes*. Retrieved from http://www.forbes.com/sites/benkepes/2013/12/04/google-users-youre-the-product-not-the-customer/

Kernighan, B. W., & Ritchie, D. M. (1988). *The C Programming Language* (2nd ed., p. 6). Englewood Cliffs, N.J: Prentice Hall.

Kerwin, D., & Stock, M. D. (2007, Fall). National Security and Immigration Policy: Reclaiming Terms, Measuring Success, and Setting Priorities. *The Homeland Security Review*, *1* (3), 1-56. Retrieved from http://www.teachingterror.net/HS/National_Security_and_Immigration_Policy.pdf

Kimhi, S. & Even, S. (2004, November). Who are the Palestinian Suicide Bombers?, *Jaffe Institute for Strategic studies, Memo 73*, Ramat Aviv, Tel Aviv University.

Korolov, M. (2015, January 13). Obama proposes new 30-day data breach notification law. Retrieved fromhttp://www.csoonline.com/article/2868096/data-protection/obama-proposes-new-30-day-data-breach-notification-law.html

Kostadinov, D. (2013, February 1). The Attribution Problem in CyberAttacks, *InfoSec Institute,* Retrieved from http://resources.infosecinstitute.com/attribution-problem-in-cyber-attacks/

Kostyuk, N. (2013). The Digital Prisoner's Dilemma: Challenges and Opportunities for Cooperation., World Cyberspace Cooperation Summit IV (WCC4), 2013, Worldwide Cybersecurity Initiative. New York, NY, USA: East West Institute. Retrieved from http://cybersummit.info/sites/cybersummit.info/files/The%20Digital%20Prisoner%27s%20Dilemma-Challenges%20and%20Opportunities%20for%20Cooperation_Nadiya%20Kostyuk%20.pdf

Kottasova, I. (2014, November 20). *Russian Website Streams Thousands of Private Webcams.* Retrieved from http://money.cnn.com/2014/11/20/technology/security/hacked-web-cameras-russia/

Krause, P. (2013). The Political Effectiveness of Non-State Violence: A Two-Level Framework to Transform a Deceptive Debate. *Security Studies. 22*(2), 259, 273.

Kuhltau, C. C. (1993). *Seeking Meaning: a Process Approach to Library and Information Services.* Norwood, N.J.: Ablex Publishing Inc.

Kwaak, J. S. (2015, March 17). *North Korea Blamed for Nuclear-Power Plan Hack.* Retrieved from http://www.wsj.com/articles/north-korea-blamed-for-nuclear-power-plant-hack-1426589324

Landi, W., & Rao, R. B. (2003). *Secure De-identification and Re-identification.* Proceedings of AMIA 2003 Symposium.

Laughl, O. (2015, January 7). FBI director stands by claim that North Korea was source of Sony cyber-attack. *The Guardian.* from http://www.theguardian.com/world/2015/jan/07/fbi-director-north-korea-source-sony-cyber-attack-james-comey

Lee, Y., & Paik, J. (2014). Security Analysis and Improvement of an Anonymous Authentication Scheme for Roaming Services. *Scientific World Journal*, 2014. doi:10.1155/2014/687879

Lemmon, G. T. (2013, April 8). The Hillary Doctrine: Women's Rights Are a National Security Issue. The Atlantic. Macmillan Dictionary. (n. d.). Retrieved from http://www.macmillandictionary.com

Levy, B.-H. (2008). *Left in Dark Times: A stand against the new barbarism.* New York: Random House.

Liaropoulos, A., & Tsihrintzis, G. (2014). *Proceedings of the 13th European Conference on Cyber warefare and Security*: ECCWS 2014 (p. 138). Academic Conferences Limited.

Lindsay, J. R. (2014). 2015). The impact of china on cybersecurity: Fiction and friction. *International Security, 39*(3), 7–47. doi:10.1162/ISEC_a_00189

Lippmann, W. (1943). *U.S. Foreign Policy: Shield of the Republic.* Boston: Little, Brown.

LoisLaw. (n. d.). *United States Code. Chapter 37. Espionage and Censorship.* Retrieved from http://www.loislaw.com.ezproxy1.apus.edu/snp/fpopwind.htm

Louis, B. (2003). The Crisis of Islam – Holy War and Unholy Terror (p. 117; p, 132). New York: Random House.

Luo, G. C., Peng, N. D., Qin, K., & Chen, A. G. (2014). A Layered Searchable Encryption Scheme with Functional Components Independent of Encryption Methods. *Scientific World Journal , 2014.* doi:10.1155/2014/153791

Maalouf, A. (2000). *In the name of identity.* New York: Penguin Books.

Macdonald, A. (aka William Luther Pierce) (1978). The Turner Diaries. Hillsboro, West Virginia: National Vanguard Books.

Machine-to-machine (M2M) is a term that digital devices of the same type communicate with one another, take measurements, and make decisions without human intervention.

Mair, P. (2013). *Ruling the Void: The hollowing out of Western Democracy.* London: Verso.

Mandaville, P. (1999, March). Digital Islam: Changing the boundaries of religious knowledge? *Newsletter 2*, 23. Retrieved from https://openaccess.leidenuniv.nl/bitstream/handle/1887/17137/ISIM_2_Digital_Islam-Changing_the_Boundaries_of_Religious_Knowledge.pdf?sequence=1

Mandiant. (2013, May 29). *Chinese motivations for corporate espionage: A historical perspective.* Retrieved from https://dl.mandiant.com/EE/library/Whitepaper_China_Motivations_for_Corporate_Espionage.pdf

Markandya, A., & Pemberton, M. (2010). Energy security, energy modelling and uncertainty. *Energy Policy*, *38*(4), 1609–1613. doi:10.1016/j.enpol.2009.01.046

Martin, D. (2014). Watch: Unraveling the great Chinese corn seed spy ring. *Al Jazeera*. Retrieved from http://america.aljazeera.com/watch/shows/america-tonight/articles/2014/10/6/unraveling-the-greatchinesecornseedspyring.html

Matsumoto, D., Hwang, H. S., Skinner, L., and Frank, M. (2011). Evaluating Truthfulness and Detecting Deception. *FBI Law Enforcement Bulletin*, (80), 1-8.

Matusitz, J. (2005). Cyberterrorism: How can American foreign policy be strengthened in the information age? *American Foreign Policy Interests*, *27*(2), 137–147. doi:10.1080/10803920590935376

Maughan, D. (2013, August). Homeland Security Advanced Research Projects Agency: *The Bigger Picture: S&T's Role in Cyber Security* (Slide 15). Homeland Security, Science and Technology division. Retrieved from http://www.dhs.gov/sites/default/files/publications/csd-ttp-finance-two.pdf

McConnell, M., Chertoff, M., & Lynn, W. (2012, January 27). China's cyber thievery is national policy - and must be challenged. *The Wall Street Journal*. Retrieved from http://online.wsj.com/news/articles/SB10001424052970203718504577178832338032176

McGregor, J. (2013, April 27). Is the specter of a 'cyber Cold War' real? *The Atlantic*. Retrieved from http://m.theatlantic.com/china/archive/2013/04/is-the-specter-of-a-cyber-cold-war-real/275352/href=

McHugh, J. (n. d.). Google vs. Evil, *Wired 11.01*, Retrieved from http://archive.wired.com/wired/archive/11.01/google_pr.html

Mellagrou-Hitchens, A. (2015) *The Global Jihad Movement in the West* [Unpublished PhD thesis]. King's College, University of London, London.

Mellagrou-Hitchens, A., & Brun, H. (2013). *A Neo-Nationalist Network: The English Defence League and the European Counter Jihad Movement*. International Centre for the.

Meux, E. (1994). Encrypting Personal Identifiers. *Health Services Research*, *29*(2), 247–256. PMID:8005792

Meyer, E. T., & Schroeder, R. (2009). The World Wide Web of Research and Access to Knowledge. *Knowledge Management Research & Practice*, *7*(3), 218–233. doi:10.1057/kmrp.2009.13

Michael, G. (1995). *Lone Wolf Terror and the Rise of Leaderless Resistance, Nashville Ten.* Vanderbilt University Press.

Michaels, J. (2014, May 19). China's theft of business secrets is beyond espionage. *USA Today*. Retrieved from http://www.usatoday.com/story/news/nation/2014/05/19/china-indictment-cyber-espionage/9289829/

Minogue, K. R. (1995). *Politics A very short introduction*. Oxford: Oxford University Press.

Mirahmadi, H., & Farooq, M. (2010, December). A Community Based Approach to Countering Radicalization - A Partnership for America, *World Organization for Resource, Development and Education (WORDE)*. Retrieved from http://www.worde.org/wp-content/uploads/2010/12/WORDE-Counter-Radicalization-Report-Final.pdf

Mittal, A., Hazra, J., Jain, N., Goyal, V., Seetharam, D. P., & Sabharwal, Y. (September, 2011). *Real Time Contingency Analysis for Power Grids.* Paper presented at the 7th International Conference, Euro-Par 2011. Bordeaux, France. doi:10.1007/978-3-642-23397-5_31

Moaz, I. (2004). Social-cognitive mechanisms in reconciliation. In Y. Bar-Siman-Tov (Ed.), *From conflict resolution to reconciliation* (pp. 197–224). Oxford: Oxford University Press. doi:10.1093/acprof:oso/9780195166439.003.0011

Montevideo Convention on the Rights and Duties of States. (1933, December 26). International Conference of American States in Montevideo, Uruguay.

Moore, C. (2014, April 18). A weak establishment is letting Islamists threaten British freedoms, *The Telegraph.* Retrieved from http://www.telegraph.co.uk/news/uknews/terrorism-in-the-uk/10775118/A-weak-establishment-is-letting-Islamists-threaten-British-freedoms.html

Moteff, J., & Parfomek, P. (2004). *Critical Infrastructure and Key Assets: Definition and Identification. CRS Report for Congress.* Retrieved from http://www.google.com/url?sa=t&rct=j&q=&esrc=s&source=web&cd=2&ved=0CCkQFjAB&url=http%3A%2F%2Fwww.dtic.mil%2Fcgi-bin%2FGetTRDoc%3FAD%3DADA454016&ei=Jgl6VMKSCrG0sAS8wYCgCw&usg=AFQjCNGnIi42ksabku3cy8G47VZdcQRtGQ

Nakashima, E. (2015, March 19). Cyber chief: Efforts to deter attacks against the U.S. are not working. *The Washington Post.* Retrieved from http://www.washingtonpost.com/world/national-security/head-of-cyber-command-us-may-need-to-boost-offensive-cyber-powers/2015/03/19/1ad79a34-ce4e-11e4-a2a7-9517a3a70506_story.html

Napoleoni, L. (2004). Money and Terrorism. *Strategic Insights*, *3*(4), 47–50.

National Security Agency. (2014). Memorandum for Staff Director and Minority Staff Director, House Committee on the Judiciary. Retrieved from http://msnbcmedia.msn.com/i/MSNBC/Sections/NEWS/nsa-snowden.pdf

National Security Strategy of the United States. (2015, February). The White House. Retrieved from http://www.whitehouse.gov/sites/default/files/docs/2015_national_security_strategy_2.pdf

Navarro, J. (2012). Detecting Deception. *FBI Law Enforcement Bulletin*, (81), 7-11.

Neame, R. (2013). Effective sharing of health records, maintaining privacy: A practical schema. *Online Journal of Public Health Informatics*, *5*(2), 217. doi:10.5210/ojphi.v5i2.4344 PMID:23923101

Negroponte, N. (1996). *Being Digital* (1st ed., p. 4). New York: Vintage.

Neumann, P. R. (2008). *Joining al-Qaeda: Jihadist Recruitment in Europe* (p. 7). New York: Routledge.

Neumann, P. R., & Rogers, B. (2007). *Recruitment and mobilization for the Islamist militant movement in Europe, A study carried out by King's College London, the 4th European Commission King's College.* London: University of London.

Norenzayan, A., Choi, I., & Nisbett, R. E. (1999). Eastern and western perceptions of causality for social behavior: Lay theories about personalities and situations. In D. D. Prentice & D. T. Miller (Eds.), *Cultural Divides: Understanding and Overcoming Group Conflict* (pp. 239–272). New York: Russell Sage Foundation.

Norris, P. (2001). *Digital Divide: Civic Engagement, Information Poverty, and the Internet.* Cambridge: Cambridge University Press. doi:10.1017/CBO9781139164887

Nye, J. S. (2010). *Cyberpower. Belfer Center for Science and International Affairs.* Cambridge: Harvard Kennedy School.

Oakeshott, M. (1962). *Rationalism in Politics and Other Essays.* London: Methuen.

Oaths of Enlistment and Oaths of Office—U.S. Army Center of Military History. Retrieved from http://www.history.army.mil/html/faq/oaths.html

Oborne, P. (2014, January 1). Europe is slowly strangling the life out of national democracy. *The Daily Telegraph.*

Oborne, P. (2007). *The Triumph of the Political Class*. London: Pocket Books.

Office of Electricity Delivery & Energy Reliability. (n. d.). *Smart Grid.* Retrieved from http://energy.gov/oe/services/technology-development/smart-grid

Office of Electricity Delivery & Energy Reliability. (n. d.). *The Role of Microgrids in Helping to Advance the Nation's Energy System.* Retrieved from http://energy.gov/oe/services/technology-development/smart-grid/role-microgrids-helping-advance-nation-s-energy-system

Office of National Counterintelligence Executive. (2011). Foreign Spies Stealing US Economic Secrets in Cyberspace: report to Congress on Foreign Economic Collection and Industrial Espionage. Retrieved from http://www.ncix.gov/publications/reports/fecie_all/Foreign_Economic_Collection_2011.pdf

Office of the President of the United States. (2010, May). National Security Strategy. *The White House*.

Oh, J. Y., Yang, D. I., & Chon, K. H. (2010). A Selective Encryption Algorithm Based on AES for Medical Information. *Healthc Inform Res*, *16*(1), 22–29. doi:10.4258/hir.2010.16.1.22 PMID:21818420

Omand, D. (2010). *Securing the State, London*. Hurst, New York: Oxford University Press.

Omand, D., Bartlett, J., & Miller, C. (2012). Introducing Social Media Intelligence (SOCMINT). *Intelligence and National Security*, *27*(6), 801–823. doi:10.1080/02684527.2012.716965

Online banking report Database. (n. d.). Retrieved from http://www.onlinebankingreport.com/

Orwell, G. (1946). Politics and the English Language. Retrieved from http://www.orwell.ru/library/essays/politics/english/e_polit

Owen, J. (2012). Man whose WMD lies led to 100,000 deaths confesses all. *Independent.* Retrieved from http://www.independent.co.uk/news/world/politics/man-whose-wmd-lies-led-to-100000-deaths-confesses-all-7606236.html

Paez, D.R., & Hou-fu Liu, J. (2011). Collective memory in conflicts. In D. Bar-Tal (Ed.), *Intergroup conflicts and their resolution: A social psychological perspective* (pp. 105-124). New York: Psychology Press.

Pagliery, J. (2014, November 18). *FBI's 10 Most Wanted Cyber Criminals*. Retrieved from http://money.cnn.com/gallery/technology/security/2014/11/18/fbi-cyber-most-wanted/

Pagliery, J., & Pepitone, J. (2014, September 5). *Five of the Biggest-Ever Credit Card Hacks*. Retrieved from http://money.cnn.com/gallery/technology/security/2014/09/05/biggest-hacks/

Paleri, P. (2008). National Security: Imperatives And Challenges. New Delhi. Tata: McGraw-Hill; Retrieved 23 September 2010.

Palmer, C. L., & Neumann, L. J. (2002). The Information Work of Interdisciplinary Humanities Scholars: Exploration and Translation. *Library Quarterly: Information, Community. Policy*, *72*(1), 85–117.

Pang, L. (2012). *Creativity and its discontents*. London: Duke University. doi:10.1215/9780822394587

Park, H. W., & Thelwall, M. (2005). The Network Approach to Web Hyperlink Research and its Utility for Science Communication. In C. Hine (Ed.), *Virtual methods: Issues in Social Research on the Internet* (pp. 171–181). Oxford: Berg Publishers.

Pennington, D. C. (2000). *Social cognition.* London: Routledge.

Perez, E., & Prokupecz, S. (2014, May 19). Inside FBI's massive cybercrime bust. *CNN Money,* Retrieved from http://money.cnn.com/2014/05/19/technology/security/cyber-crime-bust-blackshades/index.html

Perrow, C. (1999). *Normal Accidents: Living with High-Risk Technologies (Updated edition with a New afterword and a new postscript by the author edition).* Princeton, N.J: Princeton University Press.

Peterson, A. (2015, April 15). Why this national data breach notification bill has privacy advocates worried. *The Washington Post.* Retrieved from http://www.washingtonpost.com/blogs/the-switch/wp/2015/04/15/why-this-national-data-breach-notification-bill-has-privacy-advocates-worried/

Pettigrew, T. F. (1998). Intergroup contact theory. *Annual Review of Psychology, 49*(1), 65–85. doi:10.1146/annurev.psych.49.1.65 PMID:15012467

Phil Zimmermann's Home Page. (n. d.). Retrieved from http://www.mit.edu/~prz/EN/background/index.html

Pidd, H. (2014a, March 7). Alleged plot to 'take over' and run schools on strict Islamic principles. *The Guardian.* Retrieved from http://www.theguardian.com/uk-news/2014/mar/07/alleged-plot-birmingham-schools-islamic-principles

Pidd, H. (2014b, April 14). *Twenty-five Birmingham schools inspected over Islamist 'takeover plot.' The Guardian.* Retrieved from http://www.theguardian.com/uk-news/2014/apr/14/birmingham-schools-investigated-over-islamist-takeover-allegations

Pierce, E. R. (2014). *Top 9 Things You Didn't Know About America's Electrical Grid.* Retrieved from http://www.energy.gov/articles/top-9-things-you-didnt-know-about-americas-power-grid

Pinker, S. (2011). *The Better Angels of our Nature, Why Violence has Declined London.* Penguin.

Posen, B. R. (2003). Command of the commons: The military foundation of U.S. hegemony. *International Security, 28*(1), 5–46. doi:10.1162/016228803322427965

Prestowitz, C. (2013b, June). The China conundrum. *Foreign Policy.* Retrieved from http://prestowitz.foreignpolicy.com/posts/2013/06/03/the_china_conundrum

Prestowitz, C. (2014, May 25). Got intel, Uncle Sam? Share it with U.S. companies. *Los Angeles Times.* Retrieved from http://www.latimes.com/opinion/op-ed/la-oe-prestowitz-china-hacking-20140526-story.html

Prestowitz, C. (2010). *The betrayal of American prosperity: Free market delusions, America's decline, and how we must compete in the post-dollar era.* Simon and Schuster Digital Sales Inc.

Rabie, M. (1994). *Conflict resolution and ethnicity.* Westport, CT: Praeger.

RAND Corp. (2008). Terrorist Organizations Profile Aryan Nations. Retrieved from http://www.start.umd.edu/tops/

Ranger, S. (n. d.). Inside the secret digital arms race: Facing the threat of a global cyberwar. *Tech Republic,* Retrieved from http://www.techrepublic.com/article/inside-the-secret-digital-arms-race/

Ranstorp, M. (1996, Summer). Terrorism in the name of religion. *Journal of International Affairs, 50*(1).

Rayburn, D. (2007). Streaming and Digital Media: Understanding the Business and Technology (1 ed., p. 40). Amsterdam; Burlington, MA: Focal Press.

Reforms and Initiatives: We Can End Terrorism Through Quality Education. (2015). *The Tribune.* Retrieved from http://tribune.com.pk/story/818470/reforms-and-initiatives-we-can-end-terrorism-through-quality-education/

Reicher, S. D. (1996). 'The battle of Westminster': Developing the social identity model of crowd behavior in order to explain the initiation and development of collective conflict. *European Journal of Social Psychology*, *26*(1), 115–134. doi:10.1002/(SICI)1099-0992(199601)26:1<115::AID-EJSP740>3.0.CO;2-Z

Reicher, S. D. (2001). The psychology of crowd dynamics. In M. A. Hogg & S. Tindale (Eds.), *Group processes* (pp. 182–208). Malden, MA: Blackwell.

Reid, E., & Chen, H. (2008). Domain Mapping of Contemporary Terrorism Research. In H. Chen, E. Reid, J. Sinai, A. Silke, & B. Ganor (Eds.), *Terrorism Informatics: Knowledge Management and Data Mining for Homeland Security* (pp. 3–26). New York, N.Y.: Springer Link US. doi:10.1007/978-0-387-71613-8_1

Reinhardt, A. (1998, May 12) Steve Jobs on Apple's resurgence. *Business Week*. Retrieved from http://allaboutstevejobs.com/sayings/stevejobsinterviews/bw98.php

Resnick, D. (1999). Politics on the Internet: The Normalization of Cyberspace. In C. Toulouse & T. W. Luke (Eds.), *The Politics of Cyberspace* (pp. 55–56). London: Routledge Press.

Rewriting the Narrative - An Integrated Strategy for Counter-radicalization. (2009, March). Presidential Study Group Reports. *The Washington Institute for the Near East Policy*. Retrieved from http://www.washingtoninstitute.org/templateC04.php?CID=311

Reykowski, J., & Cislak, A. (2011). Socio-psychological approaches to conflict resolution. In D. Bar-Tal (Ed.), *Intergroup conflicts and their resolution: A social psychological perspective* (pp. 241–266). New York: Psychology Press.

RIPA. (2000). Regulation of Investigative Powers Act.

Risen, T. (2015). *Could Apple Compete with Tesla?* Retrieved from http://www.usnews.com/news/articles/2015/02/18/could-apple-compete-with-tesla

Ritchie, D. M. (2003). *The Development of the C Language*. Retrieved from http://cm.bell-labs.com/who/dmr/chist.html

Robb, D. (2014, December 22). *Sony Hack: A Timeline*. Retrieved from http://deadline.com/2014/12/sony-hack-timeline-any-pascal-the-interview-north-korea-1201325501/

Robbins, O. (2013, August 27). Cabinet Office witness statement of Oliver Robbins to the High Court.

Roberts, D. (2012, November 1). Confucius makes a comeback in China. *Bloomberg Business Week*. Retrieved from http://www.businessweek.com/articles/2012-11-01/confucius-makes-a-comeback-in-china

Rodriguez, G. (2013). *Edward Snowden Interview Transcript Full Text*. Retrieved from http://mic.com/articles/47355/edward-snowden-interview-transcript-full-text-read-the-guardian-s-entire-interview-with-the-man-who-leaked-prism

Roebuck, K. (2012). Application Testing as a Service (TaaS): High-impact Technology—What You Need to Know: Definitions, Adoptions, Impact, Benefits, Maturity, Vendors (p. 266). Emereo Publishing.

Rollins, J., & Henning, A. C. (2009). *Comprehensive National Cybersecurity Initiative Legal Authorities and Policy Considerations*. Washington, D.C.: Congressional Research Service.

Romm, J.J. (1993). Defining national security: the nonmilitary aspects. America's Task in a Changed World (Pew Project Series), Council on Foreign Relations.

Ronald Deibert. (2011). Ronald Deibert: Tracking the emerging arms race in cyberspace. *The Bulletin of the Atomic Scientists*, *67*(1), 1–8. doi:10.1177/0096340210393703

Rooney, B. (2014, December 5). *Hackers Threaten Sony Employees Families*. Retrieved from http://money.cnn.com/2014/12/05/news/sony-threatened-by-hackers/

Rosenthal, J. (2014, April 9). European jihadists form ISIS brigades in Syria, *ALMONITOR*. Retrieved from http://www.al-monitor.com/pulse/originals/2014/04/europe-jihadist-isis-syria-qaeda-terror-france-germany.html#

Rouhana, N. N. (2011). Key issues in reconciliation: Challenging traditional assumptions on conflict resolution and power dynamics. In D. Bar-Tal (Ed.), *Intergroup conflicts and their resolution: A social psychological perspective* (pp. 291–311). New York: Psychology Press.

Roy, O. (2007). Islamic Terrorist Radicalisation in Europe. *Centre for European Policy Studies (CEPS)*. Retrieved from http://www.isn.ethz.ch/Digital-Library/Publications/Detail/?ots591=0c54e3b3-1e9c-be1e-2c24-a6a8c7060233&lng=en&id=45688

Rubin, M., & Hewstone, M. (1998). Social identity theory's self-esteem hypothesis: A review and some suggestions for clarification. *Personality and Social Psychology Review*, *2*(1), 40–62. doi:10.1207/s15327957pspr0201_3 PMID:15647150

Runciman, D. (2013). *The Confidence Trap A History of Democracy in Crisis from World War 1 to the Present*. Princeton: Princeton University Press.

Sageman, M. (2005, Spring). The Normality of Global Jihadi Terrorism. *The Journal of International Security Affairs*, *8*, 1–10.

Samuels, D. (2012, April 6). The new mastermind of jihad. *The Wall Street Journal*. Retrieved from http://online.wsj.com/news/articles/SB10001424052702303299604577323750859163544

Sanger, D. E., & Perlroth, N. (2014, March 22). N.S.A. breached Chinese servers seen as security threat. *The New York Times*. Retrieved from http://www.nytimes.com/2014/03/23/world/asia/nsa-breached-chinese-servers-seen-as-spy-peril.html?_r=0

Schiffauer, W. (1999). Islamism in the Diaspora: The Fascination of Political Islam among Second Generation German Turks, *Transnational Communities Program Working Paper*, Oxford. Retrieved from http://www.transcomm.ox.ac.uk/working%20papers/Schiffauer_Islamism.PDF

Schmitt, M.N. (2005). Precision attack and international humanitarian law. *International Review of the Red Cross, 859*, 445-466, 445.

Schneider, S. M., & Foot, K. A. (2002). Online Structure for Political Action: Exploring Presidential Web sites from the 2000 American Election. *Javnost - The Public Journal of the European Institute for Communication and Culture*, *9*(2), 43–60.

Schroeder, R., Caldas, A., Mesch, G., & Dutton, W. H. (2005, June 22-24). The World Wide Web of Science: Reconfiguring Access to Information. *Proceedings of the First International Conference on e-Social Science*, Manchester. Retrieved from: http://www.oii.ox.ac.uk/research/project.cfm?id=22

Securing Cyber Space—President Obama Announces New Cybersecurity Legislative Proposal and Other Cybersecurity Efforts. (2015, January 13). The White House. Retrieved from https://www.whitehouse.gov/node/316726

SEED 128 Algorithm Specification. (1999). Korea Internet and Security Agency http://seed.kisa.or.kr/html/egovframework/iwt/ds/ko/ref/%5B2%5D_SEED+128_Specification_english_M.pdf

Seltzer, L. (2013, November 5). South Koreans use Internet Explorer: It's the law. *ZDNet*. Retrieved from http://www.zdnet.com/article/south-koreans-use-Internet-explorer-its-the-law/

Shanker, T. (2013). *Pentagon Is Updating Conflict Rules in Cyberspace.* Retrieved from http://www.nytimes.com/2013/06/28/us/pentagon-is-updating-conflict-rules-in-cyberspace.html?_r=1&

Sheldon, J. B. (2011). Deciphering cyberpower strategic purpose in peace and war. *Strategic Studies Quarterly*, *5*(2), 95.

Sherif, M. (1936). *The psychology of social norms.* New York: Harper & Row.

Singer, P. W., & Friedman, A. (2014). *Cybersecurity and Cyberwar: What Everyone Needs to Know* (p. 13). Oxford, New York: Oxford University Press.

Sisler, V. (2006). Islamic Jurisprudence in Cyberspace: Construction of Interpretative Authority in Muslim Diaspora. In R. Polcak, et. al. (Eds.), *Proceedings of Cyberspace 2005 conference*, Brno, Masaryk University (pp. 43–50). Retrieved from http://www.digitalislam.eu/article.do?articleId=1420

Soderbery, R. (2013, January 7). How Many Things Are Currently Connected To The "Internet of Things" (IoT)? *Forbes.* Retrieved from http://www.forbes.com/sites/quora/2013/01/07/how-many-things-are-currently-connected-to-the-Internet-of-things-iot/

Southern Poverty Law Center. (n. d.). Louis Beam. Retrieved from www.spl.org

Standing, G. (2011). *The Precariat: the new dangerous class.* London: Bloomsbury.

Stelter, B. (2014, December 14). *Sony Lawyers tell Media to Stop Reporting on Material Stolen by Hackers.* Retrieved from http://money.cnn.com/2014/12/14/media/sony-hack-lawyer-media/

Stephan, W. G., Renfro, L., & Davis, M. D. (2008). The role of threat in intergroup relations. In U. Wagner, L. R. Tropp, G. Finchilescu, & C. Tredoux (Eds.), *Improving intergroup relations: Building on the legacy of Thomas F. Pettigrew* (pp. 55–72). Malden, MA: Blackwell. doi:10.1002/9781444303117.ch5

Stephan, W. G., & Stephan, C. W. (2000). An integrated threat theory of prejudice. In S. Oskamp (Ed.), *Reducing prejudice and discrimination* (pp. 23–45). Mahwah, NJ: Erlbaum.

Sternberg, E. (2010, Winter). Purifying the World what the new radical ideology stands for. *Orbis*, 60–75.

Stewart, V. R. (2015). *Statement for the Record: Worldwide Threat Assessment.* Retrieved from http://www.dia.mil/News/SpeechesandTestimonies/ArticleView/tabid/11449/Article/570863/statement-for-the-record-worldwide-threat-assessment.aspx

Strachan, H. (2014). *The Direction of War Contemporary Strategy in Historical Perspective.* Cambridge: Cambridge University Press.

Strauss, L., & Cropsey, J. (1986). History of Political Philosophy. Chicago, IL: Chicago University Press.

Strauss, L. (1964). *The City and Man.* Chicago: Rand McNally.

Strickling, R. (2012). *Funding, Coordination, and Public Opinion: Political Obstacles to Electrical Grid Modernization in the Americas.* Retrieved from http://regulation.upf.edu/exeter-12-papers/Paper%20156%20-%20Strickling%202012%20-%20Funding,%20Coordination%20and%20Public%20Opinion.pdf

Study of Radicalisation and Political Violence. (n. d.). King's College, London.

Sutter, J. D. (2010, March 31). Why Internet connections are fastest in South Korea. *CNN.* Retrieved from http://www.cnn.com

Svendsen, A. (2010). Strategy and disproportionality in contemporary conflicts. *The Journal of Strategic Studies*, *33*(3), 367–399. doi:10.1080/01402390903189576

Tajfel, H. (1970). Experiments in intergroup discrimination. *Scientific American, 223*(5), 96–102. doi:10.1038/scientificamerican1170-96 PMID:5482577

Tajfel, H., Billig, M., Bundy, R. P., & Flament, C. (1971). Social categorization and intergroup behavior. *European Journal of Social Psychology, 1*(2), 149–178. doi:10.1002/ejsp.2420010202

Tajfel, H., & Turner, J. C. (1986). The social identity theory of intergroup behavior. In S. Worchel & W. G. Austin (Eds.), *Psychology of intergroup relations* (2nd ed., pp. 7–24). Chicago: Nelson-Hall.

Tao, Q., & Prescott, J. E. (2000). China: Competitive intelligence practices in an emerging market environment. *Competitive Intelligence Review, 11*(4), 65–78. doi:10.1002/1520-6386(200034)11:4<65::AID-CIR10>3.0.CO;2-N

Taylor, M. (1974). The Legitimate Claims of National Security. Foreign Affairs (Council on Foreign Relations, Inc.) 52 (Essay of 1974). doi:10.2307/20038070

Tedford, T., & Herbeck, D. (2009). *Amendment to the Espionage Act of 1917.* Retrieved from http://www.bc.edu/bc_org/avp/cas/comm/free_speech/espionageactof1917.html

Telegraph Video. (2014, December 23). Analyst: US possibly behind North Korea's Internet shutdown. *The Telegraph*, Retrieved from http://www.telegraph.co.uk/news/worldnews/asia/northkorea/11310314/Analyst-US-behind-North-Koreas-Internet-shutdown.html

Tellis, A. J., Bially, J., Layne, C., MacPherson, M., & Sollinger, J. M. (2000). *Measuring National Power in the Postindustrial Age: Analyst's Handbook.* Santa Monica, Calif: RAND Corporation, 28. *The PGPi scanning project.* Retrieved from http://www.pgpi.org/pgpi/project/scanning/

Terms and Definitions of Interest for DoD Counterintelligence Professionals. (2011). Retrieved from http://fas.org/irp/eprint/ci-glossary.pdf

The Daily Telegraph. (2013, May 23). Murder of Lee Rigby provokes anti-Muslim attacks.

The Guardian. (2014, January 19). Communities 'taking law into their own hands', says police chief inspector.

The Independent. (2013, May 28). Islamaphobia attacks rise dramatically after the murder of Lee Rigby.

The US Air Force. (2014, January). Dynamic Targeting and The Tasking Process, *Annex 3-60 Targeting*. LeMay Center for Doctrine Development and Education. Retrieved from https://doctrine.af.mil/download.jsp?filename=3-60-D17-Target-Dynamic-Task.pdf

Theohary, C. A., & Rollins, J. (2011, March 8). Terrorist Use of the Internet: Information Operations in Cyberspace. CRS Report for Congress, Congressional Research Service.

Thomas, T. L. (2010). *Google confronts China's "three warfares."* Carlisle, PA: US Army War College.

Tilghman, A. (2014, September 22). Active, reserve components spar over "sexy" cyber mission. *Air Force Times.* Retrieved from http://archive.airforcetimes.com/article/20140922/NEWS04/309220034/Active-reserve-components-spar-over-sexy-cyber-mission

Turner, J. C., Hogg, M. A., Oakes, P. J., Richer, S. D., & Wetherell, M. S. (1987). *Rediscovering the social group.* Oxford: Basil Blackwell.

Turner, J. C., & Reynolds, K. J. (2004). The social identity perspective in intergroup relations: Theories, themes, and controversies. In M. B. Brewer & M. Hewstone (Eds.), *Self and social identity* (pp. 259–277). Malden, MA: Blackwell.

Turton, H., & Barreto, L. (2006). Long-term security of energy supply and climate change. *Energy Policy, 34*(15), 2232–2250. doi:10.1016/j.enpol.2005.03.016

U.S. Department of Homeland Security, Government Accountability Office. (2014). Critical Infrastructure Protection. DHS Actions Needed to Enhance Integration and Coordination of Vulnerability Assessment Efforts: report to Congressional Requesters. Retrieved from http://www.gao.gov/assets/670/665788.pdf

U.S. Department of Justice, Office of Public Affairs. (2014, May 19). U.S. charges five Chinese military hackers for cyber espionage against U.S. corporations and a labor organization for commercial advantage. Retrieved from http://www.justice.gov/opa/pr/us-charges-five-chinese-military-hackers-cyber-espionage-against-us-corporations-and-labor

U.S. Energy Information Administration. (2014). *Energy in Brief.* Retrieved from http://www.eia.gov/energy_in_brief/article/power_grid.cfm

U.S. Government Printing Office. (1905). *Journals of the Continental Congress.* Washington, USA: Government Printing Office, Library of Congress.

U.S. Strategic Command. (2013). *U.S. Cyber Command.* Retrieved from http://www.stratcom.mil/factsheets/Cyber_Command/

Uimonen, P. (2003). Networks of Global Interaction. *Cambridge Review of International Affairs, 16*(2), 273–286. doi:10.1080/09557570302054

Ulph, S. (2007, May 24). The Salafist and Islamist framework for Jihadism, Manifesto Experts. *Testimony to the Open Hearing of the Senate Select Committee on Intelligence.* Retrieved from http://intelligence.senate.gov/070612/ulph.pdf

UNESCO.org. (1999). Declaration and Program of Action on a Culture of Peace. Retrieved from http://www3.unesco.org/iycp/kits/uk_res_243.pdf

United Nations E-government Survey 2014. (n. d.). The United Nations. Retrieved from http://unpan3.un.org/egovkb/Portals/egovkb/Documents/un/2014-Survey/E-Gov_Complete_Survey-2014.pdf

University for Peace Accreditation. (2015). Retrieved from https://www.upeace.org/about-upeace/accreditation

Unlocking Al-Qaeda: Islamist extremism in British prisons. (2009, February). *Quilliam, British de-radicalisation centre.* Retrieved from http://www.sunniforum.com/forum/showthread.php?52941-British-de-radicalisation-centre

Urban, F. R. M. J., Benders, R. M. J., & Moll, H. C. (2007). Modelling energy systems for developing countries. *Energy Policy, 35*(6), 3473–3482. doi:10.1016/j.enpol.2006.12.025

US Government. (2004, December 17). Intelligence Reform and Prevention of Terrorism Act 2004, Pub. L. No. 108–458. Retrieved from http://www.gpo.gov/fdsys/pkg/PLAW-108publ458/pdf/PLAW-108publ458.pdf.

US NATO Military Terminology Group. (2010). *1 (02) "Dictionary of Military and Associated Terms", 2001 (As amended through 31 July 2010). Pentagon, Washington: Joint Chiefs of Staff* (p. 361). JP: US Department of Defense.

US spy chief James Clapper highlights cyber threats. (2015, February 27). *BBC News.* Retrieved from http://www.bbc.com/news/world-us-canada-31654050

Van der Laan, D. S. (2014, April 23). AIVD: twee Nederlandse jihadisten pleegden zelfmoordaanslag, *ELSEVIER.* Retrieved from http://www.elsevier.nl/Nederland/nieuws/2014/4/AIVD-twee-Nederlandse-jihadisten-pleegden-zelfmoordaanslagen-1508028W/?cmpid=NLC%7Celsevier_dagelijks%7C2014-04-23%7CAIVD:_twee_Nederlandse_jihadisten_pleegden_zelfmoordaanslag

Van Laer, J., & Van Aelst, P. (2010). Internet and Social Movement Action Repertoires. *Information Communication and Society*, *13*(8), 1146–1171. doi:10.1080/13691181003628307

VandenBos, G., Knapp, S., & Doe, J. (2001). *Role of reference elements in the selection of resources by psychology undergraduates*. Retrieved from http://jbr.org/articles.html

VanderSchel, K. (2013). *Chinese National Arrested for Conspiring to Steal Trade Secrets*. Retrieved from http://www.justice.gov/usao/ias/news/2013/Hailong%20-%20Arrest%2012-12-2013.html

Vatis, M. (2001). Cyber Terrorism and Information Warfare: Government Perspectives. In Y. Alexander & M. S. Swetnam (Eds.), *Cyber Terrorism and Information Warfare*. New York: Transnational Publishers Inc.

Vertzberger, Y. Y. I. (1990). *The world in their minds: Information processing, cognition, and perception in foreign policy decision-making*. Stanford, CA: Stanford University Press.

Virkar, S. (2007). (Dis)connected Citizenship: Exploring Barriers to eConsultation in Europe. *Deliverable 2 of the Breaking Barriers to e-Government: Overcoming Obstacles to Improving European Public Services Project*.

Virkar, S. (2011). *The Politics of Implementing e-Government for Development: The Ecology of Games Shaping Property Tax Administration in Bangalore City* [Unpublished Doctoral Thesis]. University of Oxford.

Virkar, S. (2014). Re-engaging the Public in the Digital Age: e-Consultation Initiatives in the Government 2.0 Landscape. In M. Khosrow (Ed.), Encyclopedia of Information Science and Technology (3rd ed., pp.427-435). Hershey, P.A.: IGI Global.

Voegelin, E. (1974). Political Religions, and The Ecumenic Age (Vol. 4). In Order and History (Vols. 1–5). Baton Rouge, Louisiana: Louisiana University Press.

Waardenburg, J. (1998). *Islam et Science des Religions*. Paris: Les Belles Lettres.

Wagner, U., Tropp, L. R., Finchilescu, G., & Tredoux, C. (2008). *Improving intergroup relations: Building on the legacy of Thomas F. Pettigrew*. Malden, MA: Blackwell. doi:10.1002/9781444303117

Walker, J. (2015, February 13). Battle For Search Market Share Heats Up Again. *Media Post*. Retrieved from http://www.mediapost.com/publications/article/243791/battle-for-search-market-share-heats-up-again.html

Wallace, G. (2014, March 24). Report: Leaked Snowden documents show NSA hacked Chinese telecom company. *CNN*. Retrieved from http://money.cnn.com/2014/03/23/technology/security/nsa-china-huawei/?iid=EL

Wallace, G. (2015, February 15). *Hackers Stole from 100 banks and Rigged ATMS to Spew Cash*. Retrieved from http://money.cnn.com/2015/02/15/technology/security/kaspersky-bank-hacking/

Wall, M. A. (2007). Social Movements and Email: Expressions of Online Identity in the Globalization Protests. *New Media & Society*, *9*(2), 258–277. doi:10.1177/1461444807075007

Waltman, J. L. & Golen, S. P. (1993). Detecting Deception During Interviews. *Internal Auditor*, 50, 61-63.

Wang, B., & Chee, H. (2012, January 12). China's public sector: a different way of working. *The Guardian*. Retrieved from http://www.theguardian.com/public-leaders-network/blog/2012/jan/03/china-public-sector-leadership

Warmelink, L., Vrij, A., Mann, S., & Granhag, P. A. (2013). Spatial and Temporal Details in Intentions: A Cue to Detecting Deception. *Applied Cognitive Psychology*, *27*(1), 101–106. doi:10.1002/acp.2878

Wartenkin, C. (2001). *Reshaping World Politics: NGOs, the Internet and Global Civil Society*. Oxford: Rowman and Littlefield.

Weber, M. (2004). The Vocation Lectures. (R. Livingstone, Trans., D. Owen and T. B. Strong, Eds.) (p. 33). Indianapolis: Hackett Publishing Company, Inc.

Weimann, G. (2004, March). [REMOVED HYPERLINK FIELD]Www.terror.net: How Modern Terrorism Uses the Internet, *United States Institute of Peace Special Report 116*.

Weimann, G. (2006). Virtual Disputes: The Use of the Internet for Terrorist Debates. *Studies in Conflict and Terrorism*, *29*(7), 623–639. doi:10.1080/10576100600912258

Weintraub, W. (2005). Verbal Behavior and Personality Assessment. In J. M. Post (Ed.), *Psychological Assessment of Political Leaders: With Profiles of Saddam Hussein and Bill Clinton* (pp. 215–271). Michigan: University of Michigan Press.

Whaley, B., & Busby, J. (2000). Detecting Deception: Practice, Practitioners, and Theory. *Trends in Organized Crime*, *6*(6), 73–104. doi:10.1007/s12117-000-1007-x

What are Human Rights? (2015). Retrieved from http://www.ohchr.org/EN/Issues/Pages/WhatareHumanRights.aspx

White House. (2014A, January 17). PPD-28, Presidential Policy Directive.

White House. (2014B, January 17). President Obama's speech at the Department of Justice.

Who are Australia's radicalised Muslims? (2014, December 16). *BBC NEWS AUSTRALIA*. Retrieved from http://www.bbc.com/news/world-asia-29249462

Williams, P., Dunlevy, C., & Shimeall, T. (2013). *Intelligence Analysis for Internet Security*. Retrieved from http://www.cert.org/archive/html/Analysis10a.html

Willis, G. B. (1999). *Cognitive Interviewing: A "How To" Guide*. Retrieved from http://www.uiowa.edu/~c07b209/interview.pdf

Wrenn, C. F. (2012). Strategic cyber deterrence, (p. 25). Fletcher School of Law and Diplomacy.

Xiaomi to open India data centre to allay privacy fears. (2014, October 27). *BBC News*. Retrieved from http://www.bbc.com/news/technology-29786324

Yadron, D., & Glazer, E. (2014, October 31). J.P. Morgan Found Hackers Through Breach of Road-Race Website. *Wall Street Journal*. Retrieved from http://www.wsj.com/articles/j-p-morgan-found-hackers-after-finding-breach-of-race-website-1414766443

Yanagizawa-Drott, D. (2011). *Propaganda vs. Education: A Case Study of Hate Radio in Rwanda*. Retrieved from http://www.hks.harvard.edu/fs/dyanagi/Research/Propaganda_vs_Education.pdf

Yueh, L. (2014, October 16). Huawei boss says US ban "not very important." *BBC News*. Retrieved from http://www.bbc.com/news/business-29620442

Zimbardo, P. (2007). *The Lucifer effect*. New York: Random House.

Zinnbauer, D. (2001). Internet, Civil Society and Global Governance: The Neglected Political Dimension of the Digital Divide. *Information and Security: An International Journal*, *7*(1), 45–64.

About the Contributors

Eugenie de Silva holds a Bachelor's degree and Master's degree in Intelligence Studies with a concentration in Intelligence Analysis from the American Military University. She also holds a Master's in Liberal Arts with a concentration in Legal Studies from the Harvard University Division of Continuing Education. She is also a current Ph.D. student in the department of Politics and International Relations at the University of Leicester in England. She has given eight oral presentations at academic conferences in fields such as teaching physics and chemistry, online software programs, biometrics, intelligence studies, and Denial and Deception (D&D). Her research is mainly multidisciplinary in nature. She also holds several academic world records, and has been featured in the media around the globe due to her achievements in the academic arena. She is the founder of a non-profit known as the International Association of Child Prodigies. She is also the winner of several awards, including the Luce Leader of 2015 for global leadership from the James Jay Dudley Luce Foundation.

* * *

Galit Margalit Ben-Israel serves as Chief Scientist for project of Identity, Terror and Cyber, in the Institute of Identity Research (IDmap). Dr. Galit Ben-Israel is also an analyst of terror activity and counter-terrorism training consultant. She lectures as senior lecturer of Political Science at the Public Administration and Policy, at the Faculty of Society and Culture in Beit-Berl Academic College. Her lecturing includes courses of: World Politics and Globalization; Terror in the Digital Era; and Virtual Communities and Cyber-Terrorism. Dr. Ben-Israel extends her research to specific issues of hostage-barricade terrorism (HBT); suicide terrorism; disaster management through social media (Web 2.0); and diaspora and Internet networks.

Amanda Sue Birch is a mechanical engineer with 20 years of experience in US government leadership and policy. She has an M.S. in Mechanical Engineering from the Massachusetts Institute of Technology and an M.A. in International Relations from The Fletcher School at Tufts University. Her undergraduate studies were at the US Air Force Academy. She is a licensed professional engineer with experience in both cutting-edge research and development as well as infrastructure and facilities construction and management. She is also a certified partnership broker, speaks several languages, and has domestic and international experience in the non-profit sector. Her current duties include national-level training policy for the US military.

Tianxing Cai joined Lamar University in the Spring of 2011. He has an in-depth working experience as he served as the senior engineer in the semiconductor industry at Amkor Technology from 2006 to 2010. Dr. Cai holds a B.S. in Chemistry from Shanghai University, China and is a member of several associations, such as the Shanghai Semiconductor Association, Shanghai Electro Plating Association, Shanghai Indoor Environmental Control Association, Shanghai Chemical Analysis Association, and the Shanghai ESD Control Association.

Joseph H. Campos II is the Administrator at University Health Services Manoa and is an Affiliate Professor for the Peace Institute and Associate Graduate Faculty for the Department of Political Science at the University of Hawaii at Manoa. His interest lies in interrogating the way statist formations give voice to some issues while silencing other issues. Specifically, he asked: How is terrorism made part of the national security apparatus? How does the national security discourse conceptualize, constitute, and produce understandings of terrorism? How does the concept of security influence and constitute a discursive site that conditions responses to terrorism?

Eugene de Silva has been an educator for over 25 years. As a professor of physics and chemistry, he developed online courses in the fields of physics, chemistry, ecology, environmental science, intelligence, security, terrorism studies, research, etc. He established the National Accrediting Commission for Martial Arts (NACMA) - a registered charity- and Virginia Research Institute (VRI) – a non-profit organization in the United States in 2004. These foundations were set in place to spark the younger generation's interest in furthering their education and research. He has been the President of the Tennessee Science Department Chairs Association since 2008. He is also the Chair of Institute of Physics UK/USA Branch (South Eastern USA). He is an Executive Member of the Tennessee Academy of Sciences. De Silva has written several books including textbooks in physics and chemistry and is an internationally recognized educator with his name entered in the Who's Who in the World, Who's Who in American Education, and Who's Who in America. He developed the first Martial Arts educational degree in the world in 1993 when he was in the UK. He holds the highest Dan grade in martial arts and is the founder of an international charity known as The Society of Martial Arts, UK. He, as a practitioner of martial arts, introduced a syllabus of teaching physics through martial arts in 2007. He introduced Physics Day in the USA, which has been in place since 2005 for high school students where mechanics section of physics is taught through martial arts. He has also won the "Innovative Teaching Award," "Above and Beyond Award," and has received recognition awards from the Tennessee Academy of Sciences, USA and the Institute of Chemistry, Sri Lanka. He is a chartered chemist, chartered scientist, and chartered physicist; he was also elected as a fellow of the Royal Society for the encouragement of Arts, Manufactures, and Commerce in recognition of his outstanding work in the field of education. The World Head of Family Sokeship Council also inducted him to the Hall of Fame in 2001 in Florida, USA. His novel teaching model, "START," is now being introduced in the teaching of science through the Virginia Research Institute. He also holds two world records in breaking cinder blocks on different parts of his body.

Nicole Drumhiller joined the American Public University System in 2012 and is currently Program Director and Associate Professor in the Intelligence Studies program. Previous to this, she served as an instructor at Washington State University. She serves as an editorial board member for the Journal of Global Security and Intelligence Studies. In 2012 she carried out research in Belfast, Northern Ireland which was recently published in a co-authored work with Elena Mastors in the journal of Peace & Change. Nicole is currently working on a collaborative project which focuses on extremist group behavior within the animal right movement.

Neal Duckworth served nearly 23 years in the U.S. Marine Corps, retiring as the head of counterintelligence and human intelligence plans and policy. He served in multiple conflicts, including conducting, leading, and directing intelligence operations in Bosnia-Herzegovina, Afghanistan, and Iraq. Following his retirement, he served as a Managing Director in an intelligence consulting firm before entering federal service with the Director of National Intelligence's Office of the National Counterintelligence Executive. He left government service in 2014 and is currently employed as a Senior Director of Executive Education Programs at the Harvard Kennedy School in Cambridge, Massachusetts. Neal received a Bachelor of Arts in International Service from The American University and a Master of Arts in National Security and Strategic Studies from The Naval War College.

Latoya N. Johnson received her PhD from the Interdisciplinary Program in Molecular and Cellular Biology from Tulane University in August 2006. She completed her postdoctoral research appointment at Emory University School of Medicine's Alcohol and Lung Biology Program. She worked as a Science Writer/Editor with the National Home Office of the American Cancer Society, as a Program Coordinator in the Dean's Office of the School of Medicine, and as an Adjunct Faculty Member for Grand Canyon University and Georgia Gwinnett College. Dr. Johnson presently works in the College of Health Sciences at Walden University teaching Public Health Biology and in the General Studies department at Beulah Heights University teaching Principles of Science.

David Martin Jones' research on political theory has focused on two areas: the evolution of English political thinking on ideas of conscience and allegiance and somewhat differently the impact of traditional understandings of political obligation upon statecraft in East and Southeast Asia. In the context of English political thought his work resulted in a book Conscience and Allegiance in Seventeenth Century English Political Thought (University of Rochester 1999). More recently he has turned his attention to the problem of modern ideology and political religion which resulted in a volume on Sacred Violence Political Religion in a Secular Age (Palgrave 2014). In addition to publishing several academic pieces on terrorism in Southeast Asia in the highest quality venues, David Martin Jones has made a high profile contribution to public debate through pieces in The Australian Financial Review, The Weekend Australian, The National Interest and The World Today.

Hans Ingvar Jörgen Bengtsson has a M.A. in International Relations from the Fletcher School at Tufts University and a B.Sc. in Business Administration and Economics at Lund University, Sweden. Mr. Bengtsson is a consultant in international project financing, specialized in Emerging Market infrastructure and communications projects.

Elena Mastors, PhD is currently Dean of Faculty at the University of Phoenix. She was previously Vice President and Dean of Applied Research at the American Public University System. Previous to this, she was an Associate Professor in the National Decision Making Department of the Naval War College, and also held various senior intelligence and policy positions in the Office of Undersecretary of Defense for Intelligence and the Defense Intelligence Agency. Dr. Mastors is an expert on political psychology as it pertains to conflict, terrorism and political leadership. She writes frequently on understanding leaders and group dynamics from a political-psychological perspective. She has published on the subjects of conflict and armed groups. Her most recent books include Breaking Al-Qaeda: Political Psychological and Operational Techniques, Introduction to Political Psychology, and The Lesser Jihad: Recruits and the Al-Qaida Network.

Eriberta B. Nepomuceno holds a B.S Biochemistry- College Degree University of Santo Tomas, Manila Philippines, an M.S. Engineering -University of Tokyo, Japan and Doctor of Engineering -University of Tokyo Japan. Former Regional Director Department of Science and Technology, Former Undersecretary Department of Science and Technology, Former Director Institute of Peace and Security Studies, Bicol University, Research associate, De La Salle University Manila. Presently Professor Graduate School, Bicol University Legaspi city Field of specialization Biosensors, Bioelectronics, PEACE Science, Research and Development.

David Omand is a Cambridge University graduate in economics, has an honorary Doctorate from Birmingham University and has just completed a degree in Mathematics and Theoretical Physics with the Open University. He is a member of the editorial board of Intelligence and National Security. With Dr Michael Goodman of the Department he is responsible for delivering training to government intelligence analysts and lectures regularly to BA and MA level classes in intelligence studies. Sir David Omand was the first UK Security and Intelligence Coordinator, responsible to the Prime Minister for the professional health of the intelligence community, national counter-terrorism strategy and "homeland security". He served for seven years on the Joint Intelligence Committee. He was Permanent Secretary of the Home Office from 1997 to 2000, and before that Director of GCHQ (the UK Sigint Agency). Previously, in the Ministry of Defence as Deputy Under Secretary of State for Policy, he was particularly concerned with long term strategy, with the British military contribution in restoring peace in the former Yugoslavia and the recasting of British nuclear deterrence policy at the end of the Cold War. He was Principal Private Secretary to the Defence Secretary during the Falklands conflict, and served for three years in NATO Brussels as the UK Defence Counsellor. He has been a visiting Professor in the Department of War Studies since 2005-6.

Marina Shorer-Zeltser is founder and President of the IDmap research institute in Media and Politics. Her main fields of interest are quantitative and qualitative analysis of acquisition of identity through media and politics. She lectures in Political Science, International relations, Political Economy and Communication.

Dana-Marie Thomas is a Scholar-Practitioner with 20+ years of combined experience in health policy, biobehavioral and community health related research, and human resources management. Dr. Thomas has expertise in mixed-methods applied research; distance education policy, program management; quality program review; academic governance, learning outcome measurement; and accreditation standard adherence. Dr. Thomas earned a PhD., in public policy and administration with a concentration in epidemiology and community health at L. Douglas Wilder School of Government and Public Affairs at Virginia Commonwealth University. Dr. Thomas completed a Postdoctoral Research Fellowship in the Department of Nutrition Sciences in the School of Health Professions at the University of Alabama at Birmingham (UAB) where her research focused on biobehavioral influences of obesity–related traits, women's health, the genetic contribution of taste and gynecologic cancers, SNP Variation in the Bitter Taste hTAS2R38 Gene and Intake of Fruit and Phytochemical-Rich Cruciferous Vegetables in Women at Risk for Cervical Cancer; and health care access and delivery. While at UAB, Dr. Thomas was also a Scholar in the Health Disparities Training Program funded by the Morehouse School of Medicine and at UAB, by the Comprehensive Cancer Center – Nutritional Biochemistry and Genomics; and a Postdoctoral Trainee in the Department of Preventive Medicine. She also earned a Master's in Tourism from Temple University. Dr. Thomas is published in peer-reviewed academic journals focusing in social policy, public health, and science education. She examines the interrelationships among individual, social, and environmental factors that shape health behaviors and prevent chronic disease and public policy. Her work focuses on gene–environment interactions in health disparities. Dr. Thomas has conducted research and fieldwork on contextual determinants of chronic diseases, gynecologic cancers, taste genetics, body image in women of color. Dana-Marie has been engaged public health interventions that promote healthy lifestyles, and environmental policies which affect access to health-promoting resources. Dr. Thomas has taught courses in PA and health sciences at the graduate level; and health administration at the undergraduate level. Dr. Thomas is currently serving as Academic Program Coordinator in the School of Public Policy at Walden University. Previously, Dr. Thomas served as VP of Global Health Policy, Prevention of Chronic Diseases & Wellness Promotion at Transformational Development Consortium. Specialties: women's health; cancer prevention/control, community-based interventions; genetic and biobehavioral markers of dietary compliance; biopsycho-sociocultural factors affecting weight related behaviors, health literacy.

Shefali Virkar is a research student at the University of Oxford, UK, currently reading for a D.Phil. in Politics. Her doctoral research seeks to explore the growing use of Information and Communication Technologies (ICTs) to promote better governance in the developing world, with special focus on the political and institutional impacts of ICTs on local public administration reform in India. Shefali holds an M.A. in Globalisation, Governance and Development from the University of Warwick, UK. Her Master's dissertation analysed the concept of the Digital Divide in a globalising world, its impact on developing countries and the ensuing policy implications therein. At Oxford, Shefali is a member of Keble College.

Kirk Y. Williams, PhD, received a B.S. in Chemistry from Dillard University, and one of his M.S. degrees in Biochemistry and Biophysics from Rensselaer Polytechnic Institute. After completing his Ph.D. research in Biomedical Sciences at Tulane University, he joined the Section on Statistical Genetics within the Department of Biostatistics at University of Alabama at Birmingham. His work on one particular publication gained the interest of the Food and Drug Administration within the Center for Biologics Evaluation and Research which later led to his recruitment into the Department of Defense.

As a Contributing Faculty member for Kaplan University and Walden University, he is the Dissertation Chair for over 25 students within the School of Public Policy and Administration. His research within the area of Multidisciplinary Research has led to book chapters within Cases on Research-Based Teaching Methods in Science Education, while his knowledge of computers and computer networking has led to publications online in the International Journal of Multidisciplinary Research, and upcoming chapters in Applying Methods of Scientific Inquiry into Intelligence, Security, and Counterterrorism.

Clay Wilson is the Program Director for Cybersecurity Studies at the American Public University, and also past Program Director for Cybersecurity Policy at the University of Maryland University College (UMUC), where he oversaw development of new graduate-level courses. Prior to that, Dr. Wilson was research specialist for national defense policy at the Congressional Research Service (CRS) where he analyzed cyber intelligence reports for the U.S. Congress and NATO committees on net-centric warfare, cybersecurity, nanotechnology, and other vulnerabilities of critical civilian infrastructures and high-technology military systems. Dr. Wilson is a member of the Landau Network Centro Volta, International Working Group, an organization that studies non-proliferation of CBRN and Cyber Weapons. He has moderated panels for the National Nuclear Security Administration on nonproliferation for Cyber Weapons in Como, Italy, and has presented at the China Arms Control and Disarmament Association in Beijing. He has also presented at the US Defense Cyber Investigations Training Academy, at the US National Defense University on the topic of cybercrime, and at the Cyber Conflict Studies Association on the cyber capabilities of terrorist groups. Other projects involved research and training for Abu Dhabi government officials on computer security and network technology for defense and crisis management while living abroad in the United Arab Emirates. He received his PhD from George Mason University.

Seunghwan Yeo earned his MA Degree from the Fletcher School at Tufts University in 2015 and MA in Conflict Management from the Heller School at Brandeis University in 2008. His Bachelor's degree is from Sogang University in Korea and he also studied at Keio University in Tokyo, Japan. He is a software engineer at Virtual Research Associates and manages design and deployment of conflict monitoring and data analysis systems. He also conducts field training in conflict early warning, prevention and management in Africa, East Asia and South Asia.

Index

E

F

G

H

I

L

M

N

www.ingramcontent.com/pod-product-compliance
Lightning Source LLC
LaVergne TN
LVHW062145200926
848484LV00007B/1861